MAKING *and* REMAKING

PENNSYLVANIA'S
CIVIL WAR

PENNSYLVANIA'S
CIVIL WAR

EDITED BY

William Blair and William Pencak

The Pennsylvania State University Press
University Park, Pennsylvania

Library of Congress Cataloging-in-Publication Data

Making and remaking Pennsylvania's Civil War / edited by
William Blair and William Pencak.
p.   cm.
Includes bibliographical references and index.
ISBN 0-271-02079-2 (alk. paper)
1. Pennsylvania—History—Civil War, 1861–1865. 2. Pennsylvania—History—
Civil War, 1861–1865—Social aspects. 3. United States—History—Civil War,
1861–1865—Social aspects. 4. Pennsylvania—History—Civil War, 1861–1865—
Influence. 5. United States—History—Civil War, 1861–1865—Influence.
I. Blair, William Alan. II. Pencak, William, 1951– .

E527 .M35 2001
973.7'448—dc21   00—37330

To

G a r y   W .   G a l l a g h e r

For his
inspiration and tutelage

CONTENTS

ILLUSTRATIONS

INTRODUCTION

Oddly enough for a state so essential to the Union's war-making effort, Pennsylvania's role in the Civil War has been underappreciated. Like an old friend taken for granted, it has escaped proper attention, especially for the impact of that conflict on its communities. Although some journal articles have delved into various aspects of the state in this period, most books deal with the military aspects of the war in Pennsylvania, especially the Battle of Gettysburg. As one scholar has observed, the literature "on the battle of Gettysburg is so voluminous that it nearly smothers historians."[1] There have been exceptions to the emphasis on military personnel and battles in such noteworthy studies as Arnold Shankman's on antiwar movements, Grace Palladino's on labor unrest in the coal region, William Miller's on mobilization in the state, Michael Holt's on the Republican Party, and J. Matthew Gallman's deeply textured portrait of Philadelphia during the conflict. But only about a dozen or so volumes have highlighted Pennsylvania beyond the battlefield, and no study views the state as a whole in terms of the economic, social, and political strains for the war years.[2]

Although the essays in this volume neither completely rectify this neglect nor avoid the lure of Gettysburg, they do suggest ways to reconsider an old friend. They are not meant to plot a definitive research agenda, but rather to serve as preliminary examples of how Pennsylvania—and grassroots research in general—may lead scholars to new questions and approaches for understanding the broader war and its consequences. The studies include the battlefield but also reflect the current trends to understand the motivations of soldiers and the impact of war on civilians, rather than focusing solely on battles or leadership. The essays employ such interdisciplinary techniques as material culture and consumer theory, as well as raise gender and racial questions. They incorporate a more expansive time frame than the four years of the conflict by looking at the uses of the war in popular memory. As a whole, the authors explore not only the making of war, but also its remaking— or how a public revisits the past to suit contemporary needs.

It should come as little surprise that Pennsylvania has not held a prominent position in social, economic, and cultural studies of the nation's great struggle for survival. The same can be said for many of the Northern states. Roughly a decade ago, historian Maris Vinovskis pondered whether social historians had lost the Civil War. He observed that little had been published on civilian life in the North or the South or on the lives of veterans adjusting to conditions in the postwar world. More recently, largely because of the increased emphasis on studies that highlight the experiences of common folk, works have focused on the home front, and a few studies have looked at veterans. Additionally, scholars have explored the beliefs of common soldiers to learn their attitudes about a range of issues, in the process restoring their ideological commitment to a broader cause. *Writing the Civil War*, a recent overview of the work published on the Civil War within the past thirty years, however, has revealed that we still have a long way to go in fully understanding a range of issues regarding Northern soldiers and civilians. Historians have studied the Southern home front much more extensively than they have studied the North. And, ironically, military historians have been ahead of social historians in uncovering the impact of the war on the common folk.[3]

Pennsylvania offers a fine laboratory for broadening our understanding of how communities mobilized for the war. It was a fairly diverse state with significant immigrant populations (both old and new), rising industrialization, and isolated rural pockets especially along the northern tier and in the southwest corner. It occupied an important geographic position that made it a target of Confederate authorities, not only for the Battle of Gettysburg in 1863 but also for the burning of Chambersburg in 1864. The state ranked second only to New York in terms of soldiers who fought for the Union, contributing roughly 360,000 men to the cause. Within that total, Pennsylvania sent the highest number of black soldiers, or 8,612, into the Federal ranks. The manufacturers of the state produced about 80 percent of the War Department's iron needs, not to mention coal, textile items, and food. Various religious groups held pacifist beliefs, creating potential tensions within those communities and with the larger public.

A number of historical problems have occupied scholars interested in the broader context of the war, with most of them falling into three groupings:

the extent of change or continuity within communities; the expansion of the national state and the responses of civilians to those changes; and what motivated people to support the cause. Concerning the first issue—change or continuity—historians of the South tend to consider the war as creating a revolutionary break from the past, whereas this point seems more debatable for the North. Two synthetic works on the home front capture the spectrum of discussion among historians of the North. Phillip Shaw Paludan's *"A People's Contest"* considers the war as part of a modern industrializing process that wrought great change in individual lives as the populace advanced toward a more centralized nation with a new birth of freedom. In contrast, J. Matthew Gallman's *The North Fights the Civil War* proclaims that the conflict created no fundamental rupture with the past. The public, Gallman argues, met new challenges by expanding tried and true means of organization that never abandoned local networks or mentalities. Gallman and others cast doubt on whether the war contributed a significant boost to the economy, arguing that the conflict only accelerated changes that had been in the works for several decades. The same argument extends to women's roles, with assertions of expanding public activity challenged by others who claim that no fundamental upheaval occurred in household responsibilities. Paludan recently has offered an intriguing hypothesis that the story might not be all one way or the other, that the North itself might have contained different patterns of development, with the Northeast more firmly settled in its ways while the West experienced more accelerated growth.[4]

Historians often proclaim the Civil War as a watershed event that firmly established a new meaning to federalism, with the central government exerting new sovereignty over states. But this second grouping of problems involves a debate over the extent and permanence of this change, as well as how to assess the public response to unpopular policies. Government expanded dramatically at the time. The war resulted in the nation's first income tax, the first national conscription of soldiers, a national currency, pensions for widows, legislation against discrimination in federal offices, and social programs for the freedpeople. Slavery ended. And the constitutional amendments after the war that ended the peculiar institution and enforced new standards of citizenship and civil rights signaled a shift toward a more activist national authority. Yet some argue that the expansion of government lost momentum after the war as Congress scaled back the army. The Supreme Court later in the nineteenth century also upheld cases that reasserted state authority over civil rights.[5] At the same time, new questions have arisen about the nature of public response to government intrusion, especially whether public protest signaled antiwar sentiment or reflected more fundamental social upheaval. Dissent has typically been cast within the political terms of Democrat versus Republican when, in fact, public protest might contain dissatisfaction that crosses party lines.[6]

Finally, historians have done perhaps the most work in trying to figure out the reasons why soldiers fought in the war. The research of James M. McPherson, Reid Mitchell, and Earl Hess, among others, has restored ideology as a major force compelling the men of both armies to fight. Until fairly recently, studies suggested that soldiers fought for each other or for local issues rather than national ones. Now it appears that soldiers also consciously fought to maintain liberty or to protect the experiment in democracy.[7] Yet the content of national identity in the nineteenth century begs further inquiry. Victory has anointed Northerners with nationalism, while defeat has cast doubt on the South's national identity. During the war, however, Northerners sounded suspiciously like Southerners in their assertion of local versus national goals. And the desertion, draft resistance, and public protest in various forms have rarely been taken as a sign of incomplete nationalism in the Union. It is doubtful that Northerners had a national identity that always superseded local ties. In the nineteenth-century United States, the public considered "the nation" an extension of local, personal needs. The term "Union" itself conveyed a more complicated meaning than the definition of "a nation" in contemporary American society. The federalist structure of the Constitution created ambiguities over the question of sovereignty that had to be resolved. Most Americans in the nineteenth century used Union as a plural verb, suggesting they thought of their nation as a jointure of sovereign states. It was only after the war that the Union took on a singular form—in more than grammar.[8]

The history of Pennsylvania and its role in the Civil War contains great potential for adding to these discussions. We know the most about the economy and communities of Philadelphia and Harrisburg but have little understanding of the rest of the state. No community study exists of Pittsburgh or, for that matter, of the vast rural stretches in between the major cities. Pennsylvania mirrored many areas in the North by featuring rural manufacturing, typified by the iron-making industries that combined artisan, agricultural, and unskilled labor housed in a self-contained village setting. At least one study of the Pennsylvania economy suggests that the state experienced an industrial revolution that was more benign and with less social upheaval than in the earliest stages of this process in New England.[9] Women in the state mobilized as part of the Sanitary Commission and helped organize the largest charitable event during the conflict. Did the war nudge the people out of established patterns, or did it merely expand traditional practices and accelerate a shift toward more consolidated manufacturing in cities? Was there any difference, in fact, between rural and urban experiences of war? What happened to agricultural labor in general in the state? Were Pennsylvania farmers rushing headlong into mechanization or hanging on to old ways?

For the expansion of the national state and civilian response, few works hint of the complexity of underlying dissent in Pennsylvania. Arnold Shankman's *The Pennsylvania Anti-War Movement* follows the more traditional approach, which considers the peace movement as a function of the Democratic Party. Politics was admittedly a prominent part of dissent. The Democratic Party was strong in Pennsylvania. In the mid-nineteenth century it was the more conservative of the two, with the stated goal to keep power in the hands of the people by resisting the expansion of centralized, governmental power. As 1863 came, the state featured increased resistance to the Republican policies for conducting the war. Yet dissent existed outside of political channels as well. In Bellefonte, farmers in 1863 marched on the courthouse to protest the arrest of a man who had resisted draft enrollment. In other rural areas, snipers fired at enlistment officers. Grace Palladino has taken a fresh look at the unrest in the coal regions, arguing that what went on there was labor strife, not antiwar protest. But scholars have largely ignored explanations for the reputedly more than 1,000 deserters who hid in Cambria and Clearfield counties in 1864.[10] As historians explore these patterns more deeply for the North overall, they have tended to locate the impulse for dissent in deeply rooted social conflict that pits local and family loyalties against national ones. Can dissent best be understood as class conflict, political conflict, or resistance to modernization? Is it a combination of these factors or something else entirely?

At first the state might seem to offer little new for understanding why people supported the war; however, even here there is fresh ground to explore. In Chapter 1 Christian Keller reveals that as many as 2,000 Pennsylvanians fought for the Confederacy, and there were pockets of Southern sympathizers. But we also need to know more about the impact of ethnicity and religion on Northern ideology. Pennsylvania, for instance, featured significant communities of religious pacifists—German descendants and such newcomers as Amish and Mennonites with an established tradition of pacifist Quakers to boot. Did ethnicity matter in Northern nationalism? Did religious scruples stand in the way of participation in the war? Or did antislavery attitudes prevail? And how should we assess the actions of civilians along the southern tier? In his chapter on the marketing of Gettysburg, Jim Weeks notes that Union and Confederate soldiers during the Gettysburg campaign referred to the civilians from the region as stingy and looking only to protect their own property rather than help a broader cause. Were they less than perfect nationalists? Or did something else account for their behavior?

Pennsylvania's contributions to the war did not end with the surrender at Appomattox. For the past decade or so, studies have demonstrated the power of current political circumstances in shaping public memory of the past. Societies often build consensus by creating a history devoid of fundamental differences or deep-seated animosities. The Battle of Gettysburg has been part of this process, influencing how Americans perceived their conflict and bound up the nation's wounds. Beginning with the dedication of the National Cemetery in November 1863, the site has been used to define the character of the United States. In Lincoln's hands, the battlefield became a reason for furthering the conflict. Later generations used the location for the opposite reason: to fashion reconciliation. The process began in the late nineteenth century with veteran reunions and excursions by a host of people, including African Americans. Today, approximately two million visitors each year still flock to Gettysburg, attesting to the power the site holds with the contemporary public.[11]

The essays in this collection highlight Pennsylvania's various roles during and after the war. The writers inspect issues relevant to the war, such as how persons chose sides, the impact of the conflict on civilians, the effort of women, and the role of black soldiers. The latter essays examine facets of remembering the war, including the role of black and white veterans in this process.

Opening the wartime chapters, Christian B. Keller identifies what he calls Keystone Confederates, men who felt strongly enough to pick up a musket on the side of the Confederates. The most famous examples are Wesley Culp, who traveled with his Southern unit back home to Gettysburg only to die in the battle, and John Pemberton, who surrendered the Confederate army to Ulysses S. Grant at Vicksburg. They were by no means alone. Perhaps as many as 2,000 residents of the Keystone State joined the Southern cause. Keller examines this phenomenon more deeply, showing that support for the South was strongest in Philadelphia with a sprinkling of sympathizers in the northeastern and south-central portions of the state.

The next contribution employs cultural analysis to learn more about the nineteenth-century mentality as well as how art can assist in a political cause. In "Avenue of Dreams," Elizabeth Milroy revisits the Great Sanitary Fair at Philadelphia in June 1864. The fair itself is nothing new; however, Milroy shifts the focus to the content of the exhibits. Through an analysis of artwork, she uncovers how culture helped infuse patriotism—or at least how the manufacturers and distributors of these works consciously used them to instill identification with the nation. She adds that the use of art to help patriotism also changed the way people viewed the continuing role of art museums themselves.

Gender analysis informs the approach of the next two chapters, indicating how women stretched and redefined their positions in society during wartime. In "'We Were Enlisted for the War,'" Rachel Seidman argues that women's participation in various aid societies not only helped the war effort but also staked out a new political role that shaped the definition of citizenship. Her case study reaffirms the work of other historians who have broadened the interpretation of politics beyond the ballot box by trying to understand how people structure, distribute, and contest power. Following this effort, Christina Ericson finds that women in Gettysburg did not always act according to society's prescribed role for women. In "'The World Will Little Note Nor Long Remember,'" her study of ten women during the battle of Gettysburg, Ericson concludes that these women were not passive females who remained inside homes while men conducted the dirtier business of the world. Both essays support scholarship that underscore how women could stake out autonomy even within the constricting rules of society. And they show the two ways in which scholars have considered women during the conflict: the impact of women on the war and the impact of war on women.[12]

Three studies involving issues concerning African Americans provide a transition between wartime and postwar essays. In his essay on Pittsburgh, Henry Pisciotta shows the antislavery debate becoming enmeshed in the representation of a monument to a late industrialist. The work supports scholarship that focuses on the political meaning of public artifacts, in this case a statue to industrialist Charles Avery, who held antislavery beliefs and founded a college for African Americans. The monument to Avery represents one of the first examples in the United States of a public monument with an African-American theme. Pisciotta shows that despite the "real" character and background of Avery, the public—including African Americans—used the statue to construct meanings that served particular political ends.

Next, letters from a black soldier who served in the Army of the Potomac during the Overland Campaign of 1864 provide insight into the service of black persons in the war. John C. Brock composed these letters for the *Christian Recorder*, the official publication of the African Methodist Episcopal Church. A resident of Carlisle, he served in the rear guard during the army's advance to Petersburg and helped construct trenches outside the city for the final siege that led to the downfall of the Army of Northern Virginia. The letters reveal Brock's heady sense of helping in the liberation of slaves. Like so many African Americans, he believed that his defense of his counrty deserved recognition through full and equal rights. The material provides a rare glimpse into the mind of one black soldier, who reveals how African Americans worked not only for their own liberation but also to redefine the meaning of citizenship. But the collection also fits nicely with the emerging genre of publications that feature letters from black soldiers to newspapers.[13]

The importance of using the past to serve current political needs forms a theme in Chapter 7, where Barbara Gannon looks at the Grand Army of the Republic posts in Pennsylvania in the late nineteenth century and discovers a considerable amount of interracial activity. Her work promises to revise our notion of this organization, as it suggests another tool that African Americans employed in the struggle to maintain full rights as citizens.

The final three chapters are concerned with the various ways that the battle of Gettysburg has been represented in culture. "'A Disgrace That Can Never Be Washed Out'" by Jim Weeks traces the transformation of Gettysburg, despite its poor wartime reputation, into a modern shrine for tourists. During the war, residents of the area drew criticism from both sides for their stinginess and lack of patriotism. Many farmers wanted to charge for their goods rather than donating their family's resources to soldiers. Although an understandable reaction to preserve a family's subsistence, this behavior sparked comments about the region's "meanness." Yet the town managed to turn around its image through the examples of John Burns and Jennie Wade: the farmer who grabbed his musket to help in the battle and the young lady with the dubious honor of being the only civilian to die in the battle. Their examples of self-sacrifice contrasted with the wartime image of the region.

Mark Thistlethwaite's "'Magnificence and Terrible Truthfulness'" takes us inside the construction of one of the more famous paintings of the battle, Peter F. Rothermel's huge work now housed in the State Museum of Pennsylvania in Harrisburg. Representing four and a half years of effort, the artwork's creation contains an interesting story of an artist attempting to balance conflicting accounts in the historical record to create a painting he hoped would be authentic. The public's reception of the painting varied dramatically, seeing it first as a realistic composition then as one that was too sensational. Thistlethwaite's chapter describes how art can contribute to contemporary debate across a wide span of time. Similarly, art can reveal to us how a public views a historic event. My concluding chapter on the movie *Gettysburg* indicates that the concept of a "brothers' war" remains popular. Remembering the war in this way allows for a reconciliation between the opposing sides by diminishing areas of conflict—such as slavery—in favor of portraying the war as a brother's spat that could easily be patched with a handshake.

Overall the chapters in this book open up some new avenues for exploring Pennsylvania and the Civil War. They reevaluate what constituted political activity in the nineteenth century as they highlight the contributions of women to charity and the battlefield. They also support the view that African Americans were active seekers of their freedom rather than passive recipients of emancipation. They show the importance of history in validating current circumstances, and how artwork and other cultural forms can become allies in this invention. Most of all, we hope the essays underscore the value of reconsidering the Keystone State as a place for valid historical inquiry of this important time in our past, not only because the state has been neglected but also because it has even more worthwhile stories yet to tell.

The editors would like to thank J. Matthew Gallman of Gettysburg College for a thorough reading of the entire manuscript. Lori Ginzberg, Gary Cross, Sally McMurry, Michael Birkner, David Montgomery, Joe Trotter, Mark Thistlethwaite, and Gary Gallagher each read one or more chapters and also provided invaluable assistance. Editor-in-chief Peter Potter, production editor Patty Mitchell, designer Steve Kress, copyeditor Eliza Childs, and indexer Cynthia Bertelsen were sympathetic, professional, and prompt, as they invariably are. Our greatest debt is to the incomparable scholar, teacher, and friend to whom this book is dedicated.

William Blair
The Civil War Era Center
The Pennsylvania State University

KEYSTONE CONFEDERATES

Pennsylvanians Who Fought for Dixie

Christian B. Keller

Lieutenant George G. Junkin pondered a most uncomfortable dilemma on April 4, 1862. A prisoner of war of the Union army, he was a native Pennsylvanian who had sided with the Confederacy, served on Stonewall Jackson's staff, and been captured at the battle of Kernstown on March 23, 1862. Imprisoned at Fort Delaware, Junkin had hoped for an exchange, but on this day he confronted an unpleasant alternative. His father, the Reverend David Xavier Junkin, had hurried from Philadelphia after learning of his son's incarceration and stood before him with a Federal officer ready to administer the oath of allegiance to the United States. As he decided between the "peril of his soul" and "the respect of honorable men," Lieutenant Junkin—a cousin to Jackson's first wife and the nephew of the erstwhile president of Washington College, Doctor George Junkin, who had fled back to Pennsylvania after Virginia seceded—must have sensed the irony of the situation. This was not the first time his father had attempted to sway Junkin's loyalty away from the Confederacy. In May 1861, Reverend Junkin had journeyed to Harpers Ferry to retrieve his son from the camp of then-Colonel Thomas J. Jackson and even attempted to convince the stalwart Rebel commander that he, too, should fly from the "inexcusable" rebellion. Both Jackson and the younger Junkin politely refused the Reverend Junkin's requests. With "tears upon the cheeks of both," the elder Junkin left his "poor boy" standing next to Jackson and returned to Pennsylvania.[1]

Lieutenant Junkin gave in to his father's entreaties at Fort Delaware that April day, primarily because he was told that his mother, heartbroken by his choice to fight for the South and sickened that he was not yet paroled, would react violently to his father's return without him. "[H]e had no doubt his return to [Philadelphia] without me would produce either permanent insanity, or her death," the younger Junkin later wrote. "I went through the mockery of swearing to uphold and defend the Constitution and gov't of the U.S. against all enemies, etc. etc., remarking as I did so that 'I took it under solemn protest and only to save my mother's life and reason.'" Finding his mother to be "seemingly well" in Philadelphia, Junkin felt himself even more blackmailed than before. He escaped from his father and rejoined Jackson's command at Martinsburg in early September 1862. Jackson received Junkin's letter of explanation cordially but firmly, informing him that "his place had been filled," and accepted his resignation without punitive recourse. Aware that he had committed a crime against the Confederacy by swearing the oath to the United States, Junkin happily took a captain's commission in the 25th Virginia Cavalry and served throughout the rest of the war in southwestern Virginia. He maintained to the very end that the oath he took at Fort Delaware was not valid. Armed with the potential testimony of brother officers who witnessed his "coercion" there, he argued that he "owed no allegiance nor obligation to the United States gov't" and "was determined under no circumstances ever to live under that government."[2]

What was Junkin, a native Pennsylvanian, doing in the Confederate army in the first place? Why did he support the Southern cause, and why, after given the opportunity to distance himself from the war, did he return to Virginia to continue fighting for a cause and a state that he knowingly adopted, at the risk of forever estranging his family in the North? Was Junkin's experience an isolated case, or were there others like him?

Although his wartime record is more detailed and better documented than most, Junkin's story was representative of scores of men from the Keystone State who cast their lot with the Confederacy. Most of these "galvanized rebels" remain obscure. There are a few memorable exceptions, such as John C. Pemberton, Josiah Gorgas, and Wesley Culp, but these names are just a sampling of Pennsylvanians found on Confederate rosters. Perhaps as many as 2,000 men from the Keystone State wore gray. While their numbers are startling enough, their reasons for fighting and the conclusions we can draw from them are even more important.[3] The history of the Pennsylvania Confederates is compelling not only because of the curious novelty these men represented in a sectionally polarized conflict, but also because it provides a refreshing opportunity to reexamine traditional beliefs about the motivations and values of Civil War soldiers. Understanding why these young men enlisted in Confederate service presents a number of intriguing historical problems, among them: what effect did men like Junkin have on the Confederacy's bid for independence, and will an analysis of their role in the conflict alter our assumptions about loyalty in the American Civil War?

The Keystone State was not a hotbed of secession fever, but certain counties contained the ingredients for producing Pennsylvania Confederates. Some of these factors included large numbers of Southern sympathizers, a strong Democratic vote in the 1860 election, social or economic ties to the South, and partisans who ideologically supported the peaceful secession of the Southern states. Not surprisingly, most Confederates hailed from regions with these attributes, more typically along the eastern and south-central portions of the state. Although many of them had moved to the South before the secession crisis, the correlation between their birthplaces and the later areas of pro-Southern sentiment is striking. It is difficult to distinguish between prosecession and antiwar sentiments in the statements of many of these Pennsylvanians, but they typically professed friendliness toward the Southern states, built on associations formed during the antebellum period.

Philadelphia had long fostered economic ties with the South. As historian Kenneth M. Stampp has indicated, the financial interests of many businessmen transcended politics during the first reactions to South Carolina's secession. Even some moderate Republicans joined with Democrats in conciliating the South, he explained, when secession threatened financial prosperity. "Their commanding political and economic positions," according to Stampp, obliged many manufacturers, merchants, and financiers to support compromise with the South.[4] The city's merchants drew a lively profit in trade with Southern customers, and the factories that churned out furniture, farm implements, and foodstuffs employed thousands of workers whose jobs depended on the sale of these products to purchasers below the Potomac. Blessed with an outlet to the Chesapeake Bay, Philadelphia produced a stream of manufactured goods accessible to Southern markets. The city joined Baltimore and New York as an entrepôt for southern raw materials destined for northern industry. Philadelphia was traditionally Democratic, and though Lincoln won the city in 1860, he received barely 60 percent of the vote. The strong Republican position on the tariff, rather than its stance on slavery, had swung many Philadelphia voters into the Republican camp.[5]

Several newspapers openly supported the new Confederacy before April 1861 and demanded the federal government's immediate recognition of the new nation, often using economics as a support for their position. The *Christian Observer* proudly advertised to its subscribers that it had opened an office in Richmond. The *Pennsylvanian*—edited by James Buchanan's nephew-in-law—advocated Pennsylvania's union with the new Confederacy. The openly secessionist *Palmetto Flag*, which managed to publish only three issues before being shut down by Unionists, observed that "coercion was futile" and that Pennsylvania's economic interests were entwined with the South's. Its editor observed: "Can Philadelphia with the South cut off compete with New York in ships, in trade, and other branches of enterprise? We opine not."[6]

Immediately after Lincoln's election, many Philadelphians feared that Southern secession would not only disrupt the Union, but also their profits. Pottsville lawyer Francis W. Hughes, whose brother lived in North Carolina, enjoyed political backing from wealthy Philadelphia merchants and ranked among the more vociferous proponents of peaceful separation. He complained in February 1861 that if Pennsylvania allied with the North in the secession crisis, it risked inheriting a "place in some Northern fragment of a once-glorious Union" and would lose all its Southern customers and profits. Conversely, if allied with the Confederacy, Pennsylvania would "become the great manufacturing workshop for a people now consuming annually $300,000,000 worth of products." Hughes even volunteered to run for public office on a platform of conciliation and friendship toward the South. His nephew took one step further in June 1861 by fleeing to his father's home in North Carolina, enlisting in a Confederate company, and becoming its captain.[7]

Similarly, a letter from the firm of Atwood, White and Company, dry goods merchants of Philadelphia, sympathized with the South based partly on economic ties, although the letter also suggests that Pennsylvanians may have shared an affinity for the border region that transcended the Mason-Dixon line. In a message to Mr. D. L. Hopkins of Lexington, Virginia, on February 1, 1861, the firm assured Hopkins that his "noble old state is very dear to us, and we should regret as much as her own sons to see any wrong done to her. In this feeling we have no doubt that nine-tenths of the people of Pennsylvania share, although this may seem strange to you." Although undoubtedly exaggerated, this statement was tempered with the admission, "How to explain the great misapprehension of the feelings and designs of this section of the country toward the South, which seems to prevail here, passes our ability." The author realized that most Pennsylvanians did not sympathize with the

South. He attempted to mollify the fears of his Virginian customer by emphasizing Pennsylvanians' general feeling of kinship with the Old Dominion, which he described as a "border state": "There has been, and is considerable irritation at the boastful character of South Carolina, but toward the Border States an increased, friendly regard." Acknowledging Virginia's power to raise an army in self-defense, the author nonetheless added: "If old Virginia should be placed in circumstances of trouble she would find 100,000 men from Pennsylvania ready to take her side." Whether the author believed "trouble" to mean an attack from secessionists farther South or an invasion from the North is unclear, but his pro-Virginia sympathies are certain. Many in the border regions, whether from North or South, saw themselves as men of moderate temperament, caught between extremists.[8]

It is worth questioning if these businessmen truly sympathized with the South or if letters such as the one addressed to Mr. Hopkins merely paid lip service to clients; however, political activity in the state suggests that many held beliefs akin to their Southern neighbors. The author answers the question with "a few words as to what is called the Republican Party." He explained that "we suppose you are aware that we were decidedly opposed to it—our votes and influence were for John Bell." Bell received about 12 percent of Philadelphians' votes in 1860, a small minority compared to Lincoln's totals in the city, and fared even worse outside of Philadelphia. It appears the owners of Atwood, White and Company were similar to Virginians in their political outlook, at least compared to the majority of their neighbors.[9] These merchants clearly deplored the possibility of civil war and believed the Republican Party's victory would increase the chances of armed conflict, which would be disastrous for all involved. Like the majority of Virginians, the letter's Pennsylvania author must have hoped for a constitutional resolution to the secession crisis, one that would respect the rights of individual states and placate Southern fears of Northern political dominance. In the closing sentences of the letter, the author revealed his ambivalence toward slavery. The aversion to civil war, not the resolution of the slavery controversy, was paramount: "You have had too glorious a history and we cannot part with you upon the question whether an hypothetical negro upon some imaginary territory hereafter acquired, is to be bond or free. But should Mr. Mason and Hunter hurry the state into secession before there is time to know the truth as to the feelings of the North, by all means, let the separation be peaceful, and may God bless you. But that we think would be a sad day for Virginia and long and deeply would she regret a separation from her best interests and best friends."[10]

According to this letter, Virginia, or at least Virginian-like political beliefs, held a special place in the hearts of some Philadelphians before the war. Fraternal memories of a joint revolutionary heritage may have prompted a small part of the affection these Pennsylvanians felt for the Old Dominion, but at least in this example, more contemporary, ideological motives influenced their writings. These were conservatives who believed that the Constitution functioned well and that the crisis would be averted if the citizenry faithfully followed its precepts.

Other Philadelphians exhibited even greater sympathy for the South, going so far as to support the new Confederacy in its infancy. Among this group was William B. Reed, who gained fame as a Democratic peace agitator later in the war but in 1860 favored peaceful secession. In the event of full-scale Southern secession, he believed Pennsylvania should hold a convention "to determine with whom her lot should be cast, whether with the North and East whose fanaticism has precipitated this misery upon us, or our brethren of the South whose wrongs we feel as our own."[11] Reed had allies who echoed his sentiments. The former chairman of the Democratic Executive Committee in Pennsylvania was Robert Tyler, son of the former president from Virginia. An arch supporter of President James Buchanan—who was falsely accused of collaboration with the secessionists—Tyler went on record numerous times defending both the president and the legal right of secession, stating his opposition "to coercion as some persons daintily describe the act of civil war." Once the war began, he wrote that "should the Border States join the Southern Confederacy within one, two or three years, it would then become a most serious question to determine the political status of Pennsylvania and New Jersey in that relation." Tyler even suggested that the United States adopt the Confederate Constitution, after which a mob ran him out of Philadelphia. He moved South, lived in Richmond during the war, and served as register of the Southern Confederacy until 1865. Another prominent Pennsylvanian, George W. Woodward, chief justice of the state supreme court, supported peaceful secession and noncoercion, arguing that in the event of war, "I wish Pennsylvania could go with them." Reed, Tyler, and Woodward, pro-Confederate in some instances, all strongly supported Buchanan's legalistic, reserved approach to the secession crisis and exhorted their friends and neighbors to follow conservatives in their lead.[12]

While strongest in Philadelphia, support for the South existed elsewhere. Pittsburgh and the western counties were staunchly Unionist, but Pennsylvanians in the northeast and the south-central region lent an ear to Southern justifications for secession. Although not ardently pro-Confederate, some communities contained advocates of peaceful secession. The counties bordering the Mason-Dixon line had traditional economic and social ties with Maryland and northern Virginia, enhanced by intermarriage and migration down the Cumberland Valley and into the Shenandoah Valley. Such towns as Carlisle, Chambersburg, Bedford, Harrisburg, and even Scranton and Easton had strong Democratic parties. The Democratic press often ran editorials supporting the young Confederacy.[13] One author has concluded that of the sixty-two Pennsylvania newspapers he studied, twenty-three were Democratic, and of that number seventeen "supported some sort of secession." Most surprising, of the thirty-one Republican papers he surveyed, eight also supported Southern secession before the attack on Fort Sumter.[14] The Democratic *Harrisburg Patriot and Union* was outspoken among newspapers in its geographic area but not unrepresentative. On April 9, 1861, it carried an editorial blaming the Republicans for preempting secession: "If this Administration wickedly plunges the country into civil war, it will be a war between the Republican party and the Southern States. . . . In such a conflict the Northern Democracy can have no sympathy with the Government. . . . If the Administration is bent upon having a fight, let it be understood that they created the difficulty and their partisans must carry on the war. Northern Democrats can never shoulder a musket or pull a trigger against those whose rights they conscientiously believe have been trampled upon. . . . If this is treason, make the most of it."[15]

The *Bedford Gazette* similarly forecast doom for the Republicans because the administration failed "to yield to a fair and honorable compromise with the South." As a result, stated the editor on March 8, 1861, "we are for revolution, peaceful if it can be, forcible if it must." If war resulted from the unfair practices of the Republican government, "the steady and true-hearted yeomen of Pennsylvania will rise in their might, and in the name of the Great Jehovah, hurl from power and existence a party that has perverted the Constitution." The *Easton Sentinel* argued along similar lines, and even Harrisburg's Republican *Pennsylvania Daily Telegraph* argued in April 1861 that "war with the seceded States will not bring them back into the Union. . . . In the present juncture, a resort to arms seems utterly impracticable."[16]

Political gatherings also issued statements in support of peaceful Southern secession. On February 21, 1861, the Democratic Party of Pennsylvania met in a state convention in Harrisburg. Amid great excitement and between stirring speeches, 350 delegates passed resolutions upholding the sovereign rights of states and the fugitive slave law, as well as advocating the adoption of the

Crittenden Compromise. Further, they unanimously agreed, "by all proper and legitimate means," to "discountenance, and prevent any attempt on the part of the Republicans in power to make any armed aggression upon the Southern States."[17] Such sweeping proclamations found a willing champion in U.S. Senator William Bigler, a Democrat who avidly supported the Crittenden Compromise and later spoke for peaceful Southern secession. In a speech in the Senate on January 21, 1861, he stated his intent to "fight for their [Southern] constitutional rights to the last hour," but refused to "shed a brother's blood in a fratricidal war." He added that "Pennsylvania will never become the enemy of Virginia. Pennsylvania will never draw the sword on Virginia; and she is no less affectionate to her other sisters."[18]

After the firing on Fort Sumter on April 12, support for the South vanished overnight. Pro-Southern men found their homes threatened by angry crowds. In some cases even the display of an American flag failed to assuage the masses. Numerous fine homes were damaged and several Southern sympathizers were run out of the cities. A letter written to "Friend Joe" from an anonymous Southerner caught behind the lines on May 16, 1861, indicates that Southern sympathizers risked death if they spoke publicly. Yet the letter mentions that Pennsylvanians sympathetic to the Southern cause did exist this late in Philadelphia: "There are a great many men here who are for the South but they cannot say a word for fear of being hung or put in prison or being shot down like dogs."[19]

Yet the support shown to the South, especially to Virginia, during the secession crisis is important to note because it indicates that Southern sympathies flourished in parts of prewar Pennsylvania. The sentiments expressed in the foregoing sampling of letters, newspaper editorials, and speeches indicate that a fair number of Pennsylvanians supported peaceful secession and a few, at least, supported the Confederacy outright. Some residents of the Keystone State would even follow Lee and Jackson into battle. Most of them, however, were likely to do so as a result of practical considerations.

Bell Irvin Wiley touched briefly on the subject of Northern-born soldiers in the Confederate armies. In "a random sampling of 42 descriptive rolls covering 21 regiments from six Confederate states," eighty-six names of privates born in the North appear, and of that number, nine hailed from Pennsylvania. Attempting to place a figure on the number of "Yankee-born men who served the cause of the South," Wiley estimated that "the figure must have run into the thousands." Arnold Shankman, in his study of the antiwar movement in Pennsylvania, echoed Wiley's rough guess by giving a "subjective judgment based on a critical perusal" of newspaper accounts; letters in archives and in the papers of Senators Bigler, Cameron, and Crittenden; and records of public meetings. Although not venturing to estimate how many Pennsylvanians actually fought for the Confederacy, Shankman contended "that not less than five percent favored Pennsylvania's joining the South" during the secession crisis, and "a much larger number, at least a third of the electorate, approved the Crittenden Compromise."[20]

These impressionistic but thoughtful speculations indicate that not all Pennsylvanians immediately rallied around the flag when war appeared imminent. While most Southern sympathizers professed loyalty to the Union and remained in Pennsylvania, a certain number—how many will never be completely known—fought for the Confederacy. Their names and Pennsylvanian birthplaces are inscribed in the regimental rosters of the Confederate regiments in which they served, and it is primarily from such regimental records that the first trace of their existence can be gleaned. Popular legend and folklore has passed down the names of a few prominent or familiar men of Pennsylvanian birth who wore gray, such as Pemberton, Gorgas, and Culp, but the vast majority of their comrades from the Keystone State have remained anonymous. Discovering who these soldiers were and why they enlisted, along with providing some analysis of their better-known expatriates, will help shed new light on the motivations of Civil War soldiers in general.[21]

The rosters contained in the Virginia regimental histories published by H. E. Howard provide a beginning for estimating the number of Pennsylvanians who fought for the Confederacy. Each regimental history contains a list of the soldiers who fought in the unit. Next to the name of each soldier is usually the place and date of birth, along with other relevant biographical information. After a review of more than forty rosters it became clear that each Virginia regiment averaged two to three Pennsylvania-born troops. Some had as many as a dozen. Considering the review of rosters was limited to less than half of Virginia's known regiments and included no tabulation of rosters from other Confederate states, a conservative guess about the numbers of Pennsylvanians in each Confederate state's service would be around 200.[22] Multiply 200 by 11 (the number of seceded states) and the result is 2,200. Although imprecise, this number probably is on the low side because it does not include Pennsylvanians living in border states who fought for the Confederacy. It also does not consider the likelihood that certain states, such as Virginia and Tennessee, because of their proximity to Pennsylvania, would have had a higher proportion of Pennsylvanians than other Confederate states. Admittedly, states in the Deep South probably did not have high numbers of former Pennsylvanians in their regiments, but this probability may be at least partially counteracted by other factors: the number of Pennsylvanians in the reviewed Virginia regiments who gave no birthplace, and an unknown number who would have thought it imprudent to provide evidence of Northern birth. How many soldiers like them populated other Confederate states' regiments? An exhaustive, detailed analysis of rosters from non-Virginia regiments is impossible at this time, but it is probable that these units likewise had "hidden" Pennsylvanians.

Surviving personal narratives or letters from their wartime service indicate that some Pennsylvanians who enlisted in the Confederate armies did so for political or ideological reasons. James M. McPherson and Reid Mitchell have shown that the typical Southern soldier fought to avoid subjugation to perceived Northern tyranny; to defend hearth, home, and Southern women; to preserve the right to pursue economic opportunity (through slavery); and to maintain a distinctive Southern culture. Such words and phrases as "liberty," "glorious cause," and "our people" typically appear throughout letters written by Southern soldiers. There is usually a clear understanding of who is "right" and who is "wrong" in the authors' minds, and whose side God is bound to support. The Northern enemy is often depicted as a "Yankee horde," or "mercenary." Not surprisingly, such catchwords and phrases are scattered throughout the writings of Pennsylvania Confederates also. These adoptive Southerners unquestionably felt a kinship with their native Southern neighbors and believed in the cause. Defeat for the South meant defeat for them as well. Frequently, ideology was only one of several considerations motivating the loyalties of Keystone Confederates, but in a few instances it was a key or dominating factor.[23]

Although ideology played a prominent role in certain soldiers' decisions to enlist, many Pennsylvania Confederates fought under the "Stars and Bars" because of important economic considerations, such as a business enterprise located in the South. Marriage to a Southern woman or other strong family relations compelled some of the better-known Pennsylvanians who wore gray. In most cases, a combination of ideological, economic, and marital factors influenced their decision making. A few probably enlisted in Confederate service because they were enrolled in Southern educational institutions when war broke out; others joined for no apparent reason at all. Whatever their motivation, these men fought against their native state because they had lived in the South, usually in Virginia, directly before the war, which weakened their ties with the Keystone State while strengthening those with their adopted home. All of these men, however, also faced the common difficulty of reconciling their Pennsylvanian birth, childhood, and in some cases a large part of their adult life with the choice to renounce family and friends and fight for the Confederacy. Loyalty to their place of birth and old familial ties became secondary to the other loyalties mentioned above, and hence the Pennsylvanians who fought for the Confederacy found themselves, sometimes quite literally, fighting their relatives.

Although he did not confront his father on the field of battle, Lieutenant Junkin fought verbally with him on several occasions during the war, in part because of the younger Junkin's ideological devotion to Virginia. Junkin formed ties to the Old Dominion while attending Washington College in Lexington from 1855 to 1859. After 1859 he worked as a teacher in Christiansburg, joined a militia company there, and donned gray when Virginia seceded. His adoption of the political causes of Virginia's secession probably explain why he enlisted in the Confederate army and became an officer on Jackson's staff. A letter written to his mother by one of his friends, James H. Langhorne, captured Junkin's fervor for Virginia's rights and the Confederate cause in general: "He is very differently situated to any of us, he is fighting against the State that gave him birth, Father, Mother, Bro. & Sister, and for what? because he thinks our cause is just. His father came all the way to the [Harpers] Ferry by private conveyance, to try and get him to resign his place here and go north, but he resisted the tearful request of his father & letters from his mother."

Langhorne described the meeting at Harpers Ferry between Junkin and his father, adding: "He could not give up the loyal principals of his noble heart & made the sacrifice of all family connection, for I know his father will disinherit him, and Ma, I think that a man who would make such sacrifices as these ought to be rewarded by every show of kindness from those who know he has made them. He has not the sweet assurance that we have that we are fighting for 'our own, our native land,' but he is fighting for justice which is inspiration enough for a noble soul like his."[24] That Junkin, when released from captivity at Fort Delaware, returned to Virginia to face a possible court-martial and promptly reenlisted in another Confederate unit indicates that he was as committed ideologically to his adopted state as many native-born Virginians.

Political reasons probably played a major role in motivating another Pennsylvanian to join Confederate arms. John William A. Berry was born in Virginia but had spent most of his adult life in Philadelphia. Whether he owned a business there or was married is unknown. When war broke out, Berry remained in Philadelphia, but emboldened by Robert E. Lee's second invasion of the North in late June 1863, he traveled to occupied Chambersburg and enlisted in Company K of the 5th Virginia Infantry on June 24, 1863. Berry emerged unscathed from the battle of Gettysburg. Good fortune, however, deserted this newly galvanized Confederate when he was captured at Cashtown eleven days later. Federal records indicate that he wanted to take the oath of allegiance the same day. He apparently did, but not before being sent to Forts McHenry and Delaware in chains. But Berry, like Junkin, did not take the oath seriously, because he is listed as a Federal prisoner again after the battle of the Wilderness in May 1864. Berry must have rejoined the Confederate army and fought for another year. Interestingly, the rolls of the 5th Virginia Infantry contain no fewer than ten men with the surname of Berry. It is conceivable that John Berry had relatives in the regiment, which would help explain why he enlisted. Yet he had lived in Pennsylvania a long time and must have developed close ties through friends, family, or business in the Keystone State. The only viable reason—besides a desire for adventure—that may explain Berry's enlistment in the Confederate army is that he believed in its cause.[25]

A Pennsylvanian with unquestionable ideological motives was George McHenry, who so believed in the Confederacy that he fought for it abroad. A former director of the Philadelphia Board of Trade, McHenry was a Pennsylvania delegate to the Democratic National Convention at Charleston in 1860. He joined the Southern fire-eaters from Mississippi and Alabama when they bolted the convention and later openly campaigned for Breckenridge in Philadelphia. On March 30, 1861, certain that Pennsylvania would never join the Confederacy, McHenry fled his native state for Europe and became a rabid proponent of the Confederate cause in London. During the war he worked tirelessly on propaganda designed to convince England to recognize Confederate independence and strongly critical of Pennsylvania and the Northern cause. Among his many publications were *The Position and Duty of Pennsylvania* (1863), *The Cotton Trade* (1863), and *Why Pennsylvania Should Become One of the Confederate States of America* (1862).[26]

Some evidence exists of native-born Pennsylvanians who joined Confederate regiments because they were attending Southern colleges and universities when war broke out. An intriguing case is that of John Kennedy Hitner of Carlisle. The Hitner family name appears in numerous local contracts and wills beginning about 1820, and John Hitner, born in 1839, must have been raised there.[27] He attended Dickinson College in 1858–59, before transferring to the University of Virginia in 1859. Graduating from the latter in 1860, he attended Union Theological Seminary until 1861, and then enlisted in the 1st Rockbridge Artillery at "Camp Buchanan" on St. Patrick's Day in 1862. Why Hitner waited so long to enlist, and why specifically he sided with the Confederacy after spending only two years in Charlottesville, is hard to determine. Yet he had spent almost three years in Virginia educational institutions, and while there it is almost certain that he became friends with other students, almost all of whom would have been Southerners. He probably joined the Rockbridge Artillery for two reasons: to join college friends in the regiment and to escape the Confederate draft. Once a Confederate soldier, however, Hitner's loyalty to the Confederate cause was steadfast. A letter written to a "Miss Grattan" from camp near Culpeper on July 31, 1863, displays disappointment about the recently ended Gettysburg campaign, faith in God's support of the Confederacy, and denunciations of the Yankees. Hitner's ideological beliefs were clear: "I hope a history—and a precise one—will be written to show to the world the way in which the Yankees have acted towards our border people," he lamented. Regarding the hardships of the people of Union-occupied Winchester, he observed: "Having no servants the young ladies had to do all the housekeeping, washing, etc." In the same letter Hitner also praised army life, calling the Army of Northern Virginia his home: "I cannot feel contented out of the army. I feel there is my place and there is my duty—and so can feel better contented in camp in the midst of hardships and difficulties because I feel that I am in the right place."[28] Hitner served throughout the war, receiving wounds at Winchester, Antietam, and Gettysburg, and spending a considerable time in hospitals in Charlottesville, Richmond, and Lynchburg. Letters written by him both during and after the war exhibit the depth of his Christian faith. After the war he remained in Virginia and later became a "presiding minister" for Episcopalian congregations in Virginia, West Virginia, Tennessee, and Kentucky.[29]

Another man of the cloth who hailed from Pennsylvania but zealously served the South was Father Emmeran Bliemal of the 10th Tennessee Infantry. Ordained in Pittsburgh in 1852, Father Bliemal administered to parishes in Hollidaysburg and Johnstown until 1860. Appointed pastor of the small German parish of the Assumption in Nashville in the fall of that year, he became attached to the Southern cause through his parishioners. When Union forces occupied Nashville in spring 1862, Father Bliemal, allowed freedom of movement to carry on his priestly duties, smuggled medicine out of the city to nearby Confederate forces. He was caught twice with more than four ounces of morphine in his possession and acquitted both times because of his religious status. Professing his support of the Confederacy, Father Bliemal received permission from his bishop to serve as a field chaplain with the 10th Tennessee, an ethnically Irish regiment. He escaped through Union lines to the open arms of his adopted troops in November 1863 and was killed while hearing the confession of the regiment's colonel at the battle of Jonesboro on August 31, 1864.[30]

Many Pennsylvanians moved south in the decades before the Civil War for economic purposes. They operated small businesses of their own or worked for other shopkeepers, opened up legal and medical practices, and became accustomed to life in the South. Many of these men married into Southern families, adding familial bonds to the economic ones. When the Southern states seceded, some of these former Pennsylvanians felt obliged to enlist in defense of their adopted states and the lives they had built there.

Wesley Culp of the 2nd Virginia Infantry typifies the men in this category. Born in Gettysburg in 1839, Culp, along with his brother William, worked in his late teens for the Hoffman Carriage Works. When the business moved from Gettysburg to Shepherdstown, Virginia, Wesley accompanied it. There he joined a local militia company to acquaint himself better with young men of his own age. When the war came, Culp decided to stick with his new friends by enlisting in Company B, 2nd Virginia Infantry, commanded by Captain Henry Kyd Douglas. According to one of his comrades, Daniel Entler, Culp refused to go back North "because [he] did not wish to." He "espoused the cause of the South of [his] own free will and was as good a rebel as any of us, and as good a soldier." Douglas recalled that Culp was "very little, if any, over five feet, and when captain of the company I procured a special gun for him." Culp's cut-down musket was later recovered after the battle of Gettysburg, where, ironically, he died in the July 2 attack of the 2nd Virginia and the Stonewall Brigade against Union positions on Culp's Hill. Even more ironic, Culp probably died within sight of his birthplace on the hill owned by his cousin Henry, where he had played as a child. On the night of July 1, Culp visited the home of his sister Julia and, according to one account, resisted her pleas to desert from the Confederate army. Like George Junkin, Culp had been captured in 1862, taken the oath of allegiance to escape captivity, and returned to Confederate service before he was officially exchanged. An editorial in the *Adams Sentinel*, dated June 3, 1862, angrily confirmed this fact: "Our young townsman, Wesley Culp, was taken prisoner at the battle of

Winchester—took the oath of allegiance to the U. States—was released—then joined a band of guerrilas [*sic*], and has been captured again. He is good and ripe for summary process or at least ought to be." Local lore also maintains that Culp had met Johnston H. Skelly of the 87th Pennsylvania, another Gettysburg native and a good friend of his brother's, a few weeks before at Winchester. Skelly, mortally wounded at Winchester, was engaged to Mary Virginia Wade—the only civilian to die at Gettysburg—and had entrusted Culp with a message for Miss Wade. The message was never delivered.[31]

Men of science traveled south from Pennsylvania in the years before the war in hopes that their skills would be in greater demand there than in the Northeast. Henry Garey, born in Berlin, Pennsylvania, in 1830, graduated from Jefferson Medical College in 1860 and immediately moved to Cockrum, Mississippi, to serve as the town's only doctor. He took his younger brother Joseph with him. When war broke out, Henry enlisted in the 4th Mississippi Cavalry as assistant surgeon, and Joseph joined the Pettus "Flying Artillery." Both still had strong family ties to Pennsylvania, but no evidence of remorse may be found in Joseph's diary, which covers his service from 1861 to 1864. On the contrary, he wrote movingly of the defeated Confederacy in ideological terms on April 24, 1866: "Many of her braves lie mouldering beneath the clouds of the valley, but they rest in peace from the usurpers' wrongs & opposition. Peace to their ashes."[32] Another Pennsylvanian involved in scientific pursuits was Colonel George Washington Scott of the 5th Battalion Florida Cavalry, who had moved to Florida in 1851 for the climate's "salubrious effect on his health." He bought a small plantation, established a mercantile business in Tallahassee, and during the war managed a salt-production facility on the coast near Newport, providing tons of much-needed salt to the Confederate government. At the same time he resisted frequent Union naval raids as commander of his cavalry battalion.[33]

Many business-minded Pennsylvanians who ventured South before the war enlisted in Virginia regiments. One of them, Rufus B. McCrum, was another member of the 1st Rockbridge Artillery. Born in Mifflinburg in 1844, McCrum settled in Lexington shortly before the war and helped his brother establish a town landmark, McCrum's drugstore. The 1860 census lists him as a clerk, aged fifteen, and in March 1864 he enlisted at "Frederick's Hall," fighting with the battery in the Overland campaign and at Petersburg. He was paroled at Appomattox. A notation next to his name in the company roster states that he "made a bright record for bravery and faithfulness for duty." Private Thomas B. Mullen of the 5th Virginia Infantry also moved to Lexington in

1847 from Franklin County. Although his prewar occupation is unknown, he established a foundry and machine shop in town after the war. William M. Deane, born in Mechanicsburg in 1835, was a plumber in Kernstown, Virginia, by the time he enlisted in the 2nd Virginia Infantry. Similarly, Major Samuel B. Myer of Company C, 7th Virginia Cavalry, born in Rochtsville in 1830, moved to Shenandoah County, Virginia, in 1852 and became owner of the Union Forge there.[34]

William McComb, a Pennsylvanian who attained the rank of brigadier general in the Army of Northern Virginia, also moved to the South for economic reasons. Born in Mercer County in 1828, he went to Tennessee in 1854 and established a flour mill on the Cumberland River at Clarksville. When the war began, McComb enlisted as a private in the 14th Tennessee Infantry, was soon elected lieutenant, and rose through the ranks of his regiment while participating in all the major battles of the Army of Northern Virginia except for Gettysburg. Severely wounded twice, McComb received his promotion to brigadier general in the twilight of the Confederacy on January 20, 1865. He never returned to his native state, dying on his plantation near Gordonsville, Virginia, at age ninety in 1918. McComb ranked among the more successful Confederate Pennsylvanians, but his experiences were in many ways similar to Pennsylvanians who established businesses in the South before the war and later fought to defend them.[35]

Whereas ideological reasons motivated George Junkin to battle for the Confederacy, and economic and ideological considerations influenced Wesley Culp, Joseph Garey, and William McComb, marital ties proved decisive for the most famous Pennsylvania Confederates. For these men, loyalty to their spouse, above all other considerations, overcame devotion to the Union. Indeed, protecting their wives and families became ideological motives. Like for many other Confederates, defense of hearth and home proved the decisive factor in convincing them to fight. Josiah Gorgas, chief of Confederate ordnance; John C. Pemberton, defender of Vicksburg; and Johnson Kelly Duncan, commander of the New Orleans defenses in 1862, all married southern women. Each of these men played roles in the struggle for Confederate independence that had an important effect on the outcome of the war.

Without the leadership that Gorgas provided in the Ordnance Department, the armies of Robert E. Lee and Joseph E. Johnston would probably have been denied adequate ammunition. Gorgas, argued his biographer Frank Vandiver, "has long been regarded as the administrative genius of the Confederacy," and "the products of his industry had profound influence on the course of the war." Whereas his fellow bureau chiefs generally failed to supply the necessary shoes, uniforms, food, fodder, and transportation to the Confederate armies, Gorgas succeeded admirably in ensuring that the troops had the requisite firepower at their disposal. After the first year of the war, during which Gorgas struggled to overcome the inherent deficiencies of an agrarian economy unprepared for conflict, the Confederate Ordnance Department developed an impressive system of arsenals, armories, factories, powder works, mines, and laboratories that devised substitutes for leather, copper, and fulminate of mercury; discovered new sources of niter and lead; and created a complex network of arms purchasers and blockade-runners abroad. When Lee surrendered at Appomattox, his soldiers may have had little food and precious few shoes, but they had enough shells for their artillery and minie balls for their muskets. Without the generous and timely supply of ordnance to its armies, concluded Vandiver, "the Confederate States would have been short-lived indeed."[36]

Gorgas was born at Running Pumps in Lancaster County on July 1, 1818, and graduated from West Point in 1841. In 1853 he married Amelia Gayle, the daughter of the former governor of Alabama. Thereafter the couple traveled around the country as Gorgas was assigned to one fort after the other, mainly in the East. As war clouds loomed, Gorgas wrote in his diary of the approaching danger. He generally chastised Republican politicians (including the new governor of Maine, Hannibal Hamlin, whom he despised) for their harsh words toward the South, but his writings never foreshadowed his future choice of the Southern cause. But on March 31, 1861, he noted in his diary: "An army being organized at the South a commission was offered to me in it. I declined then, but being much urged by own sympathies & likings, & importuned by my Southern friends, I sent in my resignation on the 27th, to take effect on the 3d of April. I might have passed the summer here on account of . . . mother's health, but that I was ordered away from here (very wrongfully) & so I thought I might as well make one move of it & go where I should ultimately have to go, I doubt not."[37]

Gorgas finished the entry describing how he would leave his family in Charleston for safekeeping and then proceed to meet the new Confederate secretary of war, Leroy Pope Walker of Alabama.

At first glance, it appears that Gorgas was persuaded by his own feelings and his friends' suggestions to side with the South, but his statement "I thought I might as well make a move of it & go where I should ultimately have to go" warrants further examination. Gorgas's birth family lived in Pennsylvania and the North, and his allegiance to the Union was unquestionable. He had a secure job in the United States army—although, significantly, he had recently complained about his immediate superior Colonel Henry Knox Craig, who had refused repeated requests for leave and preferred post transfers and was about to send him to demeaning "foundry duty." Moreover, Gorgas had only limited contact with prosecession Southerners before the attack on Fort Sumter.[38] Why would he fight for the South? One reason could be that he believed he had to "go where [he] ultimately had to go"—to the defense of his wife's land. He could not remain in an army that might invade his Southern home and threaten his Southern family. Earlier in March, Gorgas had received a letter from General P. G. T. Beauregard suggesting to him a possible Confederate commission. Gorgas politely declined. "All my sympathies are with you," he informed Beauregard, adding: "I hesitate to act, unless I am wanted, or unless I am tempted greatly to my advantage."[39] For Gorgas to desert the Union, much more than friends' persuasion, disgust at a superior, or an uncertain offer would be necessary. In the end, Gorgas fought for the Confederacy because he had married a Southern woman, and like native Southerners ideologically driven to defend hearth and home, Gorgas became a Confederate to protect what he held most dear: his wife.

Brigadier General Johnson Kelly Duncan, born March 19, 1827, in York County, was another exemplary Confederate officer who based his military service on marital allegiance. After graduating from West Point in 1849, Duncan became friends with George B. McClellan on an exploring expedition in the Northwest for the Northern Pacific Railroad. McClellan later frequented New Orleans while officially surveying the Texas Coast. P. G. T. Beauregard was also stationed in New Orleans, and Braxton Bragg owned a sugar plantation nearby. It was through McClellan's association with either Beauregard or Bragg that Duncan received the job in 1855 of superintendent of repairs of New Orleans. Working on the Branch Mint, the Marine Hospital, and other prominent structures in the city, Duncan became well known there and married Mary Grimshaw, daughter of a successful Crescent City merchant. He conspired with McClellan, then director of operations of the Illinois Central Railroad, in possibly aiding William Walker's filibustering operation in Nicaragua in 1857. By 1860, Duncan had firmly settled into New Orleans society and his new post of chief engineer of public works. He was positively devoted to his wife, Mary, and warmly embraced by her prominent family. When Louisiana seceded in January 1861, Duncan's influential connections offered him a colonel's commission in the Provisional Army of the Confederacy, and he unhesitatingly accepted.[40]

He was given command of coastal defenses in and around New Orleans, including Forts Jackson and St. Philip. When residents of the city learned of his appointment they had confidence he would defend them from attack. Confederate authorities believed the Federal army would advance up the Mississippi River. Duncan, however, realized the vulnerability of the city's seaward defenses and repeatedly attempted to use his influence to secure adequate artillery for the two forts, enlarge them, and take command of the makeshift naval squadron stationed nearby. His herculean efforts did not go unrecognized. His immediate superior, Major General Mansfield Lovell, whose assistant, Brigadier General Daniel Ruggles, had fallen ill, wrote Jefferson Davis on October 31, 1861, that "Duncan is worth a dozen Ruggles." He had "rendered most efficient service, with a zeal, untiring industry and ability, which entitle him to your high consideration." Promoted to brigadier general on January 7, 1862, Duncan's rank proved insufficient to override the bureaucratic objections of Commander John K. Mitchell of the naval squadron, who answered only to Secretary of the Navy Stephen R. Mallory, or the obdurate demeanor of the various civilian captains, who refused to follow any orders except those issued by Louisiana Governor Thomas D. Moore. As a result, the powerful ironclad CSS *Louisiana*, newly constructed in New Orleans, and the steamboat-rams that accompanied it were not allowed to pass below Forts Jackson and St. Philip and engage the mortar flotilla of Rear Admiral David Dixon Porter. Federal ships so damaged the two forts during the bombardment of April 18–23, 1862, that when David Farragut and the Northern deepwater fleet steamed up river on the 24th, only three vessels failed to pass the forts.[41]

Crestfallen, General Duncan surrendered the forts shortly after the fall of New Orleans, was captured and officially exchanged, and was later assigned the position of chief of staff to General Braxton Bragg, who appeared cognizant of Duncan's abilities. Unfortunately for the Confederacy, Duncan caught typhoid fever and died at Knoxville on December 18, 1862. A general order proclaimed Duncan as "among the brightest and bravest spirits of the many who have given their lives to the holy cause of freedom." Duncan's old regiment, the Louisiana Regular Artillery, decreed him to be one of the Confederacy's "most able, gallant and efficient generals."[42] One can only wonder how and where Duncan might have served his adopted cause had he lived longer.

Probably the best-known Pennsylvanian who fought for the Confederacy was Lieutenant General John C. Pemberton. Although numerous enlisted men from the Keystone State contributed significantly to the Southern cause and other officers proved talented (or in Gorgas's case, indispensable), Pemberton, by virtue of the fact that he commanded a most important Confederate stronghold at one of the critical junctures in the war, was unique. His decisions at Vicksburg had a monumental impact on the fate of the Confederacy. The loss of the southern Gibraltar allowed Union control of the Mississippi, split the Confederacy in two, badly damaged Confederate morale, and, most important, caused the loss of more than 30,000 Southern troops. Pemberton has had his defenders and critics through the years, but the fact remains that he lost Vicksburg to Ulysses S. Grant. This fact coupled with his birthplace make him one of the most important and unusual Confederates of the war.

Born in Philadelphia on August 10, 1814, the son of a respected family, Pemberton graduated in the class of 1837 at West Point, fought gallantly in the Mexican War, and became close to both Jefferson Davis and Joseph E. Johnston. His friendship with these two men, who personally despised each other, contributed greatly to his advancement through the ranks, often at the expense of native Southern officers. Yet Pemberton's decision to resign from the United States army rested not on friendship with Southerners, but almost completely on the basis that he had married a Southerner, Martha "Pattie" Thompson, the daughter of a respected shipper in Norfolk. After the Mexican War he had served stints in Florida, Louisiana, New York, and the West, and Pattie accompanied him everywhere. They had seven children and an extremely close relationship.[43]

He also kept strong relations with his brother and sister in Philadelphia, and during the secession crisis maintained a lively exchange of letters with his brother Israel. A resolute Union man politically, Pemberton had resolved not to resign unless his wife's native state, Virginia, seceded. Even after Virginia left the Union, he refused to follow his earlier preset course, plagued by his conscience and worried about the effect his resignation would have on the Pembertons in Philadelphia. On April 19, 1861, he received orders to "seize and hold possession of, in the name of the President of the United States" all the steamers found between Washington (where he was stationed at the time) and Acquia Creek. He unswervingly performed this duty. Having previously sent his family south to Charleston, Pemberton received almost daily letters from his wife urging him to resign. "My darling husband," Pattie wrote on April 23, "why are you not with us? Why do you stay?" Sensing his brother's wavering loyalties, Israel desperately tried to persuade him to remain true to Pennsylvania, arguing that he would lose all his friends, could never return home again, and would deeply embarrass the Pemberton family name. Israel traveled to Washington in a last-minute attempt to sway his brother's course but had to admit that his brother's "ideas of duty & honor are all the other way." When Pemberton resigned from the United States army on April 24, his sister responded, "I have been more wretched in this horrid state than words can tell." Yet she respected her brother's decision, claiming that "I must accept it . . . we have done all we can."[44]

In the end, argues Pemberton's biographer Michael Ballard, despite strong feelings for Virginia that Pemberton possessed even before meeting Pattie, it was she who ultimately compelled him to side with the South: "The only reasonable conclusion is that Pemberton left the Union because of his marriage. . . . His choice ultimately came down to fighting for the North or fighting for Pattie, and for John Pemberton that was no choice at all."[45]

How do we assess Confederate Pennsylvanians and place them in the proper historical context? First, Pennsylvania was not unabashedly Unionist during the secession crisis. Many regions of the state, particularly Philadelphia, contained outspoken advocates for peaceful secession if not outright union with the new Confederacy. Democrats led the way in their critique of the Republicans, yet business leaders also saw merit in continuing friendly ties with the South. Second, when war broke out, the vast majority of Pennsylvanians immediately supported the Union, but an important and little-known group of men severed their ties with their native state and enlisted in the Confederate armies. Their reasons varied from ideological support of the Southern cause, to defense of homes and businesses established in the prewar South, to a devotion to wives and family that outweighed allegiance to Pennsylvania and the Union. Some of these men, such as Josiah Gorgas and John Pemberton, rose to positions of prominence and responsibility in the Confederacy, and the immediate impact of their service was readily visible. Others, such as Wesley Culp, became legends, but most faded into anonymity with their service as Confederate enlisted men and officers practically forgotten. Third, the number of such "Keystone Confederates" will probably never be fully known, but their efforts should be remembered. These Pennsylvanians fought for reasons similar to those that led their former friends to support the Union: home, family, friends, economic prosperity, and belief in the righteousness of their cause. Yet their motivations were not exactly the same as those of blue-coated Pennsylvanians. These men fought for the

South, not the North, and offer a new perspective into understanding why men fought and what values were most important to them. Loyalty to one's respective section or state, in this case Pennsylvania, was not necessarily a foregone conclusion. New ties outweighed devotion to older ones, and place of birth did not always predetermine national identity.

AVENUE OF DREAMS

Patriotism and the Spectator at Philadelphia's Great Central Sanitary Fair

Elizabeth Milroy

Between 1863 and 1865 more than two dozen sanitary fairs were organized in various Northern cities to raise money for the United States Sanitary Commission. Not simply entertainment or money-making ventures, these fairs were "lessons in loyalty" staged in exhibition spaces selected or constructed and decorated to elicit patriotic fervor and national pride.[1] The largest of these events took place at Philadelphia in June 1864 and was grandly titled the Great Central Sanitary Fair. When filled with domestic and manufactured goods, military souvenirs, artworks, and other items donated by the citizens of the Delaware Valley and then decorated throughout with tricolored bunting and battle flags, the exhibition complex specially built to house the Great Central Sanitary Fair became a wondrous space of patriotic consumerism (see Fig. 2.1). In an official history of the fair published soon after the event, Charles Stillé likened the displays to a religious sanctuary: "the light reflected from countless

I first presented some of the ideas developed in this essay while a faculty fellow at the Center for the Humanities at Wesleyan University. Funding for further research on the history of cultural institutions in Philadelphia came from the National Endowment for the Humanities, the American Philosophical Society, and The Library Company of Philadelphia. My sincerest thanks to the following individuals: Nancy Armstrong, Beth Carroll-Horrocks, Jacqueline Clark, Diane Dillon, Ken Finkel, Roy Goodman, James Green, Elizabeth Kornhauser, Phil Lapsansky, Cheryl Leibold, Diana Linden, Charlotte Emans Moore, Richard Ohmann, Darrel Sewell, Linda Stanley, John Van Horne, and Sarah Weatherwax. Special thanks to Elizabeth Anderson for her generous hospitality and to Jennifer Burwell who patiently and perceptively critiqued the final drafts.

Fig. 2.1 Robert Newell, *Union Avenue* (frontispiece to the *Philadelphia Photographer,* October 1864). The Library Company of Philadelphia.

objects of every variety of form and hue, was a sight like that of the illumi-nation of Saint Peter's, the sight of a lifetime."[2] The act of touring the exhibi-tion buildings assumed a ceremonial dimension as visitors were urged to view and buy the commodities accumulated in the cause of Union victory.

Despite the frequency and popularity of the Civil War sanitary fairs, and the many descriptions and reports of these events published during and soon after the war, they disappeared from Civil War historiography for almost a century. This situation corrected itself starting in the 1950s when historians began to devote more energy to documenting and interpreting activities on the home front. But only in the past decade have the sanitary fairs, and indeed the Sanitary Commission itself, received rigorous and sustained study. Among these recent works are J. Matthew Gallman's valuable account of wartime Philadelphia, which includes a chapter on the Great Central Sanitary Fair, and a new monograph by Beverly Gordon on the history of American fund-raising fairs from the early nineteenth century to the present—published while this essay was in the final stages of preparation—which provides an informative overview of the sanitary fair movement throughout the Northern states, with short discussions of the art galleries and other special exhibits in the various "fair" cities.[3]

Philadelphia's sanitary fair deserves another visit for what it can tell us much about how specific objects produced political meaning and how the fair may have contributed to the postwar development of public space and cul-tural institutions in the city. The displays at the Great Central Sanitary Fair embodied changes in modes of visual consumption prompted by specific his-torical circumstances and ideological needs. These changes can be discerned in particular in the presentation of works of art, which were among the most popular and lucrative components of these events. And because these art exhi-bitions showcased local tastes and treasures, they differed significantly from one fair to the next. Moreover, because valuable and unique artworks usually are carefully preserved, it is possible to reassemble at least some of the objects displayed in these galleries. Using the catalogues of the exhibitions sold at the various fairs, we can learn a great deal about mid-nineteenth-century American taste and exhibition design and also gain some sense of how specific artworks were put to use during the Civil War.

The Philadelphia fair showcased more than one thousand paintings, sculp-tures, and watercolors, as well as dozens of prints and photographs by both professional and amateur artists. The largest art exhibition ever held in North America, it was also among the first to be photographed. The Fine Arts

Committee mined artists' studios and private collections in Philadelphia and other cities—in America and throughout Europe—both to tout America's artistic riches and to instill in its citizenry a patriotic fervor modeled on its past, especially the War for Independence. The success of the Art Gallery of the Great Central Sanitary Fair inspired these men and women after the war to reassess the role particularly of art museums in the postwar period.

In structure and purpose, the Great Central Sanitary Fair marked an important stage in what British scholar Tony Bennett christened the "exhibitionary complex," a nineteenth-century movement that simultaneously helped to form a new public and to regulate that public through new relations of sight and vision. The institutions comprising this exhibitionary complex—among which Bennett includes art, science, and history museums; department stores; and international exhibitions—formed a network of disciplinary and power relations directed to the systematic transfer of objects and bodies from display in the enclosed or private domains where they had previously been exhibited only to a restricted public into progressively more open and public arenas. Once arrayed in these arenas, such objects and bodies became vehicles for inscribing and broadcasting messages of power throughout society.[4] By enacting the power to command and arrange things and bodies for public display, these institutions "sought to allow the people, and en masse rather than individually, . . . to become, in seeing themselves from the side of power, both the subjects and the objects of knowledge, knowing power and what power knows, and knowing themselves as (ideally) known by power, interiorizing its gaze as a principle of self-surveillance and, hence, self-regulation."[5]

Like Michel Foucault, Bennett is concerned with understanding the problem of social and political order. But whereas Foucault locates solutions to this problem in discipline and surveillance, Bennett conceives the exhibitionary complex as a counter to Foucault's "carceral archipelago." The problem to which Foucault's "swarming of disciplinary mechanisms" responded was that of making extended populations governable. But, as Bennett goes on to note, "the development of bourgeois polities required not merely that the populace be governable but that it assent to its governance, thereby creating a need to enlist active popular support for the values and objectives enshrined in the state." Foucault locates one embodiment of state power in the penitentiary, "even at the very center of the cities of the nineteenth century, the monotonous figure, at once material and symbolic, of the power to punish." Bennett counters this with the museum, also typically located at the heart of the city which both as architecture and as an institution functioned as the symbol "of a power to 'show and tell' which, in being deployed in a newly constituted open and public space, sought rhetorically to incorporate the people within the processes of the state."[6] Here power was expressed through rhetorical effect rather than incarceration, promoting a technology of vision that regulated a broad audience rather than marginalized individuals.[7]

The Civil War caught the Union unprepared to fight a conflict of such magnitude. Before the war began, the United States maintained a standing army of approximately 15,000 men, served by the Medical Bureau of the War Department. By the end of 1861, Abraham Lincoln had sent out calls for a half million volunteers. Most men who responded, officer and enlisted alike, had little or no military training or experience. Specifically, few of the volunteers were familiar with proper methods of bivouacking and sustaining large numbers of men. Army camps were often hastily constructed and badly administered, with only the most primitive sanitary facilities. When the inevitable battle casualties arrived, the capabilities of the Medical Bureau were severely taxed. Indeed, the Washington bureaucracy in general was woefully unprepared to meet wartime demands. Logistical systems were rudimentary and lacking in proper accountability. Supplies and appropriations frequently were misdirected or became tangled in political infighting.

Civilian relief agencies helped the government meet the increased need for health care. Since the early part of the nineteenth century, managers of various benevolent organizations throughout the United States had developed systematic methods for tapping local philanthropic resources. Religious, charitable, patriotic, and humanitarian causes competed for public sympathy and support. When war erupted, philanthropy and patriotism fused. As local regiments marched off to war, support groups, composed primarily of women, were formed. By war's end, some 7,000 independent relief groups operated throughout the North, with members busily sewing garments; knitting scarves and socks; or assembling packages of food, tobacco, and other delicacies for the men in uniform.

The proliferation of relief groups and societies throughout the North following the fall of Fort Sumter occasioned calls for some kind of central supervisory organization. At the urging of Dr. Elizabeth Blackwell, a delegation led by Henry Bellows, the influential minister of New York's All Souls Unitarian Church, traveled to Washington to propose that a committee of civilians be appointed to assist the inefficient and overtaxed Medical Bureau. Although Abraham Lincoln and several members of his administration questioned the viability of such a group, the lobbying succeeded. In June 1861, the president approved the creation of the United States Sanitary Commission.[8]

Although never receiving the policy-making authority that its founders had envisioned, the Sanitary Commission became a formidable advocate for the Union soldier and sailor. Agents hired by the Sanitary Commission looked for ways to improve the medical inspection of recruits and enlisted men, as well as to ensure that soldiers enjoyed a good quality of life through the proper provision of cooks, nurses, and hospitals. Commission physicians devised new surgical techniques, medical treatment, and procedures for transporting the wounded; commission agents and physicians investigated and reported on the living conditions of prisoners of war; and commission nurses—both men and women—provided improved levels of care.[9]

The commission played a significant role in the design and construction of the spaces where wounded soldiers recuperated or, more often, died.[10] Commissioners fought for the construction of larger and better-equipped hospitals and battlefield convalescent camps, the formation of ambulance brigades, and the establishment of Soldiers' Homes. The sick and wounded were transported away from the dirt and chaos of the battlefield, by train, wagon, or hospital ship to hospitals. Soldiers on furlough or passing through cities were entertained and occupied at refreshment centers, in the hope of keeping them away from the temptations of saloons. By war's end, the Sanitary Commission had supervised the distribution of more than $15 million worth of supplies to soldiers in the field and in prison camps.

The Sanitary Commission sought to transcend state borders and local interests. Commissioners encouraged workers to take the broad national perspective needed to reestablish the Union. The author of an 1863 pamphlet entitled "How Can We Best Help Our Camps and Hospitals?" noted: "The Commission has done the country some service, in relieving the sufferings and saving the lives of its soldiers; still more in teaching the Army the importance of Sanitary laws; but its highest office has been, and is, to nationalize the Sympathy of the People with the sufferings and privations of the People's Army." Initially relief efforts had been local in focus, this writer noted, but as the war dragged on civilians "were gradually compelled to enlarge their views and look beyond community and state. Soldiers' aid became a prime force for unifying the nation." By spearheading the "nationalizing" of the "people," the Sanitary Commission became a powerful political organization.[11]

As several historians recently have demonstrated, the history of relief efforts during the Civil War was an unending struggle between the myriad local relief committees, organized in numerous American cities and towns and run predominantly by women, and the efforts of the Washington-based and male-dominated Sanitary Commission to establish and maintain control over a centralized distribution system.[12] From its beginnings, the Sanitary Commission relied on cash donations collected by agents throughout the North and sent to the central treasury located in New York or to the various branch offices.[13] By summer 1863, contributions had totaled almost three-quarters of a million dollars. But the rate of expenditure far outpaced donations. Months of heavy fighting both in the east and the west had severely taxed the resources of local relief agencies and the commission itself. As supplies diminished, the situation worsened.

An apparent solution to the shortage of money came in early fall 1863 when Chicago women organized a charity fair to benefit the Sanitary Commission. They appealed for donations from fellow citizens and solicited contributions of money or consumer goods from the mercantile, industrial, and agricultural communities, not only in Chicago but in all the Northern states.[14] Male directors of the Sanitary Commission's branch office in Chicago initially belittled the women's efforts. Their attitudes changed, however, when the Northwest Fair proved an unqualified success and inspired relief committees in other cities to organize similar "sanitary" fairs. By the end of 1863, fairs had been conducted in Boston, Rochester, and Cincinnati, and fair committees were at work in New York, Cleveland, Pittsburgh, and Albany.[15]

Although organizers advertised that the fairs benefited the Sanitary Commission, the "sanitary fair movement" was not welcomed by the organization. Commission members worried that these events subverted their centralizing efforts and distracted much-needed woman- and manpower. And they feared that reports of the large financial proceeds garnered at the fairs might lead the public to assume the commission had more than enough funding when, in fact, no effective system was ever established to forward such proceeds to the commission's coffers. Still the sanitary fairs enabled men and women in various communities to work for the war effort and to advertise the virtues of a reunited nation in at least a semblance of unity, even if commitment to the Sanitary Commission was only nominal. By war's end, sanitary fairs had become regular events on the Northern calendar.[16]

Planning for Philadelphia's Great Central Sanitary Fair began in January 1864, when the executive committee of the Women's Pennsylvania Branch of the Sanitary Commission passed a resolution to hold the event. This resolution was seconded by their male colleagues of the Union League, who then urged the executive committee of the Philadelphia branch of the Sanitary Commission to authorize a fair, "the proceeds of which shall be given to the Sanitary Commission, to be applied by it to promote the health, comfort and efficiency of the army of the Union."[17] As in other cities, the activities of male and female organizers were segregated: contributions were organized by departments or categories, each administered by two committees, one all female the second all male. An all-male executive committee was formed to oversee planning: the members included bankers, industrialists, machinists, merchants, attorneys, physicians, and academics. John Welsh was appointed chairman, Caleb Cope the treasurer, Charles Stillé the corresponding secretary, and Horace Furness the recording secretary. Eleven women, including Mrs. Charles Stillé, formed a committee of organization to supervise the formation and membership of the women's committees sponsoring displays and sales booths.[18]

As J. Matthew Gallman has recounted in his history of wartime Philadelphia, the Great Central Sanitary Fair both continued and expanded established patterns of benevolence in the city.[19] Many of the men and women who volunteered for the fair already had experience producing public displays and exhibitions. Most of the members of the executive committee, for example, had served on the boards of directors of such institutions as the Franklin Institute, the Pennsylvania Academy of the Fine Arts, and the Pennsylvania Horticultural Society, each of which regularly sponsored significant public exhibitions.

In late March 1864, solicitations for donations printed on flyers or in newspaper advertisements were distributed throughout Philadelphia and southeastern Pennsylvania as well as to neighboring communities in New Jersey and Delaware. Because the executive committee wanted to keep overt politics out of the fair as much as possible, it discouraged participation by private groups. Instead, eighty subcommittees were organized, most around particular trades, products, or types of displays, including "Carpets, Oil Cloths, and Mattings," "Furs, Hats, and Caps," "Hardware," "Paper-hanging," "Plumbing," and "Umbrellas, Parasols, and Canes." Several of these groupings repeated exhibit categories used at the American Manufactures Exhibitions, organized by the Franklin Institute since 1824 to stimulate domestic manufacturing. This similarity reflected the fact that many of the same merchants and industrialists who came together to plan the Central Fair had worked for or had exhibited at the Franklin Institute fairs before the war. Like all nineteenth-century expositions, the sanitary fair showcased displays of machinery, finished products, and objets d'art as material signifiers of progress. The wartime event celebrated the achieved power and progress of the Northern industrial economy, with leaders of the capitalist establishment coordinating the collective patriotic effort.[20]

Organizers initially planned to hold the Central Fair at the Academy of Music on Broad Street, but reports from other cities of large crowds pressing into inadequate spaces prompted Philadelphians to rethink the fair's venue.[21] Organizers foresaw that the regularity of "exhibitions of articles of interest or curiosity under the denomination of Fairs" had accustomed the public to think of these as "hackneyed" affairs. They thus had determined to make the Great Central Sanitary Fair something "calculated to fix the imagination by its magnitude, the novelty and variety of its preparations, the picturesqueness of the scene, and the unequalled rarity and attractiveness of the display."[22] Reports that New Yorkers had raised more than a million dollars at their Metropolitan Sanitary Fair in April doubtless also encouraged the Philadelphians to surpass their upstart rivals with a fair larger and more lucrative than anything ever before attempted. Whereas in other cities the fairs were housed in existing structures, such as armories or concert halls, the Philadelphians decided to build a massive temporary exhibition hall expressly for the sanitary fair.

The committee first selected Logan Square for the exhibition hall, an area northwest of Centre Square and the last of the original six squares laid out in William Penn's original plan of Philadelphia.[23] Strickland Kneass, a local engineer best known for his innovative bridges, designed a temporary exhibition complex of sixteen buildings set atop the existing layout of lawns and walkways on Logan Square. Lithographer James Queen's contemporary view of the Great Central Sanitary Fair records the impressive scale of the fair complex (see Fig. 2.2). The central block, nicknamed "Union Avenue," ran from east to west the width of the square, some 540 feet long and 64 feet wide, with a height of 51 feet to the point of a cast-iron ogive vault. Great care was taken to protect trees on the square: the branches of several trees extended through the roof, making a natural decoration, "which harmonizes very agreeably with the red, white and blue drapery with which the roofs of the buildings are profusely hung."[24] At the center of the avenue, extending through the roof, stood a 216-foot-high flagpole donated by the city's shipwrights. To the south of Union Avenue was a wooden-roofed round building housing the restaurant; to the north a similar structure, with canvas canopy,

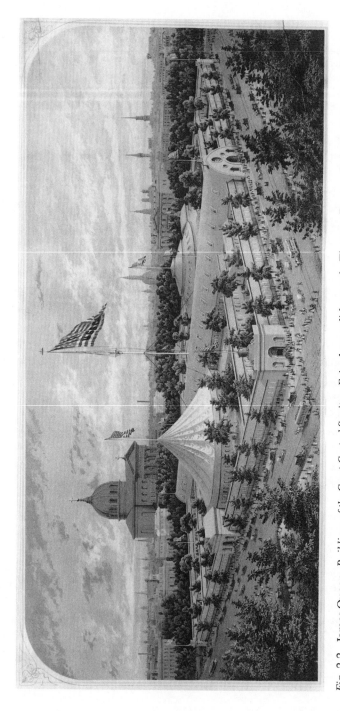

Fig. 2.2 James Queen, *Buildings of the Great Central Sanitary Fair*, chromolithograph. The new Roman Catholic Cathedral of Saints Peter and Paul can be seen at the left; the Wills Eye Hospital is right of center, just beyond the wood-roofed restaurant section of the fair complex. The Library Company of Philadelphia/Historical Society of Pennsylvania.

housed the Floral Department. Four subsidiary buildings extended from both the north and south walls of the central avenue; running parallel to Union Avenue along Race and Vine Streets respectively were buildings 29 feet wide, 18 feet high, and 500 feet long. Construction of the complex started in March 1864. Local construction workers donated their labor, completing the 200,000-square-foot complex in forty days.[25]

The Great Central Sanitary Fair opened on June 7, 1864, with more than 15,000 people attending the opening ceremonies. Many arrived by the new trolley lines that ran along the north and west sides of Logan Square.[26] Admission cost fifty cents—a season ticket five dollars—with an additional fee (twenty-five or fifty cents) to enter such exhibits as the Art Gallery, the Horticultural and Arms and Trophies departments, and the Penn Parlor. A floor plan of the fair was published in guidebooks, and in the first issue of *Our Daily Fare*, a newspaper printed on premises (see Fig. 2.3). The complex included a children's playground; a "Turkish Smoking Divan" for gentlemen wishing to relax away from the crowds; and a bank, post office, and police station at the midpoint of Union Avenue. Although community neighborhoods sponsored some booths (the Eighteenth Ward and West Philadelphia), as did the states of Delaware and New Jersey, the majority of booths were organized according to the trades or industries for which committees had been appointed. These were sited throughout the complex in no apparent sequence, most of them along Union Avenue. The public could use one of six entrances. For example, a visitor entering Union Avenue from Eighteenth Street to the east (according to the numbering on the floor plan), could turn to the right or left to view the New Jersey or Delaware sections, respectively, or by going ahead would first encounter the displays contributed by students of the School of Design for Women to the left, the Eighteenth Ward display in the middle of the exhibit hall, and the "Paper and Stationery" booth to the right; then the editing committee's desk, the booksellers' booth, a display of "Fancy Articles," the West Philadelphia booth, and the "produce" exhibit.

The Great Central Sanitary Fair combined the basic structure of traditional county fairs and antebellum mechanics' institute fairs, such as those sponsored by the Franklin Institute, with an overlay of patriotic purpose and decor.[27] Visitors paid admission to see and shop for items in donated exhibits; attend dramatic performances and musical concerts; and sample the offerings of various restaurants and food emporia. Tricolored bunting and regimental battle flags were always in evidence. The majority of volunteer workers at the fair were young upper-middle-class women—often the daughters of the fair

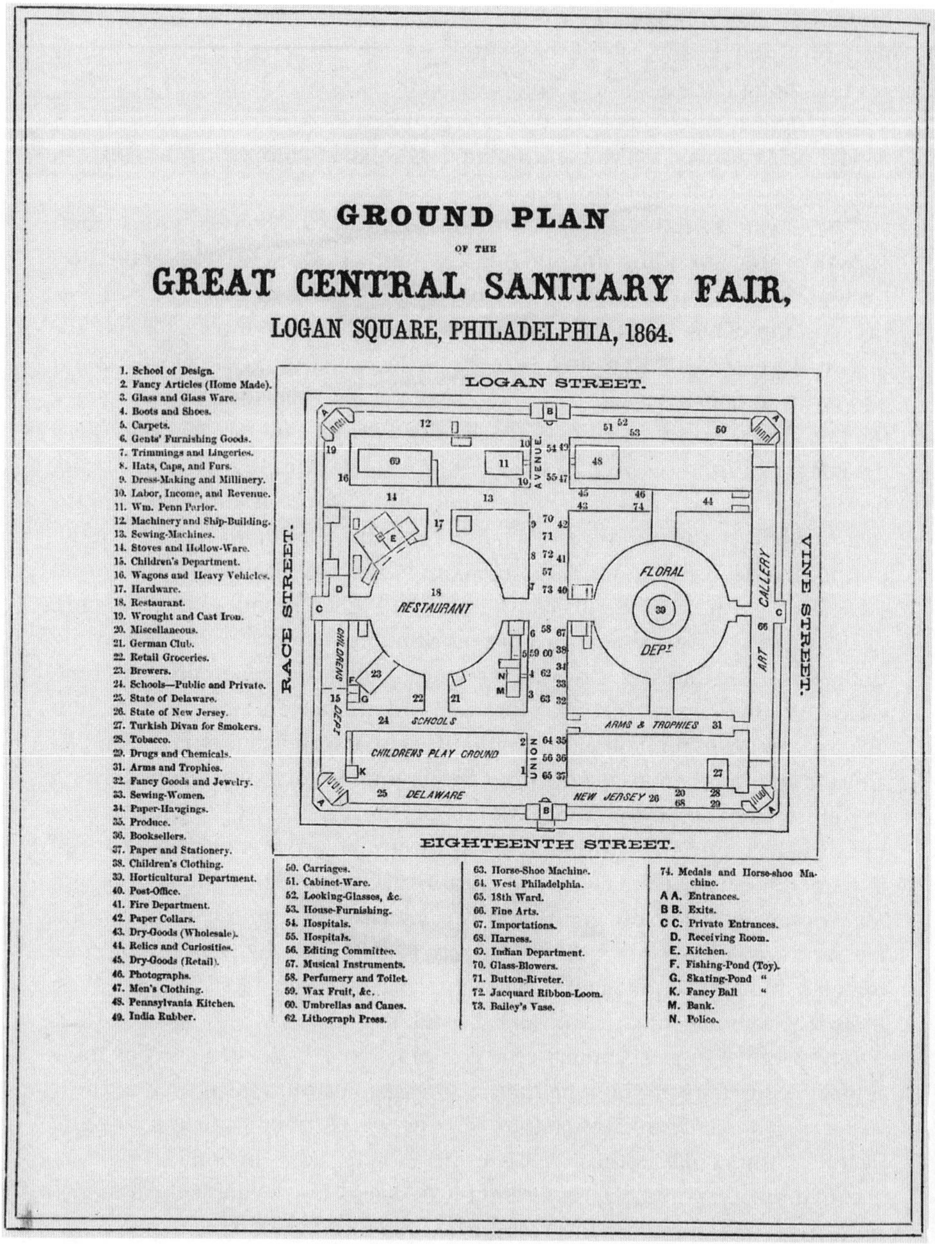

GROUND PLAN

OF THE

GREAT CENTRAL SANITARY FAIR,

LOGAN SQUARE, PHILADELPHIA, 1864.

1. School of Design.
2. Fancy Articles (Home Made).
3. Glass and Glass Ware.
4. Boots and Shoes.
5. Carpets.
6. Gents' Furnishing Goods.
7. Trimmings and Lingeries.
8. Hats, Caps, and Furs.
9. Dress-Making and Millinery.
10. Labor, Income, and Revenue.
11. Wm. Penn Parlor.
12. Machinery and Ship-Building.
13. Sewing-Machines.
14. Stoves and Hollow-Ware.
15. Children's Department.
16. Wagons and Heavy Vehicles.
17. Hardware.
18. Restaurant.
19. Wrought and Cast Iron.
20. Miscellaneous.
21. German Club.
22. Retail Groceries.
23. Brewers.
24. Schools—Public and Private.
25. State of Delaware.
26. State of New Jersey.
27. Turkish Divan for Smokers.
28. Tobacco.
29. Drugs and Chemicals.
31. Arms and Trophies.
32. Fancy Goods and Jewelry.
33. Sewing-Women.
34. Paper-Hangings.
35. Produce.
36. Booksellers.
37. Paper and Stationery.
38. Children's Clothing.
39. Horticultural Department.
40. Post-Office.
41. Fire Department.
42. Paper Collars.
43. Dry-Goods (Wholesale).
44. Relics and Curiosities.
45. Dry-Goods (Retail).
46. Photographs.
47. Men's Clothing.
48. Pennsylvania Kitchen.
49. India Rubber.

50. Carriages.
51. Cabinet-Ware.
52. Looking-Glasses, &c.
53. House-Furnishing.
54. Hospitals.
55. Hospitals.
56. Editing Committee.
57. Musical Instruments.
58. Perfumery and Toilet.
59. Wax Fruit, &c.
60. Umbrellas and Canes.
62. Lithograph Press.

63. Horse-Shoe Machine.
64. West Philadelphia.
65. 18th Ward.
66. Fine Arts.
67. Importations.
68. Harness.
69. Indian Department.
70. Glass-Blowers.
71. Button-Riveter.
72. Jacquard Ribbon-Loom.
73. Bailey's Vase.

74. Medals and Horse-shoe Machine.
A A. Entrances.
B B. Exits.
C C. Private Entrances.
D. Receiving Room.
E. Kitchen.
F. Fishing-Pond (Toy).
G. Skating-Pond "
K. Fancy Ball "
M. Bank.
N. Police.

Fig. 2.3   Ground Plan of the Great Central Sanitary Fair from *Our Daily Fare,* no. 1 (June 8, 1864). The Library Company of Philadelphia.

organizers. Although such women would never have engaged in the retail trade in normal times, social restrictions relaxed because of the war. Many worked diligently to persuade fair visitors, especially males, to part with their money. The money-making talents of these women "for the cause" became the subject of some comment and derision, as contemporary cartoons and commentaries attest. The voluntary labor provided by these women was needed and appreciated, but many men feared the outcome of their aggressive, public behavior. Moreover, many female relief workers expressed concern that local women devoted more time to organizing charity events than to the more pressing duties of relief work.

The Logan Square complex was a proto-shopping mall (see Fig. 2.4). Indeed, the commercial aspects of the Central Fair were so pronounced as to create confusion among visitors and concern among local merchants who feared the loss of customers. "The amount of 'shopping' already done at the Fair is very great, and money is flowing at a rate that caused us no small degree of surprise," reported one newspaper within two days after the opening. "Though all goods were displayed in plain sight of the people, inquiries were made for all sorts of things not in the Fair. At the china counters, where exquisite vases and porcelain are displayed, people were all day asking for common dishes, spittoons, castor bottles and other trifles. . . . Many people entered with the idea that the Fair was nothing more than a series of stores, keeping complete stocks in the respective branches of business."[28] For many visitors the urge to shop was stronger than patriotism.

The sanitary fairs introduced new kinds of displays in response to current events. Among the most popular in all the fair cities, including Philadelphia, was the "Arms and Trophies" department. Here were showcased souvenirs and regimental memorabilia—typically not for sale—loaned by local regiments, individual veterans, or private collectors. Rifles, small arms, sabers, and even large-caliber ammunition were neatly arrayed in the space alongside flags, contemporary and vintage uniforms (including one said to have been worn by George Washington), and prints and photographs of celebrated military commanders of the past and present. Artifacts on display in Philadelphia included Revolutionary War-era weapons and ammunition, an Albanian pistol from Constantinople, John Brown's spear "of Harper's Ferry notoriety," and a claymore said to have been owned by the father of Scottish hero Rob Roy.[29]

Two other innovative exhibits were housed in small buildings adjoining the western end of Union Avenue. To the north was the "Pennsylvania Kitchen," where visitors could "ruminate upon how their grandfathers lived in

Fig. 2.4 A. Watson, *The Great Sanitary Fair*, 1864, from a stereograph. The Library
Company of Philadelphia.

their primitive homes" while sampling Pennsylvania Dutch cuisine served by
women in colonial costume. In the corners of this "kitchen" stood "antique"
cupboards filled with pewter, china, and crockery. Dominating one wall was a
stone fireplace, beside which sat "the venerable grandmother plying her
spinning-wheel."[30] Across Union Avenue was the "William Penn Parlor," furnished to re-create the period of Philadelphia's founding and filled with relics
of William Penn, "more curious and valuable than ever gathered before" and
lent by the Historical Society of Pennsylvania, the City of Philadelphia, and

various private collectors, including Penn's descendants. Among the souvenirs on display were original letters and documents signed by Penn, the original charter of the city of Philadelphia, Benjamin West's painting of *Penn's Treaty with the Indians* (lent by Joseph Harrison), and the wampum belt presented to Penn by the Delaware sachems at the treaty's signing in 1682.[31] The cult of George Washington was well represented by artifacts assembled in the "Washington Department," including a lock of Washington's hair, portrait busts and paintings, and a leaden spoon marked G.W., found at Mount Vernon.[32]

To the west of "Arms and Trophies" was the "Floral" or "Horticultural" department, housed in a circular canvas-roofed building 190 feet in diameter. Deer and a peacock grazed on a small patch of lawn just outside this building, lending a parklike atmosphere to the complex. Inside local amateur and professional horticulturists showed their prize specimens on tables set up along circular walkways lit by more than 500 gas jets. Rare orchids graced the table contributed by industrialist Matthias Baldwin. Mrs. George Carpenter donated several palm trees in tubs set in various parts of the space. At the center of the hall, flowering plants and shrubs were arranged in concentric circles around an artificial lake. A rustic bridge led to an island at the center of the lake, on which stood a fountain surrounded by a pyramid of exotic plants, including a date palm, Australian tree ferns, a Bourbon palm, two banana trees "in full fruit," Norwegian pines, the rare "Diffenbachia," and pineapple plants (see Fig. 2.5). Contrasting displays provided the chief attractions of the Floral Department: a "Torrid Zone" of tropical plants with stuffed birds and animals, and a "Frigid Zone" constructed of mountains of ice made of crystallized alum. In the midst of the latter "down upon the frozen sea . . . amid these arctic horrors" could be seen the wreck of a ship "fast locked in the embrace of an ice-drift." Purple filters lighted the Frigid Zone to reproduce the arctic atmosphere described by explorers.[33]

From the Floral Department participants passed directly into the Art Gallery (see Fig. 2.6). Here Philadelphia again surpassed every other sanitary fair.[34] A 500-foot-long gallery featured more than 1,000 artworks, with an insured value of more than $700,000. As was typical, two "Fine Arts Committees"—one all female, the second all male—supervised the selection and installation of the exhibition. Thirty-eight women formed the ladies' committee, chaired by Mrs. Henry Gilpin. Among their ranks were such noted community leaders as Elizabeth Duane Gillespie, Mrs. Bloomfield Moore, and Mrs. George Meade, wife of the general who led the Army of the Potomac. The men's committee was chaired by industrialist Joseph Harrison and counted among its

Fig. 2.5   Robert Newell, *The Great Central Fair, Horticultural Department*, 1864, from a stereograph. Robert Dennis Collection of Stereoscopic Views, Miriam and Ira D. Wallach Division of Art, Prints and Photographs, New York Public Library. Astor, Lenox and Tilden Foundations.

twenty-five members such artists as Thomas Sully, Christian Schussele, John Sartain (who acted as secretary), and Thomas Moran; collectors Henry C. Carey, William Wilstach, George Whitney, and James Claghorn; as well as the influential Unitarian minister William Henry Furness, father of Horace.[35]

In early April 1864, the members of the Fine Arts Committee met with several local artists to explain the scope and purpose of the fair and to solicit loans and donations or any assistance the artists might provide. The committee

Fig. 2.6 John Moran, *Picture Gallery, Sanitary Fair,* from a stereograph. The Library Company of Philadelphia.

suggested that each artist prepare a list of works desirable for exhibition from which contributions would be selected. The artists were responsible for obtaining loan permissions from the owners of their works.[36] Claghorn, who had run an auction house before the war and was an art dealer as well as collector, had charge of contacting artists and collectors outside Philadelphia. He sent solicitations to selected artists in Europe and in several American cities.[37]

Assured by Harrison and Claghorn that the brick walls and tin roof of the Art Gallery would withstand the danger of fire (the art gallery of New York's Metropolitan Fair had been installed in rooms of the Fourteenth Street Armory, a wood building), artists and collectors throughout the North seized this opportunity to advertise their talents or their fine taste and material assets, while at the same time demonstrating their dedication to the Union cause. Few artworks were made expressly for this exhibition and many works by European painters and sculptors were included, thanks to the generosity of private collectors. Although most were by contemporary artists, many of the paintings and sculptures on view had been exhibited more than once before at the Pennsylvania Academy of the Fine Arts. This sanitary fair exhibition, however, was three times larger than the academy's annuals. Indeed, the display probably reminded the several academy directors who worked for the Fine Arts Committee of the inadequate display space in the aging academy facilities.

The Fine Arts Committee did not accept every donation. A week before the fair opened, Harrison called an emergency meeting to deal with "the embarrassment of riches" that resulted from the unexpected response. So many paintings had been submitted to the fair that they exceeded the available wall surface. During previous meetings, the committee had debated various arrangements of the assembled artworks: some members advocated grouping works by nationality, other members suggested groupings by artist or by owner. Realizing that "some principle of arrangement had to be adopted to control the rejection of the surplus," the committee rejected copies and pictures "of doubtful originality" as well as portraits unless the subject was particularly noteworthy (several images of George Washington were accepted). Preference was given to contributions from Boston and New York because these had been solicited, and in cases of about equal merit between "old and modern art," preference was given to the latter.[38]

As the Philadelphians collected works for the exhibition, they were doubtless thinking back to the art gallery of New York's Metropolitan Sanitary Fair, held two months earlier. Assembled by a committee that included such well-known artists as John F. Kensett, Eastman Johnson, and Emanuel Leutze, the New York exhibition also presented paintings, sculpture, and photographs by American and European artists, loaned by private collectors or donated by working artists, and featured several paintings already regarded as American masterpieces. This exhibition was smaller than the Philadelphia display, with about 350 works on view. A portfolio of photographs produced by Brady's studio documents how the New Yorkers arranged the artworks to create a powerfully allusive decorated space. Dominating the northern wall of the gallery was Emanuel Leutze's *Washington Crossing the Delaware* (then owned by Marshall O. Roberts). On the flanking walls hung such works as Thomas

Cole's *Italy*, William Sidney Mount's *The Power of Music*, Daniel Huntington's *Mercy's Dream*, and Frederic Edwin Church's *Niagara*. The care that went into the arrangement of works on view was signaled by the pairing of Church's *Heart of the Andes* and Albert Bierstadt's *Rocky Mountains, Lander's Peak* hung directly opposite one another on the east and west walls (see Fig. 2.7a). Contemporary accounts record that visitors read these two landscapes together as signifying the contrast of South and North.[39] Between them, Leutze's *Washington Crossing the Delaware* made a visual and ideological transit throughout the display to reinforce the theme of fighting for the nation (see Fig. 2.7b). The art gallery was a profoundly moving experience. One soldier recalled that he left the New York fair's art gallery with particular regret: "Many a poor fellow at this moment experiences the blessings which that money has brought and yet I do not know if that money were the chief or greatest good done by the 'Arms and Trophies' or the 'Art Gallery' for what man or woman left either room without a nobler inspiration of Patriotism?"[40]

The Philadelphia fair had a larger gallery area, but one which was singularly unsympathetic as an exhibition space: running parallel to Union Avenue, the art gallery was 500 feet long but only 30 feet wide (to avoid destroying trees), a corridorlike space that may have reminded some visitors of the Long Gallery of the Louvre. Contemporary photographs show an impressive space but one that was also narrow and cramped (see Fig. 2.8). Oil paintings, watercolors, and drawings had to be hung in multiple tiers along 460 running feet of wall. For the last 40 feet of wall, photographs hung on each side. Sculptures were placed on the floor or on tables set in the center of the gallery. Many more artworks were displayed here than at New York's Metropolitan Fair. Not until the Centennial Exhibition would an art exhibition of comparable size be assembled again in the United States. "Connoisseurs speak of it as the finest collection ever gathered together in America," George Fahnestock, a merchant and accomplished amateur scientist, noted in his diary: "Many of them are from choice private collections in New York and this city, and represent high prices. I saw one little thing, simply a man at full length, the whole picture about 5 by 7 inches [worth] $3100. . . . No figures were alluded to on [*sic*] the catalogue, but [a friend] was familiar with many of the works and the owners and artists, and gave us a running commentary as we went along. We remained nearly two hours, elbowing through an immense crowd."[41]

The contents of the art gallery, most effectively of all the exhibits at the fair, embodied the nationalist and internationalist sentiments of the organizers. The oil paintings, watercolors, and sculptures selected for exhibition were typical

Fig. 2.7a Mathew Brady, *West Wall of the Art Gallery, Metropolitan Sanitary Fair*, 1864, albumen print. Worthington Whittredge Papers. Archives of American Art, Smithsonian Institution. Bierstadt's *Rocky Mountains, Landers' Peak* can be seen at left.

Fig. 2.7b Mathew Brady, *North Wall of the Art Gallery, Metropolitan Sanitary Fair*, 1864, albumen print. Worthington Whittredge Papers. Archies of American Art, Smithsonian Institution.

Fig. 2.8 John C. Browne (?), Bierstadt's *Rocky Mountains*, 1864, albumen print. Free
Library of Philadelphia.

of well-informed and well-endowed collections of mid-century Americans, mixing history and genre pieces by fashionable European painters (including Thomas Couture, Jean-Léon Gérôme, Ernest Meissonier, and William Powell Frith) with landscapes, portraits, and history and genre subjects by such American artists as Thomas Sully, Asher Durand, George Inness, and Eastman Johnson. Most private collectors only loaned works for the duration of the fair, but the majority of artists sent works for sale or auction.

As one visitor observed, a good deal of thought went into the installation: "for be it known to the uninitiated that a picture is not hung merely by attaching it to a nail in a wall, and, harmless as a picture seems, artists do not esteem each other's work. To prevent a general massacre and War of the Roses among a thousand rivals, the committee has displayed admirable tact in reconciliation."[42] Although the selection and hanging of the artworks in this exhibition may appear from surviving stereographs to have been arbitrary, Harrison, Claghorn, and the Fine Arts Committee, assisted by contributors, made judicious, provocative, and purposeful selections.

The art gallery was designed to inspire and to educate the spectator. The committee selected paintings and sculpture that eloquently embodied the history and inestimable cultural promise of the traumatized young republic. "Every epoch of modern art has here its type and expression," wrote a reviewer for *Forney's War Press*. "The whole range of art is included and the student of the historical and national development of art could scarcely have a fairer opportunity of examination and comparison."[43] By including works attributed to such European old masters as Rembrandt, Anthony Van Dyck, and Murillo, the committee sought to place American creativity within the context of European tradition and to confirm the pedigree of such American "old masters" as Gilbert Stuart, John Vanderlyn, Raphaelle Peale, and Thomas Sully.

As with sanitary fair art exhibitions in other cities, a significant core group of works on view in Philadelphia functioned not only for aesthetic effect, but also because their subject matter resonated with the political agenda of Unionism. Portraits of the Founding Fathers and subjects from American history, especially those most pertinent to the Delaware Valley, were particular features of the display. Emanuel Leutze and Peter Rothermel, who with eleven and twenty canvases on view respectively were given the largest representation, provided a thorough pictorial history of the nation. Leutze's paintings included *Landing of the Northmen, Vinland* (lent by John H. Towne), *The Departure of Columbus* (lent by B. Frodsham), and *Columbus Landing at America* (lent by W. F. Leech); Rothermel's included *Sir Walter Raleigh Spreading His*

Fig. 2.9 Peter F. Rothermel, *State House on the Day of the Battle of Germantown,* 1862, oil on canvas. Pennsylvania Academy of the Fine Arts. Bequest of Henry C. Gibson.

Cloak for Queen Elizabeth (lent by Mrs. Van Syckel), *The Landing of the Pilgrims* (lent by Matthias Baldwin), *The First Reading of the Declaration of Independence,* and *Franklin at Versailles* (both lent by the artist). In particular, Rothermel's *State House on the Day of the Battle of Germantown* (lent by Henry Gibson; see Fig. 2.9) clearly and emphatically used local history to urge upon viewers the need for immediate political action through financial sacrifice. The painting depicts the women of Philadelphia, "wives, daughters, or sisters of Tories, aroused to the assistance of their unfortunate and, as they thought, misguided country-men," ministering to wounded American prisoners taken at the infamous defeat in October 1777. As Mark Thistlethwaite has noted, the composition effectively urged Northern women to follow in the footsteps of their Revolutionary foremothers. It also demonstrated the elegant interweaving of genealogy and public history cherished by the many members of Philadelphia's old families who had assisted in organizing the fair.[44]

Few paintings on display at the Metropolitan Fair in New York explicitly treated a Civil War theme. In Philadelphia, by contrast, a city directly threatened by the enemy in summer 1863, the organizers of the art gallery accepted works with such titles as *Raw Recruits; The Departure for War; The Widow, or Spirit of '64; Sailor's Requiem; Slain for His Country;* and the intriguingly entitled *High-Mettled Confederates Going to Northern Pastures,* contributed by one E. Smith. Eastman Johnson sent a painting called *Working for the Fair* and Winslow Homer sent his wry study of a malingerer entitled *Playing Old Soldier.* Among the thirteen plaster tabletop groups by John Rogers were the *Wounded Scout* and *Sharpshooters* as well as the ever-popular *Checker Players.* References to the war could be implicit as well. Philadelphia artist James Hamilton contributed an allegorical composition, inspired by a poem written by Oliver Wendell Holmes. Called *The Shipwreck of Old Ironsides* (see Fig. 2.10), Hamilton's composition portrays the venerable warship the USS *Constitution,* built at Philadelphia, as the ship of state, now buffeted by the winds of war and in danger of sinking (an image echoed by the shipwreck exhibit in the Frigid Zone in the Floral Department).

Unfortunately, it is impossible to determine whether suggestive juxtapositions of paintings comparable to the placement of Leutze's *Washington* or the pairing of Church's *Heart of the Andes* and Bierstadt's *Rocky Mountains* at the New York sanitary fair art gallery were attempted in Philadelphia. The narrow tunnel-like art gallery was difficult to photograph, and the exact location of only a few canvases can be ascertained. One surviving photograph does show Bierstadt's canvas, shipped to Philadelphia after the close of the New York fair, swathed in drapery and hung in a place of honor at the midpoint of the gallery. "If it is not the master-work of the artist," wrote one reviewer, "we should be glad to see the picture which surpasses it."[45]

The sanitary fair's art gallery was a popular attraction. Contemporary photographers do not record the jostling crowds numbering in the hundreds that packed the art gallery from early in the morning until closing. "The most difficulty is found in gaining entrance to the picture gallery and the horticultural exhibition," reported one eyewitness. "A sight of these two departments is omitted by scarcely any one. People with the most limited pocket-books shape their finances in this direction. Once inside them they remain there. An entire day may be profitably spent in the picture gallery alone. Persons who get into the horticultural department feel an equal reluctance to depart."[46] So great was the demand that during the last week of the fair, the fine arts committee opened the gallery at seven o'clock in the morning to selected

Fig. 2.10 James Hamilton, *Old Ironsides*, 1863, oil on canvas. Pennsylvania Academy of the Fine Arts. Gift of Caroline Gibson Taitt.

"connoisseurs and the judicious who may desire a comparatively private view of these treasures."[47]

It must have been extremely difficult to see, much less to appreciate, the hundreds of artworks packed along these walls. Yet exhibition-goers reported experiencing an emotional and intellectual release when they entered this space. "Why, this picture gallery excels anything ever seen here before, and everything that is scanned excites an intelligent curiosity and wonder," exclaimed celebrated orator Edward Everett, who delivered an address when Abraham Lincoln visited the fair on June 16. "I had expected something unusual, but was prepared for nothing near like this."[48] "It is like standing in a hollow prism," wrote another visitor, adding: "One is walled in by color, shut out from the common life by a wilderness of splendor . . . a panorama of the world's beauty. . . . Whoever has the mental energy to realize a picture, to live for the moment in its illusion, will find among these scenes paths that will lead him to many a lovely dream."[49]

The magic of the art gallery pervaded the space of the entire fair. "The Fair is a world in itself," declared the editor of Philadelphia's *Daily Evening Bulletin*. "In the countless articles exhibited, we see the collective advancement of all civilization."[50] In particular the form and content of works exhibited in the art gallery informed the entire space of the fair. As one local journalist exulted: "Light, music, female beauty, with every adornment which surrounds a woman with loveliness like a luminous cloud, flowers filled with the passionate life which burns beneath the equator, and flinging forth incense to mingle with a thousand other delicate perfumes; together with pictures from every realm of art to enchant the sense of the beholder, and to carry him in imagination over every age and clime, from heathen Rome to the virgin Rocky Mountains. . . . 'The sense aches at it,' and we wander from avenue to avenue like one in a dream."[51]

Similar hyperbole had been used to describe the wondrous effects of London's Crystal Palace exhibition thirteen years before. "Wonderful, amazing, fairylike! are the words that come uppermost to [the visitor's] mind as the full glories of that famous vista break for the first time on his astonished sight," announced one guidebook. "For a few moments he is so lost in astonishment and absorbed in pleased wonder, that he can do nothing but gaze upwards on the noble proportions of that vast central hall. . . . Above the long lines of beauty arrest the eye and fix the wondering mind; below, the moving crowd, passing and re-passing among the sculptured forms of beauty on either hand, confuse and almost bewilder the visitor."[52]

Like London's Crystal Palace, the Great Central Sanitary Fair was a vision of utopia promising, as Tony Bennett notes for the earlier event, the imminent dissipation of social tensions once progress reached the point that its benefits might become universal. "Out of the Industrial Jubilee in Hyde Park," the Crystal Palace exhibition guidebook had avowed, "we see rising up before us . . . a fair edifice of which a free, happy, moral, educated and enlightened people, shall form the broad and smiling base. . . . Nothing like this has existed in the memory of any living man, and we, as a people, may be said to have thrown aside our home feelings and national prejudices, and grown quite citizens of the world."[53] Similarly, the Great Central Fair embodied the reconciliation of a young nation divided by civil war.

Bennett identifies two significant changes introduced at the 1851 Crystal Palace exhibition that decisively influenced the form of later displays. Both of these developments were evident at the Great Central Sanitary Fair. The first was a shift of emphasis from the processes to the products of production, presented as signs of the productive and cooperative power of capital and the state. After 1851, world's fairs functioned less to educate the working classes than to "stupefy" them with the results of their labors. Like the more than two dozen sanitary fairs produced in other Northern cities, the Great Central Sanitary Fair at Philadelphia enabled visitors to escape the brutal reality of a civil war by buying or paying admission to see the artifacts of American history and culture. The awestruck reactions of visitors quoted above document the "stupefying" effect of the fair.[54]

The second change identified by Bennett involved the subordination of a progressive taxonomy based on stages of production to principles of classification based on constructs of race and nation. Daily attendance at the sanitary fair numbered in the tens of thousands, confirming the existence of a large, enthusiastic, and generally well-behaved public.[55] The characterization of that audience by the fair's organizers, however, belied their visions of a classless utopia. Rejean Attie has observed that at New York's Metropolitan Sanitary Fair, "the fair's public was expected to consume more than articles for sale: it was also to absorb the vision of a diverse, interclass, harmonious culture, efficiently run by the city's ruling class," an observation echoed by Beverly Gordon.[56] At Philadelphia, the Great Central Sanitary Fair also asserted the civic authority of the elite. Karal Ann Marling points out that exhibits such as the "Pennsylvania Kitchen" and the "William Penn Parlor," by assuming a common ancestry among fairgoers, represented "the first constricting twinges of a new and increasingly self-conscious exclusivity, grounded in ancestry and a cult of 'antiques' connoting hereditary superiority."[57] In spite of the calls for participation by any and all loyal citizens, the sanitary fair became an arena for the playing out of power relations of gender, class, and race in a nation disrupted by civil war.

The politics of race was similarly mediated. Participation by African Americans was limited. In April 1864, William Forten and Ebenezer Bassett, both leaders in the African-American community, wrote to executive committee chair John Welsh to ask that African Americans who were anxious "to render some substantial aid in the benevolent enterprise" be permitted to sponsor a table attended "by the ladies among us whose fathers, brothers, sons and friends, have shared the blessings of the . . . Commission's care." Welsh declined, however, responding that the fair could house only booths sponsored by the established subcommittees.[58] Such exclusionary attitudes meant the loss of experienced volunteers. Philadelphia's African-American community had long nurtured a system of benevolent institutions with charity fairs just as much a tradition as at white churches. In November 1863, at the start of the fair movement, the First Baptist Church had sponsored a "Grand Annual Fair" at the Masonic Hall. Some African-American congregations formed Sanitary Commission auxiliaries, and late in 1864 the ladies of the Sanitary Committee of the St. Thomas [African] Episcopal Church, an auxiliary to the United States Sanitary Commission, held a fair for the benefit of sick and wounded soldiers.[59]

Although African Americans offered private, individual contributions to the various fair committees, none participated in their administration. African Americans also worked at the fair as waiters and waitresses or custodial staff, but they received only limited access as visitors and consumers. Indeed, evidence suggests that they were not even allowed in as visitors during the first week. And many whites complained when the managers designated a special day for African-American visitors during the final week.[60]

The presence of Native Americans within the fair's utopia also was carefully managed. Only contemplative, peaceable, or assimilated Indians appeared, either on canvas or as novelty performing acts. Among the many landscape paintings featuring Indians, the most explicit depiction of "primitive" aboriginal culture was found in the foreground of Bierstadt's *Rocky Mountains, Lander's Peak*, in which the artist depicted a Blackfoot encampment (see Fig. 2.11). In the "Indian department," housed just south of the William Penn Parlor, a troupe of men and women—variously described as Sioux or Iroquois by visitors although they were actually Onondaga—performed courting and

Fig. 2.11 Albert Bierstadt, *The Rocky Mountains, Lander's Peak*, 1863, oil on canvas. The Metropolitan Museum of Art. Rogers Fund, 1907.

war dances and a dramatic tableau of Pocahontas rescuing John Smith. Published descriptions assured readers that these "children of the forest" were not dangerous and that their "manager," one Clement Barclay, ably succeeded "in reconciling their little 'eccentricities' with the requirements of modern civilization." As Charles Stillé recorded in his history of the Philadelphia fair, "It certainly was very suggestive of the universality of the attractions which the Fair presented, . . . that even a representation of savage life was made to help forward the great cause which all had in heart."[61] Tellingly, when Barclay's troupe was booked for the Philadelphia fair, they performed in a space initially assigned to the children's department.

The Great Central Sanitary Fair ran for fifteen days. During the last two days, organizers reduced admission from fifty to twenty-five cents "so that the poor as well as the rich may be able to enjoy what is really one of the wonders of the age," though actual attendance figures did not increase substantially.[62] Auctions were conducted to dispose of donated artworks and other exhibits for several days before the close of the fair; afterward objects on loan or unsold went back to their owners. Within days the fair buildings were demolished. The lumber, bricks, stone, and tin roofing were purchased by the Pennsylvania Railroad as materials for the construction of a depot building at the West Philadelphia terminal.[63] All that remained on Logan Square was the shipwrights' flagpole.

The fair was an unqualified success. In fifteen days 400,000 visitors had toured the Logan Square complex, an average of more than 25,000 per day. Eighty-four committees reported a total income of $1,154,897.50; the largest amounts, excluding admissions, came from the committees on Labor, Income, and Revenue ($247,500); Wholesale Dry Goods ($53,814.67); and Fine Arts ($33,333.09). After expenses, net proceeds from the fair to be forwarded to the Sanitary Commission totaled $1,010,976.68. Philadelphians were disappointed to learn that this sum fell short of the record income of $1,183,506.23 contributed to New York's rival Metropolitan Sanitary Fair. Organizers could take comfort, however, that the Philadelphia fair outstripped any of the other sanitary fairs in scale and in attendance.[64]

Both as an event and as an architectural space, Philadelphia's Great Central Sanitary Fair embodied three defining aspects of Bennett's exhibitionary complex. First, the fair was a self-consciously staged spectacle of artworks, souvenirs, and commercial goods assembled in a grand architectural setting in order to be admired and consumed by and for "the people." The organizers were familiar with the great European world fairs of the previous decade and consciously sought to equal if not surpass these events. They succeeded in attracting unprecedented attendance.[65] Second, although neither the federal nor state governments played a direct role in its creation, the "state" or nation was implicit in the purpose of the fair to reestablish national unity in wartime. And third, although it lasted less than a month, the success of the sanitary fair spurred the expansion of permanent cultural institutions in the city in response to a broadening public audience and served as an important training opportunity for the male and most especially the female members of Philadelphia's governing elite.

Scholars have assessed the significance of the Great Central Sanitary Fair only in connection with Philadelphia's hosting of the Centennial Exhibition of 1876. J. Matthew Gallman has enumerated the links between the two events. Although produced on a much grander scale as befitting its international scope, the Centennial Exhibition was also a temporary installation built around special exhibitions devoted to manufacturing, horticulture, and the fine arts. Both events were produced under the direction of men and women from the city's elite, assisted by hundreds of local volunteers with the financial support of the city's businesses, fraternal societies, and private citizens. Chief among the central fair managers who went on to work at the Centennial were John Welsh, appointed chairman of the powerful Centennial Board of Finance; Frederick Fraley, secretary and treasurer for the same committee; and Elizabeth Duane Gillespie, who led the Women's Centennial Executive Committee.[66]

But indications that Philadelphia's cultural leaders were rethinking the structure and scale of cultural spaces within the city actually emerged much sooner in the immediate postwar period, long before planning for the Centennial had begun. After the war several institutions in the city initiated or revived plans for relocation or expansion. By 1867, a consortium of cultural institutions had petitioned the city councils for permission to build new facilities on Penn (or Centre) Square. Before the war, the Pennsylvania Academy of the Fine Arts, the Academy of Natural Sciences, the Philadelphia Library (now The Library Company of Philadelphia), the American Philosophical Society, and the Franklin Institute had operated independently at dispersed sites in the eastern section of Center City, though all drew many of their members from the same ranks of Philadelphia society and some individuals sat on several boards of directors.[67] Now these institutions desired to come together at a central site, thereby creating a kind of island of culture within

Penn's grid. The city government passed a resolution supporting this petition, and it was duly referred to the state legislature at Harrisburg.

The plan was still active in 1870 when a public referendum on the site of a new city hall was held. The alternatives were Washington Square, at Sixth and Chestnut Streets just north of Independence Hall, and Penn (Centre) Square, subdivided by the intersection of Broad (Fourteenth Street) and Market Streets. If Washington Square were selected by a majority of voters, the four subsidiary squares at Penn Square would be granted to four of the above-named institutions: the Academy of Fine Arts, the Academy of Natural Sciences, the Franklin Institute, and the Philadelphia Library. When voters selected Penn Square for the new city hall, these four institutions had to abandon the Centre Square proposal.[68] Two of the four—the Franklin Institute and the Philadelphia Library—remained for the time being in the eastern section of the city. But the other two institutions relocated into the Logan Square district, signaling the beginning of a shift in the city's cultural institutions into the northwestern quadrant. The board of directors of the Academy of Natural Sciences selected Logan Square for their new building, which opened in 1876; that same year, the Academy of Fine Arts reopened in a new building designed by Frank Furness (brother of Horace) and located just four blocks from Logan Square at Broad and Cherry Streets.[69]

The largest public project of the postwar period was the development of Fairmount Park. Also in 1867, authorities created the Fairmount Park Commission to supervise the development of the municipal park, with the entrance gates located at Twentieth and Green Streets near the Fairmount waterworks, one of Philadelphia's most popular tourist sights. Officials wanted the park to provide "an open public place & a park for the health and enjoyment of the people of said city, and the preservation of the purity of the city water supply."[70] By the early 1870s the park had been expanded to encompass almost 2,500 acres throughout central Philadelphia, making it the largest urban park in the United States. Seven of the founding members of the Fairmount Park Commission had served on the executive committee for the Central Sanitary Fair: John Welsh, John Cresson (who became chief engineer for the park), N. B. Browne, Frederick Graff, Strickland Kneass, Theodore Cuyler, and Joseph Harrison.[71]

Within the precincts of Fairmount Park developed the chief institutional offspring of the Great Central Sanitary Fair. Just as the Art Gallery of the fair had reflected most explicitly the ideological agenda of the fair's organizers, so too in the immediate postwar period did the public exhibition of works of art and design manifest the changing attitudes of Philadelphia cultural elite. Although the Pennsylvania Academy of the Fine Arts had been in existence since 1805 and had presented annual exhibitions for more than fifty years, it primarily served a limited number of stockholders and attracted few visitors: at this time the permanent collection was quite small and there was no professional curatorial staff. Plans to build a new museum and art school facility were under way by 1867, but not everyone was satisfied with this plan and a movement developed to establish a new art museum in the city. Spearheading this effort was Joseph Harrison, erstwhile chairman of the Fine Arts Committee for the Great Central Fair, who, in 1871, urged fellow members of the Fairmount Park Commission to approve the construction of a free art gallery and museum in Fairmount Park: "owned by, enjoyed by and cared for by the people. Being the property of the people, [it] will stimulate a just pride through all classes, in their maintenance, their conservation and their endowment."[72]

Harrison's plan may well have been inspired by events unfolding in New York. In 1867 William Cullen Bryant delivered a speech to fellow members of New York's Union League Club—several of whom had assisted in organizing that city's Metropolitan Sanitary Fair—in which he advocated the founding of a permanent public art museum in the city to offset the harmful vulgarity of the nouveau riche. Bryant applauded the country's postwar prosperity but warned of the annual plunder of "immense sums by men who seek public stations for their individual profit," alluding to wartime profiteers and to the increasing power of populist Tammany Hall. Political corruption not only robbed Americans in general—and New Yorkers in particular—of revenue, Bryant avowed, it robbed them of culture. "If a tenth part of what is every year stolen from us in this way, in the city where we live, under the pretence of the public service, and poured profusely into the coffers of political rogues, were expended on a Museum of Art," the poet declared, "we might have, deposited in spacious and stately buildings, collections formed of works by the world's greatest artists, which would be the pride of our country." The influence of works of art is wholesome, ennobling, instructive, the poet urged: "Let it be remembered to the honor of art that, if it has ever been perverted to the purposes of vice, it has only been at the bidding of some corrupt court, or at the desire of some opulent and powerful voluptuary. . . . When intended for the general eye, no such stain rests on works of art."[73] Because art could build ideological cohesiveness, as Bryant noted, it was incumbent upon members of the city's upper class to build permanent display spaces to confirm their own cultural leadership.[74] The National Academy of Design had existed as an exhibiting society and art school since 1826, but like the Pennsylvania Academy, it was a private organization with no requirement to serve the public at large. In 1870 several members of Bryant's audience would answer his call when they became founding trustees of the Metropolitan Museum of Art.

Members of Philadelphia's elite also worried about the rising influence of "new money" and the growing corruption of municipal politics.[75] The Fairmount Park commissioners endorsed Harrison's proposal with enthusiasm, recognizing that no such truly public institution existed in Philadelphia: "private owners possess collections of great merit and value; the Academy of Fine Arts has steadily added to its paintings and statuary; and in some of its departments the Academy of Natural Sciences is confessedly without a rival. But none of these are the property, or subject to the control, of the general public, and hence they are accessible only to limited numbers and on special occasions."[76] When a temporary gallery building was constructed in the park in 1872, Harrison loaned the site paintings from his own collection. The facility also showcased Peter Rothermel's six paintings of the Battle of Gettysburg, dominated by the sixteen-by-thirty-two-foot canvas of *The Battle of Gettysburg: Pickett's Charge*.

Harrison died in 1874, but his vision for the new art museum was kept alive. In 1875 a committee, which included sanitary fair workers John Sartain, Henry C. Gibson, Coleman Sellers, and James L. Claghorn, petitioned the Fairmount Park Commission for permission to take over Memorial Hall, the permanent structure housing the international art exhibition during the Centennial, after the close of the world's fair for the purpose of establishing a "Museum of Industrial Decorative and Antiquarian Art." Modeled on London's successful South Kensington Museum, the new institution would combine display with education, presenting "the best examples of Industrial Art, manufactures, free lectures to artisans upon subjects connected with their work and schools for proper education upon all subjects which are essential to the successful production of works into which design in every way enters." "Such a purpose," the committee stated, "would combine with the cultivation of the public taste, the still more valuable feature of our education of a sort which our large manufacturing state sorely needs."[77] The petition was successful, and in 1877 the Pennsylvania Museum and School of Industrial Art was opened, with founding bequests by the Wilstach and Bloomfield Moore families, both of whom had contributed to the sanitary fair.

The Great Central Sanitary Fair was produced in response to specific historical circumstances and ideological needs. But the organization and structure of the fair and the constituent displays also reflected broader changes in modes of visual consumption within the nineteenth-century audience, and the fair had a far-reaching impact on the subsequent history of cultural institutions both in Philadelphia and nationally. The success of Philadelphia's fair, as well as those in other Northern cities, demonstrated the receptivity of the American public to political as well as cultural messages conveyed within environments combining commodity displays with entertainment and didactic exhibits. The elite organizers recognized this and returned to directing the city's cultural institutions with a revised approach to programming, applying their new expertise in the formulation and administration of large-scale public cultural events and display spaces, which would build ideological cohesion and confirm their superior position in the cultural hierarchy. They were joined by contemporaries who had organized the sanitary fairs in New York, Boston, Chicago, and other Northern cities. In the postwar period, with the reunification of the nation, cultural leaders in the United States would transform the mandates of the country's cultural institutions, moving outward to develop broader perspectives on the international stage.

THREE

"WE WERE ENLISTED FOR THE WAR"

Ladies' Aid Societies and the Politics of Women's Work During the Civil War

Rachel Filene Seidman

In the spring of 1861 Jennie Sellers was seventeen years old and living on her father's farm outside West Chester, Pennsylvania. As the secession crisis deepened in the South, Jennie read Democratic newspapers avidly and by the time the fighting erupted, she was deeply interested in the war. While she gleaned what information she could from the papers, Jennie relied on her father, Samuel, and her brother, Escol, to keep her up-to-date on the changing local and national scene. On April 15 she noted in her diary that her father had been to "the Lion store" in the morning and at a neighbor's house sale in the afternoon. "Papa brought home word from the sale, said to be the latest news, that Major Anderson has made an unconditional surrender." On April 17 Samuel went back into West Chester and "brought home word" that a rifle company was being raised in the city and that sixty men had enlisted. In addition, there was "a great deal of excitement about W. Chester, several democratic printing offices have been broken up in Philadelphia." Her father had also heard about a man who had "stabbed his wife several times and then cut his own head nearly off." Meanwhile, in stark comparison to the tumultuous world of news that her father entered when he went into town, Jennie noted "I washed today."

As the month wore on—and her father and brother constantly brought home news of the exciting war developments they heard—Jennie grew ever more frustrated about having to remain at home, cut off from the flow of information except for what she heard through the two men. On April 30 she tried to break the pattern. "I wanted to go to the parkerville store this afternoon a horseback," she wrote in her diary. "Papa said I might." But her father changed his mind. "I got ready to go," Jennie noted dryly, "but had to stay, of course I was pleased very much." These last sarcastic words she underlined heavily with a series of short, angry pen marks.[1]

Eventually, Jennie found a source of information and conversation that did not depend on her father and brother. By spring 1862 she had joined a debate society, the Union Literarie Society of Pocopson, which gave her a chance to meet with others of her age on a regular basis, discuss the important topics of the day, and keep up-to-date on local and national developments.

Like Jennie Sellers, a young Philadelphian named Susan Trautwine found herself swept up in the anxious, nationalistic uproar that followed the attack on Major Anderson's troops at Fort Sumter.[2] "I feel so interested in Major Anderson," wrote Trautwine on the morning of April 13. "I hope this mrng's news is not true. 'Lord, have mercy upon us!'"[3] Two days later she reported feverishly: "News of Major Anderson's surrender! People much excited! Quite a mob collected today. Flags of Union flying every where. Lincoln orders the raising of 70,000 men—'Lord have mercy upon us!'"[4] For the next few days, news of the war and the city's preparations displaced Susan's usual comments on chores, visits, and religion. By the first week of May, the women of her church had begun to make arrangements "for working for the soldiers."[5] Trautwine joined them, eager to channel her excitement and her political energy into a useful vein.

Amanda Meshler, another young single woman, living with her father in Philadelphia, also read the newspapers eagerly, like Sellers and Trautwine, but she invested more energy in tracking the war than the other two. She kept daily accounts of the battles in her journal and copied a chronological list of each major fight and political development into the back of the book.[6] Meshler articulated her own analysis of the causes of the war and its likely outcome: "Since the Election of A. Lincoln the South has arisen in Rebellion against their Government," she wrote in July 1861. She pinpointed the two sides' disagreement over the extension of slavery as the cause of "all this Difficulty." She felt strongly that the South was at fault: "They would not listen to reason and Justice and finally they declared themselves to be a separate and distinct people. But we where [sic] not going to let them go so easily. Our president is a Man for the Times. He is Firm as a Rock." Amanda had educated herself on the issues involved in the war and, at least in the privacy of her journal, she voiced her own opinions.

Soon her diary could not satisfy Meshler's urge to partake in the political discussions of the day. She visited the Philadelphia Ladies' Aid Society, a military hospital, and the Cooper Shop Refreshment Saloon, where women provided hundreds of soldiers with meals as they passed through the city. After witnessing the work done in these large organizations run in large part by women, Meshler gathered her neighbors together at her own house to sew for the soldiers, forming the Spring Garden Hospital Aid Society.[7]

As the national drama of the Civil War unfolded, Jennie Sellers, Susan Trautwine, and Amanda Meshler each demonstrated an urgent desire to keep up-to-date on the events. The petulant Sellers, the excitable Trautwine, and the serious Meshler revealed not only their individual personalities in their journals, but also common themes among women across Pennsylvania and the Union. Thousands of women experienced the same thirst for information, the same reliance on neighborhood networks, and the same urge to participate in the civic response to the war.[8] These three women's actions can be seen as part of a much wider continuum of women's participation in the war. From debating the political issues with friends and family, to providing essential food, medicine, and clothing to the army, to nursing the soldiers, to fighting alongside the men, women made many decisions about how they wanted to help the Union war effort. As historians continue to plumb the depths of the Civil War crisis for what it reveals about American social, political, and cultural history, these stories offer important insights into how gender shaped people's experiences of the war and into the war's impact on women's ideas about being American citizens.

The Civil War offers a particularly rich moment for exploring the suggestion recently made by several women's historians that in order to understand more fully the complexity of American political culture, we must expand our definition of "politics" beyond campaigns and elections. We need to transform our image of political culture to incorporate all the ways in which people try to shape the distribution and use of power in society. As Lori Ginzberg has pointed out, benevolent women "worked hard to influence the leadership of local, state, and national governments" long before the women's suffrage movement.[9] Thousands of antebellum women formed voluntary associations for a variety of goals, from benevolent aid to the needy, to radical political causes like abolition. During the Civil War many women turned to ladies' aid societies, voluntary associations aimed at providing food, medicine, and clothing to soldiers, as a means of supporting the Union war effort. As had their ante-bellum precedents, ladies' aid societies combined elements of benevolence and political participation.

As Sara Evans has argued, women in the nineteenth century created an organizational life for themselves that existed between the formal realm of governmental institutions from which they were banned and the private, domestic sphere to which societal values tried to bind them. In voluntary associations women created a new type of public space for themselves, a "new arena for citizenship and collective decision making that ultimately reshaped the state." Although both men and women joined voluntary associations in the nineteenth century, for women they represented a "new kind of free space" where they "practiced the basic skills of public life—to speak and to listen, to analyze issues in relation to structures of power, and to develop agendas and strategies for action." As Evans argues, as women participated in public life in their communities through these groups, they "reworked privatized defini-tions of femininity and demanded admission into the more formal realm of politics."[10]

A close examination of Civil War era ladies' aid societies in Pennsylvania offers a richly textured case study of Evans's theory and will add to our under-standing of wartime political culture. For many Northern women, ladies' aid societies constituted not an alternative to but a form of politics during the Civil War. By studying these groups we can see how the war intensified the political significance of women's information and support networks, and how women's activities helped to shape the political mobilization of the region. By examining Pennsylvania ladies' aid societies, we can begin to understand how the Civil War reconfigured Northern women's understanding of their political identities in both their own neighborhoods and in the nation as a whole.[11]

Women's experiences in ladies' aid societies echoed in many important ways their antebellum voluntary association work. But the context of a national crisis shaped the meaning of their work in new ways. Tied as they were to the federal government's war effort, ladies' aid societies gave women a new sense of direct participation in the nation's work. Membership in ladies' aid societies shifted women's relation to both the local and national political scene. Some women used their participation in ladies' aid societies to increase their prestige and power in their neighborhood's or town's cultural and political arena. Other women, represented most famously by Elizabeth Cady Stanton, argued that the support women provided the Union during the war warranted giving them a formal political voice in the nation's government. Through the efforts of ladies' aid societies to supply the army, the women created a direct link between themselves and the federal government, and in forging this new relationship, they began to articulate a new understanding of their status as citizens and of the rights to which this status entitled them.

Thousands of women across the Union formed as many as 20,000 ladies' aid societies in order to send goods to soldiers. These groups ranged greatly in size and organization. Some were small, informal gatherings of women who came together in the first heady weeks of war to can a few peaches and knit some socks before fading away. Others grew into grand institutions like the Ladies' Aid Society of Philadelphia, which by 1863 estimated that it had received and distributed more than $60,000 worth of goods. Whereas some arose in direct response to the shots fired at Fort Sumter, others were drummed up later by agents of the United States Sanitary Commission. They sprouted up in large cities and in tiny rural hamlets, wherever women hoped to participate in their country's tremendous struggle.[12]

To understand fully the meaning of women's participation in ladies' aid societies requires exploring the changing nature of life on the home front. In Pennsylvania, Jennie Sellers, Susan Trautwine, and Amanda Meshler each grasped at the very start of the war one of the most immediate changes—the heightened importance of their neighborhood networks as sources of information. The war understandably intensified women's reliance on news and emotional support. The wartime burgeoning of ladies' aid societies reflected this new reality; they formalized the avenues for information that already existed between family, friends, and neighbors.[13]

As the war progressed from the initial feverish preparations to the harsh realities of long marches, disease-ridden camps, and devastating battles, the families and friends of soldiers grew ever more dependent on information, whether it came by word of mouth, newspaper, or letter. People learned to be wary of the rumors that constantly surged up and down lines of communication and of the newspaper reports that were often no more accurate. Those at home considered personal letters from soldiers to be the most reliable source of information. These letters themselves became material embodiments of the neighborhood information networks. Because of the locale-based recruitment patterns of the Civil War, soldiers served in regiments alongside their townsmen and family members. When soldiers wrote home, they included news of these other men; every soldier knew that his letter might for some reason get home while his comrades' did not. Battles, the destruction of railroads, long marches, and Confederate occupations of Pennsylvania cities could disrupt the delivery of mail. Writing to her husband Robert after the battles at Fredericksburg in which his company had fought, Mary Browne told him: "Our news . . . is only vague and unsatisfactory. We long for a reliable letter, from some of you. No deaths are reported from [your company], nor wounded. God grant it may be so, Oh, what sad, anxious hearts beat in many bosoms here."[14] Mary and her neighbors wanted a letter to confirm what they had already heard and read.

The arrival of a letter, proving that the writer still lived, provided cause for celebration. Rachel Cormany, who boarded in Chambersburg, received a letter from her husband after a long delay in May 1864. She told her diary: "I was so glad I scarcely knew what to do with myself. I kissed the little missive, run all through the house proclaiming my fortune." She then hurried to tell her neighbor Mrs. Snyder (another soldier's wife) about the letter, "but she having had the same good fortune was on her way to tell me & I met her a few doors from [here] so we returned together." On another occasion Rachel noted that a Mrs. Wordabaugh had walked four miles into town, carrying her heavy child, "to see whether I had heard from Mr C.," because Mr. Wordabaugh was in the same company. "What will woman not do or endure for the man she loves," Rachel commented.[15] To Mary Browne, Rachel Cormany, and their neighbors, letters were an essential link to their loved ones, the only kind of information they trusted. When a letter arrived, they considered it a communal event.

By piecing together the bits of information each one had, women tried to keep abreast of military developments and the fates of their family members. Women gathered in each other's homes or at local stores to share news and to counter the isolation many of them felt living without their husbands or fathers or sons. Returning home one day after running errands, Rachel found "three country women whose husbands are in the co[mpany] Mr C is in were here for dinner."[16] The women had turned up uninvited, probably in town to gather information about their husbands. When Rachel's husband Samuel was home on furlough in February 1863, the wives of two men in his company came to visit to "hear direct from their soldier husbands" through Samuel.[17] In towns across Pennsylvania, neighbors expected everyone to share any available information.

The news that reached the home front, of course, was not always good. When women shared information concerning the loss of loved ones, death took on a communal, public character that bound families and neighborhoods together in grief. Catherine Fair wrote to her husband, William, after hearing he had survived the battle of Petersburg: "O that news is priceless to me these are heart rending times." She then relayed sad news regarding the man who helped her with her farming. "Mr. Moorheads son is gone to his last resting place he fell on the 2nd . . . they take it verry hard about him they dont know whether he was buried . . . or how if at all." Mr. Moorhead's wife had asked Catherine whether William might "find out what had been done" with the young man's remains. Catherine had received similar requests from other neighbors because "there has not been one letter got by any person but myself since the Battle people verry uneasy."[18] After the same battle, Samuel Cormany wrote an obituary of a soldier and sent it home with a letter to Rachel, asking her to read the obituary to the soldier's wife. It is unclear whether the woman was illiterate or whether Samuel simply thought that dealing with grief should be undertaken with female company. Bad news as well as good bound women together in networks of shared information on the home front.

The intensity of wartime bonding through information networks did not necessarily produce harmony and cooperation among the women at home. Rachel Cormany had long been friends with Mrs. McGowan and was boarding with her in early spring 1864. Samuel Cormany meanwhile noted often in his diary that the other woman's husband, Sam McGowan, was not exactly a model officer. Samuel was in fact caring for McGowan, who claimed to be sick. "Doc H. and I and some others are tired of sore or lame backs—when it looks like business or a fight looming out in the near future,"[19] he commented. The previous summer McGowan had been considered absent without leave, and Samuel had written up an order for his arrest. In November of that year, Samuel had been promoted to quarter master sergeant at the same time that McGowan was reduced in rank for "inefficiency."[20] When Rachel received a letter from Samuel in June 1864 informing her that he had received a lieutenant's commission, she immediately shared the news with her friend Mrs. McGowan. Rachel did not get the reaction she expected. Mrs. McGowan "did not seem to like it," she noted, adding, "She said a good many things that were meant to cut—& were hard to take."

Rachel tried to fix the friendship. When she weeded her own garden she also tended to Mrs. McGowan's "little onions." She told her diary, "I want to show her that being a Lieut's wife does not change me."[21] Throughout the summer, though, Rachel continued to have trouble with her friend, who remained "crusty" and "ugly." When Mrs. McGowan blamed Samuel for her husband's confiscated pay, Rachel lost her patience: "That gets my du[t]ch up," Rachel confided. "As long as she picks at me I can grin & bear, but she had better not pick at my Samuel or she may get some back."[22] Women's intimate knowledge of each other's news and their reliance on each other for information did at times draw them together, but it could also foster tension and discord.

During the war, women's knowledge of each other's lives had political ramifications, as they used it in their dealings with local, state, and federal officials. When women appealed to the government for the release of husbands or sons from the army, they often called upon each other to serve as witnesses. They relied on the federal officials' belief that women had access to intimate information about their neighbors' and family members' lives. Margaret Lipplinger lived in Cumberland County and wanted to get her son out of the army in 1861. She sent a petition to her congressman, asking him to present it to the secretary of war, which he agreed to do. When more information was requested of her, she filed a deposition with a justice of the peace. She brought with her both her mother and Mary Lineed, "a close neighbor," as witnesses to her son's birth to prove that he was, indeed, a minor. The three women were successful, and the boy was discharged.[23]

In another instance, Thankful Hipwell of Luzerne County resorted to similar means to have her son discharged from the army. Her second husband had died in 1859, leaving her with "no property or means of subsistence except the household furniture." Her three oldest sons were in the army out West, and her younger son, Henry, had "left her home with a recruiting officer without her knowledge or consent" in October 1861 when he was seventeen years old. He had been taken prisoner in 1862 and released. Although his captain had sent him home on Hipwell's request, the young man was arrested for desertion four weeks later. Hipwell had traveled to Scranton to get him released but had been treated "very uncivilly" by the officer in charge, who had ordered her "to be taken out of the room, and would not listen to any thing she wanted to say." When Hipwell took her case before her alderman, she brought Jane Mariah Whitnesy with her. Whitnesy swore that she had lived "a near neighbor" of Hipwell "for upwards of twenty years and has during that time been intimate and well acquainted with her and her family." She went on to swear that Hipwell "is a credible person and worthy of belief," and that the facts in Hipwell's deposition were true. Sergeant Bradford, the provost marshal of the 12th District, was satisfied with the women's story. A special order of the secretary of war discharged young Henry Hipwell.[24]

Although women often supported their neighbors' claims on the government, they could use the same access to private information to undermine another woman's efforts. Anna M. Bicking of Chester County turned Melissa Smith in to the authorities in 1865 on the charge of false pretenses. Smith charged that Bicking had obtained twenty-one dollars of pension money from the government "alleged to be due her as the widow of one David Birney, who died in the military service . . . with intent to cheat and defraud said government."[25] Because the case was later dropped, the details were never divulged. Clearly, however, the women could use their intimate knowledge of their neighbors' lives against one another as well as in each other's favor when dealing with the government.[26]

The Civil War not only gave women chances to use information about their individual neighbors in political ways, but it also sharpened their understanding of the general political layout of their neighborhoods. The call for army volunteers practically demanded that families announce their loyalty to their community by sending a husband or son to the front. Those who did not send anyone were sometimes suspected of being less than enthusiastic patriots. Sarah Murphy of Pine Grove Mills wrote to her brother in the army thanking him for the money he had sent home. "We have sent most of our men to the defence of our state," she noted, adding "there are few copperheads about yet[,] in fact about all that are here are that sort with a few exceptions."[27] Especially in a politically divided state like Pennsylvania, women drew political conclusions from their observations of local families.

With the Confederates actually inside state lines in summer 1863, civilian actions became even more overtly political. Rachel Cormany watched from her window as the rebels invaded Chambersburg, sawed down telegraph poles, destroyed the bridge, and took possession of warehouses. The soldiers demanded that residents bring them extra food, especially bread and meat. "Some dumb fools carried them jellies & the like," Rachel nearly spit in her journal. "Not a thing went from this place."[28] A few days later she ruminated on the difference she hoped it would make that the Confederates were in enemy territory. "Scarcely any are willing to give them anything—in fact none give unless they have to[,] except perhaps the Copperheads."[29] War thrust people's political beliefs into the public eye, and Union women took careful note of their neighbors' actions.

The Civil War intensified women's need for information and sharpened the political implications of their shared knowledge of each other, and the rapid spread of ladies' aid societies across the state and the Union reflected these new realities as well as women's desire to participate in the war effort. Ladies' aid societies performed several functions for the women who joined. They offered a way to focus productive energy and for the women to feel they were being useful to the war effort. They provided important emotional support to members. In addition, as members gathered food and clothing and secured cash donations, they gained access to the information they craved and they honed their organizational and political skills.

Ladies' aid society members collected materials from neighbors and merchants, sewed and knit clothing, prepared foodstuffs, and packed hospital supplies. They incorporated the extra work needed to supply the army into their already labor-intensive lives.[30] On October 16, 1861, Mrs. Furman of the Richmond (Pennsylvania) Ladies' Aid Society took home some rolls of wool. One week later she had spun the wool into yarn, dyed it, and knit five pairs of socks.[31] As Anne Scott has pointed out, ladies' aid societies "transferred to the community the production women had always carried out for their own families."[32] In the record books' long lists of shirts, drawers, bandages, overcoats, quilts, jellies, jams, currant wines, vinegar, dried apples, and barrels of butter made at home can be read almost incredible hours of extra work taken on by women already burdened by the loss of male hands to help with their farm work or small businesses.

When sadness and tragedy so often filled daily life during the war, cheerful sociability became immensely important to those trying to survive. The work itself and regular meetings brought women together and members seemed to thrive on the camaraderie involved in their labors. In January 1864 the Ladies' Aid Association of Weldon learned that the Sanitary Commission wanted quilts for sick and wounded soldiers and immediately took action. They arranged for a grand "quilting bee," where members would gather in one large room to sew quilts. They decided to bring their meals with them, "in order to lose no time by returning home." The twenty-five quilters assembled "at an early hour" and soon were "filling the Hall with frames and busy workers to its utmost capacity." By evening they had finished twenty quilts. The day had been full of "work and entertainment," with "not only substantial food but delicacies . . . a handsome dinner and tea."[33] Two weeks later fifty women assembled again to repeat the success: "Although there was a perpetual buzz of cheerful voices resounding throughout the apartment, old and young seeming to have thrown away all care for the day, so industriously was the needle plied that by evening all the work previously cut out, and much more, was either finished or in a way soon to be. Agnes Paxson facilitated the work very much by bringing her sewing machine." Some "reen-listed veterans" had been invited to the social, and "several young ladies added much to the entertainment" by singing the "Star-Spangled Banner" and "other patriotic songs."[34] Combining much-needed productive work for the army with much-craved companionship for those on the home front, ladies' aid societies found a highly successful formula.

The support networks forged in regular discussion groups and labor served women well when the war invaded their families most harshly. Mrs. Shafer lived in Montgomery County. All four of her sons served in the Union army. In December 1864 her son Morris fell in battle. The Weldon ladies' aid society tried to comfort her and help her deal with her loss by placing her son's death in a broader perspective. They wrote: "The loss of a son in the prime of manhood is at all times a severe affliction but when in addition to his many other virtues, that son has bravely battled amid all the dangers and trials of war, in defense of our liberties, our country and peaceful homes, his death becomes a public loss; and we, as loyal, sympathizing, neighbors and helpers in the cause, most earnestly deplore it."[35] Mrs. Shafer's membership in the aid society assured her of a loyal support group and helped her view the death of her son not simply as a private loss, but also as a public one.[36]

Ladies' aid societies often brought needed emotional relief not only to their individual members but also to whole communities as well. Attesting to the widely felt need for gaiety and camaraderie during the long years of war, the Richmond aid society noted that they found "entertainments" to be the most successful form of fund-raising. They organized socials centering around picnics, "oysters, ice-cream, and hot-maple-sugar-syrup, each very popular in their appropriate season."[37] In Weldon, too, fairs and other sociable events were usually extremely popular. In September 1863 the secretary drew up a long report on the fair they had recently undertaken. She noted its "complete" success, suggesting that "the constant succession of chances . . . the passing around of the 'Fortune Teller' the 'Dorcas Lady' and the 'Grab Bag'. . . and the cutting of the large cake which contained the ring, added greatly to the spirit and cheerfulness of the Fair, whilst they increased its profits in no small degree."[38]

Using a variety of methods, ladies' aid societies raised significant amounts of money for the Union. As they had done in antebellum voluntary work, women practiced the skills needed for political movements and gained insights into the political layout of their communities. Amanda Meshler called it "beggin," but her efforts at door-to-door canvassing of her neighborhood for funds were surprisingly successful and encouraged her to organize other women.[39] Many societies worked to mobilize their regions. The members of the Richmond Ladies' Aid Society sent notices to all the ministers in their area, requesting that they announce the society's meetings from the pulpit. Using a popular reform movement technique, the group divided the town into districts and assigned one or two women responsible for covering each one. On their rounds the women requested money, food donations, and membership in their society. Mrs. Smith and Miss Vanderen, for example, were to cover Pickle Hill, while Mrs. and Miss Wilson took Lamb's Creek.[40]

When women came across neighbors unwilling to donate time or money, their hesitancy took on political overtones by suggesting a lack of patriotism. Fannie Dyer of Covington, Tioga County, wrote to Mrs. Morris, the secretary of the Richmond Ladies' Aid Society, about the difficulty she had in getting women in her town to contribute. She was frustrated by "sluggish souls" who did not contribute "like true women" to "this wonderful system of 'home-help' to our over-burdened Government." Underscoring her astute recognition of the financial and political significance of women's labor for the country, she added that she hoped every town where women did so little would be "the very first to feel the heavy pressure of taxation" that she was sure the war would bring.[41] Fannie Dyer, like many others, articulated a new understanding of the link between women's actions and the federal government.

Ladies' aid societies offered women a political education in other ways as well. One of the most important functions ladies' aid societies performed was as a conduit of information about current events and an arena for discussion of political issues, providing women with what Sara Evans has described as a school for citizenship.[42] Some ladies' aid societies formalized this educational function into a regular segment of their meetings. The hamlet of Weldon, in Montgomery County, about fifteen miles northwest of Philadelphia, was home to a remarkably active ladies' aid society. The Ladies' Aid Association of Weldon regularly assigned one woman to be "reader" for each meeting. The selections they read aloud to the group were usually of a patriotic or political nature. On February 25, 1863, the president read "in a spirited manner, a poem, entitled 'Union is Strength,' written by a young lady of Norristown, full of patriotic and benevolent sentiments."[43] On March 11 the secretary read an "Appeal to My Country-women" from the *Atlantic Monthly*.[44] The essay, which challenged women to "do more than sew" by helping husbands and sons stay virtuous and brave in the face of danger and sacrifice, "gave satisfaction" to the society. Later that month, the president read "a very amusing satire on the

'Peace Party' of the north, from the pen of Artemus Ward."[45] Other pieces read included extracts from a speech by Confederate Vice President Alexander Stephens and letters from soldiers describing the military campaigns.[46] The Weldon's Ladies' Aid Association provided its members with exposure to a wide range of political and military information, both of which the women craved, and a forum for discussing these important issues. While reading to each other was not a new activity for women, the political content and context of their material had changed, and its significance to their sense of national citizenship was therefore heightened.

Through their membership in ladies' aid societies, Pennsylvanian women were also drawn into new political networks, giving them a sense of participation in a broader movement of women's political activism. In August 1863, for instance, the secretary of the Weldon association received a letter from the Woman's National Loyal League (WNLL) requesting her help in obtaining one million signatures on a petition to Congress to free all the slaves "at the earliest practicable day." The Woman's National Loyal League had been founded by Elizabeth Cady Stanton and Susan B. Anthony early in 1863 in response to the limitations of Abraham Lincoln's Emancipation Proclamation, which freed slaves in the Confederacy in theory only, because in reality they lived in an area over which the Union had no control. Many abolitionists were disappointed, and Stanton and Anthony formed their group to prove to Congress that the public supported complete and immediate abolition of slavery. Through their contact with the WNLL, the Weldon women found themselves dealing with a group that Wendy Venet argues represented a "new type of organization," a national group run by women "from a decidedly feminist perspective."[47]

The WNLL secretary asked whether the Weldon society wanted to take on the challenge of collecting signatures for the petition as a group or leave it up to "individual responsibility." This question forced the aid society to discuss whether or not they unanimously supported immediate emancipation. Perhaps already antislavery activists—Montgomery County included several stops on the Underground Railroad—the Weldon women decided to treat the petition as a "Society measure," which each one signed. The treasurer and the secretary offered to visit the neighborhood to gather more signatures.[48] Through their efforts, the Weldon women contributed to the 8,625 signatures collected in Pennsylvania.[49]

Another national network that many ladies' aid societies joined was that formed by the United States Sanitary Commission.[50] Although some ladies' aid societies were formed under the umbrella of the national commission, others remained independent. During winter and spring 1863, the Sanitary Commission faced a crisis as rampant rumors spread throughout the North that it was a money-making scheme rather than a philanthropic endeavor.[51] This rumor threatened to erode the commission's control over the national effort to supply the soldiers. To counteract the rumors and bring local societies into closer contact with the national institution, the commission established a system of "female associate managers," women chosen to coordinate the activities for a county or a region and report back to their branch office. Their role encompassed a "delicate mixture of public relations and spying."[52] Not only did their role benefit the commission, it also offered rural women a chance to establish a semiprofessional career and to make contact with other Unionist women in their region.

Mrs. Morris of the Richmond Ladies' Aid Society was named to such a position in spring 1863, reporting to the Pennsylvania branch office in Philadelphia. A Sanitary Commission circular informed her that the duties of an associate manager included ascertaining whether a local soldiers' aid society existed in every town and village in her region, and "if so, for what they are working." If they were not part of the Sanitary Commission's network, she was to "use all her influence to induce them" to join, "meeting all objections by bringing forward in a kindly spirit the convincing proofs furnished by the published documents of the Commission." She was to visit all the societies from time to time, give them information, answer questions, dispel doubts, and encourage the workers. She was to keep informed about the work of the commission and to send the Philadelphia branch a "friendly letter" once a month about her progress.[53]

Mrs. Morris attended regularly to her duties, maintaining a correspondence with other local societies and visiting them on occasion. A high point for her must have been the Woman's Council she attended in January 1864, in Washington, D.C., where sixty-five other delegates from ladies' aid societies joined officers of the United States Sanitary Commission. There she met national figures, talked with the other delegates, and learned how local societies across the North functioned.[54] As an associate manager, Mrs. Morris expanded her knowledge of the political layout of her region, honed her organizational skills, and made contact with other women working toward similar goals. Like hundreds of other associate managers, Mrs. Morris was drawn into the national organization of the Sanitary Commission and gained assurance from its officers that her work was essential to the Union's success.

Even women who did not become as intimately involved with the Sanitary Commission as Mrs. Morris found that the national organization satisfied some of their wartime needs. The commission provided ladies' aid society members with access to information and a sense of belonging to a national network of active, patriotic citizens. The corresponding secretary of the Sanitary Commission, Mrs. Moore, sent the Weldon society a copy of the *Saturday Evening Post* in which she had published a piece "setting forth the efforts that are being made by different Aid Societies" for the benefit of the Sanitary Commission. She volunteered to furnish the society with a weekly subscription to the *Post*.[55] Maria C. Grier, the chairman of the Women's Pennsylvania Branch, sent the Weldon women a personal letter of thanks for the boxes of clothing they sent to her office in Philadelphia. The letter gave "great satisfaction, each member feeling that her efforts had met with a warm and liberal appreciation." The Weldon women had not expected such a response from the large, national, and seemingly impersonal Sanitary Commission. The "earnestness and cordiality" of Grier's letter, the Weldon secretary Mrs. Smith assured her, would have "two important results." It would establish "a more complete confidence in the Sanitary Commission," and it would stimulate the group to "further efforts in the great cause."[56] The Sanitary Commission offered rural women a new source of critical information, a chance to feel connected to the rest of the country, training in political organizing techniques, and a sense of recognition and gratitude not only from their local communities but also from a national organization.

Ladies' aid society members desired and cultivated public gratitude for their work during the war.[57] Not content to take this recognition for granted, women expended great effort in publicizing their labor. When, for example, the secretary of the Chanceford aid society sent a box of goods to the Ladies' Aid Society of Philadelphia for distribution, she included a list of the contents and their value. Nine comforters were valued at $15.75, and ten pillows were worth $2.50. Altogether she estimated their contribution came to a net worth of $53.50. She asked that the Philadelphia women acknowledge their gift not in the city newspaper, the *Philadelphia Inquirer*, as they normally did, but in the *York Pennsylvanian*, so that "more of our people will see it."[58] Women recognized and relished the stature that their participation in ladies' aid societies could earn them.

These women created for themselves a public persona imbued with patriotism and loyalty to country. Ladies' aid society members often became representatives of their communities, civilians with a role in the male-dominated public ceremonies surrounding the war. This public participation by women benefited both the men who invited it and the women who accepted. Historian Elizabeth R. Varon has recently shown that in the antebellum South, the Whig Party consciously courted women's participation in their political activities, such as parades and meetings, to lend an aura of dignity and to protect "'domestic virtues' such as fairness, harmony, and self control." By doing so, Varon points out, men eased their anxiety about the nature of party politics.[59] Similarly, Northern men heading off to the Civil War requested women's public blessing to prove that women supported their decision to leave home and risk death in battle. For example, Joseph Hoard invited the Richmond Ladies' Aid Society to "confer a name upon the company of volunteers now forming in this place." In the middle of October 1861, the society met with the captain, the lieutenants, and some of the privates of the company. "After considerable debate," the women voted and chose the name "Tioga Mountaineers." They decided to present the company with a flag "as a memento of our esteem and the deep interest felt in the sacred cause." They raised the money, ordered the flag, and presented it in a formal ceremony the following week. Speeches were made,[60] patriotic songs were sung, and then everyone partook of a supper the women had prepared. Throughout the war, the women tried to keep close track of the flag they had given to the company as it faced battle after battle. They relished the idea of the soldiers carrying a physical symbol of women's patriotism and involvement in the war effort.[61] The men literally and symbolically obtained the women's blessing, and the women gained an increased public role.

Mary Ryan has argued that women's presence at wartime rallies served mainly to "fill the air with cloying gender stereotypes and recruit women to traditional roles on the sidelines of the public sphere."[62] But the Weldon women's experience may complicate this picture by suggesting that women could recast the significance of their participation and gain more public influence from it. The women in the Ladies' Aid Association of Weldon consciously parlayed their public status into a heightened collective position of power in the community. They did so by building a permanent public hall and by seeking a corporate charter from the state legislature. The story of the decision by Ladies' Aid Society of Weldon members to incorporate offers a fascinating glimpse into the world of women's benevolent work during the war. It reveals how some women used the status they gained through their participation in ladies' aid societies to shift their relation to their communities. It also illuminates the role that class played and shows one way that upper-middle-class women made use of politics long before they had the vote. Finally, the story of the Weldon hall reveals the intensity of women's dedication to their wartime societies, even after the end of the war, and thus suggests their importance to women's wartime experiences.

In 1864 members of the Weldon association declared themselves unsatisfied with the amount of money they had raised by donations alone and decided to build a hall where they could sponsor lectures, concerts, exhibitions, and other public events. They felt confident that the money they raised by selling tickets to these performances would substantially increase their funds. They also knew such a hall would situate their group at the cultural center of their community.

The women planned to build a hall that could accommodate six hundred people. Russell Smith and Ellwood Tyson, husbands of the secretary and treasurer, respectively, drew up a petition to obtain subscriptions for the building, and in the space of a few days these two comfortably well-off men had raised about five hundred dollars.[63] The society purchased a half-acre lot on which to build, wrote a series of resolutions and bylaws, outlined their purpose, and declared themselves "a body corporate, by the name of the Ladies' Soldiers' Aid of Weldon."[64]

Their success illustrates the political clout women of considerable social standing and financial status had in their communities, and their ability to use it for their own political ends. The secretary, Mrs. Smith, noted that she knew "several strong personal friends of the Governor" and together with the treasurer she visited one of them—Henry Bumm, the city treasurer. Mr. Bumm had read the society's annual report and "looked very favorably upon the enterprise." He suggested that the two women call on Thomas Cochran, a member of the legislature, the following Saturday. Their mission was successful. Mr. Cochran promised to use his influence to get the charter and even to draw up the bill itself, which he would forward to them for approval. Mrs. Smith used her class-based political connections to gain access to the halls of the legislature and affect policy in her society's favor.[65] When she returned home after the meeting with Mr. Cochran, Mrs. Smith worried she had left a mistaken impression. She immediately sat down and wrote him a letter, saying: "As I did not in my interview with you state with sufficient clearness that the object of our Society in applying to the Legislature for a charter was to obtain one which would enable ladies to be the sole managers, I now write to say that I hope you will use your influence, which we know is very great, to attain that end." She pointed out that precedents existed for this endeavor, including the Rosine Association of Philadelphia. The Weldon women just a few weeks earlier had received several pamphlets and reports from the Rosine Association, which may have prompted the decision to incorporate.[66] Mrs. Smith added that they thought because their society had "simple" purposes—sewing for soldiers and giving relief to their widows and orphans— it "could very properly be managed by women, and thereby save much complication and trouble." But, she went on, if the legislature found the request impossible, then they would prefer to continue without a charter rather than obtain one that included a management or ownership role for men.[67] Clearly, the women of the Weldon association felt strongly about maintaining control of their society.

Control of the ladies' aid society did indeed have important ramifications for the women of Weldon. Ownership of the new hall provided them with significant social power and control in their community. They doled out use of the building, bestowing favor on groups of which they approved and from which they felt no threat, while refusing others. On October 12, 1864, they agreed to let the Union League of Abington hold their meetings there, and later that month decided that Mr. Fields could hold his singing school in their building.[68] When Mr. George Cole applied to use the hall for "an entertainment for the benefit of the Odd Fellows," the board declined, "not being certain of the character of the entertainment" and fearing "it would interfere with the Exhibitions of the Society."[69] An October 1864 application to use the hall for "an address to be delivered for the benefit of the freedmen," was turned down, "since it seemed to conflict with similar means used by the Society for raising funds for the soldiers."[70] By the beginning of the next year, however, they responded differently to the same request. This time they decided that "it could be let for that purpose for the sum of $35.00."[71] By building the hall, the women had created one of the neighborhood's major resources, and through their control of it, they gained a significant amount of leverage in their community.

As the end of the war finally drew near, the whole North rejoiced. Four long years of bloodshed were over. When the news of Richmond's surrender reached Philadelphia, "all the Bells were rung, flags were put out of all Public Buildings and many private residences . . . every body seemed joyous and Happy," Amanda Meshler reported. But peace could not wash away all the sorrow and grief. "Hundreds of Thousands have found a Warrior's Grave and thousands to day mourn for Loved ones. . . . Thousands have met Death from Starvation and Cruelty at the hands of the Rebels, and thousands to day live Maimed for Life,"[72] Meshler noted. The North had to face the reality of reconstructing the country and its relationship to the former slaves as well as to the rebels. And then the entire Union was thrown into confusion and shock by the assassination of Abraham Lincoln.

For women who had structured much of their wartime lives around working for the soldiers, peace brought mixed emotions as well. Those who had been the most active often felt depressed or frightened at the thought that they might face what Rejean Attie has described as "a complete rupture of the elaborate network of relationships among like-minded women the war helped foster."[73] Some women tried to carry on their aid societies after the war. Their tenacity suggests that working with other women on behalf of their country had given these women a profound sense of satisfaction and direction in their lives that they were loathe to give up.

At one time, the Weldon society had been one of the most active and well organized in the state. In summer 1865 the president of the Philadelphia committee to aid the Chicago Sanitary Fair sent the society two silk flags as an award for the largest donation from any ladies' aid society in the state of Pennsylvania. The goods they had sent had raised $310.00 at the fair.[74] By the time they received their reward, however, the society was experiencing a decline in membership and participation that continued for ten years. In August 1865 its members decided to meet less than once a week and to reduce the dues.[75] By 1869 meetings were held only monthly, but still there was so "seldom a sufficient number of members present" to transact business that members decided to meet "from time to time" as needed.[76]

A few women held on to the group that had given so much meaning to their lives during the war. They continued to rent out the hall and to donate money and goods to needy individuals. But slowly members started to die and the end became unavoidable. In 1872 the treasurer was instructed to sell off the society's ice cream cans. In 1873 the quorum was reduced to five. In 1876 thieves broke into the hall and stole a dressing gown, some muslin, and some cash. Despite these setbacks, the women continued to make improvements to the hall, finishing the basement, constructing outbuildings, and extending the front steps. Susan Lukens's death in 1877 marked the end of the organization. She had been going to meetings since the founding of the society. The secretary, Mrs. Russell Smith, had died in 1874. The president "looked over some dishes in the closet and thinking they were no longer of any use there, proposed that they should be distributed amongst the members, which was agreed to, each paying twenty five cents for their lot." All the officers were unanimously reelected, but there the minutes of the Ladies' Soldiers' Aid Society of Weldon stopped.

The dedication of the few remaining members of the Weldon society suggests the importance their participation in that group must have held for them. Thousands of women joined ladies' aid societies, either for a brief, impetuously patriotic moment or for the long months and years of the war and even after. Acting together, they raised millions of dollars and provided Union soldiers with the varied diet and extra clothing that saved lives. The military relied heavily on their labor; without it the forces could not have been maintained through four years of war.

In the public space of ladies' aid societies, women of the Civil War era reshaped their relationship to their local communities. Ladies' aid societies provided a formal, public channel for the information and support networks that existed in neighborhoods and that became so important during the war. They provided women an arena in which to discuss political issues together and to gain an education from each other. In canvassing their neighborhoods to convince people to sacrifice more for the nation, women played a significant role in the political mobilization of their areas. Within an organization they had political clout, and they often controlled significant amounts of property and could operate as a major cultural institution in their town.

Although many of their day-to-day activities echoed those of earlier voluntary efforts, the context of the Civil War shifted the implications of women's actions. Women's wartime work in ladies' aid societies not only changed their relationships to their own communities, but to the nation as well, and altered women's sense of their own citizenship. Some women joined national political networks, such as the Woman's National Loyal League. When others joined the United States Sanitary Commission, they sensed that their work was part of a national effort. Because the fruits of their labor directly aided the federal government, women expressed pride in their work and a deep sense of connection to their country's cause. "We consider it both a duty and a privilege to contribute our mite towards the grand total" of goods sent to the government, noted the secretary of the Richmond Ladies' Aid Society. Women knew their work was an essential part of the war effort. "Were it not for the 'drops of water,' there would be no 'mighty ocean,'" the Richmond secretary mused. The Ladies' Aid Society of Philadelphia pointed out that women's efforts had "no doubt doubled the number" of soldiers who returned to battle from the hospitals rather than going home. They suggested that women's labors therefore had saved not only men's lives but "millions upon millions" of dollars to the public treasury.[77]

Russell Smith, husband of the Weldon society's longtime secretary, noted in a typewritten frontispiece for the society's minute book that "a true record of the great efforts the members of the Society and other loyal and generous women of the neighborhood, made to help the soldier during one of the greatest struggles a people ever made to raise the downtrodden and save their country" should be "of great interest to the future historian, and to all loyal Americans."[78] He was right. The workings of ladies' aid societies represent an important piece of the richly textured world of Pennsylvanian and American politics and culture during the Civil War. Elizabeth Cady Stanton, writing in the 1880s, called attention to the work women did in ladies' aid societies during the war. She argued that their wartime experiences helped women learn that "they had an equal interest with man in the administration of the Government."[79] Stanton believed that women's sacrifice for the government earned them the right to suffrage. While not all women joined Stanton in her demand for the vote, many considered their work for ladies' aid societies an important part of the national effort, and their language suggested that they equated it in importance to the service of soldiers. "We confess," wrote the Richmond secretary, Mrs. Moore, "to a degree of pride . . . that we were *enlisted for the war!*"[80] By comparing themselves to soldiers, ladies' aid society women recognized their new relation to the federal government and highlighted their newly sharpened sense of themselves as full American citizens.

"THE WORLD WILL LITTLE NOTE NOR LONG REMEMBER"

Gender Analysis of Civilian Responses to the Battle of Gettysburg

Christina Ericson

On the morning of July 3, 1863, twenty-year-old Mary Virginia Wade was shot dead while making bread in her sister's kitchen. This unfortunate occurrence gained Wade the distinction of being the only civilian killed during the Battle of Gettysburg. Jennie Wade was at the home of Georgia Wade McClellan to provide aid and comfort to her sister who had given birth to a son three days earlier. Despite the danger of stray bullets and shelling, Jennie had insisted on baking bread for hungry Union soldiers. After reading her morning devotional from the Bible, she had begun to mix the ingredients for biscuits.[1] Before her work could be completed, a bullet pierced two doors and struck her in the back, killing her instantly.

After the Battle of Gettysburg, Jennie Wade was hailed as a heroine throughout the Union. "The maid of Gettysburg" became the subject of countless poems, songs, and sentimental prose.[2] Rumor of her engagement to a Union soldier who, unbeknownst to Wade, had been killed shortly before the battle added to the pathos of the story. In addition to being immortalized in the pages of popular literature, her tragic story was preserved for the ages by an appropriation from the Pennsylvania state legislature for "a monument to

The author wishes to acknowledge the invaluable assistance of personnel at both the Adams County Historical Society and the Gettysburg National Military Park, as well as the guidance of Professor Robyn Muncy (University of Maryland, College Park), who directed the master's thesis that formed the core of this essay.

Fig. 4.1 A monument to Jennie Wade stands above her grave in Gettysburg's Evergreen Cemetery. The front panel reads, "Jennie Wade. Aged 20 yrs, 2 mo. Killed July 3, 1863, while making bread for the Union soldiers." Photograph by Tipton studio, Gettysburg, Pennsylvania (n.d.). Courtesy of Special Collections, Musselman Library, Gettysburg College.

Jennie Wade." Erected in 1900 over her grave in the Evergreen Cemetery, adjacent to the Soldiers National Cemetery, the monument includes the words: "With a courage born of loyalty, she hath done what she could" (Fig. 4.1).

Although Jennie Wade was the only civilian killed during the three-day battle, she was not the only civilian hero of Gettysburg. John Burns, the sixty-nine-year-old patriot who grabbed his gun and ran out "to fight the rebs," was also lauded as a symbol of loyalty and courage. A veteran of the War of 1812, Burns fought bravely alongside the Union forces to the west of town on July 1, 1863, and ceased his defense of home and country only when he fell thrice wounded. Burns's wounds were not fatal, and he lived to see his name immortalized in much the same way as Jennie Wade. Newspaper accounts praised him as the embodiment of American valor and patriotism (Figs. 4.2a and 4.2b). Popular nineteenth-century author Bret Harte wrote a poem in his honor.[3] He, too, has a monument on the Gettysburg battlefield. And Abraham Lincoln was so impressed with Burns's exploits that he asked to meet with the old man when he traveled to Gettysburg for the dedication of the Soldiers National Cemetery.

The images of Jennie Wade and John Burns, the heroine and hero of Gettysburg, boosted the morale of Northern soldiers and civilians in the summer of 1863. Military defeat and the strength of antiwar propaganda, combined with the threat of European intervention on the side of the Confederacy, had made the spring of that year a dark time for the Union war effort. Demoralization had reached "epidemic proportions" in the Union army after the defeat at Fredericksburg the previous December, and the Northern press carried debates over the extent of women's patriotic convictions. Men were deserting the army, female loyalty was uncertain, and many had begun to despair that no true symbols of "manly" or "womanly" loyalty remained.[4]

The psychological boost offered by simultaneous victories at Gettysburg and Vicksburg was crucial to the Union. These victories renewed faith in the ability of both the Union armies and President Abraham Lincoln. But it was the human interest stories, such as those of Jennie Wade and John Burns, that captured the collective imagination of the North.

As the civilian heroine and hero of the Battle of Gettysburg, Jennie Wade and John Burns epitomized the dominant nineteenth-century gender ideology of separate spheres that located women in the home—concerned with family and domestic tasks—and men in public arenas, such as business, electoral politics, and, when necessary, on the battlefield.[5] The staying power of these images of Wade as a selfless, domestic woman-girl and of Burns as a martial,

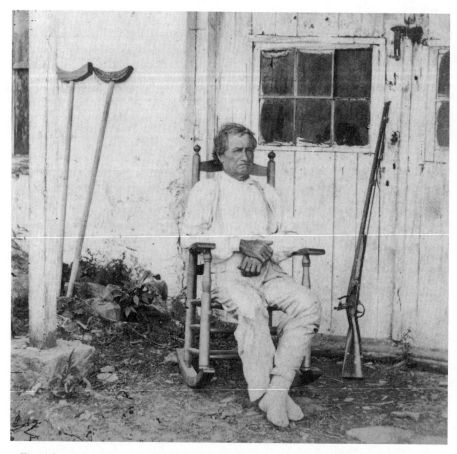

Fig. 4.2a A popular image of John Burns. This famous Mathew Brady portrait is a stereopticard of the "old patriot" convalescing at his home ca. July 15, 1863. Brady intentionally included Burns's gun and his crutches—symbolic badges of his manly valor. Courtesy of Special Collections, Musselman Library, Gettysburg College.

protective man has been immense. These highly gendered symbols continue to color our view of the Battle of Gettysburg, suggesting that women were passive inside their private homes during battles while men were active in the public exercise of martial valor.

Eyewitness accounts written by women living in and around the town of Gettysburg suggest a very different configuration of female and male gender roles during the battle. A study of these accounts indicates that the response of Gettysburgians during the battle challenges the ideal of the dominant

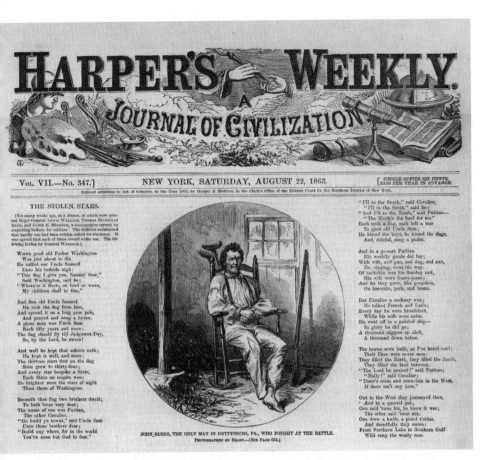

Fig. 4.2b A reproduction of Mathew Brady's photograph, entitled "John Burns, the Only Man in Gettysburg, Pa., Who Fought at the Battle," which appeared on the front page of the August 22, 1863, edition of *Harper's Weekly*. Courtesy of Special Collections, Musselman Library, Gettysburg College.

gender ideology of separate spheres, suggesting new insights into life on the Northern home front.[6] To understand these accounts and the actions of the citizens of Gettysburg in context, one must be familiar with the circumstances surrounding the Gettysburg campaign.[7]

In the summer of 1863 Confederate forces under the command of General Robert E. Lee poured into Pennsylvania with hopes of taking the war to Northern territory, thus relieving the beleaguered environment and economy of battle-scarred Virginia and securing badly needed supplies from the abundant local landscape. Gettysburg, the county seat of Adams County and a thriving village of 2,400 people, had its first taste of invasion on June 26, 1863, when Lieutenant General Jubal Early's Confederate cavalry raided the town. As one town resident described it, "About 4 o'clock the long looked for Rebels made their appearance, and such a mean looking lot of men I never saw in my life. . . . How exasperating the thought that tonight we are under the control of 'armed traitors.'"[8] Although Early requisitioned a wide variety of supplies (or, as an alternative, $10,000 in cash), he did not "force" compliance when the local authorities claimed they were unable to meet his demands. Before leaving town the following morning, however, Early's men burned rail cars and the bridge over Rock Creek, severing Gettysburg's rail connections until after the battle.[9]

After two days "in Rebeldom" many citizens of Gettysburg were elated when advance pickets of the Federal army reached the town on Sunday, June 28. Most observers considered the Union forces now streaming in to southern Pennsylvania "Hooker's army," but they were actually portions of "Meade's army": President Abraham Lincoln had replaced Commander of the Army of the Potomac Major General Joseph T. Hooker with Major General George Gordon Meade in the early hours of that day. In spite of the comfort generated by the presence of the Federals who controlled the town, Gettysburg citizens were uneasy about the proximity of Confederate troops. During the nights of June 28 and 29, Confederate campfires were clearly visible along the eastern slopes of South Mountain, barely nine miles west of town.[10] On Tuesday, June 30, Gettysburg residents spotted Confederates along the Chambersburg Pike, at the top of the hill overlooking town from the west. These men paused to survey the town briefly but turned back to their camp at Cashtown when they saw a Federal cavalry unit entering Gettysburg from the south. That night Gettysburg was occupied by Union forces under the command of General John Buford.

On Wednesday, July 1, the Confederates attacked from the west and north of town and the Battle of Gettysburg began in earnest. Union troops were forced to retreat through the town, often hiding behind—or in—any building that offered protection from flying shot and shell. By early evening the Confederates had occupied the town while the Union forces regrouped and amassed along Cemetery Hill and Cemetery Ridge, high ground to the south of town. The Confederates would control the town, and all in it, for three days. Most of the second day's fighting took place south of town. Because Confederates still occupied the borough of Gettysburg, much of the firepower directed at them from Federal guns smashed into the streets and buildings. To escape the danger of shot and shell, citizens had been advised by both armies to take to the cellars of their dwellings. This advice was particularly well heeded on July 2 and 3.

The fighting continued to the south of town on the third day of the battle. The town was awakened when the day's fighting began at 4:00 A.M. at the base of Culp's Hill. On July 3 General Lee decided on a frontal assault of the Federal line, assuming that the previous day's attacks on Meade's left and right flanks had weakened the middle of the Federal line. An artillery bombardment was ordered to "soften" the Union defenses, to be followed by a major infantry assault upon the middle of the Union line on Cemetery Ridge. The bombardment of Cemetery Hill began around 1:00 P.M. The ensuing cannonade between the artillery of the Union and Confederate lines lasted well over an hour. One resident of the town described the sound "as if the heavens and earth were crashing together."[11] The Union line ultimately repulsed Pickett's charge, but Meade—perhaps sensing the exhaustion of his troops—did not order a counterattack.

On July 4, 1863, the Confederates began their retreat. Most had vacated the town by morning, although the presence of sharpshooters in certain parts of the borough temporarily prevented those residents from moving about freely. By nightfall of Saturday, July 4, Federal troops had once again secured the town, but the joy of Union victory was tempered by the daunting tasks of caring for the myriad wounded and burying the dead that littered the ravaged landscape of the town and surrounding countryside.

Eyewitness accounts written by Gettysburg women reveal a disjuncture between the ideal of separate spheres and the reality of life in the area before and after the battle. Although their experiences differed because of such factors as age, marital status, geographic location, class, occupation, and ethnicity, their recollections contain several themes that suggest a decidedly nontraditional response to the exigencies of battle.[12]

Sarah Broadhead, John Burns's neighbor, is perhaps the best known of the ten women studied in this chapter.[13] Broadhead was a thirty-year-old wife and mother, as well as a public schoolteacher in 1863.[14] She and her husband, Joseph, had a four-year-old daughter, Mary. Her diary of events from June 15 to July 15, 1863, was printed in 1864 under the title, *The Diary of a Lady of Gettysburg, Pennsylvania.*[15] The Broadhead home was located on the western end of town in the "Warren Block," a row house that stood on the north side of Chambersburg Street.[16] John Burns lived across the street.

Just down the north side of Chambersburg Street from the Broadheads lived Mary McAllister. Forty-one and unmarried, McAllister was a spinster residing in the household of Martha and John Scott, her sister and brother-in-law. The brick building housed both their residence and the general store that Mary ran.[17] Mary McAllister's account of the battle was published posthumously in a series of articles in 1938.[18]

Both Sarah Broadhead and Mary McAllister had the dubious honor of living on a street that served as a main artery for the Confederate advance (and corresponding Union retreat) through town on July 1 and the retreat of Lee's forces on July 4. The street witnessed intense sniper fire for days. Sarah Broadhead noted this in her diary entry of July 5, complaining that everyone else in town could walk around unmolested, but her family remained virtual prisoners in their home.[19]

Elizabeth Salome ("Sallie") Myers lived on Baltimore Hill, four blocks south of Mary McAllister's home and general store. A Gettysburg schoolteacher like Sarah Broadhead, Sallie was twenty-one in the summer of 1863. She published her account of the battle of Gettysburg in the San Francisco *Sunday Call* in summer 1903. Ten years later she recounted her story to Clifton Johnson, who included it in his 1915 book, *Battleground Adventures.*[20] At the time of the battle, Sallie lived with her sister in the household of their father, Peter Myers, a justice of the peace.[21] Sallie was among a group of young women "brimming over with patriotic enthusiasm" who greeted the Union army's First Corps on July 1 with refreshments and songs.[22]

The excitement and romance of uniformed troops marching to battle also impressed young Matilda "Tillie" Pierce. A fifteen-year-old schoolgirl, Tillie was a pupil of the female seminary run by Miss Carrie Sheads. In a postwar account titled *At Gettysburg: Or What a Girl Saw and Heard of the Battle*, Pierce recalled that she and a crowd of her friends stood on the corner of Washington and High Streets and sang patriotic songs as the Union men of Brigadier General John Buford's cavalry rode into town shortly after noon on June 30. She also described singing again on July 1, and it is possible that Tillie Pierce was a member of the group that included Sallie Myers.[23]

Like Sallie Myers, Tillie Pierce belonged to one of the wealthier families of Gettysburg. Although a butcher by trade, her father, James Pierce, appears as a "Gentleman" on the 1863 septennial census of taxable inhabitants. Despite the relative safety and comfort her home provided, Tillie did not remain with her family during the ordeal. Instead, she left town on the afternoon of July 1 with family friends, a woman and her two small children.

Her journey eventually led to the Jacob Weikert farm one mile south of town, where, ironically, Tillie spent most of the battle in a position much more exposed than that of her father's house.

Fannie Buehler was another wealthy woman who later wrote a book about her experiences during the battle of Gettysburg.[24] The wife of David A. Buehler, Fannie was thirty-seven and the mother of six in 1863. All but the oldest and youngest of her children had been sent to visit her sister in New Jersey at the time of the battle. Her husband—a lawyer, politician, editor of a Republican newspaper (a real "leader among the leaders," according to his wife) and postmaster of Gettysburg—had fled town on July 1 with the mail, leaving his wife in charge of the Baltimore Street building that housed both the post office and their home. After aiding her husband's escape (he was running out the east end of town as the Confederates were entering from the west), Fannie quickly took action to thwart Confederate access to the federal office. She closed the shutters, took down the "post office" sign, locked the door, and buried the keys.[25]

Like the Pierces and the Buehlers, Jennie McCreary's family possessed considerable wealth. Jennie's father, widower Smith S. McCreary, worked as a hat maker and owned a workshop just off "the diamond" on the south side of Chambersburg Street. The McCreary family also lived in this building, located adjacent to the social, if not the geographic, center of Gettysburg. The youngest of three daughters, Jennie was only seventeen years old at the time of the battle. On the first day of fighting she and her sister Kate went up on to the roof to watch the opening salvos. A short while later the sisters, undoubtedly realizing the roof offered little protection from flying debris, joined their father downstairs in the safety of their home's interior. Clearly restless, the girls then made their way to the home of a neighbor where they helped to roll bandages, which a group of wounded Union soldiers later used. When the fighting became too intense to remain upstairs, the girls joined neighbors, the Weaver family, in their cellar. A few hours later Jennie and Kate McCreary returned home in a journey filled with the sight of the carnage. At their home they found not only their anxious father, but also a group of wounded officers and hungry soldiers. Jennie spent the rest of the battle either tending to the needs of these men or seeking shelter in the basement. She wrote an account of the battle in a letter to her sister Julia a few weeks later.[26]

Unlike Jennie McCreary's experience as a young woman in the relative safety of the household of her wealthy father, Sarah Barrett King left home and struck out on her own. Although King lived with her father and mother in 1863, she was twenty-seven and the mother of five. Sarah's husband, William T. King, served in the Union army. A sergeant in Captain Robert Bell's cavalry, William was convalescing on a couch in his own living room when the Confederates raided Gettysburg on June 26. Sarah alerted him and other members of his company to the impending danger—timely advice that apparently saved them. In her words, "They barely escaped."[27]

Although she had enjoyed the excitement of standing on her front porch and watching Confederate General Jubal A. Early's division chase the remnants of Bell's cavalry out of town, Sarah decided she did not want to be in Gettysburg for the impending battle. She prepared some pies and biscuits and assembled an impressive array of items that she stuffed into her bodice.[28] She then set out for a friend's cabin at Wolf Hill with her mother and five children in tow. Her father had decided to stay at their home, which stood on the corner of York and Liberty Streets. All of Sarah Barrett King's subsequent adventures took place at the homes of neighbors in the countryside northeast of town. She published her account, "Battle Days in 1863," in the *Gettysburg Compiler* in 1906.

Liberty Hollinger's family also lived at the eastern end of town. Their home stood across York Street, approximately one block to the east of Sarah Barrett King's. Liberty, a sixteen-year-old schoolgirl, lived with her merchant father, mother, three younger sisters, and one younger brother. Financially comfortable, Jacob Hollinger made his living in the grain and produce business and owned a warehouse adjacent to the railroad. Unlike the King family (with the exception of Sarah's father), the Hollingers did not flee their home. Consequently, they "viewed" the battle mostly from the cellar. Liberty's reminiscences of the battle remained a private memoir until editor Elsie Singmaster published the account in the *Pennsylvania History* journal decades later.[29]

Joseph and Harriet Hamilton Bayly owned a farm three miles north of town. Because the Bayly farm lay behind enemy lines throughout the battle, Harriet experienced the battle in a far more immediate way than Liberty Hollinger. A forty-three-year-old farm wife with five sons, Harriet had more than one spirited exchange with Confederate soldiers and even managed to get herself briefly arrested. Her accounts of the battle were later published in the local Gettysburg press.[30]

Like Harriet Hamilton Bayly, Elizabeth Thorn had extremely close contact with a large military contingent in her backyard. But whereas the Confederate troops had allowed the Baylys to remain on their farm relatively unmolested, the Union army commandeered the Thorns' home, forcing Elizabeth and her family to seek refuge elsewhere. Elizabeth's husband, Peter, had been the gatekeeper of the Evergreen Cemetery before he enlisted in the Union army in 1862, and the Thorns lived in the gatehouse of the cemetery.[31] Upon her husband's departure, Elizabeth took over the duties—and the salary—of gatekeeper.

Elizabeth and Peter Thorn had emigrated from Germany. Elizabeth's mother and father, Catherine and John Masser (neither of whom spoke English), lived with the Thorns. Elizabeth had three sons and was six months pregnant with her fourth child at the time of the battle.[32] Ordered from their home at the gatehouse, which was strategically located just to the east of what would soon be known the world over as Cemetery Ridge, Elizabeth and her family sought shelter in the countryside south of town. When finally allowed to return to their home, the Thorns faced ruined bedding, pilfered belongings, and the grim task of burying 105 dead bodies. Elizabeth Thorn recorded her experiences in two accounts published many years later in local Gettysburg newspapers.[33]

Four important themes emerge from these women's writings. Men fled the area with livestock and government property, leaving women and children behind. Civilian men who did stay behind often insufficiently protected their wives and children. Women became assertive and insistent in confrontations with men, and war work offered the opportunity to provide much-needed aid (including nursing, food preparation, lodging, and so on) to the armies as well as opening the possibility of demanding recognition for this vital role in the war effort. These reactions to the battle show that the ideal of separate spheres, so carefully cultivated in the personae of Jennie Wade and John Burns, was far from a reality in Gettysburg.

Of the ten women who wrote these eyewitness accounts, five had the head of their household or other male members leave at some point before or during the battle.[34] Some of these men, such as the husbands of Sarah Barrett King and Elizabeth Thorn, enlisted in the army. Others had gone for different reasons. One left Gettysburg to protect United States government property. Fannie Buehler's husband, David, took his job as the town postmaster seriously. Upon learning of the Confederate invasion, he quickly removed the mails from Gettysburg to a safer location. The majority of men who fled Gettysburg moved their horses to safer areas in order to keep them away from Confederate "reckless raiders."[35] The threat of pilfered livestock was widespread. Thus this practice, although seemingly at odds with the dominant gender ideology that celebrated men as protectors of women, was common in and around Gettysburg during the three Rebel scares of the war.[36]

Sarah Barrett King's account illustrates what happened to the women who stayed home as their men fled with their horses. Although her husband served with Bell's cavalry thus had not "fled," Sarah spent the days of the battle with women and children whose menfolk had. Along with her mother and children, Sarah spent the day and night of July 1 at the John Bender farm. Because her husband had already departed the area with the most valuable of his stock, it was Mrs. Bender who greeted and extended hospitality to the weary refugees. After the Bender farm had been completely overrun by Confederates, the women and children, which now included Mrs. Bender, moved on to the Rhinehart farm on July 2. Mrs. Rhinehart and her four daughters were "glad to have company," for their men also had fled with their stock.[37] None of the women condemned the male exodus. In fact, many made a point of mentioning the constant threat of losses faced by the owners of livestock.[38] Perhaps no one explained the justification for this practice better than Harriet Hamilton Bayly: "Why a farmer needs a horse as much as a house."[39] A man could leave his wife and children because the extenuating circumstances of war made protecting horses the most important duty for ensuring the economic safety of his family. Traditional gender roles may have eased the decision for many men who were faced with the choice between economic ruin and temporary absence from their family. If men were the natural protectors of families, women and children would not be in danger if left alone because other men would protect them. The very troops who might steal a man's goods would be chivalrous enough to refrain from harming his dependents. This assumption turned out to be true. Union and Confederate troops generally behaved well toward civilians of both sexes, with the majority of the destruction occurring through pilfered property.[40]

Fleeing with horses and other valuables may have been widely practiced in and around Gettysburg, but it was not accepted without question in other areas of the North. *New York Times* correspondent Lorenzo L. Crounse branded the men of Gettysburg cowards and indicted them for utterly failing in their manly responsibilities both during and after the battle. In an article widely reprinted in the Northern press, Crounse contemptuously claimed: "In the first place the male citizens mostly ran away, and left the women and children to the mercy of their enemies." He went on to accuse them of "indecent haste" in presenting their bills for losses inflicted by the battle, "instead of lending a helping hand to our wounded, and opening their houses to our famished officers and soldiers." Crounse also railed against the "exorbitant" prices charged for food, lodging, and even bandages for the wounded.[41]

In spite of these stinging rebukes to Gettysburg's men, the guidelines of what constituted honorable, manly behavior were far from rigid. Separate spheres constituted a powerful ideology, but many men and women recognized the divergence between the ideal and the reality in wartime. Gender roles fluctuated throughout the war. An indignant letter to the editor of the *New York Times*, written to protest Crounse's slander of the men of Gettysburg, furnishes an example. Signed by no less than twenty leading professional men of the North, the document defended the men of Gettysburg (and, by extension, no doubt the rest of the North). The letter argued that men left town during the battle not due to "cowardice, meanness, or a lack of patriotism," as Crounse had argued, but because, "there are times when 'discretion is the better part of valor.'" These men argued that far from being a static, timeless trait, manly behavior was subject to the constraints of time and place. The letter pointed out that the men fulfilled the role of protector in leaving, which allowed them to safeguard government property and their own bodies from impressment. And although this letter did not acknowledge the role of farmers or the economic significance of the horses (it claimed, "but very few" of the townsmen actually left, and those that did "were chiefly men of official positions . . . and others of that class"), the eyewitness accounts of Gettysburg women clearly did.[42]

Certain of the women, however, viewed men as falling short of their responsibilities as they grappled with reconciling the domestic ideal against the wartime actuality. The men who fled town were not the only ones singled out as inadequate. Civilian men who stayed in town also failed to provide sufficient protection. In cases where the male head of household remained, women often portrayed them as protectors: younger women, such as Liberty Hollinger and Jennie McCreary, especially presented their fathers in such flattering roles. However, many of the older women made a point of mentioning the shortcomings of this protection. Forty-one-year-old storekeeper Mary McAllister, for instance, was generally disappointed with civilian men. For example, her brother-in-law, John Scott, did not leave town but was of little use as a protector because he was recuperating from an illness and ended up fainting just as the battle began on July 1. McAllister also recalled a man on the street who shouted to warn her of sharpshooters and got shot himself. Similarly, twenty-seven-year-old Sarah Barrett King found amusement in telling how her father hid behind a bed in the house when he learned that the Confederates had entered the town. Only Fannie Buehler, the wife of a wealthy politician, appeared overly concerned with exalting the protective qualities of her husband. According to Fannie, "There was no lack of provisions in our home, thanks to the prudent forethought of my very thoughtful husband." Thus, David Buehler provided for his family, protecting them from hunger and want despite the fact he had fled town with the mails.[43]

Whereas civilian men were ineffective protectors, military men generally lived up to the challenge. Accounts of the fighting abound with images of Union men safeguarding both the psychological and physical well-being of Gettysburg's frightened populace. Many narratives recalled feelings of relief produced by the arrival of Union troops on June 27, and their triumphant return to town after their victory on July 4. According to Sarah Broadhead, their presence in the public square on that Independence Day offered comfort because "I knew we were now safe."[44]

The Union army also provided physical protection. When Elizabeth Thorn showed Union scouts the roads in the area, an unnamed officer directed her to walk "to the east or southeast of the horse" so he could protect her from any bullets that might fly her way. Liberty Hollinger recounted how she appealed to two wounded soldiers for help and advice on the first day of the battle. They advised her to go to the cellar, and then carried her mother, who had fainted, to that protected area before joining the Union retreat. Finally, Jennie McCreary told of how a wounded Union officer called out to a group of menacing men that her home was a hospital and how the threatening Confederates "went away."[45]

In spite of belonging to an invading army, Confederate men also protected the women of Gettysburg. This is intriguing in light of the fact that many of the townsmen who were not invaders had been denied this manly role. Does the fact that Confederates willingly protected Pennsylvania's women and children mean that they, too, were bound to the same prescriptive ideology of separate spheres? No doubt General Orders Number 73, issued by General Robert E. Lee just days before the battle, had a salubrious effect on the behavior of the Confederate troops. These orders stressed that war should be made "only upon armed men" and denounced the "barbarous outrages upon the unarmed, and defenceless [sic] and the wanton destruction of private property that have marked the course of the enemy in our own country." By using the depredations of the Union army as a negative example, Lee cast the Confederates as protectors of noncombatants.[46]

One result of Lee's orders was the posting of Confederate soldiers to guard the homes and property of Gettysburg's townspeople.[47] In two accounts women used the image of the Confederate guard to great effect. Sarah Barrett King described how she and her companions felt "perfectly safe" when two Confederates said they would sit on the doorstep and guard the house where she stayed. And Mary McAllister, who had a problem with the first men assigned to guard her home, was eventually rewarded with two satisfactory men and "not molested any more."[48]

Assertiveness in women is the third theme that recurs in these eyewitness accounts. These women acted without the consent of men, and occasionally against men's wishes. Surprisingly, Gettysburg townswomen, as did Southern women confronting Union troops, stood up to soldiers much more often than to civilian men.[49] Even when women asserted themselves with civilian men, they did so typically over questions of personal safety rather than in an attempt to thwart male authority. Women's defiance of armed soldiers raises several questions. Did they find it easier to overturn gender hierarchies with unfamiliar men? Why was military authority questionable whereas local power relations were not? Were women more inclined to challenge the authority of Union or Confederate troops? What role did military rank play in these situations?

Spirited exchanges with military men were usually initiated by older women and took place with both Union and Confederate troops. A pair of confrontations with Union men illustrates this point. In defiance of the soldier who insisted upon a male guide, Elizabeth Thorn asserted that she could show the Union troops roads in the area. Sarah Broadhead displayed even more stridency. While caring for wounded soldiers at the Seminary hospital on July 5, she demanded to see the surgeon in charge and then insisted that he provide an explanation for the neglect of a patient whose leg was "covered with worms." By invoking their traditional role as caregivers, women could give themselves authority in these instances.[50]

Gettysburg women also asserted themselves with Confederate men. Sarah Barrett King refused to leave when Confederate soldiers recommended that she and her companions vacate a house where they had found shelter. Harriet Hamilton Bayly recounted how she "rose up in my wrath" against Confederates, demanding water for wounded Union troops who had been without drinks for twenty-four hours. Similarly, Mary McAllister twice reported "sassy" Confederates to their commanding officers. Women also stood up to

Confederate men by refusing to accept views or actions that violated their worldview. Sarah Barrett King matched wits with a belligerent old soldier sent to guard the farm where she stayed. To his incessant inquiries about why the men of the town were absent and not protecting the townswomen, she finally retorted, "They know we can do that ourselves." Perhaps no account revealed the spunk of its author so much as Harriet Hamilton Bayly's. She recalled blatantly telling Confederate men she was an abolitionist when they "talked their slavery and secession notions." She also refused Confederate money offered for bread she had distributed to them. This action became less altruistic when she told them, "I would take the genuine article—good greenbacks—if they had it; and they paid me well."[51]

The fact that many older Gettysburg women asserted themselves better against soldiers than against civilian men may point to the significance of daily contact in constructing and maintaining power relationships between men and women. The soldiers who entered Gettysburg in summer 1863 had power in terms of weapons and sheer numbers, but the civilian men who remained in town retained their longstanding positions of authority within the family and the larger community. The women who confronted soldiers, such as Sarah Barrett King and Harriet Hamilton Bayly, were apparently more comfortable standing up to unfamiliar men. But these confrontations were ultimately counterproductive: although women asserted their autonomy, men who witnessed these assertions left when the battle was over. The women of Gettysburg temporarily overturned a few gender hierarchies, but the civilian men who were in power before and after the battle neither witnessed nor recognized these spirited exchanges with military men.

A final theme in eyewitness accounts is that of women who empowered themselves through war work. All ten women aided the soldiers, some on the battlefield and others in their homes. Going out and ministering to the wounded embodied a certain level of autonomy, as Harriet Hamilton Bayly no doubt realized when her husband forbade her to return to the risky work. A certain degree of authority also accompanied caring for wounded men within the confines of one's own home. Although these women were catering to the needs of men—a decidedly uncontroversial aspect of the domestic ideal—the power dynamic had shifted because these men were vulnerable and in some cases in need of protection, two decidedly unmanly traits.

Wounded men reacted to their dependency in different ways. Many thanked the women for their assistance. A few, including the officers nursed in the homes of Mary McAllister and Sallie Myers, were demanding and haughty. As accounts of Sarah Broadhead and Sallie Myers suggest, at least some of the men appeared to be aware of a line between being self-sufficient (manly) and being helpless (effeminate). Thus, some men submitted reluctantly to first aid by women. When Sarah Broadhead asked Union soldiers at the Seminary hospital if any would like their wounds dressed, one mentioned a man on the floor "who cannot help himself, you would better see to him." Perhaps merely wanting to help Broadhead make the best use of her time, this soldier nonetheless proclaimed his self-sufficiency and drew a distinction between himself and his helpless fellow comrade. A second example of this reluctance to grant women control occurred when Sallie Myers assisted a wounded Union officer in dressing his wounds. She recalled his assurance that "he would take the responsibility and superintend the job if I would do the work."[52]

Ultimately, women did have a large degree of control over the fate of many of these men. Sarah Broadhead, for instance, helped relocate wounded men from the wet basement of the Seminary hospital to more sanitary quarters four flights up.[53] Nursing wounded soldiers empowered Gettysburg women. At least some of the men recognized this, especially the wounded Union men who made such a point of being able to help themselves.

As these varied experiences of stepping up (and in some cases physically stepping out of the home) to the challenge of nursing suggest, the women of Gettysburg lived a reality far removed from the popular image of female passivity. Nursing and feeding many of the 21,000 wounded men who littered the town and countryside gave them a vital military role. Their service was an indispensable part of the war effort. Because this service fit with the nurturing domestic role of women, the nontraditional aspect of the experiences of Gettysburg's women too often has been hidden behind Jennie Wade's ample domestic (and inherently passive) shadow. Domesticity became equated with passivity. Instead of being recognized for their active public labor, real work in service to their country, these women were patted on the head and thanked for their sentimental assistance, understood simply as a natural outpouring of their feminine charity and not really "work" at all.[54] Ultimately, none of these women demanded recognition for her service.[55]

How women dealt with these expanded roles during and after the battle varied. Although the conditions were present, not all of the women recognized that they might have been empowered, and still fewer acted upon this possibility.[56] In fact, the only woman who exhibited extraordinary behavior following the battle was Elizabeth Thorn, who had the grim task of burying 105 bodies.[57] Most of the women found great personal satisfaction and pride in the work they did for those wounded at Gettysburg. Sallie Myers captured the mood succinctly: "While I would not care to live over that summer again . . . I would not willingly erase that chapter from my life's experience." Many of the women of Gettysburg expressed surprise at being able to handle the responsibilities placed upon them. Jennie McCreary found she actually had "a little more nerve than I thought I had." And Sarah Broadhead discovered that "we do not know until tried what we are capable of."[58]

In addition to this sense of personal growth, a few of these women recognized that their responsibilities during the battle had offered them a greatly augmented role. Fannie Buehler realized that it was she who must run her household and take care of those who gathered in her home. With her husband gone, she had assumed the responsibility for herself and for the lives of others. With the importance of her role in mind, she recalled, "so much depended upon me, and what would happen if a stray shot or shell should strike me. No, no, whatever others did I must run no risks, and so I staid [sic] in the house and yard."[59] According to Buehler's account, domesticity did not equal passivity: instead, domestic responsibilities gave married women power. In her 1903 account, Sallie Myers recognized the power her role as a nurse had bestowed. She articulated the great pride she took in the "passes which admitted me to any hospital at any time." She considered enlisting as a nurse but decided against it, as "I could not see my way clear to leave home at that time."[60] In fact, all these women returned to their traditional, prebattle roles after the battle had ended. None was ready to leave home, either in the literal or figurative sense.

One can understand the necessity of remaining in Gettysburg. An immense influx of visitors came to the town as soon as railroad lines were repaired on July 10. Within days the town overflowed with volunteers, family members searching for loved ones, and the simply curious. The women of Gettysburg, some of whom were relieved of their nursing duties by the arrival of the United States Sanitary and Christian Commissions and the establishment of the general United States Army Hospital, were now expected to provide food and other accommodations for these guests. And if the demands of the battle's immediate aftermath did not tax even the sturdiest constitution, the stench of rotting human and equine flesh and the fear of pestilence necessitated keeping one's windows closed in the stifling heat of summer. No wonder these women stayed indoors.

When the first trains arrived in Gettysburg after the battle, agents of the Sanitary Commission (USSC) and members of the Christian Commission

(USCC) swarmed into town. By assuming care for the wounded men, the men and (primarily) women of the USSC and the USCC relieved the burden of grateful townswomen. Some local women were upset to see their wounded moved out to Camp Letterman, the general hospital established a mile and a half outside of town.[61] Many, such as Sallie Myers, had formed close relationships with the men in their care and were reluctant to give them up. But the majority was too occupied with the immediate demands of accommodating the multitude of guests in their household to put up much of a fight. Within days the local women—many of whom had braved shot and shell and held their own against two armies—once again found themselves consigned to the home. But just because these women did not ultimately seize the opportunities that the Battle of Gettysburg offered to expand their gender roles does not mean the opportunities did not exist.[62]

While the women of Gettysburg cooked, cleaned, washed, and generally supported the hordes of visitors, the men also busied themselves. Many helped with clean-up efforts, both for individual property and for the health of the town. Others were interested in the profit to be made from the battle. These profits ranged from the immediate (such as charging wounded men for a wagon ride from the battlefield into town or demanding exorbitant prices for goods) to the long-range (such as the "gentlemen" who purchased many acres of farmland and started a Gettysburg Battlefield Memorial Association).[63] It seems that these men, some of whom had been absent during the battle, prepared to reap any rewards that might come from the unfortunate event.

As the behavior of Gettysburg's men and women during June and July 1863 shows, the simplistic images history has assigned to Jennie Wade and John Burns are far from representative. Although each legend has some basis in fact, details that did not quite fit with the sterling images of the heroine and hero of Gettysburg were widely ignored by the national press. For instance, the town held the Wade family in no great esteem because of a number of sexual and legal transgressions. Jennie's father, James Wade, was a less than reputable character, and in 1852 Jennie's mother committed him to the Adams County Alms House. He remained in the asylum until his death in 1872, which has raised questions about the paternity of Jennie's youngest brother, born in 1855. Both Jennie and her mother worked for wages. Jennie helped to support the family by taking in work as a seamstress.[64] Soon after the battle, stories that questioned her loyalty to the Union and even her virtue circulated through the town.[65] A number of Gettysburg's citizens resented Jennie's posthumous role as a heroine. And the voice that rang out above all others was none other than that of John Burns.

John Burns's best-known attack on Jennie Wade's reputation came in response to a letter from Frank Moore, a man who was writing a book "to set before the world the noble acts of our loyal women in this war." In his letter of January 17, 1866, Moore asked Burns if he knew anything of Jennie Wade, and if so, would he kindly supply "the name of some person who may be acquainted with the particulars of her life, character and the manner of her death." Apparently this inquiry about Jennie Wade, along with the painfully obvious lack of interest in his own heroics, struck a nerve in John Burns. Writing his reply on the same sheet of paper as the original letter, the frugal Scotsman's indictment was short and sweet: "The less said about her the better." And despite claiming that "Charity to her reputation forbids any further remarks," Burns concluded by labeling Jennie Wade a "she-rebel," implying she could have been either a Confederate sympathizer or a local troublemaker.[66]

The reality of John Burns also fell far short of the ideal immortalized by the Northern press. Accounts of local townsfolk who knew the hero of Gettysburg described "a Scotchman lacking in humor and the subject of practical jokes," who enjoyed a reputation as a "local controversial character" even after he had held the position of town constable.[67] Although he freely acknowledged a wild and intemperate past, his application for a pension from the U.S. army in 1864 made clear that he had changed his ways.[68] Burns was evidently an exasperating man to live with, even in his abstemious incarnation. His wife, Barbara, was less than thrilled with Burns's battlefield heroics. Instead of expressing concern when a neighbor told her that John was wounded and he wanted her to fetch him in a wagon, Barbara flatly stated, "Him, I told him to stay at home." And she left him to find his own way home.[69]

Gender roles in Gettysburg at the time of the battle were considerably more complex than the images of Jennie Wade and John Burns would suggest. Events surrounding the Battle of Gettysburg fostered considerable debate over appropriate womanly and manly roles. Men abandoned their families to flee with horses, and even those who remained proved unable to protect their wives and children. Women, in turn, frequently became assertive and empowered (however temporarily) by war work. Images of Jennie Wade and John Burns have smoothed over these rough edges, obscuring the complex, dynamic gender negotiations that took place during the battle.

In Gettysburg, as in the rest of the North, the war caused fluctuations in the exercise of proper manly and womanly roles. And it is precisely this uncertainty, this ambiguity, that can ultimately enrich our understanding of social relationships between and among men and women on the Northern home front. In order to understand that complexity, not only for Gettysburg but for the rest of Northern society as well, we need a new way of looking at gender relations in the mid-nineteenth century.

THE AVERY MONUMENT

The Elevation of Race in Public Sculpture and the Republican Party

Henry Pisciotta

I have appointed a Secretary of Semantics—a most important post. He is to furnish me with forty- or fifty-dollar words. Tell me how to say yes and no in the same sentence without contradiction. He is to tell me the combination of words that will put me against inflation in San Francisco and for it in New York.
—Harry S. Truman, memorandum, December 1947

You can campaign in poetry. You govern in prose.
—Mario Cuomo, New Republic, April, 8, 1985

The text itself is no more than a series of "cues" to the reader, invitations to construct a piece of language into meaning. . . . The work is full of "indeterminacies," elements which depend for their effect upon the reader's interpretation, and which can be interpreted in a number of different, perhaps mutually conflicting ways.
—Terry Eagleton, Literary Theory, 1983

The quips of Harry Truman and Mario Cuomo mock, but also recognize as necessary, the ambiguous rhetoric sometimes employed in political campaigns. Specificity and clarity may not be the best means of attracting voters with divergent interests and opinions to a single ticket. To "campaign in poetry" is to indulge in the same "indeterminacies" that reception theorists

Many thanks to Kirk Savage for bringing the subject of this paper to my attention as part of his seminar on the representation of race at the University of Pittsburgh and for generously permitting me to develop his discovery for publication—and also for finding the important 1869 description of the monument in the *Christian Recorder* and reading my manuscript at several stages. Joe Trotter may not realize how important his brief comments on this work have been and how grateful I am for them.

observe in the arts—the reader, listener, or viewer determines meaning not only from the clues in the work, but also from personal experience. A proliferation of meanings may result. The word "polarizing" is often used to describe divisive political issues, such as school integration in the 1960s or abortion today, as if only two interpretations of these controversial topics were possible. In fact, support for either side in such a dispute often consists of an amalgam of people with divergent and sometimes contradictory reasons for taking the same stance. This type of awkward coalition characterized both sides of the debate over slavery in the United States.

Shortly before the Civil War contention over slavery reached its boiling point, with arguments presented in speeches, sermons, newspapers, and most other public media. But the least likely medium for addressing such an unresolved and unsettling topic may have been permanent public sculpture, typically the choice for commemorating the ennobling, the inspirational, and the widely accepted. So it is remarkable that the tomb of the wealthy industrialist Charles Avery, designed and constructed between 1858 and 1860, was apparently the first large public memorial to depict African-American slaves and the only example preceding the Civil War. This heavily damaged sculpture still stands in Pittsburgh's Allegheny Cemetery. It has received little historical attention but has much to offer our appreciation of the political poetry of its time.[1] Commissioned by men who were active in the formation of the Republican Party, the Avery Monument celebrated the achievements of Charles Avery and offered a vision of the potential of the freed slave. Although this vision made some precise references to education, religion, geography, and even specific historical events, it was a picture capable of supporting several interpretations. Particular confusion resulted from the monument's images of the education and emigration of people of color. These representations, contained in a well-publicized relief panel on the face of the monument, confronted the most heated issue of the day, but did so enigmatically. In this way, they paralleled the ambiguous rhetoric employed by the Republican Party in building a coalition in the years preceding its victories in the 1860 elections.

The Cemetery and Public Sculpture

The grave of a forgotten Pittsburgher may seem an odd site for political commentary, especially since the twentieth-century notion of a gravestone usually involves a neutral, private, and perhaps devotional object. But the tomb for Charles Avery clearly functioned as a didactic public sculpture. Political readings of its imagery resulted partly from this function, since public sculpture is seldom entirely free from politics. Understanding the civic prominence of the Avery Memorial requires consideration of the role of "rural" (or "garden") cemeteries in the nineteenth-century city as well as some of the particulars of this sculptural commission. Little of antebellum Pittsburgh remains, but one experience that can be reconstructed is a visit to Allegheny Cemetery, which was incorporated in 1844 as one of America's first rural cemeteries. Before the rural cemetery movement, churchyards provided most of the burial sites in American cities. During the last half of the century rural cemeteries moved this function to interdenominational landscaped gardens located on the outskirts of the city. In addition to easing concerns about urban crowding and sanitation, these large cemeteries served as recreational facilities—predecessors of the large city parks. Pittsburghers of all classes might enjoy a buggy ride or a hearty walk from the central city three or four miles to the east to the nicely groomed cemetery for a picnic.[2] In 1860 they entered Allegheny Cemetery through the main gate on Butler Street, designed by John Chislett in a romanticized Gothic style, then turned and paused at the first fork in the road. At this first juncture, people were greeted by a view of the Avery Monument on the hill just to the right (see Fig. 5.1). This sequence of gateway, fork, and figural sculpture also welcomed those entering Mount Auburn Cemetery in Cambridge, Massachusetts, the first of America's rural cemeteries and the model for many others. There the large seated portrait of mathematician and navigator Nathaniel Bowditch by Robert Ball Hughes watched visitors from atop a monument erected in 1847. By 1860, similar figures had been stationed in key positions at other rural cemeteries.[3] Major monuments in these predecessors to large city parks acted as public sculpture. The Avery Monument was the centerpiece of this new type of public space in Pittsburgh.

In its scale, materials, and form, the Avery Monument resembles major civic sculptures of its day more than the obelisks and tombstones of Allegheny Cemetery. The formula of a large, decorated pedestal holding a larger-than-life-size portrait figure well above eye-level typified such outdoor civic monuments as Henry Kirke Brown's equestrian statue of George Washington in New York's Union Square (1853–56) or Thomas Crawford's Washington Monument in Richmond (1857) or numerous European models.[4] The handful of early biographical sketches of Charles Avery all mention the monument and

Fig. 5.1   Louis Verhaegen, Avery Monument, 1860. Allegheny Cemetery, Pittsburgh. Photo: George Bekich.

several begin and end with contemplations on this stone commemoration of his character. It attracted compliments as the most elaborate tomb west of the Alleghenies; one parochial journalist thought it the finest in the world.[5] Roughly thirty feet high, the effigy commanded a view of much of the cemetery as its tallest construction. Only a few architectural structures in the cemetery compared in scale: a couple of mausoleums, the Gothic receiving vault, and Chislett's entry gate. Made entirely of imported Carrara marble, the Avery Monument cost about $12,000, a very large sculptural commission for the United States at mid-century. Sculptors of funerary works were seldom identified, but the plinth of this example bears the inscription "L. Verhaegen. Sculptor, N.Y. 1860." Louis Verhaegen was a little-known artist, listed as a sculptor in New York business directories from 1851 through 1860. He exhibited sculptures, mostly portraits, at some of the industrial trade shows of the American Institute in New York, where he won a bronze medal in 1856 for a portrait of the late Daniel Webster.[6] An 1859 New York article about the Avery Monument characterized Verhaegen's oeuvre as "several busts of distinguished statesmen" completed "for some gentlemen of this city."[7] Insofar as Verhaegen had a reputation, it seems to have been because of portraits of political personalities. Verhaegen may have based his designs for the Avery Monument on a monument to a New York politician: Henry Kirke Brown's bronze monument to DeWitt Clinton placed near the entrance to Brooklyn's romantic Greenwood Cemetery in 1852, which is similar in its combination of full-length portrait in-the-round and didactic relief and its mixture of naturalism and allegory (see Fig. 5.2). The raising of Avery's costly marble tomb sculpture in Allegheny Cemetery, designed by a Belgian-born New York sculptor, must have been a major event in the visual arts of antebellum Pittsburgh.

Charles Avery: "The Tree Is Known by Its Fruit"

Charles Avery was an early Pittsburgh industrialist. He invested in many public works, brought important industries to Pittsburgh, and acted as a civic leader, particularly in Allegheny, the municipality a short walk north of Pittsburgh's central business district. He made his fortune during the presteel era of Pittsburgh's development—the period before Andrew Carnegie and Henry Clay Frick—beginning in the 1820s and 1830s with a start in pharmaceuticals and white lead. During the early 1840s, his larger source of income became one

Fig. 5.2   Henry Kirke Brown, DeWitt Clinton Monument, 1852.
Greenwood Cemetery, New York. Courtesy Library of Congress,
Manuscripts Division.

of Pittsburgh's half dozen cotton mills. By the end of that decade he had amassed an astonishing fortune in copper mining and smelting.[8] Throughout this time he collected diversified investments in bridges, roads, shipping firms, and railroads. The trajectory of his career suggests that he was an aggressive and clever businessman. Yet nearly all the information available on Avery, especially the obituaries and posthumous biographies, portray him not as a shrewd investor, which must have been the case, but as a devout evangelistic Christian leader and an exceptionally generous philanthropist—the very model of moral conscience in control of the capitalist drive of self-interest.

In the context of antebellum race relations, Avery's philanthropy stood out because of his active support of antislavery causes and education for African Americans. Even among abolitionists, Avery had unusually strong confidence in the intellectual abilities of blacks. At a time when such anthropologists as Josiah Nott fabricated "proofs" of white superiority, Charles Avery apparently trusted his own judgment and experiences with the African-American community. One example of this confidence touches on the visual arts. The first work of art that Avery commissioned was an 1848 painting of his phenomenally profitable copper mine. He sought out a young African-American painter from Cincinnati—Robert Scott Duncanson—and sent him to Michigan's Keweenaw Peninsula to produce the oil painting. Grateful for this crucial early commission, Duncanson made a much-publicized gift to Avery of his first ambitious historical painting: the *Garden of Eden* (1852), based loosely on Thomas Cole's painting of the same title.[9] In 1849 Avery funded a scholarship for African Americans at Oberlin College, the first of many across the nation later established in his name by bequest. In the Pittsburgh area, Avery is best remembered for starting the area's first college exclusively for black people, apparently acting upon the suggestion of John Peck and perhaps other leaders of western Pennsylvania's African-American community. The Avery Institute (named the Allegheny Institute in its early days), opened its doors in 1850 and survived, through a series of hardships, until 1912.[10]

Charles Avery's tomb memorializes him as an exemplar of morality and generosity. The portrait sculpture that tops the monument and an allegorical figure of Charity on one side emphasize these aspects of his character. The portrait depicts Charles Avery as a man of religion. His hand rests upon two books, probably the Old and New Testaments, presenting himself in nearly the same pose as Verhaegen's portrait of Webster, the nation's greatest orator (see Fig. 5.3). The Bible and posture refer to Avery's status as a "local preacher." In fact, he was often referred to as the "Reverend" Charles Avery, though his

Fig. 5.3 Louis Verhaegen, *Daniel Webster*, undated. Courtesy of the Saint Louis
Mercantile Library Association, Saint Louis.

was an honorific title bestowed upon active laymen in the Methodist church and not an ordained or degreed status. Nonetheless, Avery did preach and teach Bible classes throughout his life. Moreover, he worked as one of a handful of leaders in the formation of his denomination. Adamant about the rights of the laity to govern local churches cooperatively, he helped to found a sect of Methodism known as the Methodist Protestant Church, which split from the Methodist Episcopal Church in 1828.[11] Avery devoted much of his time and wealth to his church. His evangelism was a catalyst for his concern for blacks in the United States as well as his support for Christian missions in Africa. But his Methodist sect contained activists on either side of issues like slavery, so Avery's philanthropic concentration upon race must also have been a matter of individual conscious.[12] To Avery, good works were requirements of Christian association but also statements of personal identity. Four biblical quotations fill the broad expanse of stone below the Avery portrait. In the eulogy, Rev. John Cowl, the pastor of Avery's congregation, reported that the first of these inscriptions recorded the last words from the lips of this busy Methodist: "The tree is known by its fruit" (Matthew 12:33).[13] "Fruit" in this case might as well have signified both good deeds and material wealth. In both realms Charles Avery's tree was exceptionally productive. Estimates of the value of his estate at the time of his death ranged from $300,000 to $700,000. One obituary suggested that a roughly equal amount had been donated to charitable causes during his lifetime.[14]

Representing Avery's generosity, an allegorical female figure of Charity stands in a niche on the north side of the sepulchral monument (see Fig. 5.4). The allegory follows a long tradition of representing Charity as a woman with a baby held near her breast. This breast-feeding was often rendered more frankly, but Verhaegen's version for Pittsburgh risks no nudity. Nor does it explore the multicultural scope of Avery's philanthropy by including children of different ethnicity. That would have been unusual but not unprece-dented. Such a group of children clustered around *La charité universelle* in the 1845 painting of that title by the French artist Alexander Laemlein.[15] For the Allegheny Cemetery monument Charity was personified as simply and conven-tionally as possible and accompanied by an equally straightforward inscrip-tion on the front facade: "It is better to give than to receive" (Acts 20:35). Causes that Avery supported included conventional ones, such as his church and local hospitals, but also less typical gifts to individuals (both white and black), donations of real estate that were instrumental in establishing the African Methodist Episcopal Church in Pittsburgh, and many others.

Fig. 5.4   Louis Verhaegen, Avery Monument, detail of Charity. Photo: George Bekich.

The Patrons: "Without Undue Pomp or Display"

In 1859 the Avery Monument looked to the past by memorializing a life, but it also physically introduced a new program of philanthropy that was to be conducted over the next two decades. This program, Avery's greatest act of charity, was embodied in his will. That document, written in late 1857 and amended twice before his death in February 1858, began by making the customary provisions for burial and bequests to family and other close associates. Few relatives survived him and no offspring. Less than one-fourth of his great wealth was distributed in this manner, and the remainder constituted a huge charitable bequest for its time. Avery divided it into two equal funds dedicated to these separate purposes: "for disseminating the light of the Gospel of Jesus Christ and the Blessings of Christian Civilization amongst the benighted Black and Colored races of people inhabiting the Continent of Africa. And to this end, I direct my Executors to pay over said fund to . . . the 'American Missionary Association,' located in the City of New York . . . and . . . for promoting the education and elevation of the Colored people of the United States of America and the British Provinces of Canada . . . free from all bias on account of sect or party and limited only by the general principles of Christian morality."[16] The money directed toward the Christianization of Africa was fully managed by the executive committee of the American Missionary Association, an interdenominational organization dedicated to spreading the Gospel. The fund devoted to American blacks was administered and distributed by the three associates named by Avery as his executors: William M. Shinn, Thomas M. Howe, and Josiah King. These three executors commissioned Louis Verhaegen to create the Avery Memorial.

Of the three, Thomas M. Howe stood out as the most visible public figure. He established his reputation as a banker and was president of Pittsburgh's Exchange Bank until 1859. By that time he had involved himself in many other business interests, including iron and steel manufacturing, railroad investments, and copper mining and refining through a partnership with Charles Avery and others. He served as the first president of the Pittsburgh Chamber of Commerce from the 1850s until his death. As a Whig he was elected to the U.S. House of Representatives in 1850 and again in 1852. When the Whig Party disintegrated in the mid-fifties, Howe, like Avery, became active in the newly formed Republican Party—so active that by the end of 1859, his name appeared frequently in Pittsburgh's most Republican newspaper, the *Gazette*, as a potential candidate for the party's gubernatorial nomination.[17]

Josiah King owned one of Allegheny's cotton mills in partnership with Avery. Although a more obscure figure, King had a role in the first Republican National Convention in 1856 and presided over the Allegheny County Republican Party conference that endorsed Howe for governor in early January 1860. By 1866 King owned a major share of the *Gazette*.[18]

William Shinn was the son of the Reverend Asa Shinn, a principal theologian of the Methodist Protestant Church and longtime friend of Avery. A lawyer, the younger Shinn had handled many of Avery's business transactions. His political preferences in the late 1850s are less clearly documented than those of his coexecutors, but he was active in the Free Soil Party as late as 1856. He probably became a Republican by 1860, like so many other Free Soilers in Allegheny County. Shinn aspired to improve Pittsburgh's cultural amenities. He chaired Pittsburgh's Philological Institute in 1839, dabbled in publishing, and founded an early romantic suburban community, Evergreen Hamlet, in 1851.[19]

While all three men stood in, or at least near, the Republican camp, their views on slavery differed to some degree. Howe might be described as a Northern centrist. For example, he opposed the Fugitive Slave Act in his campaign of 1850 but felt obliged to support its enforcement after its passage.[20] King's stance on slavery is not recorded. One abolitionist described William Shinn as "the only Anti-Slavery man of the three Executors."[21] In their failure to agree on the question of chattel slavery, Avery's executors typified the variety of opinions that had collected within the new Republican Party.

The executors of the estate shaped the monument to Avery more than did the wishes of the surviving family, the other heirs, or Charles Avery himself. Friction quickly developed between the three trustees and Avery's family. The intensity of Charles Avery's charitable pursuits conflicted with the security of his wife. Martha Avery did not join Charles to rest beneath the monument until 1865. Upon her husband's death in 1858, she contested the terms of his will in an attempt to improve her share of the inheritance, and this suit paralyzed the estate for a number of years.[22] Avery directed in his will that he be interred "without any unnecessary pomp or display," yet his tomb was exceptionally ostentatious by any measure.[23] In a letter of May 6, 1858, to George Whipple, the secretary of the American Missionary Association, William Shinn described the impetus for a monument and expressed willingness to pay as much as $20,000 from the estate "if less will not carry out the object."[24] Shinn specified, in a subsequent letter, that the association was "the only party having a legal right to interpose . . . advice or objection" regarding the funerary monument, since the expenses incurred would reduce the association's income from the bequest.[25] This interpretation excluded Avery's wife or other family members and there is no record of any immediate family involvement with the commission. Nor was the American Missionary Association involved with the monument. Indeed, the sequence of letters exchanged suggests that the association's officers may have been outwitted, either by accidental events or by clever manipulation, into accepting the substantial costs of the tomb for Charles Avery.[26]

Why then did Avery's executors interpret so broadly the amount of "pomp and display" required? There are at least three likely answers to this question, one centering on the promotion of philanthropy, another on the successful development of Allegheny Cemetery, and a third on the Republican campaigns of 1860.

Philanthropy: "We Want More Men Like Mr. Avery"

In his letter to George Whipple justifying the expense of the monument, William Shinn emphasizes the encouragement of philanthropy:

Something is due to that aspect of the subject which presents the man himself, as a bright *example* to the race of man; not in the light of the old heathen idea of personal fame, not to deify Charles Avery, but to perpetuate the fact that God raised up such a character—one whose ambition (so to speak) turned aside from the applause of his peers, to seek the approval of that higher One who condescends to look in compassion and love upon these the down trodden and despised of man—the lowly and neglected. . . . We want more men like Mr. Avery: he was a very rare specimen. Many men we have who, out of their abundance, give liberally to charitable objects: many who, dying, make up the shortcomings of a lifetime by munificent bequests to the Lord's treasury: multitudes, who, from benevolent and Christian impulses, from their scanty poverty, under a solemn sense of duty, drop their mites into the lap of the poor. But few—very few, who in the spring time of life, deliberately choose a field for cultivation *because* it is unruly, and barren and overgrown with bramble and neglected & rejected of other husbandmen, and toilsomely, & perseveringly, through summer, harvest, autumn, winter & against all opposition & with slight hopes of fruit, dig and grub and plant it, looking to God only to give increase. Verily they have their reward, but our duty is to give permanency and prominence to their example.[27]

The model to perpetuate was not simply one of generosity, which might have been embodied in sculpture simply by the allegory of Charity and the portrait of the deceased. More particularly the letter underscores a lifetime of consistent effort made more worthy by its focus on "the lowly and neglected." Shinn ranks social commitment and moral conscience as the highest motives for philanthropy. In this view, exemplars like Avery provided the necessary "safety net" for the lowest stratum of a free-market society—those who were owned and could not advance by ownership. This contrasts sharply with one of the common arguments in defense of slavery—the critique of the industrial capitalist and his avoidance of responsibility for his laborers. Antislavery arguments typically pitied slaves as the least privileged class, whereas slavery's defenders pointed to Northern factory workers as the most economically imperiled group. The economic strata suggested in Shinn's letter takes the Northern, industrial point of view.

Interestingly, Shinn disguises Avery's occupation. The letter's extended analogy to clearing and planting land associates African Americans with nature and imagines the good philanthropist in the role of homesteader. The first association, the theme of blacks as primitives who enjoy a more natural state of existence, was a variation on "noble savage" imagery, a common projection rooted in ancient traditions of connecting the sociological "other" with nature.[28] The characterization of the conscientious industrialist as a farmer drew upon the agrarian myth of the independence that had long been a central theme in America's nationalist ideology. By further specifying "unruly" ground, Shinn casts Avery in the role of the heroic homesteader—an image consistent with the lawyer's Free Soil politics. Free Soil rhetoric enshrined the yeomanly settler, cursed the baronial slaveholder, and avoided addressing the role of the industrial capitalist. Republicans adopted very similar messages in the late 1850s.[29] The text of Shinn's call for more philanthropists like Avery assumed some political and economic qualifications for the job.

Allegheny Cemetery: "All the Essential Requisites of a Rural Cemetery"

The Avery Monument may also be understood as part of a program to ensure the success of Allegheny Cemetery. In this context, the construction of the monument becomes associated with Howe's activities as a leading Republican. Pittsburgh's rural cemetery was only the sixth or seventh of this type in the country, but its development lagged somewhat because of the Great Fire that burned a large portion of the city's business district in 1845. Several of the cemetery's forty corporators (who functioned as board members and stockholders) resigned during the hardships of the following year. Each of the executors of the Avery estate, and Avery himself, had been corporators of Allegheny Cemetery at one time or another. More important, Howe served as president of the cemetery from 1846 until shortly before his death in 1877.[30] Directing the cemetery was among the most visible public works in his portfolio of commercial and civic activities.

During the two years between Avery's death and the completion of his memorial the cemetery grew and improved dramatically. Howe and his board of managers added adjoining properties, installed low fences around major monuments, and petitioned the state for a change in the articles of incorporation that would permit the cemetery to accept grants, bequests, and endowments. In January 1859, one year after Avery had been interred, Howe transferred $200 from the estate in order to expand the size of the Avery burial lot by 600 square feet, apparently in preparation for the grand monument and its surrounding fence. The following month, the cemetery's board voted unanimously on "opening up the Main avenue of the Cemetery (called Tour Avenue) the coming season," which most likely passed by the Avery Monument in order to reach the gatehouse.[31] By 1873, near the end of Howe's leadership of the cemetery, a report published by its corporators boasted that there was no "other locality in the country where all the essential requisites of a rural cemetery are present in a higher degree of perfection."[32] These types of improvements in a rural cemetery lured both the casually curious and wealthy buyers of large burial lots. Managing these visible successes for this civic amenity could do no harm to Howe's simultaneous gubernatorial bid.

The Campaign and the Courts: "The Memory of the Just"

Whether intended or not, the iconography of the monument resonates with two of the values of the young Republican Party. First, the sculpture was cautious in its stance on the recent controversial laws and court decisions. Second, its images of blacks called direct attention to the national issues of race. By focusing on a scene of black emigration, the memorial envisioned a future for blacks that was understood differently by distinct groups in the sculpture's audience. Like most Republican proposals related to race, this emigration scene suggested a world in which elevation from slavery and racial prejudice were potentially compatible.

The allegory of Justice on the southern side of the monument alerts us to the political sentiments in the sculptural program. Unlike the image of Charity, Justice is depicted indirectly and uncomfortably, apparently in reaction to political events of the 1850s. The statue is now so badly damaged that the difficulty of interpretation begins with simple recognition of what was carved. The female figure is certainly blindfolded, but other attributes have been obliterated (see Fig. 5.5). Her left hand may have held a flattened ovoid object, or simply an awkwardly fashioned tuft of her drapery. A fading photograph of the work, taken in 1873, reveals that her right hand rested upon the hilt of a sword, the blade extending down to the base near her right foot (see Fig. 5.6).[33] The blindfold and sword were common attributes of Justice, and descriptions of the monument published in 1859 before its completion supported this interpretation.[34] Intriguingly, a description by an African-American "Pittsburgh Correspondent" dating from 1869 called the figure "Liberty," offering no explanation for this identification.[35] Allegories of Liberty, particularly those displaying the Phrygian cap, were frequently tied with the abolition movement at mid-century.[36] If the object in the left hand was once discernible as a cap, then Verhaegen may have combined the traditional attributes for Justice (the blindfold and sword) and Liberty (the Phrygian cap). This would have been a novel and interesting use of allegory, but so unusual that it is less likely than a simple mistake on the part of the anonymous journalist. One of the scriptures quoted on the front of the pedestal draws upon Solomon's wisdom: "The memory of the just is blessed" (Proverbs 10:7). Justice seems an appropriate tribute to the man who was alleged to have maintained the highest ethical standards in his business practices and who displayed such concern for the educational and spiritual opportunities of the "downtrodden race."[37]

Louis Verhaegen's representation of Justice does not fully conform to convention, apparently because of political sensitivities. During the middle of the nineteenth century, the most recognizable allegory of Justice was a blindfolded female holding forth a set of balancing scales, as found in Luigi Persico's 1826 central portico pediment for the east facade of the U.S. Capitol and in the figures which decorated many nineteenth-century courthouses. But the scales connoted jurisprudence, a theme less relevant to Avery's life. Indeed, an allusion to jurisprudence might have been particularly awkward in the late 1850s because of unpopular laws, such as the Fugitive Slave Act, or

Fig. 5.5 Louis Verhaegen, Avery Monument, detail of Justice. Photo: George Bekich.

Fig. 5.6 Louis Verhaegen, Avery Monument. Photograph by Seth V. Albee from *Allegheny Cemetery: Historical Account of Incidents and Events Connected with Its Establishment . . .* (Pittsburgh: Bakewell & Marthens, 1873), facing p. 73. Photo courtesy of the Historical Society of Western Pennsylvania.

legal interpretations, such as the Supreme Court's decision in the *Dred Scott* case—both shocking disappointments for Republicans. Avery himself spoke against the fugitive slave law at a large public rally in fall 1850, calling it unconstitutional and declaring that its enforcement would "trample under foot all Divine Authority."[38] Martin Delany, the African-American leader and one-time Pittsburgher, shared the speaker's platform with Avery that evening and his impassioned oratory demonstrates how the most traditional icons of American justice and government had been devalued for many:

A man has the right to defend his castle with his life, even unto the taking of life. Sir, my house is my castle; in that castle are none but my wife and my children, as free as the angels of heaven, and whose liberty is as sacred as the pillars of God. If any man approaches that house in search of a slave,—I care not who he may be, whether constable or sheriff, magistrate or even judge of the Supreme Court—nay, let it be he who sanctioned this act to become a law, surrounded by his cabinet as his bodyguard, with the Declaration of Independence waving above his head as his banner, and the constitution of his country upon his breast as his shield,—if he crosses the threshold of my door, and I do not lay him a lifeless corpse at my feet, I hope the grave may refuse my body a resting place, and righteous Heaven my spirit a home.[39]

The problem of personifying justice in these years was magnified in parodies, which often included some misuse of the traditional scales. Around 1860 the Pittsburgh genre painter David Gilmour Blythe painted a series of satires on the courts. The scales of Justice in his 1859 *Lawyer's Dream* hoist aloft a bleeding heart, outweighed in the balance by "a purse and a bottle of something supposed to be strong."[40] In George Cruikshank's illustration of "Emmeline About to Be Sold to the Highest Bidder" for *Uncle Tom's Cabin*, blindfolded Justice holds her balancing mechanism over the slave auction, apparently unaware that the two dishes have vanished, rendering it inoperable (see Fig. 5.7).[41] In the Avery Monument, the scales may be represented by the odd oval shape in the maiden's left hand. This eroded form was probably the dishes folded upon one another like a closed clam shell—jurisprudence still operable, but deferred. This mode of allegory was expressive but not as inflammatory as the parodies nor as adamant as Delany's speech.

Although Avery and many others questioned the efficacy of the nation's legal system, he held deep respect for properly constituted authority, especially at the local level. The key principle of his Methodist Protestant Church was

Fig. 5.7 George Cruikshank, "Emmeline About to Be Sold to the Highest Bidder," illustration from Harriet Beecher Stowe, *Uncle Tom's Cabin* (London: J. Cassell, 1852). Photo courtesy of Carnegie Mellon University Libraries.

the right of each congregation to self-governance. Early nineteenth-century defenders of the Methodist Protestant schism argued their religious case with quotations from the Constitution of the United States on the guarantees of states' rights. Of course, state sovereignty also guided legal arguments in the South's defense of slavery.[42] The tension between Avery's antislavery convictions and his respect for local sovereignty was not an unusual difficulty, though his ideas for its resolution may not have been widely held. In a letter of 1854, he sought a solution for the nation comparable to the rupture of the Methodist churches: "Slavery is likely to triumph again in our National Councils. I am discouraged but will not despair while Jehovah reigns. *We must separate from the South.* Would to God this feeling was more general in the free states."[43] Rather than dictating policy to the Southern states or bending to their domination, Avery wished to assign questions about slavery to local polity, assuring democratic principles for each side, even at the expense of abolishing slavery itself.

In spite of his radically separatist views, supporting the new Republican Party was a logical choice for Avery. He had never supported the abolitionist Liberty Party, which exhibited no qualms about dictating policy to Southerners and which placed moral concerns above legal ones by condoning civil disobedience. These ideas were at odds with Avery's high regard for orderly self-governance. Clearly, the Democratic Party's support for slavery and its expansion in the West would have been unacceptable to Avery. On these moral issues, the Republican approach probably represented an acceptable compromise to Avery, as it did for so many others. In regards to slavery, the coalition needed for the formation of the Republican Party included those opposed to its existence, those against only Southern domination of the federal courts and Congress, and others with positions in between.[44] This indeterminacy in the appeal of the Republicans may underlie the less-than-typical allegory of Justice on the Avery Monument. It was certainly at play in the choice of motifs for the relief panel and their reception.

The Campaign and Slavery: "The Wrongs of Their Oppressed Race"

The most unusual and interesting portion of the sculptural program is the central relief panel at eye level on the front of the monument (see Fig. 5.8). Before deciphering the components of this odd tableau, the very act of including images of slaves and free blacks requires consideration. By directly addressing the most controversial national issue of its day, the relief sculpture conformed to the Pittsburgh Republican Party's attempt to avoid local issues. The carvings of slaves must have seemed particularly audacious because of the lack of precedent in such a permanent, public setting and because of the heightened tensions resulting from such contemporary events as the *Dred Scott* decision, John Brown's raid at Harpers Ferry, and the many predictions of impending war. The conventions of public sculpture would certainly have permitted some indirect, allegorical method of representing Avery's concern for the downtrodden race, but instead a fairly realistic mode was chosen. One could imagine sculpted tributes to Charles Avery that bypassed issues of race altogether. For example, the memorial to DeWitt Clinton emphasized that politician's economic contributions in two relief sculptures celebrating his role in building the Erie Canal and the resulting prosperity for New York.[45] (One of these is seen in Fig. 5.2.) Clinton's monument omits references to his work to abolish slavery in New York. More so than Clinton, Avery's wealth backed many of his city's important public works, such as the gasworks that provided light for Allegheny, the major bridge linking it with Pittsburgh, the lock and dam system on the Monongahela, the newer railroad lines, and others. His factories figured prominently in the industrial economy. But these types of investments were precisely what western Pennsylvania's Democratic Party had exploited for scandal in recent elections. In 1848 Avery joined other local cotton mill owners in locking out workers (mostly women and many quite young) in protest of a new law mandating a ten-hour workday. The lockout led to the city's first recorded labor riot,[46] which was one of several events that helped the local Democrats to position themselves as the party of the workers, an identity that the party cultivated throughout the 1850s. During that decade, railroad investments became the more explosive issue. The combination of new lines being built in and out of Pittsburgh actually had the potential of reducing rather than increasing trade in the city. Investments in these new companies enjoyed protection at the taxpayer's expense. In the elections of 1857 and 1859 Democrats fanned public ire toward the scheme of railroad bonds, to the point where anyone with railroad investments (and that was most Republican candidates) carried heavy political baggage.

For Pittsburgh Democrats, local issues could win elections. On the other hand, local Republican strategists knew that the Democrats were vulnerable on national issues and, in the minds of the public, were tied closely with the unpopular "slave power" of the South. Historian Michael Holt has demonstrated that Pittsburgh Republicans understood this dynamic and purposely

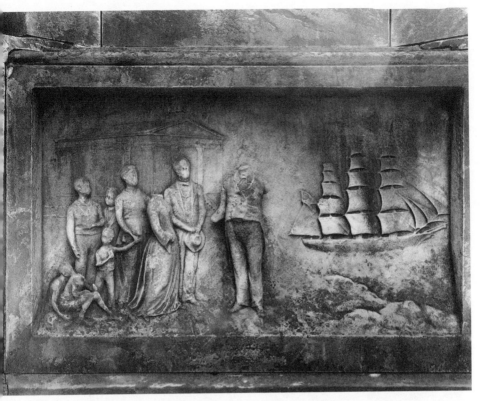

Fig. 5.8 Louis Verhaegen, Avery Monument, detail of relief panel. Photo: George Bekich.

focused public attention on national matters. This crucial strategy helped to make Pittsburgh an early stronghold for the newly ascendant party.[47] This party predilection may help to account for the frank inclusion of slaves and free blacks on Avery's tomb—and perhaps the introduction of this imagery to American public sculpture.

Even though slaves are depicted, the relief panel is free from the imagery of radical abolitionism. It contains none of the symbols that had become well established in political tracts, books, and sometimes paintings, such as the kneeling figure with the motto "Am I Not a Man and a Brother?" (see Fig. 5.9), or the broken and discarded shackle, the slave auction, methods of slave punishment, or the chasing of an escaped slave. The absence of this type of direct reference to full and rapid emancipation was congruent with

Fig. 5.9 "Am I Not a Man and a Brother?" detail of undated broadside, ca. 1835. Photo courtesy of the Moorland-Springarn Research Center, Howard University.

the Republican strategy of maintaining a respectful distance from the abolition movement.[48]

The Campaign and Emigration: "Waiting to Convey"

Although the stonework has suffered severe damage, records and remnants
reveal that the relief carvings depicted specific details of Avery's support for
the education of African Americans and missionary work in Africa. The panel
is more than two feet tall and some of the foreground figures are carved in an
extremely high relief. The foremost figures lack heads and hands. Severe
erosion has emaciated the remaining limbs and heads and erased facial features so that recognizing the gestures and actions in this scene is difficult. The
"Pittsburgh Correspondent" facilitates this effort with a description of the relief
panel in the lead editorial of an 1869 issue of the *Christian Recorder*, an organ
of the African Methodist Episcopal Church:

Mr. Avery is represented in the act of giving with his right hand, a Bible, to
one of Africa's dusky maidens—while with his left he points to a ship in the
distance, with sails unfurled, waiting to convey her to her native shore. —
Immediately behind her are a group of colored ladies and gentlemen that
appear to bear her company. These are gazing earnestly at their noble benefactor and espouser of the wrongs of their oppressed race. Near by are two little
slave boys seated in a recumbent position,—the foremost the very picture of
despair, with his head bowed, and looking down on the heavy shackles fastened
upon his limbs, while a third figure on the right represents a little fellow newly
liberated and his young life first coming into perfect consciousness of puberty,
is putting forth its first efforts to acquire knowledge. With book in hand, he is
advancing in the direction of "Avery College," which with its spacious environs
is plainly seen in the background.[49]

From the faded albumen photograph of the sculpture taken in 1873 (see Fig.
5.6) and from a close examination of the worn carvings, most of the statements in this description can be verified.[50] Some license must be allowed for
the elaboration of the description of the "little fellow" who clutches a book to
his bosom. He does not, in fact, seem to advance toward the college. But concluding the description with such a narrative sufficed as a transition for the

Fig. 5.10 Avery Institute, built 1849, Allegheny (now Pittsburgh). Undated photograph. Courtesy of the Pittsburgh History and Landmarks Foundation.

writer, whose editorial solicited funds for Wilberforce College.[51] A photograph taken before the demolition of the Avery Institute confirms that it is the building in shallow relief on the panel (see Fig. 5.10).[52] The three-masted ship was a type used for transatlantic passenger voyages at mid-century. The placement of Avery in the center of the relief panel divides it into two equal areas comparable to the two major stipulations of his will. The ship to Avery's left in the panel alludes to his interest in the African missions. The school to his right stands as an example of "the education and elevation of the Colored people of the United States." With this divided background composition, Louis Verhaegen fulfilled the instructions that he received for the commission. These survive only in a portion quoted in a letter from one of the executors to Lewis Tappan, the treasurer of the American Missionary Association: "The directions given to the artist in relation to the Bas Relief were, to 'give expression to the two prominent ideas of Mr. Avery's will.'"[53]

The group of carvings in the foreground divides less clearly between these two themes. These figures enliven the panel with their gestures and poses. They enact two different narratives: the Bible presentation toward the center relating a specific highlight among Avery's good deeds, and another more allegorical sequence of elevation from the degradation of slavery, indicated by a procession of bodies from left to right. This ambiguous composition permitted viewers to construct three potential identities for African Americans. One of these featured blacks as the ideal missionaries to Christianize the fever-ridden jungles of West Africa. Another interpretation centered upon self-improvement through education. A third reading of the relief sculpture, which was scattered widely through the popular press, suggested that the future for African Americans lay in mass colonization—sending them "back to Africa."

The Missions: "White Men Are Not the Men"

The reading emphasizing black evangelism in Africa concentrates upon the Bible presentation by Avery. As an image of a white man offering his Bible and gesturing broadly before a group of attentive people of color, the sculpture repeats elements from the engraving used on the masthead of the *American Missionary*, the monthly magazine of the American Missionary Association (see Fig. 5.11). This promotional publication would have been available to Verhaegen and was doubtlessly sent to each of the estate's executors. Avery

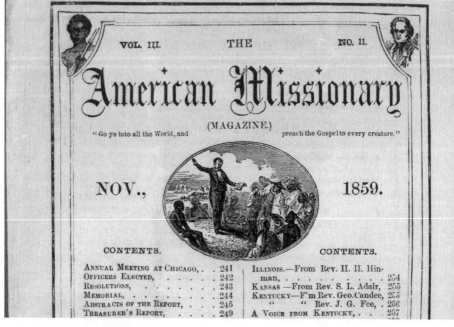

Fig. 5.11 Masthead of the *American Missionary*, November 1859. Note the portrait of Cinque in the upper left corner above the title. Photo courtesy of the Pittsburgh Theological Seminary.

had been an enthusiastic supporter of the American Missionary Association's work in Sierra Leone since the *Amistad* incident of 1839, when captive Mendian Africans seized control of the slave ship *Amistad* that was smuggling them into the United States. The resulting Supreme Court case became a well-known rallying point for antislavery supporters in the country, but it also helped link the Mende missions in Sierra Leone with the American abolition movement. The Amistad Committee, which raised funds for legal costs and return passage to Africa, evolved into the American Missionary Association and some of the *Amistad* victims chose to help in the missions started by the association in Sierra Leone. Even in the late 1850s, the American Missionary Association was still publicizing the activities of the *Amistad* celebrities to interested donors. (Notice in Fig. 5.11, on the masthead of the *American Missionary*, that the African in the upper left corner is based upon a portrait of Cinque, the leader of the mutiny.)[54] One of the four Biblical passages above the relief panel was taken from the letters of the great missionary Paul. It may refer to Avery's enthusiasm for the African missions: "He hath dispersed abroad. He hath given to the poor. His righteousness remaineth forever" (2 Corinthians 9:9).

After the portly Avery, the second most prominent figure in the panel is a woman to whom he presents a Bible. This "dusky maiden" stands in the foreground and shares the highest level of sculptural relief with the celebrated white man. She probably represents an African-born woman named Margru, one of the thirty-five captives returned to Africa after the *Amistad* trial. One of three who stayed at the Mende mission where they landed, Margru became a Christian missionary. Within a few years, she returned to the United States to study at Oberlin College in Ohio. After studying from 1846 through 1849, she took residence in Mende to teach and proselytize. In 1855 Margru married an African, Edward Henry Green, who joined in her work. (Green might be the figure standing between Avery and Margru.) Some sources report that the American Missionary Association financed her education at Oberlin and others credit Charles Avery. Records show payments from the association, but Avery may have helped because many donors to the association earmarked their gifts for specific purposes.[55]

Avery certainly maintained an interest in Margru's work and supported it in some manner. His library contained a copy of *Thompson in Africa*, an 1851 journal of George Thompson's tenure as leader of the Mende mission that reported on Margru's teaching and demeanor.[56] A letter dated January 28, 1854, from Margru to Avery, addressed to "her friend and benefactor," was published in the *Pittsburgh Gazette* and also appeared in the *American Missionary*.[57] A subsequent letter from Avery to Lewis Tappan, the treasurer of the association and Margru's "godfather," asked that a portion of an enclosed donation be used for clothing for Margru.[58] The *Gazette* deemed Avery's relationship with Margru newsworthy: "as an evidence of the wonderful strides which may be made in one generation in the elevation of a debased and heathen people by Christianity and education. Such as Sarah Margru Green is now, Christianity and education can make millions of Africans, whether they doze away their lives in Africa or groan under the driver's lash in America."[59] Standing in the foreground of the relief panel, Margru's presence exemplified success in the goals of education and Christianization and illustrated a notable achievement in Avery's life.

Charles Avery was clearly devoted to sending black missionaries to West Africa. Margru's work interested him partly because so many white missionaries died within a year of reaching Africa, which had become known as "the white man's grave." In one letter Avery warned the executive committee of the American Missionary Association: "The death of Mr. Garnick is another indication of Providence, that *White* Men are not *the* men by whom the Colored People of Africa are to be converted to God. *Colored* Men of the *right* kind must be sent. It is presumptuous to suppose that God will work Miracles, and change the Country & climate, to suit the constitution of the Whites. . . . We ought not to sacrifice valuable lives, and spend our strength for naught."[60] Avery accepted the popular myth that race protected African Americans from the diseases common in the missions. Leaders of the American Missionary Association apparently shared this belief and had attempted to recruit African-American clergy to lead the missions in Sierra Leone since the time of the *Amistad* trial. Those in charge of other missionary boards had made similar efforts, including an earlier, less successful attempt by Avery through his own Methodist denomination.[61] Reading the sculpted narrative as a celebration of black missionaries and Avery's support for them would have come easily to those most involved in the West African missions. Ancel Bassett, writing his 1877 history of the Methodist Protestant Church, described the relief sculpture solely in terms of Avery's assistance to Margru as an advancement in the effort to Christianize Africa.[62]

Education: "Many Shall Be Raised"

The only known contemporary African-American interpretation of the sculpture emphasized education and self-improvement as the future for the black community. In the panel, the Bible presentation, the small boy's book, and the school in the background touch upon the issue of education for African Americans. In many Southern states, and only a few hours away in Virginia, teaching slaves to read was outlawed.[63] Education was even questioned for free blacks in the Northern states: their inclusion in the Pittsburgh and Allegheny public school systems came slowly and only after protest and threats of legal actions. In 1837 Avery joined John Peck, George Vashon, and other local blacks in requesting complete school integration as a simple and cost-effective measure. But the city chose separate and drastically unequal school facilities, which became the subject of periodic uneasiness during the 1840s and 1850s.[64]

Higher education for African Americans raised even more perplexing questions. Because few colleges accepted black people, and only a small fraction of white people in the region had this level of formal education, Avery's estab-lishment of an all-black college in Pittsburgh must have surprised many. Even among the African-American leadership, no consensus existed on what type of advanced education was appropriate. The recommendations of the National Negro Conferences in these decades shifted between practical training for business and the more classical liberal arts curriculum. The Avery Institute began by featuring the classical approach. The venture might have been char-acterized as quixotic with Avery, who had little formal schooling, as its presi-dent. Few students were ready for its proposed course work, so it had to perform chiefly as a preparatory and trade school until well after Avery's death. By 1871, not a single degree had been conferred.[65] Although governed by a racially mixed board, the school's impact on the African-American community may have been primarily symbolic. Avery's last will and testament suggested that even he eventually lost faith in this effort: his bequest to the institute was relatively small.[66]

The Avery Institute did produce at least a handful of notable students. One of them was the journalist who interpreted education as the key theme in the relief sculpture. Benjamin Tanner, the father of painter Henry Ossawa Tanner, had attended preparatory classes at Avery before obtaining his degree at the Western Theological Seminary and becoming a bishop in the African Methodist Episcopal Church. As a former Pittsburgher and the editor of the *Christian Recorder*, he may have been the "Pittsburgh Correspondent" who provided the detailed description of the relief panel in 1869.[67]

Fully half of that text focuses on the boys at the lower left of the composi-tion and especially embellished the "first efforts to acquire knowledge" of the youngster with the book. Although a bit strained toward the solicitation for Wilberforce College, this African-American reading of the relief sculpture places as much emphasis as possible on elevation through education—a topic of increased importance during the Reconstruction years. In this telling of the sculpture's story, the explanation begins at the center, only briefly men-tions the ship at the right side of the panel, and concludes at the left. In this description the purpose of education at such a school as the Avery Institute is unspecified and unconnected to the missionary activity shown at the center and right side of the scene. In fact, there seems to have been no actual link between the Avery Institute and training for the missions. The top floor of the school housed an African Methodist Episcopal Church congregation, but neither the preparatory school nor the college offered any courses in religion or theology. Among the few known students of the Avery Institute, none was a missionary or an emigrant during the 1850s or 1860s.[68] Nonetheless, Margru's letter in the *Gazette* seemed to wish for such students: "I should like to hear how your Institution is going on. I hope many shall be raised from it who will love to go to Africa."[69]

Colonization: "He Hath Dispersed Abroad"

Formal analysis of the composition of the relief sculpture supports a third, procolonization interpretation. The *Christian Recorder* account of the actions in the sculpture concluded with the boy at the left side of the panel, but to achieve this sequence, Tanner resisted the visual cues in Verhaegen's carved procession. These suggest continuous movement from left to right. They communicate a process of elevation and emigration. In the lower left corner, the two slave boys are dressed only in a nondescript cloth about their waists. Such a garment corresponded to that worn in the "Am I Not a Man and a Brother?" emblem more than the clothing actually used by slaves as seen in antebellum photographs (see Fig. 5.9). But these two sculpted figures evoked neither the same direct pathos as the famous emblem nor its direct statement of racial equality. Instead the unrealistic waist cloth signals an allegorical mode of depiction. Seating the two boys on the ground associates slavery with nature and uncivilized forces, as in Shinn's "unruly field" metaphor.[70] The foremost of these seated slaves has his left elbow on his left knee with the arm jutting upward to where it must have once supported the chin. Traces of the shackle on his right ankle are barely visible. The description of this figure as "the very picture of despair" places it within a general type of what might be called "despairing thinkers," some notable precedents being the dejected sufferer whose eyes nearly meet ours in Théodore Géricault's *Raft of the Medusa* (1819), William Rimmer's *Seated Man (Despair)* (1832), or the despondent Native American in Thomas Crawford's *Progress of Civilization* for the Senate pediment of the U.S. Capitol (1855; see Fig. 5.12).[71] In the relief panel, the despairing figures present slavery as a sorry condition. The figures closest to Avery are the best dressed and most mature, illustrating growth and improvement. In this way, the elevation of the race is illustrated as a sequence of increasingly vertical, well-dressed, and individualized figures.

Even by strictly compositional means, Verhaegen has suggested movement from the lower left to the right. A shallow diagonal crosses the top row

Fig. 5.12 Thomas Crawford, *The Dying Chief,* 1856 (originally sculpted as part of the *Progess of Civilization* figural group for the Senate pediment of the U.S. Capitol). Photo courtesy of the New-York Historical Society.

of heads. A steeper diagonal once extended from the seated pair up through the arms of the "little fellow" and through both of Avery's arms toward the ship. (Some of these missing arms may be seen in Fig. 5.6.) This pattern of movement from left to right is amplified by crowding the left of the composition and a gradual increase of open spaces to the right. One general description of this movement may be from a group of pitiful slaves, to a group of educated youngsters, to a group of respectable adults—from despair to dignity—or from slavery to freedom . . . and then to Africa.

The form of black emigration most widely publicized was colonization, the organized effort to settle freed slaves in colonies on foreign soil. A pro-colonization reading of the relief sculpture soon appeared in the press and seemed to harmonize with one faction of the Republican Party. Eric Foner and others have shown that Republicans attracted more votes by focusing on limiting the territorial expansion of slavery rather than promising abolition. For an enormous number of voters, a crucial part of America's promise of upward mobility lay dormant in the undeveloped western territories. To many workers, the best insurance against the costs of a growing family or the poverty inflicted by a closed factory was to become a homesteader—to take Horace Greeley's remedy and "go west." Many saw the legal battle to prevent the expansion of slavery as a matter of competition for resources rather than a moral issue. Growth of the slave-labor plantation system threatened smaller or would-be landowners, but complete emancipation also worried many Northern operatives because of the potential effect of transforming the large slave population of the South into a mobile force of low-wage laborers.[72] Beyond this economic problem, less rational concerns—such as the fear of racial amalgamation—also clouded the issue of abolition. Even some staunchly antislavery groups feared the potential demographic effects of complete manumission. For example, in 1854 William Shinn spoke in Pittsburgh's courthouse at a rally opposing the Kansas-Nebraska Act. The Free Soilers and Whigs who dominated that assembly saw no inconsistency in passing one resolution that objected to "the curse of slavery" and another "opposed the Africanization of the American Continent."[73] For a successful political party to oppose slavery, some palatable vision of the future of the freed slave was needed. Colonization could fill that need.

Throughout its long history, colonization had the curious ability to appeal to people with divergent views on slavery. Martin Delany, for example, was intensely interested in colonization in the years preceding the Civil War. At the time Avery's tomb was being completed, Delany toured Africa scouting for prospective sites for a new colony. Most African Americans, however, opposed colonization, whereas many slaveholders supported it. Such abolitionist organizations as the American Missionary Association accused groups like the American Colonization Society of perpetuating slavery by providing a useful personnel management tool to slaveholders—a disposal system for old, rebellious, or otherwise unprofitable slaves.[74]

Interest in this systematic emigration or deportation of African Americans declined in the 1840s but was rekindled during the tumult of the 1850s, partly by the Republicans. During the 1858 congressional campaigns Republicans published an edition of *The Impending Crisis of the South* by the Southern white supremacist Hinton Rowan Helper, who opposed slavery on economic grounds and who proposed shipping all slaves to colonies in Liberia, Latin America, or restricted "settlements" in the United States. Abraham Lincoln listened closely to those Republicans who attempted to install a colonization plank in the party's 1860 platform. But as an election strategy, party interest in colonization had peaked during the winter, before the platforms were written in the spring.[75] At the local level, the *Pittsburgh Gazette*, during the same winter months that it was printing endorsements of Thomas Howe for governor, published news of colonization efforts, letters from Liberia with word of prosperity there, glowing accounts of Martin Delany's African expedition, and procolonization editorials. One example called for the Pennsylvania legislature to appropriate five to ten thousand dollars to the colonization cause.[76] For local Republicans one popular view of the future of the freed slave included mass emigration.

Some saw colonization sculpted in the relief panel. During the first week of December 1859, while the Avery Memorial was nearing completion but still housed in Verhaegen's studio in lower Manhattan, a brief article appeared in *Scientific American* with news about the sculptural commission. It described the scene in the panel as "Mr. Avery surrounded by negroes and pointing to a ship at anchor in the distance, as if in the act of designating the conveyance that will transport them to their native land." The article included this striking epitaph for Charles Avery: "He was a gentleman of great wealth, and noted for his benevolence, both of which were directed mainly to the relief of negroes, principally in sending them to Africa; Mr. Avery being an active colonizationist."[77] Either the artist or the reporter must have been mistaken or misinformed—Avery did not support colonization.[78] This news item reappeared in most of the Pittsburgh newspapers with startling rapidity.[79] Avery was labeled a colonizationist in each of these articles. The American Missionary Association leader Lewis Tappan found the error repeated in the *Boston Congregationalist* and quickly sent the clipping to William Shinn. Given the competition between the association and the American Colonization Society, the mistake must have alarmed Tappan. Shinn invited Tappan to interpret the images for himself by visiting Verhaegen's studio as the sculptor continued his work on the relief panel—apparently the last piece of carving for the monument. The invitation included this assurance: "The misconstruction of the Bas relief and the wrong inference drawn from it were promptly corrected by one of our local newspapers."[80]

The correction appeared in the December 6 *Pittsburgh Daily Dispatch,* which may have been the only paper in town that had not published the erroneous news. The *Dispatch* generally supported Republican efforts, but insisted that it was not a party mouthpiece and regularly conducted editorial combat with the *Gazette.* The letter read, in part: "The editor says of the deceased Mr. Avery: 'He was an active colonizationist.' He was no such thing. The late Rev. Charles Avery was an active, earnest, intelligent and intrepid *Abolitionist,* who utterly repudiated the colonization scheme, as fraudulent humbug."[81] The letter then assured readers that Avery would turn in his grave should he learn of this mistake. It was not sent by one of the executors but was signed simply "Blanchard." Strangely, the executors had remained silent about this barrage of inaccurate reporting. This was particularly odd for Shinn, who wrote letters to editors with some frequency.

The identity of Blanchard is uncertain but the most likely prospects were Republican politicos. If the shortened name was supposed to be recognizable, it might have belonged to the noted abolitionist orator Jonathan Blanchard, who spoke in Pittsburgh against colonization at a well-attended, two-day debate, refereed by Charles Avery in 1837. At the end of 1859, Jonathan Blanchard was flirting with a run for the House of Representatives as an Illinois Republican and would have been very interested in Avery's estate, as the newly appointed president of Wheaton College.[82] Another possible "Blanchard" was Edmund Blanchard, a central Pennsylvania businessman, "well known throughout the state," who practiced law in partnership with Andrew G. Curtin, Howe's opponent for the Republican nomination and the winner of the 1860 gubernatorial race.[83] Whether by accident or intrigue, interpretation of the relief sculpture became embroiled in campaign posturing before it was even completed.

"The Right of Private Judgment"

The three potential roles for African Americans projected upon the enigmatic sculpture can be associated with important constituents at the periphery of the Republican Party's widening influence. Giving education and self-improvement the highest priority was not unusual among the African-American leadership and was also important to many radical white abolitionists. Most Christians, if they recognized Margru, could approve of her exemplary missionary endeavors regardless of their opinions about slavery. The reading of the relief sculpture that posited a future for African Americans in colonization could appeal to segregationists, who could be found on both sides of the polarizing slavery question. Although least accurate as a commemoration of Charles Avery, this was the interpretation that found the widest circulation in the newspapers and magazines. Nothing in the carved stone denied it. The sculpted riddle offered only the sort of "elements which depend for their effect upon the reader's interpretation," called "indeterminacies" by Terry Eagleton.

Other responses to Avery's tomb must have existed, but few have been found. Its unveiling may have been crowded out of the newspapers by the series of crises and preparations that led to civil war. One reaction to the sculpture was probably vandalism. Not all of the damage to the Avery Monument seems due to erosion. Physical examination and documentary evidence indicate that the tomb was damaged during the 1870s, in apparently one or more acts of racist violence.[84] In 1867 or early 1868, the popular journalist of the *Atlantic Monthly*, James Parton, complimented the craft exhibited in the Avery tomb but misunderstood or avoided the topical relief panel. He described it only as the "gentleman figured with ships and other indications of commercial activity" and criticized the expensive stone assemblage as a waste of the estate's funds and an inappropriate commemoration of a man so concerned for using his money to help others. Oddly, Parton blamed this waste on "the colored men who permitted this diversion."[85] (In fact, a group of Pittsburgh's black leaders had attempted to poll influential African Americans to identify more important uses for the bequest.)[86] The photographer of the 1873 albumen print (see Fig. 5.6) must have had to climb a ladder to get a complete view of the monument because of a dense ring of evergreen trees surrounding it—planted either to protect the eroding marble or to hide a feature of the cemetery that had fallen out of fashion. After the hard realities of war and the setbacks for blacks during Reconstruction, the effort "to give permanence and prominence" to Avery's ideals may have seemed less than successful. Or perhaps the political scene had changed so much that the poetry of the sculpted images had become meaningless.

To some extent, all memorials attempt to write history. But in the nineteenth century, monuments including blacks were also forced into the position of predicting the future. A series of attempts to commemorate emancipation in public sculpture followed the Civil War. Some of these were completed, such as Thomas Ball's Emancipation Monument (1876), but many more languished as unrealized plans. In his study of these efforts, Kirk Savage observes that the sculptors faced the impossible task of giving permanence to the role of the African American even though society had never resolved that role: "Sculptors struggling to represent emancipation in public monuments were out on the cultural forefront, working to visualize what was still unfolding, still unwritten. They were coming to grips with a new social paradigm that seemed clearly defined in principle but was yet to be absorbed into the hearts and minds of the citizenry. Their task was profoundly paradoxical, at once conservative and progressive. They were charged with conserving the memory of something that had not yet taken form, that might never take form."[87] The Avery Memorial was a prototype for memorials to emancipation in that it struggled with this same central paradox. To avoid offending public sensibilities, Verhaegen and his patrons had to move cautiously between controversial topics. The path they chose, "at once conservative and progressive," resembled the steps taken in the venture to form a new political party. The differences in the recorded responses to the Avery Monument demonstrate the variety of viewpoints in its audience, but they also show that this paradox of commemorating the future placed even more of the burden of interpretation on the viewer than it did on the artist. Meaning was more a matter of interpretation than convention. Individual judgment was required to develop an understanding of the artwork, the political speech, or the best path to the future. Perhaps Charles Avery himself would have been comfortable with the necessity of delegating this responsibility to the individual. His colleague William Shinn touched on the significance of private conscience for Avery: "The testator has committed large discretion . . . in the management of his estate and I trust we shall always exercise a portion of that liberality shining out through his whole life which claims for all men the right of private judgment and allows all men freedom of thought and conscience without impeachment of motives."[88] In the interest of "the right of private judgment" perhaps a monument to Charles Avery that supported only one interpretation would have been entirely inappropriate.

THE CIVIL WAR LETTERS OF
QUARTERMASTER SERGEANT JOHN C. BROCK,
43RD REGIMENT, UNITED STATES COLORED TROOPS

Edited by Eric Ledell Smith

The letters of African-American soldiers represent an underused genre of Civil War historiography. Rich in social history, they provide a counterbalance to Civil War history written more typically from the white officer's perspective.[1] Their relative omission has special implications for Pennsylvania history. Camp William Penn, outside Philadelphia, was one of the nation's major training camps for black soldiers during the Civil War. Many of the soldiers from Camp William Penn wrote letters to editors of such newspapers as the *Christian Recorder*, the *Weekly Anglo-African*, *Pine and Palm*, and the *Liberator*. It is regrettable that the black soldier is missing from major history textbooks of the state, such as Philip Klein and Ari Hoogenboom's synthesis that continues to serve as a principal work on the Commonwealth.[2]

In the late twentieth century, however, the twin emergence of social history and multicultural awareness has caused a growing number of historians to include the black perspective in Civil War narratives. One of the first to draw upon these resources was Herbert Aptheker, who reprinted three black soldiers' letters in his *Documentary of the Negro People in the United States*. More than a decade later, James M. McPherson's collection on African-American writings about the conflict cited eight letters from black soldiers. In the 1980s, the Freedmen and Southern Society Project at the University of Maryland began to publish documentary materials that focused, among other things, on the black military experience. Edited by Ira Berlin and others, the project reprinted letters found in the National Archives rather than in newspapers and reissued a more condensed version in 1998 notable for its fine illustrations. More recently has come a small flurry of publishing of additional resources, such as the letters of Corporal James Gooding of the 54th Massachusetts Volunteer Infantry, Edwin S. Redkey's compilation of the black military experience, and Noah Andre Trudeau's book that cited newspaper letters of black soldiers. During the last half-century, therefore, letters of United States Colored Troops (USCT) soldiers finally have found their way into Civil War scholarship.[3]

The letters of John C. Brock provide an additional window into the experiences of black soldiers and show the value of paying attention to the letters that veterans wrote to newspapers. Brock served in the 43rd Regiment of the USCT, rising to commissary sergeant and quartermaster sergeant of the regiment. Because few personal papers of Brock's are extant, what is known about his life comes primarily from his military records, pension records, and wartime correspondence. Fortunately, nine of the Civil War letters of John C. Brock survive, and they are reprinted here from the *Christian Recorder*. Brock's letters take us back in time to describe what it was like to be a black Civil War soldier from Pennsylvania. As part of the Ninth Corps of the Army of the Potomac, the unit in which he served saw important service in the Petersburg theater during the latter stages of the war. He reveals the impression that black soldiers had about the South and Southerners and reaffirms that African Americans were keenly aware of their own agency in ending slavery and changing the meaning of freedom in this country.

Pennsylvania's African-American participation in the Civil War had two distinct phases: (1) 1861 to 1863 when blacks in the North had to agitate for the right to serve because policy makers denied their use in the war; and (2) 1863 to 1865, which featured recruitment and training efforts at Camp William Penn. During the first phase, President Abraham Lincoln refused to permit African Americans to enlist in the Union army, despite pressure from Frederick Douglass and a number of other abolitionists, both black and white. Northern racism and the need to retain the four Border States that still had slavery affected how fast the administration moved on emancipation. By summer 1862 momentum built to take the war in a more radical direction, one that included freedom for slaves. Southerners appeared less than willing to return to the Union, and the war effort that had started promisingly turned sour as the campaign to capture Richmond from the Virginia peninsula failed. In July Congress authorized the recruitment of black soldiers, and Lincoln himself came to the decision to emancipate slaves. Yet advisers counseled him to wait because, with the reversal in military fortunes, the action would seem to be an act of desperation. Thus, in a letter to Horace Greeley written in August 1862, Lincoln still maintained: "If there be those who would not save the Union unless at the same time they would save slavery, I do not agree with them. If there be those who would not save the Union unless they could at the same time destroy slavery, I do not agree with them."[4] With the victory at Antietam on September 17, 1862, and the advent of the Emancipation Proclamation on January 1, 1863, the North turned to recruiting African Americans into the military.

African Americans, however, were employed early in the war as support personnel in noncombat functions, such as "fatigue duty" gangs or, on occasion, as cooks. Southerners more naturally turned to this resource in the beginning, which spurred some Union supporters not only to do the same but also to attempt to organize black regiments. However, these regiments—the 1st South Carolina Volunteers, the 1st Kansas Volunteers and the 1st Regiment Louisiana National Guards—were formed without approval from Lincoln or the War Department.

During this first phase, Pennsylvania's African Americans lobbied Harrisburg and Washington to recruit black troops in the state and sometimes formed units even without national authority. Black Philadelphia schoolteacher Alfred M. Green spoke for many in 1861 when he pointed out: "Many persons in the North—perhaps strong friends of the Union—are not prepared to endorse the idea of admitting colored regiments into its service. [But] it might be well for us to remember that every effort is being made in the South to make their black population efficient aids in defending their soil against our army."[5] In Pittsburgh the "Hannibal Guards" formed on April 18, 1861, and its captain, Samuel Sanders, declared: "We consider ourselves American citizens and interested in the Commonwealth of our white fellow citizens. Although deprived of all political rights, we yet wish the government of the United States to be sustained against the tyranny of slavery, and are willing to assist in any honorable way or manner to sustain the present administration."[6] The Hannibal Guards, however, were not mustered in to Federal service. Nevertheless, Allegheny County's Twelfth Pennsylvania Volunteers *were* mustered in on April 25, 1861. The regiment's Company "I," the Zouave Cadets, under Captain George W. Tanner, contained the only men of color. The cadets were assigned to guard the Northern Central Railroad from the Mason-Dixon line to Baltimore. In contrast, in Philadelphia in 1861, at least two companies of African Americans were called together but were not allowed to enlist.[7]

When Congress passed the Second Confiscation Act and the Militia Act on July 17, 1862, it prepared the way for Lincoln to receive African-American men as soldiers. Lincoln waited until he had issued the Emancipation Proclamation before permitting official black enlistment. Secretary of War Edwin M. Stanton authorized the governors of Rhode Island and Massachusetts to raise black regiments. These were the 14th Regiment Rhode Island Volunteer Heavy Artillery and the 54th Massachusetts Volunteer Infantry, familiar to many persons today as the regiment featured in the movie *Glory*. Abolitionist George L. Stearns, working with Massachusetts Governor John A. Andrew, commissioned such black leaders as Martin R. Delany, John Jones, and John M. Langston to help enlist black men for the 54th Massachusetts.[8]

Another recruiter, Frederick Douglass, urged Pennsylvania Governor Andrew Gregg Curtin in February 1863 to create black regiments in the Keystone State. Curtin declined. It is unclear how Douglass and Curtin communicated on this subject because there is no extant correspondence from Douglass in Curtin's papers and Douglass's allusion to this incident in a speech given in New York City suggests that he had spoken to Governor Curtin in person. It is possible that Curtin was awaiting direct orders from the Lincoln administration on this question. A Southerner by birth, Lincoln feared the racial discord that might result from African Americans and Northern whites fighting in the same regiments. The only solution, he thought, was to create all-black regiments staffed by white officers and managed by a distinct bureau in the War Department

The Bureau of Colored Troops was formally established on May 22, 1863. It would oversee the recruiting of Union colored troops, commissioning of white officers, forming of regiments, and coordinating their activity in the war. Pennsylvania's adjutant general declared that African-American volunteers would no longer join black regiments in other states but instead would enlist in Pennsylvania under the auspices of the War Department.[9]

In June 1863, a state of emergency was declared in Pennsylvania as General Robert E. Lee's army moved northward toward an eventual showdown with the Union army at Gettysburg. When Governor Curtin called for volunteers to defend the Keystone State, white and black persons alike responded. There was great excitement in black Philadelphia where an instructor for the Institute for Colored Youth, Octavius V. Catto, formed a company that included some of his colleagues and students. Under Captain A. M. Babe, Catto's company received uniforms and arms at the city arsenal and headed for Harrisburg. But Union Major General Darius N. Couch, commander of the

Department of the Susquehanna, turned them away, claiming that army enlistment required a three-year commitment and that Catto's company was only prepared to serve several months. This was strange since several white Pennsylvania regiments were signed up for three months' service. Catto's company returned to Philadelphia dejected. Stanton roundly criticized Couch for his action. "You are authorized," commanded Stanton, "to receive into the service any volunteer troops that may be offered, without regard to color."[10]

Many Philadelphia citizens, both blacks and whites, were indignant about the rejection of Catto's company. Major George L. Stearns, Pennsylvania's recruiting commissioner for the USCT, appealed to the Union League of Philadelphia for help. With the league's support, a group of seventy-five Philadelphians formed the Supervisory Committee for Recruiting Colored Regiments, headquartered at 1210 Chestnut Street in Philadelphia. It petitioned Stanton for permission to raise three black regiments. The War Department agreed, advising the committee's chairman Thomas Webster, "The troops raised under the foregoing instructions will rendezvous at Camp William Penn, Chelten Hills, near Philadelphia." Lieutenant Colonel Louis Wagner, from the 88th Pennsylvania Volunteer Infantry, was named camp commander.[11] The second phase of Pennsylvania African-American participation had begun.

Camp William Penn was located eight miles north of Philadelphia in what is now La Mott, Cheltenham Township, Montgomery County. Civil War financier and abolitionist Jay Cooke (1821–1905) owned the original land for the camp at the junction of Church Road (now Pennsylvania Route 73) and Washington Lane. Cooke's estate was near a major transportation route, the North Pennsylvania Railroad, and it was in a neighborhood sympathetic to abolitionism, one settled by Quakers. The first eighty recruits who entered Camp William Penn were housed in tents. Soon it was discovered that the Cooke land "was not parade ground level" and the camp was moved to the junction of Cheltenham and Penrose Avenues, in Cheltenham Township, close to "Roadside," the home of the famous abolitionist Lucretia Mott (1793–1880). By December 1863, army regulation wooden barracks were built for the colored troops and Mrs. Mott commented that "the barracks make a show from our back windows."[12]

But the work of the supervisory committee was not over. It was responsible for the transportation and subsistence of the recruits from the time they left their respective homes until they arrived at camp. Furthermore, since Pennsylvania had not provided bounties for the raising of African-American troops as had other states, the committee had to raise funds for the cause. It did so through newspaper advertisements throughout the Commonwealth as well as in Delaware, Maryland, and New Jersey. The committee helped to start the "Free Military School for Applicants to Command Colored Troops" to train white Union army officers for Camp William Penn. The school, under the direction of Major George A. Hearns and Colonel John H. Taggart, was located at the supervisory committee headquarters, 1210 Chestnut Street in center city Philadelphia.[13]

By the end of July 1863, Thomas Webster informed Stanton that "the first recruits were mustered in on the 27th of June and the 3rd Regiment USCT made full [on the] 24th [of] July; that two Companies of another regiment have also been mustered in."[14] Eventually, eleven regiments—the 3rd, 6th, 8th, 22nd, 24th, 32nd, 41st, 43rd, 45th, 127th, and one independent company— were trained at Camp William Penn. From these regiments, Lieutenant Nathan N. Edgarton, Captain Albert Wright, First Sergeant Alexander Kelly, and Sergeant Major Thomas R. Hawkins distinguished themselves in combat and won the Congressional Medal of Honor.[15]

Recruiting stations for conscripting African Americans were set up across Pennsylvania and from these "stations" the supervisory committee in Philadelphia brought in recruits to Camp William Penn. Before the Battle of Gettysburg, Harrisburg blacks were summoned to a meeting announced in the *Harrisburg Daily Telegraph*: "The black men of Harrisburg are to hold a meeting this evening at the Masonic Hall, Tanner's alley, for the purpose of organizing and offering their services to the Governor."[16] Fifty-four men came to the meeting, at which Union army Captain Henry Bradley spoke. Many of the men were refugees from the South and were anxious to enlist for three years' service in the USCT. Several days later two companies of black men, one headed by Captain Bradley and one led by Harrisburg native Thomas Morris Chester, were learning military drills. Bradley's company paraded on the state capitol grounds and the *Harrisburg Patriot and Union* commented that "the men looked strong and determined, and went through the drill quite as creditably as the generality of raw troops on their first parade."[17] Historian R. J. M. Blackett contends that "neither company was pressed into service, for in early July, the emergency [in Harrisburg] was lifted when [Confederate army leader Richard] Ewell's forces withdrew to prepare for the bloody and decisive encounter at Gettysburg." After Gettysburg, many African-American men in central Pennsylvania enlisted in the USCT. One of these men was John C. Brock of Carlisle, Cumberland County.[18]

Brock was born April 12, 1843, in Carlisle, Pennsylvania, to William and Elizabeth Donaldson Brock.[19] William Brock was a farmer. The Brocks appear first in the 1850 United States Census for Cumberland County; John is listed as being eight years old.[20] Devout Protestants, the Brocks worshiped at the local African Methodist Episcopal (AME) Church and enrolled their children in the AME Sabbath School in Carlisle. The 1860 census describes John as a "farm laborer," yet by 1863 he was also secretary of the AME Sabbath School.[21] In a school report published April 25, 1863, in the *Christian Recorder*, Brock wrote, "The Sabbath school at present consists of one superintendent, one librarian, one secretary, one treasurer, [and] eight teachers. Average attendance [is] fifty-five scholars."[22] So it was natural that when he enlisted in the United States Colored Troops Brock made friends with several black chaplains. Brock's letters contain references to these men as well as his thoughts about God, salvation, and morality. Brock's letters, therefore, have both a literary and a spiritual quality to them.

Brock was mustered into service on April 5, 1864, as a private in Company F of the 43rd Regiment, USCT, at Camp William Penn.[23] On April 12, 1864, Brock was promoted to commissary sergeant and was made quartermaster sergeant on January 5, 1865. Mustered out with the 43rd Regiment on October 20, 1865, Brock returned to Carlisle. There he fell in love with an African-American woman named Lucinda Jane Dickson, whom he married in Carlisle on Christmas Day 1867.[24]

By 1870 the Brock family included two-year-old Mary Elizabeth and six-month-old William. Lucinda Brock, listed as housekeeper, employed a fourteen-year-old black girl named Emma Fisher as a live-in servant or possibly a nanny.[25] In 1870 the census taker reported Brock as being employed as a gardener, but other sources claim that he was a schoolteacher in the schools of Harrisburg, Steelton, and Marietta.[26] The Brocks had altogether seven children. One died as an infant and six survived childhood: Mary Elizabeth born September 27, 1868; Rachel Alcinda born February 3, 1874; Maria Louisa born May 8, 1879; John Robert born October 31, 1880; Ralph Elwood born February 15, 1883; and Howard Faunteroy born July 23, 1889.

In the 1870s, the Brocks moved to West Chester in Chester County. Their home at 530 East Miner Street was near the center of a thriving black business community.[27] For instance, there was Spence's Restaurant and Burn's Great Oyster House on Gay and Fortune Streets and Fullerston's Oyster Bar in the Mansion Hotel on Market Street. Down the street from the Brocks, at the corner of Franklin and Miner, Moses G. Hepburn ran the Magnolia House Hotel. "Hepburn was one of the first blacks to set up business on the East End of the borough; his hotel guests included the orator and abolitionist Frederick Douglass."[28] Further down Miner Street, near present-day Everhart Park, was Bethel AME Church. Brock was ordained an elder in June 1881 and later served as minister of West Chester's Bethel AME Church.[29] Brock filed for an invalid pension with the federal government in 1890, citing "kidney disease and shortness of breath." He died eleven years later on August 16, 1901, of kidney disease in West Chester.[30]

The Civil War began for John Brock on April 18, 1864, when the 43rd USCT left Camp William Penn for Virginia. The regiment was first assigned to the First Brigade, Fourth Division, Ninth Corps of the Army of the Potomac, and acted as its guard en route to Petersburg in mid-June 1864. Brock's regiment fought in the "battle of the Crater" at Petersburg on July 30, 1864. In September 1864 the 43rd was assigned to the First Brigade, Third Division, Ninth Corps of the Army of the Potomac, and in the following months it was engaged in Union military operations at such Virginia sites as Weldon Railroad, Poplar Grove Church, Boydton Plank, Hatcher's Run, and Bermuda Hundred. In January 1865, the 43rd was assigned to the Third Brigade, Third Division, Twenty-Fifth Corps. It shuttled between Hatcher's Run and Richmond before joining the Appomattox campaign in late March and the pursuit of Lee's army in early April. Then the 43rd went to the Rio Grande Valley in Texas until muster-out in Pennsylvania, October 20, 1865.[31]

The *Christian Recorder*, published in Philadelphia, was the official newspaper of the African Methodist Church. Many African-Americans soldiers, including Brock wrote to the newspaper from the Civil War battlefield. In his first letter to the *Recorder*, Brock displays different emotions: he is both excited about being in the Union army and angry about slavery.

Camp near Annapolis, Md.[32]

April 21, 1864

DEAR RECORDER:

As we are about to move out to join our hearts, hands, and fortunes in the great contest, I think it proper to let the world know something about our regiment's movements. It has scarcely been six weeks since this regiment's organization. It had been recruited up to seven companies, which the first six received orders to march. We broke camp at Chelton Hill,[33] near Philadelphia, on Monday morning April 18th. The regiment, however, did not leave the camp till about 2 o'clock. We arrived in the city [of Philadelphia] about 4 o'clock and left in an hour afterwards for Baltimore. The citizens of Baltimore cheered us lustily as we moved away from the wharf on the stately steamboat *Columbia.* We sailed about three hours over very smooth water; the vessel glided along so lightly that its movement was scarcely perceptible.

After a while we reached Annapolis, which we found to be our destination. We moved off the boat, and we found ourselves on the soil of a State which was once under the despotic sway of slavery, but which we soon hope shall never more allow human bondage to prevail on its borders. After we reached the town, we took up the line of march for our camp, which is four miles from town. We found the road, as we went out, lined with tents and soldiers, all of which cheered us as we passed.

When we got to our camping ground, we found great many colored troops there. The 30th Connecticut (Colored) Regiment was there. Three regiments arrived from Baltimore the day before we came, and the next day after we arrived, there was another regiment arrived from Ohio. God speed the glorious work, and may this accursed rebellion, that has been producing so much sorrow and distress, be brought to its proper doom.

We are now attached to the 9th Army Corps, 4th Division, under the command of General [Ambrose Everett] Burnside.[34] We are proud to be under such a distinguished leader, and we hope, under the leadership of this great General, to burn the sides of the rebels so badly, that they will never wish to rebel against the government anymore, nor to raise for their escutcheon the foul emblem of slavery.

Adieu now, dear *Recorder,* till we make some more movements; and I shall endeavor to keep the public in knowledge of where we are going and what we are doing.

JOHN C. BROCK
Commissary Sergeant
43rd Reg. USCT

During the first year of the USCT, the Union army rarely assigned African-American soldiers to combat duty. Public opinion and racial prejudice in the military was against allowing blacks to engage in actual fighting. Consequently, fatigue duty and guard work were the lot of these men. The 43rd Regiment was exceptional in being assigned to the rear guard of the Army of the

Potomac. When the colored soldiers arrived in Confederate territory, the Virginians were surprised. In his second letter Brock describes the reactions of both black and white Virginians while also observing their desolation, illiteracy, and suffering.

Camp near Milford Station, Va.[35]
May 26, 1864

DEAR RECORDER:

It has been some time since you have heard from me. We have been formed into a brigade since I wrote to you last, which consists of the 30th and 39th [colored regiments] which were raised in Maryland, the 27th, which was raised in Ohio; and the 43rd which was raised in Philadelphia. The Brigade is commanded by Colonel Seafried.[36] We have got away down in the secession Territory; all the way down, until we get to Fredericksburg.[37] The rebels have taken the most of their slaves and driven them South; but those that were left, welcomed us with tokens of rejoicing.

After we left Fredericksburg, the rebels left in such a hurry, that they were glad to get away themselves, and left the slaves to take care of themselves as best they could. Some of the masters had told their slaves such frightful tales about the Yankees, they were actually afraid of us. Again, some of them, their owners could not get impressed with that fear; and as soon as we come along, fathers, mothers, and their little children, picked up their bundles and marched along with us, carrying them on their heads.

Where the contending armies have been, the desolation of war is plainly visible; but after we leave Fredericksburg, southward, the countryside is in a fine state of cultivation; the rebels having planted large crops of corn, evidently confident that [General Robert E.] Lee would fulfill his promise, which was "If they would feed his armies, he would keep the Yankees back."[38] But his boast, this time was more than he could stand to; for our brave army marches on like an overwhelming flood. You cannot imagine with what surprise the inhabitants of the South gaze upon us. They are afraid to say anything to us so they take it out in looking. They pretend to be great Union people, while we are present; but it is hard to tell what they [really] are when we are gone. What a wonderful change [we see among black folks]! The very people, who three years ago, crouched at their master's feet, on the accursed soil of Virginia, now march in a victorious column of freemen, over the same land. The change seems almost miraculous. Yet through the mysterious workings of Providence, it is so.

So far, the 1st Brigade has not been engaged with the enemy; but we do not know how soon we may be. At present we are acting as rear guard of the wagon train of the Army of the Potomac. We can plainly see, here, the blasting influences of slavery. Instead of energy, thrift, and the spirit of improvement being manifested, as it is in the North, we see nothing here but desolation and destruction, visible on every hand. You will see large farms, and old houses with thatched roofs, every here and there. The distance between the different places, in this country, is very often two miles or more. There are marks of civilization, nowhere. We very often see white children, and even men and women that cannot read a word. Surely this is a land of darkness, and gross darkness covers the people thereof.

The health of the Brigade, so far, is very good. I cannot write anymore this time, but I will endeavor to write more in my next [letter].

Yours respectfully,

JOHN C. BROCK
Commissary Sergeant
43rd USCT

By June 1864, the 43rd Regiment and the Army of the Potomac were closing in on the Confederate capital of Richmond. Brock refers to several African-American men from central Pennsylvania in this letter. One senses the loneliness and homesickness of the soldiers in Brock's plea for mail. Soon after writing this letter, Brock and the 43rd Regiment crossed the James River where they were put to work digging trenches around Petersburg, Virginia.

Camp near Hanover, Va.[39]
June 5, 1864

MR. EDITOR:

As it has been some time since we have had an opportunity of writing to you, we thought that, as we now have leisure, to let your readers know something about the movements of the Forty-third. We are now encamped about fourteen miles from Richmond. We have had some considerable marching to do to reach this point. We have been instrumental in liberating some five hundred of our sisters and brethren from the accursed yoke of human bondage. The slaves come flocking to us from every part of the country. You see them coming in every direction, some in carts, some on their masters' horses, and great numbers on foot, carrying their bundles on their heads. They manifest their love for liberty by every possible emotion. As several of them remarked to me, it seemed to them like heaven, so greatly did they realize the difference between slavery and freedom. They were all sent to White House Landing in wagons.[40] From hence they are to be taken to Washington in transports.

We are now formed into the First Brigade, consisting of the Twenty-seventh Regiment raised in Ohio, the Thirtieth and Thirty-ninth raised in Maryland, and the Forty-third raised in Pennsylvania. We are now the rear guard of the [Army of the] Potomac.

The slaves tell us that they have been praying for those blessed days for a long time, but now their eyes witness this salvation from that direful calamity, slavery, and, what was more than expected, by their own brethren in arms. What a glorious prospect it is to behold this glorious army of black men as they march with martial tread across the sacred soil of Virginia! They cause what few inhabitants yet remain to look and wonder.

Rev. Mr. Sterritt,[41] of the Baltimore Conference, is sergeant major of the Thirty-sixth. I have become acquainted with him, and find him a very fine and agreeable gentleman. Rev. Morgan, of the Forty-third, has been a little indisposed, but is now recovering. The brigade generally has been enjoying very good health.

The Second Brigade consists of the Twenty-third raised in Washington, the Nineteenth raised in Maryland, and the Thirtieth in Connecticut. This brigade is reported to have been in several skirmishes. What a glorious record will these two brigades have! The members of them can refer with exultation and say, "I was one of that noble band that marched through the wilds of Virginia, through privation and sorrow, for the liberation of my brethren." No longer can we be reproached as being afraid to take up arms for the defense of our country. No longer can it be said that we have no rights in the country in which we live, because we have never marched forward to the defense. All these accusations and other objections to our rights of citizenship are repudiated by the noble action of the colored volunteers. God bless them in their endeavors! Who refuses to say, Amen?

For the benefit of those that have friends here and wish to write to them, I will give the directions: "Mr._____, Co. A. Forty-third Regiment, First Brigade,

Fourth Division, Ninth Corps, Washington, D.C." and your letters will be forwarded to us.

Adieu, dear Recorder, for the time [being]!

JOHN C. BROCK

Commissary Sergeant

43rd USCT

In his fourth letter, Brock tells of his regiment's travels in the South. He expresses the high self-esteem and pride African-American soldiers felt about liberating the slaves and gaining freedom for themselves as well.

Camp near Manassas Junction, Va.[42]

3rd ultimo [July] 1864

DEAR RECORDER:

I think it is now about time that I should again be letting you and the folks know the present whereabouts of the 43rd Regiment. We are now encamped at a very pleasant place in Virginia between Manassas Junction[43] and Brandy Station. We have been moving considerably since I last wrote to you. We were then lying at Annapolis, Maryland. We left there on the 23rd of April, on Saturday. We were delayed a considerable length of time in starting, as there was a large division. It took a long time for all of us to finally get under way.

Well, we marched all day on Saturday, and also on the Sabbath (how different that Sabbath to some we have formerly spent) and on Monday evening we arrived at Alexandria, Va. How horrible it must have been to the rebels that their "sacred soil" should have been polluted by the footsteps of colored Union soldiers! We lay at Alexandria all day on Tuesday, and on Wednesday morning we commenced the march farther into the interior.

On Wednesday evening we reached that historic village named Fairfax Court House.[44] The inhabitants, what few there were, looked at us with astonishment, as if we were some great monsters risen up out of the ground. They looked bewildered. Yet it seemed to be too true and apparent to them that they really beheld nearly 10,000 colored soldiers filing by, armed to the teeth, with bayonets bristling in the sun. And I tell you, our boys seem to fully appreciate the importance of marching through a "secesh town." On [and] on we came, regiment after regiment, pouring in, as it seemed to their bewildered optics, by countless thousands with colors flying and the bands playing; and without intending any disparagement to other regiments, I must say that the 43rd looked truly grand, with the soldierly and imposing forms of our noble and generous Colonel [H. Seymour] Hall and Adjutant C. Bryan riding at the head.[45]

The next day, being Thursday, we crossed the memorable stream known as Bull Run. It had been raining considerably, and the stream was swollen, so that the men were obliged to roll their pants up to their knees in order to cross it, which they did amidst great shouting and cheering from the men. On the same day we passed by the famous town of Centerville, which comprises some eight or ten houses, surrounded by fortifications. This is the spot where the gallant (though unjustly abused) McDowell,[46] sword in hand, vainly endeavored to check the progress of the panic-stricken and flying army at the time of the first Bull Run fight.

Next day we arrived at the place where I am now writing. It is a very pleasant grove. We are doing guard duty here on a railroad, the older veterans having been sent to the front on the same day that we arrived to take their place. So you will see now that we have performed considerable marching for a new regiment, and one that was hardly formed. But the boys bore up with great perseverance and fortitude under the task. We have been regularly detailed for picket duty both day and night since we came here. The boys halt a man very quick, and if he does not answer quickly, he gets a ball sent through him.

Now, Mr. Editor, I herewith enclose two dollars, and you will, if you please, send me the Recorder, and I shall endeavor to do all I can for you. Direct to John C. Brock, Commissary Sergeant, 43rd Reg. USCT, Fourth Division, 9th Army Corps, Washington, D.C., and they will be forwarded to me. I am getting along remarkably well at the present time.

JOHN C. BROCK
Commissary Sergeant
43rd Regiment

The remaining companies of the 43rd Regiment—Companies H, J, and I—left Camp William Penn on July 11, 1864, bound for Camp Casey, Virginia. In his fifth letter Brock writes of the hardships his regiment endures. This is one of the few times Brock speaks about the deaths of his fellow soldiers. He pleads for, as soldiers have always done, food, supplies, newspapers, and letters from home.

Camp near Petersburg, Va.[47]
July 16, 1864

DEAR RECORDER:

Having a few leisure moments, I again devote myself to writing to let your readers know how we are coming on. We have been marching for the last two weeks from one point to another along the front, engaged in picket and fatigue duty. Our division has built two immense forts, connected by a long chain of breastworks. Sometimes they were in the trenches; in very dangerous places, the bullets whistling over and among our troops all day and all night long, while the men were engaged in digging.

On last Sunday Sergeant George Mahoney of Baltimore was killed while engaged in the trenches. He belonged to Company G, 39th Regiment [United States Colored Troops]. He is represented as being a very religious young man, and at the time of his death was sitting under a tree, engaged in reading the last chapter of Revelation, which was his favorite one to read, and on yesterday Corporal Brewster[48] of Philadelphia, belonging to Company C, 43rd Regiment, was badly wounded, one ball passing through his hand and another wounding him in the head. But notwithstanding all those dangers, the boys shoulder their shovels and picks merrily every day, and go out front to the trenches, ready and willing to do everything in their power that will lead to the capture and overthrow of the rebel stronghold.

On last Sabbath I visited the division hospital in company with Reverend Mr. Underdue[49] of Philadelphia, who is now chaplain of the 29th Reg. We found the sick and wounded doing as well as could be expected in the field. Just as the cold weather is now coming on, would it not be well for the ladies and gentlemen of the North to form benevolent associations for the purposes of sending bed-clothing to their brave husbands and brothers who get wounded through the misfortunes of war. They can be forwarded to us through the Christian Commission, that noble institution which has supplied our brigade with fresh vegetables once and very often twice a week. It receives the prayers and blessings of every soldier in the army. It has been very dry here; the dust has been so thick and heavy that it is very fatiguing for the troops to march in the daytime, when old Sol sends forth his rays in his strength.

One more thing the boys complain of very much, that is that their friends never write [but] only when they receive a letter from them. Now sometimes it is very difficult for a soldier to write: sometimes he is so tired that he falls asleep and forgets all about home, very often without the means to write with.

Now, we hope, that you who have sons, husbands, and brothers, will consider these difficulties which beset the soldier in the way of writing, and act accordingly; write often, no matter whether they write [back] or not; for nothing is so cheering to a soldier as to receive a letter from home. Send papers as often as you can, for we have a great deal of leisure time, which might be spent profitably in reading instructive papers and books. We wish to increase in knowledge and wisdom, so that part of our lives, which we may devote to our country's service, may be days of instruction, to fit us for good citizens when the balmy days of peace shall return again and bless our land, when the desolation of war shall no longer be visible, and no sounds mar our ears except the din of industry and the hum of mechanical skill. Then shall we return to our homes again with beating hearts, glad that the cruel war is over, and that the gentle influence of virtue, liberty, and independence, rules our once distressed country.

J. C. BROCK
Commissary Sergeant
43rd Reg. USCT

On July 30, 1864, the 43rd Regiment fought its first major battle—the battle of the Crater. This battle achieved notoriety due to later allegations of miscalculation by the Union forces. The battle centered on a Confederate fort known as "Elliott's Salient" near Petersburg, Virginia. Lieutenant Colonel Henry Pleasants of the 48th Pennsylvania Volunteers told his regimental officers: "That God-damned fort is the only thing between us and Petersburg, and I have an idea we can blow it up."[50] In Pleasants's regiment were many coal miners from Schuylkill County. With General Grant's consent the Pennsylvanians began digging a tunnel beneath the Confederate fort. The original military plans were for the colored troops to lead the attack into the crater immediately after the explosion on June 30. At the last minute, the colored troops were pulled back ostensibly because the Union army did not want to be accused of using the African Americans as "cannon fodder." But when the black Union soldiers followed their white comrades into the crater, the Confederates trapped them. An anonymous report in the *Christian Recorder* about the Crater disaster described the horror: "Before our wounded were removed from the Crater under a flag of truce, their sufferings during the day and a half they remained in it were absolutely frightful. Their groans and cries for water could be distinctly heard in our intrenchments. [We were] without the power to relieve [since we feared] of being shot [if we tried to help them]."[51] Many men died. In the 43rd Regiment, casualties and MIAs totaled 47. Total Union losses were 3,798 to about 1,500 for the Confederates. Afterwards, Congress conducted an investigation into the Petersburg siege to determine why the Union army lost that battle.[52] It is unfortunate that Brock does not discuss the battle of the Crater in his sixth letter; hence one can only speculate about how he experienced this traumatic episode. Brock, however, is more eager to talk about his pay raise. After numerous complaints from black soldiers and black civilian leaders, Congress voted to upgrade the pay of colored troops to that of white Union soldiers. Brock tells how thrilled his regiment was to be finally paid the equivalent of white soldiers.

Camp in front of Petersburg, Va.[53]

August 13, 1864

DEAR RECORDER:

I again take my pen in hand to inform you how we are coming on. Yesterday was a joyful day in our brigade on account of the presence of the Paymaster. We have been expecting him for some time, and at last he came, with greenbacks in abundance.[54] He commenced immediately to pay us off—that is, early the next morning after he arrived on the ground. The boys fell in the ranks with more alacrity than they ever did on any other occasion. They were paid at the rate of sixteen dollars a month that is the privates were, while the noncommissioned officers were paid more according to their rank.

The boys had heard a great deal of talks about seven dollars a month, but they never believed that they would be offered such wages. So the Paymaster told us. He said that we received the same pay as any other soldier since the 1st of January; and as none of our regiment was enlisted before that time, we all received the full complement of Government pay. Every regiment had a Paymaster. Consequently our brigade was paid off very quickly.

We had been on the skirmish line ever since the battle of the 30th of July, and only got relieved from our arduous post there a couple of days ago. Yesterday, by some means or other, the rebels discovered our camp, and at once commenced to shell us. They had it so uncomfortably hot for us that we were obliged to find another stopping-place.

Our thinned ranks have been filled up by the reinforcement of three more companies, among whom we were happy to find our old friend James Hardin, Quartermaster Sergeant of the 43rd [Company C] adding one more to the noncommissioned staff of our regiment.

There is one more thing that I wish to speak of, as I believe that large numbers of those who have friends in this regiment are readers of your newspaper. Will they please, in directing their letters, be careful to state the company to which their friends belong? This will save a great deal of trouble and time. I must now come to a close. So, adieu, dear *Recorder*, until the next time.

JOHN C. BROCK
Commissary Sergeant
43rd USCT

From August 3 to November 29, 1864, the 43rd Regiment was commanded by Captain [later Major] Horace Bumstead. In his seventh letter, Brock complains that his regiment does not have an army chaplain to conduct religious services. Although ecstatic over the emancipation of the slaves, Brock empathizes also with the wartime suffering endured by white Southerners.

August 28, 1864[55]

DEAR RECORDER:

There is nothing of importance that has occurred among us since my last letter. Our regiment has mostly been on fatigue service since that time. We have marched round to the left of Petersburg, near the Weldon railroad, and have been engaged mostly in felling trees, and building breastworks and forts.

I see in last week's *Recorder*, that there is much inquiry as to whether Rev. Mr. [John R. V.] Morgan is dead or alive. He is still alive, and was in the terrible charge of July 30th, where he acted very bravely, and came out without a scratch. He was taken ill soon after the charge, and is now in the hospital, from which we hope he may soon return. This is a splendid Sabbath morning! But no sound of the church-going bell greets our ears. It reminds me of the words of the poet—"The sound of the church-going bell/These rocks and valleys never heard."[56]

It is a painful fact that this regiment has not heard a half a dozen sermons since they have been out. We have no chaplain. Is there not an opportunity here for some enterprising minister to improve? Under the present circumstances, the moral improvement of the men in this regiment is not very great. Profanity has reached such a pitch, that it very often shocks the ears of even wicked men.

We are now encamped on a splendid farm, which contains a large house, and is surrounded by a number of small ones, which were used as the slaves' quarters. There is a large orchard on the place, which had just been set out three or four years ago. Nor more than forty yards distant from the house is the family graveyard, surrounded by an iron railing. The whole place shows signs of wealth, affluence, and ease. How much joy—at the same time, how much misery has been experienced beneath the roof of this lordly Southern mansion!

But alas! The desolation of war—fences broken down and destroyed, houses disfigured and burned, gardens that were once modern Edens, now torn up, their beauty and decorations scattered to the four winds! All this is the result of slavery. God hasten the day when war shall cease, when slavery shall be blotted from the face of the earth, and when, instead of destruction and desolation, peace, prosperity, liberty and virtue shall rule the earth!

Yours,

> JOHN C. BROCK
> 43rd Regiment USCT

Brock's eighth letter to the *Christian Recorder* describes the fighting of the 43rd Regiment at Hatcher's Run, Virginia, on October 27, 1864. His writing painfully records the anxiety and confusion experienced by his regiment. The war has also taken an emotional toll on Brock and he openly wishes for the Civil War to end.

> Camp near Petersburg, Va.
> October 30, 1864[57]

DEAR RECORDER:

Since the last letter that I wrote to you, we have been engaged with the enemy. On last Tuesday we were ordered to take six days' ration, three in our knapsacks and three in our haversacks. On the same afternoon, I saw that each man had the provisions ordered. Everyone thought that a move would be made immediately. All night Tuesday every ear was on the *qui vive* [i.e., lookout] to hear the order to move, but no order came. All day Wednesday the camp was quiet as usual. I don't believe we are going to move at all, says a youngster. You will sing a different tune from that, replied an older soldier, before twenty-four hours.

On Wednesday evening we went to bed as usual. At two o'clock on Thursday morning a single horseman rode into camp, with a dispatch to our commander.

Every man was ordered to strike his tent and get ready to march immediately. Soon afterwards long columns of troops commenced to march out, past our camp. In about ten minutes every man was ready to march. But the order to move had not yet arrived; we lay there till broad daylight, before we moved.

Meanwhile, the 2nd and 5th Corps continued to pass us in one continuous column. Many a man lay there with an anxious heart. They shook hands with each other, bidding each other farewell, in case they should not meet again. One corporal from the State of Maine handed me a letter, together with his money and watch. "Write to my wife," said he, "in case anything should happen [to] me." He was only one out of the many that told me the same thing. What a time for reflection! How many who are now well and hearty going out into the fray will never return again, and how many will return bruised and mangled! Alas! Alas! The desolation of war.

At last, after many hours of delay, the order was given to move forward. The whole division was soon in motion, the first brigade leading. We proceeded along slowly and cautiously about a mile before we met any signs of the enemy. "The Johnnies are all gone," says a new recruit. "You will hear them soon enough," replied an older and wiser soldier.

"Hark! What was that?" cried one, as the report of musketry was heard in the distance. His companion told him that our skirmishers were chasing in the enemy's pickets. Our brigades advanced in gallant style, driving the rebels before them all day. Towards night the enemy fell back to his works, where he was strongly fortified. Our boys built breastworks along their line while our skirmishers were busily engaged in watching the enemy.

On Thursday night it commenced to rain, and the boys had to take it rough and ready, without tents all night. [The] next morning many of them were dripping wet. Soon after dark, on Thursday night, the rebels attempted to surprise us but we were not to be caught napping. They found the boys ready and waiting to welcome them with hospitable hands to bloody graves. On Friday morning everyone thought that the order of the day would be an attempt to make still further advances, but contrary to everyone's expectations, we were ordered to fall back. The Second Corps fell back from their position early in the morning, we following soon afterwards.

Now we are in our old camp where we started. What was accomplished, we have yet to learn. The loss in our brigade was not very heavy. In our regiment (the 43rd) we had one officer and several men killed, and some 12 or 14 wounded. Fortunate it was that we lost no more as our regiment was outflanked several times. Most of the men that were lost belonged to Company

B,—as they were first thrown out as skirmishers, and consequently were most exposed to the enemy's fire.

Of our behavior in this battle, it is spoken of as being very good. The First Brigade was more constantly engaged than the Second was. But all receive the highest merit, and have added one more laurel to their brows. The colored soldiers of the 18th Corps have well established the reputation of our soldierly abilities. And when peace shall once more return and bless our land, we can take each other by the hands, and say, together we have toiled for the rights of man, and elevation and liberty of our race. God speed the day, when these things shall be accomplished, and we shall enjoy the blessings of peace, liberty, and prosperity, and look back on the days of our trials and tribulations, and behold the record of our deeds on the pages of our national history, bright and unsullied.

JOHN C. BROCK
Com. Sergeant
43rd USCT

For a month and a half until New Year's Eve 1864, the 43rd Regiment was involved in the defenses of Bermuda Hundred, Virginia. The regiment then crossed the James River and camped near Fort Harrison until it entered Richmond on April 3, 1865. While writing this letter, Brock was waiting for orders to march into Richmond. Literate soldiers passed the time studying Scripture, reading, and writing letters. A white chaplain, Jeremiah M. Mickley, had been assigned to the colored regiment in late 1864. Mickley's "chapel" served alternately as a school for the black soldiers. "Seventy of the whole number [of the regiment] were able to read; but very few could understand intelligently what they did read," wrote Mickley to the U.S. adjutant general.[58] Others, said Mickley, could write but had poor grammar but some didn't even know the alphabet. Brock is cheerful in his ninth letter to the *Christian Recorder*. He is overjoyed not only by Mickley's work but also the opportunity to worship in services conducted by a chaplain.

Camp near Richmond, Va.[59]
March 9, 1865

DEAR RECORDER:

Having been a long time since I have written to you, I now seize the present opportunity to inform your readers where we are, and what we are doing. We are now encamped on the north bank of the James River, where we have been since New Year's Day. We have spent the greater portion of the winter in our quarters, not having been engaged in any skirmishes with the enemy. A large portion of the regiment have been going to school during the winter months, where they have made marked and rapid improvement, under the superintendence of our able and efficient chaplain, who manifests a great interest in our soldiers. May he live to see the day, when he shall behold the results of his labor with pride.

We have heard with joy of [General] Sherman's triumphant march through Georgia and the Carolinas; of his success in compelling the evacuation of their principal cities; of the release from the chains of slavery of thousands of our fellow-creatures, and of the establishments of schools and churches among them. Civilization and knowledge bursts forth, with his refulgent rays, from behind the dark cloud, which has been hiding its brightness from the earth.

Surely this is a mighty and progressive age in which we live. The hydra-headed monster slavery which, a few short years ago, stalked over the land with proud and gigantic strides, we now behold drooping and dying under the scourging lash of universal freedom. In the once greatest strongholds of rebeldom the *institution* of slavery is now the weakest and the rebel congress are now frantically appealing to that weak *institution* to prop up the sinking fortunes of their darling *confederacy*. But it is too late—the bondmen of the South have heard that single word "liberty," and they will not heed the siren voice of their humbled masters.

But what a great change this war is working! Where once the dark mantle of ignorance hung heavily over the land, we now behold churches, school houses, ministers and teachers springing up, as if by magic, and the bright light of knowledge surely dispelling the gloom of ignorance and bigotry. More especially is this so where our armies have gone before and by their power and bravery dispersed or beaten down that devilish institution, slavery. Our boys are in good spirits, and expect soon to be called upon to strike a final blow to this inglorious rebellion.

We had the pleasure of hearing Rev. Jake [John] R. V. Morgan, Orderly Sergeant of Co. C., of our regiment, preach, on Sabbath evening last. It revived our memory of days past and gone, when we often had the pleasure of listening to "the Old Man Eloquent." We find that he has lost none of his enthusiasm, but is still as eloquent as ever. He held the audience spellbound, for almost one hour, listing to his stirring remarks. The bright sparkle of his eyes is as natural as ever, and we do sincerely hope that he may live for many years, to advocate the cause of Christ, and Him crucified, and may be as a bright and shining light, setting an example of good will to all.

JOHN C. BROCK

Quartermaster Sergeant, 43rd USCT

SITES OF MEMORY, SITES OF GLORY

African-American Grand Army of the Republic Posts in Pennsylvania

B a r b a r a   A .   G a n n o n

The review of the Grand Army of the Republic passed down the broad avenues of Washington, with tens of thousands of veterans, black and white, marching together in commemoration of Northern victory in the Civil War. One newspaper proclaimed that "the entire nation unites to celebrate the valor and patriotism of the brave soldiers who fought in defense of the Union." The correspondent singled out for praise a group of black Philadelphians, members of the Charles Sumner Post, for "they marched as they fought, nobly." He added that the white and black spectators recognized the "colored troops" with "hearty applause." This report is not an erroneous version of the famous 1865 grand review of the victorious Union army, which excluded African-American soldiers. Appearing in the *Washington Post* in 1892, the item described the second great review in which 80,000 members of the Grand Army of the Republic (GAR), the Union army's largest veterans' organization, re-created the 1865 spectacle at its twenty-sixth national reunion. Because of their status as members of the Grand Army of the Republic, African-American veterans were not excluded from this second parade (Fig. 7.1).[1]

Stuart McConnell's modern examination of the GAR argues that the exclusion of African-American soldiers from the 1865 review was emblematic of their

This examination of African-American veterans was made possible by the financial support of the Civil War Era Center of Penn State. The author would like to thank the contributors to this center for helping scholars to realize their dreams.

treatment in this veterans' organization. Further, McConnell characterizes the GAR as segregated, indicating that "where the black veteran population was large, as in Philadelphia, African-American and white veterans maintained separate posts." Based on the exclusion of black veterans from the 1865 review and the existence of all-black posts, McConnell contends that "as in the Grand Review, as in the Union Army itself, black veterans were accorded separate and unequal status." McConnell's association of racially exclusive GAR posts in Pennsylvania and African-American soldiers' exclusion from the 1865 review is ironic. These black Pennsylvanians received a belated acknowledgment of their Civil War service—recognition they did not receive when they were banned from the earlier review—because of their membership in this Philadelphia-based post.[2]

This appreciation came at a time when African Americans were under siege in almost all other aspects of their political, social, and economic life. An African-American veteran marching in this parade had lived through the end of Reconstruction, when the federal government removed troops from the South allowing the South to be "redeemed" by a Democratic Party dedicated to white supremacy. In 1883 this same man would have seen the Supreme Court render impotent the Civil Rights Act of 1875, the culminating legislative act of their namesake Charles Sumner's political life. If this former soldier lived until 1896, he would lament the most infamous Supreme Court decision of the post–Civil War era, *Plessy v. Ferguson*. This ruling formulated the separate but equal doctrine and sustained the fundamental inequality of Jim Crow laws. The new century would bring the end of significant Southern black voting due to grandfather clauses and other, more subtle, attacks on the Fifteenth Amendment. Each year, African Americans had their most precious liberty, their right to life, taken away by white vigilantes. Southern racism allied with Northern indifference led to the triumph of the three horsemen of the black apocalypse—segregation, disenfranchisement, and lynching—making this era, as one of its most prominent chroniclers has called it, the nadir of black life in America.[3]

Civil War memory was crucial to Southerners' battle to ensure Northern acquiescence to their answer to the race question—black oppression. Propagandists of the "Lost Cause" wanted Northerners to remember a Civil War that had nothing to do with emancipation and the social and political rights of African Americans. The "War Between the States," the rubric of Southern apologists for this conflict, was waged by gallant white soldiers, all Americans who fought for their beliefs as African Americans stood idly by as "faithful

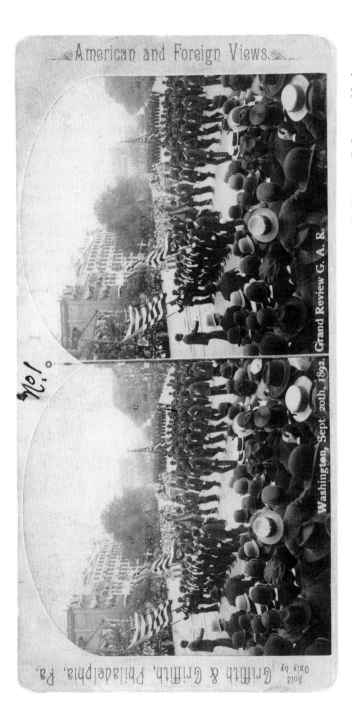

Fig. 7.1 This picture of an unidentified African-American post in the 1892 grand review in Washington, D.C., was sold, along with a handful of other stereoscopic images of the event, by Griffith and Griffith Company, a prominent purveyor of these types of reproductions. Although unidentified, this post may have been a Pennsylvania unit, given that Griffith and Griffith was based in Philadelphia. Further, the uniform worn by these men—a single-breasted coat, white shirt, and tie—was similar to the attire worn by Pennsylvanians in this parade. Courtesy of Library of Congress.

slaves" uninterested in fighting for freedom and unable to appreciate political and civil equality.[4]

The African-American community resisted the Southern effort to mold history. Frederick Douglass was particularly active in the fight to shape Civil War memory. In *Frederick Douglass' Civil War*, David Blight maintains that the black leader wanted Americans to remember that the primary cause of the war was slavery and its most important consequence was black freedom. Blight argues that Douglass tried "to forge memory into action that could somehow save the legacy of the Civil War for blacks—freedom, citizenship, suffrage, and dignity—at a time when the nation appeared indifferent or hostile to that legacy." Other elements of the African-American community, including black veterans, joined Douglass in this struggle. African-American GAR posts were particularly effective because they represented tangible and undeniable evidence that African Americans had served in this conflict and that the freedom struggle formed the central drama of the Civil War.[5]

The postwar service of black veterans in this battle for memory epitomizes a tradition in African-American history, the "site of memory." In *History and Memory in African American Culture*, Geneviève Fabre, Robert O'Meally, and others apply the theories of French historian Pierre Nora concerning sites of memory, or *lieux de mémoire*, to explain important phenomena in black history. Based on his study of French history, Nora counts among sites of memory "museums, archives, cemeteries, festivals, anniversaries, treaties, monuments, sanctuaries, and fraternal orders" and even veterans' organizations. Nora maintains that these sites "originate with the sense that we must deliberately create archives, maintain anniversaries, organize celebrations, pronounce eulogies because such activities no longer occur naturally" in the modern world. Nora's theory is readily applied to African-American history if one realizes that white Americans deliberately, and in their minds naturally, refused to include black Americans in the nation's archives, anniversaries, and celebrations. In a cross-cultural and interdisciplinary analysis of African Americana, Fabre and colleagues went further than Nora, classifying a number of unusual phenomena as sites of memory of the black American experience. Among the sites of memory catalogued by these scholars were events, such as antebellum emancipation celebrations and their modern incarnation, the Civil Rights movement; cultural developments, such as the blues; books, such as Ralph Ellison's *Invisible Man*; and even an entertainer who lived in France for much of her life, Josephine Baker. These scholars contended that Nora's theories were particularly useful as a means to include the common man and woman, those "'black and unknown bards,' historians without portfolio, who inscribed their world with landmarks made significant because men and women remembered them so complexly and so well that somehow traces of their memory survive to become history."[6]

Among the "black and unknown bards" of the battle for Civil War memory were African-American veterans. Black Pennsylvanians consciously created African-American posts to thwart the efforts of those who would forget the black experience in the Civil War. Black veterans focused on two distinct aspects of this ordeal: first, that African Americans fought and died for their own freedom; second, that the black struggle for freedom constituted the central drama of the Civil War. Black former soldiers and Nora understood the "fundamental truth" of sites of memory was "that without commemorative vigilance, history would sweep them away." When old soldiers, black and white, faded away and died, the memory of black soldiers fighting in a war for freedom almost disappeared with them. These men were forgotten until the noted African-American historian W. E. B. Du Bois wrote *Black Reconstruction*, his seminal, revisionist assessment of Civil War and Reconstruction in 1935. Du Bois's work, also identified as a site of memory, challenged but could not replace such images as the faithful slave as icons of white public memory of the Civil War.[7]

As members of an interracial organization, the GAR in Pennsylvania, black veterans acted as tangible reminders of the military service of the unfaithful slave. Their status as members of this larger, predominantly white organization allowed these men to represent their race on local, state, and even national stages. Locally, black GAR men named their posts to remind their community, black and white, of the African-American experience in the Civil War. African-American posts played prominent roles in communal Memorial Day observances. Black Pennsylvanians agitated for recognition of black military service among their white comrades. Finally, their status within the Pennsylvania GAR guaranteed African-American veterans' inclusion in GAR events that reached statewide and national audiences, such as the 1892 review.[8]

None of this would have happened had the GAR not broken with one nineteenth-century social norm—racially exclusive social organizations. According to Mary Clawson's examination of social and fraternal organizations, "racial exclusion was a hallmark of mainstream American fraternalism throughout its history." Clawson explains that all-white social organizations ensured racial exclusivity by explicitly proscribing black membership. This proscription included refusing African Americans the right to form all-black units within their organization. The admission of black men into the GAR, however, represented an unprecedented departure from this rule.[9]

The GAR consciously maintained a race-blind admission policy, using Civil War service and an honorable discharge from the army or navy as the only qualifications for membership. From its earliest years, the Pennsylvania GAR welcomed black veterans. In 1872 the Pennsylvania state commander, Howard Reeder, explained that "we care nothing for a man's nationality, race, politics, or religion. The fact that a man was ready at the call of his country in her hour of danger when stout hearts quailed and brave men faltered . . . is all the Grand Army of the Republic seeks to know." His predecessor, Major A. R. Calhoun, state commander in 1870 and 1871, explicitly included African Americans as qualified for membership. Calhoun argued that "we applied only one test that is that he [the veteran] went into the Army with a proper motive. We do not ask to what nationality he belonged. We care not whether he be a son of Jacob or a down-trodden son of Ham. We grasp his hand, and call him friend. We have no distinction of color."[10]

Pennsylvania GAR men may have welcomed black former soldiers because two prominent state officials had been affiliated with colored troops. Robert Beath, who served as Pennsylvania commander, national commander in chief, and GAR historian, had served with the Sixth United States Colored Troops (USCT). Another GAR loyalist, Louis Wagner—a state commander in 1867 and later commander in chief of the GAR—had supervised Camp Penn, a training facility near Philadelphia. According to his obituary, he "sent into the field, fully organized, drilled and equipped, nearly 14,000 colored soldiers, who as a distinguished General said, 'filled a soldier's place in the ranks and dying filled a soldier's grave.'"[11]

Although black veterans "filled a soldier's place," that place was usually not in a racially mixed post, at least not in Pennsylvania. Most black Pennsylvanians belonged to African-American posts. While racially mixed posts were rare in Pennsylvania, they were common in other states. The death records for the departments of Ohio, Massachusetts, and Illinois reveal that membership in a racially mixed post was an experience shared by many African-American veterans. For example, over a seven-year period, at least 50 percent of the black veterans who died in Ohio reportedly came from racially mixed posts. One such post in Cleveland was founded and chartered jointly by black and white veterans.[12]

When racial exclusion prevailed, it probably resulted from the racial attitudes in this era compounded by the use of a "blackball" system for voting on potential members. Under this system, an individual could reject a prospective recruit by anonymously placing a black ball in a box. In the early years of the GAR, regulations stated that a successful applicant could receive no more than one black ball in twenty. In later years, an applicant could receive no more than one black ball from ten voting members. The acceptance of African-American members in an all-white post required a very high consensus among its members. Despite this barrier, Pennsylvania posts accepted African Americans, for example, the Ezra Griffith Post in Scranton.[13]

One of the most important and enduring all-black units in Pennsylvania formed because a white post in Harrisburg was less receptive to black comrades than the Griffith Post. An African-American comrade named John Simpson, who had been elected to one of the highest positions in the Pennsylvania GAR, the council of administration, moved from Philadelphia to Harrisburg. Simpson recruited new black members for Harrisburg's GAR posts. One of the two predominantly white GAR posts in the city, Post 116, received one of his recruit's applications. According to Simpson, the application of this "honorably discharged and otherwise qualified comrade . . . has been virtually set aside and a withdrawal of it forced by announcement of the fact that the application would be rejected simply on account of the color of the applicant." Because of this threat of rejection, Simpson proposed chartering a new post at Harrisburg that "Comrades of color might join." Another Harrisburg post tried to block the post's formation. Simpson successfully appealed to the state leadership to issue a charter for a new African-American post in Harrisburg. Official documents often record the unusual and the controversial—such as the formation of Harrisburg's all-black post—while neglecting less controversial events. The formation of this black post was recorded because it was an unusual case that merited the attention of the state GAR leadership.[14]

Although the specific circumstances behind the creation of most all-black posts remain obscure, Pennsylvanians may have formed African-American GAR posts as an extension of established practices in the Keystone State. Gary Nash's study of the African-American community in antebellum Philadelphia demonstrates that black Pennsylvanians created their own social and religious organizations because they demanded autonomy in some aspects of their life. In Philadelphia, black people formed the African Methodist Episcopal Church, opened African-Americans schools, started literary and debating societies, and chartered benevolent associations. The well-established social activism of black Pennsylvanians may explain why this state had more all-black posts than any other Northern state.[15]

The acceptance of African-American comrades by the Pennsylvania GARs, combined with black veterans' willingness to ally themselves with this predominantly white organization, led to the creation of at least twenty-one all-black posts (see Table 7.1). Among the first GAR posts in Pennsylvania, Post 27 in Philadelphia was founded in the birthplace of so many other African-American social organizations. West Chester veterans formed Post 80, the second African-American post established in this state. Twenty-one all-black posts formed over four decades in Pennsylvania, and four black posts were organized in 1883 and 1884 alone. Black posts varied in size. Whereas the small black post in Delta, a town in southeastern Pennsylvania, never had more than 22 members, Post 80, in Philadelphia had 295 black veterans in its ranks in 1896.[16]

The names of these posts illustrate African-American veterans' conscious effort to create sites of memory. The numbers of the GAR posts were assigned, but members chose their names. Black former soldiers often named their posts to emphasize the African-American Civil War experience. Post 194 in Chester memorialized John Brown, while post 494 in Chambersburg commemorated a black statesman, Major Martin Delaney. Lesser known African-American heroes were also remembered. In Wilkes-Barre, the Keith Post recognized a local soldier, the first black veteran buried in that city. African-American veterans of the Sergeant Joel Benn post in Lancaster honored a local resident killed in action with the Third USCT.[17]

The most popular fallen hero memorialized by African-American GAR members was Robert Gould Shaw. Two different posts, existing at different times, honored the commander of the 54th Massachusetts Infantry. The records of the Shaw Post in Pittsburgh explicitly asserted that they established a site of memory not only for Shaw but for his entire unit: "To perpetuate his memory and to cherish his bravery and loyalty to his country and flag and to his loyal colored regiment the 54th Mass. Vol. For he fell with scores of them leading the desperate charge at Ft. Wagner." Shaw Post members spoke for many anonymous former soldiers who named their post for Charles Fribley, the late commander of the Eighth USCT, or the Robert Bryan Post, named for a black hero of the Roanoke Island campaign.[18]

The Robert Bryan Post and the Shaw Post persevered well into the twentieth century as did other all-black posts. Although it would be impossible to make a general statement on the duration of Pennsylvania's African-American posts, these organizations seem to have been extremely resilient. Post 27, chartered in 1867 or two years after Lee's surrender, endured until 1925. Post 80 in West Chester did not survive the 1870s; however, a new black post was created in

Table 7.1. African American posts in Pennsylvania, 1867–1930[a]

Post	Name	Location	Years in Existence	Largest Number of Members[b]
27	John W. Jackson	Philadelphia	1867–1925	75
80	R. G. Shaw	West Chester	1867–1877	—[c]
80	Robert Bryan	Philadelphia	1878–1930	295
103	Charles Sumner	Philadelphia	1878–1930	130
130	George F. Smith	West Chester	1879–1929	55
138	Elizabeth Temple	Kennett Square/ Avondale	1879–1924	56
194	Old John Brown	Chester	1880–1923	61
206	R. G. Shaw	Pittsburgh	1881–1930	100
365	Richard W. Dawson	Uniontown	1883–1886	24
369	David E. Small	York	1883–1916	42
390	Col. Charles Fribley	Williamsport	1883–1920	46
412	Maj. James McCorkey	Delta/ Peachbottom	1883–1917	22
440	Jesse G. Thompson	Carlisle	1884–1920	35
444	Keith[d]	Wilkes-Barre	1884–1903	25
487	William Roberts	Christiana	1885–1930	33
494	Maj. Martin Delaney	Chambersburg	1885–1893	24
520	David R. Stevens	Harrisburg	1886–1930	62
535	T. M. Jones	Brownsville	1886–1897	19
577	David Atchenson	Washington	1888–1916	41
593	George Elliot	Uniontown	1889–1904	20
607	Sgt. Joel Benn	Lancaster City	1892–1909	35

[a] Published encampment records chronicling the life and death of these posts appear to end in 1930. I would like to think that, like old soldiers, these posts did not die but merely faded away.

[b] The size of a post varied from year to year. This figure represents the highest membership recorded.

[c] No membership data were recorded in the state records for any GAR post, white or black for this period.

[d] GAR posts did not always use the full name of the individual being honored by its members.

Philadelphia using this number. The second Post 80 would be more tenacious; it existed in 1930, as did Post 103, the unit heralded by the *Washington Post* in the 1892 parade. In contrast, Post 494 in Chambersburg disbanded in 1893, only eight years after it was organized. The survival of the all-black post in Christiana whose elderly members struggled on through the 1920s with fewer than seven members, might be the most impressive testament to the tenacity of these African-American organizations. In 1930 this post and four other black posts survived: two in Philadelphia, one in Harrisburg, and the Shaw Post in Pittsburgh. In 1930 at least twenty-five aged African-American veterans still clung to their GAR charters when the entire Pennsylvania GAR had only 2,058 members and 190 surviving posts. The youngest of these men must have been eighty years old.[19]

Why would aged black veterans strive so mightily to maintain their membership? These men may have recognized that the larger predominantly white community had to grant them the status accorded to all GAR members. Membership in this interracial organization made race-based exclusion from any local, state, or nationwide Civil War commemorations impossible. As members of the Pennsylvania GAR, these all-black organizations compelled their white neighbors, both veterans and nonveterans, to acknowledge their contribution to Northern victory. On Memorial Day, GAR members of all races took center stage to remind Americans of the triumph of Federal forces. African Americans and their white comrades attended separate and integrated religious services and held racially exclusive or interracial ceremonies. Overall, black and white posts usually held some type of joint memorial exercise; for example, parades were always multiracial.[20]

Racial unity may have ruled at parades, but it did not always extend to Memorial Day religious services. Much of this separation was a product of the racial exclusivity of nineteenth-century Protestant sects. The church service celebrated the Sunday before May 30 represented the first Memorial Day activity observed by GAR posts each year. In 1899 a "very efficient and able pastor of the colored Presbyterian congregation" in Carlisle extolled the virtues and "the valor of the colored soldiers at Ft. Wagner under Col. Shaw and at Ft. Fisher under General Butler." At a service in Wilkes-Barre in 1886, a "colored preacher" described by a local paper as "one who fought to uphold the Union" reminded his listeners that the war was about more than preserving the status quo. "The first gun at Sumter," he explained, "echoed the death knell of slavery." Thus at least once a year, black GAR posts inspired African-American churches to memorialize their community's Civil War experience when organizing these services.[21]

Separate services and ceremonies highlighted the role played by other elements of the black community in Memorial Day observances. The 1890 ceremonies of the Robert Bryan Post, Post 80, for example, were typical in that although they were supervised by the post, they involved more than black former soldiers. The Bryan Post's ceremonies included the Gray Invincibles, a black militia organization; its Sons of Veterans Auxiliary, composed of the male descendants of Union soldiers; and its two ladies' auxiliaries. In 1895 the pattern was repeated in Pittsburgh, with two ladies' auxiliaries participating. A white newspaper recognized these ceremonies

as involving the entire black community. The *Harrisburg Patriot* complimented the 1891 ceremonies in Steelton by crediting, "the colored people,"
and not merely the all-black David Stephens Post, for preparing "excellent
memorial exercises."[22]

The presence of women's auxiliaries in these Memorial Day activities underscores the importance of African-American posts to all the "colored people."
An analysis of the 1892 inspection records for Pennsylvania's GAR posts
reveals that twelve of sixteen black posts reported an association with a
women's group, while only one in three predominantly white Pennsylvania
posts associated with a female organization. One of the three posts without a
ladies' auxiliary, Post 607 in Lancaster, reported the creation of a woman's
organization on Memorial Day 1896. The timing of this announcement reveals
a direct connection between the existence of these women's units and black
posts' roles in remembering the Civil War experience. A pamphlet welcoming
"colored comrades" to the 1899 national encampment in Philadelphia illustrates the importance of the ladies' organizations by including pictures of
local African-American women, leaders of the women's auxiliaries of black
GAR posts, in this publicity (see Fig. 7.2).[23]

Although black posts and their ladies' auxiliaries held separate religious
and secular ceremonies for Memorial Day, they frequently participated in
interracial ceremonies as well. In 1887 Post 201 in Carlisle "in pursuance of
an invitation from (the all-black) Post 440 . . . proceed[ed] in a body to the
Opera House to attend divine services to be held by Rev. Parker of the Baptist
church." In Washington, both the black and white posts attended two services
each year together, one at a white church and the other at an African-American
church. In 1898 both posts heard a sermon at the local AME church that was
"principally of an historical character and referred to the important part that
the colored race . . . played in American wars."[24]

Just as separate services did not preclude integrated liturgies, all-black
commemorations did not preclude racially mixed ceremonies on Memorial
Day. In Washington, the "Old Graveyard" housed the final remains of local
black veterans, and the African-American post supervised Memorial Day
observances at this graveyard. Each year, the local white post accompanied
the black veterans as they performed these ceremonies, and afterward both
units marched to another cemetery where the white post conducted services.
In Chester, the local white post, "following the usual custom," was in charge
of Memorial Day exercises. These ceremonies, however, included the all-
black Old John Brown Post.[25]

MRS. MAGGIE J. HARRIS,

Secretary of the Women's Relief Corps, John W. Jackson Post No. 106,
A well-known and most ambitious and energetic young woman. Mrs. Harris is well
known in G. U. O. of O. F. and G. A. R circles. She is a P. M. N. G. of the
Household of Ruth, and a Past Officer of the Relief Corps. Mrs.
Harris is the wife of Commander Edw. F. Harris.

MRS. MARY J. BERRY,

President of J. W. Jackson Woman's Relief Corps, No. 106.
Mrs. Berry is a very energetic woman, possessing fine business qualities. She has been
very prominent in this and other Orders; having obtained the office of National
Grand Presiding Daughter of the Order of Good Samaritans, and
this year was elected without opposition as President
of this Corps.

Fig. 7.2 The prominent role of ladies' auxiliaries in the life
of African-American posts is demonstrated by their inclusion in a special souvenir handbook and guide to the 1899
national encampment in Philadelphia. This pamphlet,
which includes a picture of the commander of an all-black
post in Philadelphia (see Fig. 7.3) also contains these
portraits of the secretary (top) and president (bottom) of
the Women's Relief Corps. Courtesy of Daniel A. P. Murray
Collection, Library of Congress.

Black posts both participated in ceremonies at white cemeteries and occasionally supervised observances at predominantly white graveyards. In 1892 the Shaw Post directed an interracial ceremony at Allegheny National Cemetery. In Philadelphia, an African-American post regularly commanded the services at predominantly white cemeteries. Post 27 regularly decorated the Third German Baptist Church and Trinity Lutheran cemeteries, denominations unlikely to have cemeteries composed solely of African Americans. Therefore, these graveyards were either racially mixed or conceivably the final resting place of only white veterans.[26]

Although black veterans supervising ceremonies at predominantly white cemeteries was an unusual observance, Memorial Day parades were a common interracial GAR activity. In areas that supported both black and white posts these units always marched together. These integrated processions were sometimes controversial. In 1898 the Uniontown Democratic paper complained that the Memorial Day parade marshal had "directly and intentionally insulted the colored Grand Army organization . . . by ordering them to take the rear of the line, and fall in behind the boy's brigade." Consequently, "the colored Grand Army boys . . . dropped out of the parade." The next Memorial Day parade in Uniontown may have been designed to apologize for this slight. In the 1899 procession, the all-black post, number 593, marched in front of the white post, number 180. In other years these posts paraded in numerical order. The Uniontown incident is notable because it was so unusual. The parade marshal's actions represented such a dramatic departure from the accepted treatment of African-American GAR members that the local Democratic newspaper, representing a party that generally refused to support black civil and political rights, repudiated this action.[27]

In contrast to the Uniontown incident, the Memorial Day parade order in Pennsylvania was almost always a function of seniority or rotation among units. The processions' sequence was often determined by the number of the post, the lower number being the senior post. For example in York, the African-American post, number 369, marched behind Post 37, the white post. Occasionally, parade order alternated among GAR posts. In Williamsport, the posts rotated their positions in the Memorial Day parade. In 1889 the all-black Fribley Post led the three Grand Army posts in Williamsport. At the next Memorial Day procession the Fribley Post was in the middle; in 1891 the African-American veterans brought up the rear. Post 577 of Washington usually marched in the vanguard of the parade in front of the more senior Post 120. This position represented an unusual honor, unexplained in articles describing this city's Memorial Day activities.[28]

Even in areas with no black post to march in their Memorial Day parade, cities and towns could be affected by black GAR members. In the 1880s no African-American post existed in Lancaster City; however, local white veterans interacted with New York-based black comrades on Memorial Day. Lancaster was the resting place of Thaddeus Stevens, "friend of the colored race" and namesake of a number of African-American GAR posts. In 1886 a representative of the all-black New York City post named for Stevens came to Lancaster to place a wreath on his grave. According to a newspaper report, representatives from the local white posts met the Stevens Post's member, Mr. Henderson, at the train. The newspaper described the scene. "He was at once escorted to the cemetery, where they assembled about the graves of Thaddeus Stevens and his nephew. Mr. Henderson then gave the command to uncover, which all obeyed." Rarely in this era did African Americans either command the actions of white Americans or get them to literally "remove their hats" to honor either a man or an idea that black Americans cherished. Henderson then eulogized Stevens: "It is right and proper that at least once a year the representative of the people for whom with tongue and pen through long years of oppression at a great personal risk, should assemble to honor his memory and drop a tear on his sod." Henderson's speech both honored Stevens and reminded these white veterans that the struggle for black freedom was the central issue of the Civil War. This was not the end of Lancaster's relationship with this African-American organization. In 1891 the entire Stevens Post came to Lancaster for the Memorial Day parade, and it led the parade by marching in front of Posts 84 and 405. The visit of the Stevens Post acted as a catalyst for local black veterans; by Memorial Day in 1892, an African-American post had formed in Lancaster City.[29]

Like New York's Stevens Post, Pennsylvania's black posts affected white Americans outside their immediate community. As active members of the state GAR, African-American veterans acted as sites of memory to a much broader audience. Campfires and reunions held at departmental events represented one venue in which African-American veterans memorialized their Civil War experience. At these campfires, GAR men regaled their comrades and the public with songs, stories, and speeches recalling their military service. In 1872 at a GAR reunion, the main speaker invited "Mr. Hood, a colored member of this organization" to address the audience. According to this account, Mr. Hood "showed a great unwillingness to appear on the stand but the audience persisted in their call until he slowly walked to the stand." General Pearson explained that Mr. Hood "had been in all the battles before Richmond and fought valiantly for his country." When Mr. Hood spoke, he explained "that he was not a speech maker. He only came that all might see the stature of [his] post."[30]

Other black GAR men were much less reluctant to address predominantly white GAR audiences on black military service. Comrade Hector, commander of an African-American post in York and a popular orator at mixed race GAR gatherings, spoke at the 1885 encampment's campfire about the need to remember the black contribution to the Civil War. "He was here to remind the hearers that they had homes churches and schools to fight for, while the dark-skinned people of his race had neither flag nor country and a very poor home, nevertheless they went shoulder to shoulder with the white man" to war. At a campfire in 1880, James A. Junior of Post 103, described by a Philadelphia paper as "one of the first seventy-five colored men who offered his services to the state," maintained that black military service may have been even more meritorious than white soldiers' because it was so dangerous. "The colored troops," he explains, "knew death was certain if they were captured but they said, My God first, my country next, and my family last." After Junior spoke, the next speaker, a white former department commander, Major Bosbyshell, agreed: "Colored troops never straggled, they dared not." Major Bosbyshell "bore witness to their bravery."[31]

Black Pennsylvania veterans expected white comrades to attend their campfires and acknowledge their military service. In 1885 the New York *Freeman* reported that the Keith Post in Wilkes-Barre held a campfire; however, "the big guns, white Republican generals, failed to come and do the speaking." One of these generals, W. H. McCartney, was running for attorney general. The *Freeman* attributed the general's absence to his racist views. According to the report, the general exclaimed that "he was not going . . . to speak for them d——n niggers." The refusal of McCartney to appear may have been worthy of comment because it was unusual. Attendance at these events by prominent white veterans was routine. McCartney's remarks at another Keith Post campfire in early 1886 support this interpretation. At this meeting, the general "eulogized the bravery of the colored soldiers, and said that they fought like the devil." He denounced the *Freeman*'s report as a lie, the product of "a miserable cur" and denied that he had ever used "scurrilous language towards" black veterans. McCartney's appearance at this second campfire and his reply to these charges may or may not have been influenced by his political aspirations. Regardless of his motive, the African-American population insisted he attend their campfire and deny the charges. He complied.[32]

Black veterans demanded more of their white colleagues than eloquent rhetoric. African Americans exhorted white veterans to assist them in their efforts to commemorate black military heroism. In 1890 African-American veterans from Harrisburg insisted that their service in colored regiments be accorded the same treatment as Pennsylvanians who served in state organizations. In this case, they demanded the preservation of the regimental colors of black units. The colors of a regiment were more than cloth to these men; the emotional attachment and reverence felt by either black or white veterans for any regimental flag cannot be overestimated. In a resolution presented to the state encampment, these African-American veterans noted that although the regimental colors of Pennsylvania state regiments were honored in the state flag room, "there were ten regiments of soldiers who served as the portion of the quota of the state whose flags are not preserved by the state." To remedy this slight, these petitioners asked that the encampment urge the legislature to "have the flags of the colored troops placed in the Flag Room of the State of Pennsylvania." The encampment agreed to support this proposal. This was no small victory given the importance of these relics to black and white veterans.[33]

Black GAR men did not always obtain their white comrades' assistance. In 1888 the "Colored Soldiers and Sailors Monument Association" of Philadelphia, a group composed of African-American GAR members and other black citizens, submitted a resolution to the annual encampment or state meeting "to raise funds for the purpose of erecting a monument commemorative of the valor of our comrades who gave their lives in defence of the flag of our country." They demanded as "a matter of equal rights and even handed justice an appropriation similar to those previously granted [to the] Pennsylvania Regimental Association" for their monument. State officials rejected this request because "the state had never contributed to any monument, except to mark the battlefield at Gettysburg, within her border and that there never has been any distinction as to color in any monument erected by the State." This excuse was somewhat disingenuous. Because no black units fought at Gettysburg, and this monument would not be placed on this field, all monuments placed at Gettysburg were de facto to white regiments. Black veterans, however, had the right to offer this resolution and white veterans were required to respond to this demand, although they did so in the negative. African Americans' demands for "equal rights and even handed justice" received little formal consideration in any other nineteenth-century organization.[34]

African Americans reminded white veterans that the monuments they built honored military exploits in a war to end slavery. The ever-popular Comrade Hector spoke at an 1885 campfire and "referred to the shackles struck from the limbs of 4,000,000 slaves, and said he was a slave until the army set him free." At an 1886 campfire in Pittsburgh, Reverend Lafayette of the Shaw Post addressed 2,500 people celebrating Grand Army Day. Lafayette saluted the GAR and the men who "brought about the liberation of his race." This panegyric to his comrades managed to both compliment his audience and remind them of slavery and emancipation. Lucius Fairchild, a white GAR man and commander in chief of the GAR, seconded Lafayette's remarks. According to an observer, he "placed his hand on the head of a negro who stood near the stage, and said that it was the Grand Army that had ransomed, with its courage, 4,000,000 of his kind." While Fairchild's actions and rhetoric were condescending toward African Americans, this incident demonstrates the influence black GAR men had on the highest level of GAR leadership.[35]

White GAR members would have viewed Fairchild's rhetoric as an acceptable interpretation of the Civil War's meaning; African-American comrades were not the only veterans who argued that the Civil War was a struggle against slavery. Many white veterans rejected the notion that they had fought merely to preserve the antebellum status quo because they believed that slavery fundamentally flawed the prewar union of states. Commander in Chief Raisseiur, in a speech to Pennsylvania GAR men, maintained that it was Union soldiers that "made it possible to keep [the] flag stainless as it is to-day as it was not in '61 in the South where human beings were held in bondage, just as much human beings as we who are white." In 1901 another GAR man, a Pennsylvania minister named Adams, reiterated this notion but argued that the entire nation was blemished by human bondage: "America was under false colors. We posed as a free people, but were not because throughout all our Southland we had humanity under the bonds of slavery." Comrade Mahon, future Pennsylvania departmental commander, endorsed this idea arguing that although "we were the whippers of women and the sellers of babes" the United States had liberty, "but [it] was not liberty in the fullness of its meaning as understood by all the magnificent men of the Revolutionary War and our magnificent Washington."[36]

Mahon and other white veterans believed that emancipation redeemed the Founding Fathers' vision and justified all the war's destruction and death. In

1874 a veteran identified only as Captain Brum maintained that Union soldiers sacrificed their lives to ensure that "the theories inculcated by our forefathers put into practice by immortal Lincoln" would succeed. Brum defined the result of these men's sacrifice: "Three millions of slaves were liberated and clothed in the panoply of freedom." Nearly thirty years later the commander in chief of the GAR, John Black of Illinois, made a similar argument when speaking at the Pennsylvania encampment. After describing the carnage of Gettysburg where men lay "down beneath the crushed wheat, bent down by the iron heel of war, there to fill unknown and unmarked graves," he maintained that these men died so that "our land might live, destined forever to Union and Liberty." The final word on the meaning of this conflict must be given to an interracial group. In 1889 the black and white veterans representing Allegheny County's GAR posts complained about Southerners' treatment of African Americans. These veterans asserted that "as ex-Union soldiers we regard Universal liberty and equal rights as trophies worthy of the Union Army," implying that anything less, such as preserving the antebellum status quo, would not have justified their service and sacrifice.[37]

It is impossible to delineate the origin of these white veterans' understanding that black freedom was the fundamental issue of this conflict, but the efforts of African-American comrades must receive partial credit for this wisdom. Such black veterans as comrades Hector and Lafayette reminded white comrades that the Civil War was more than a struggle to preserve the Union. These white veterans remembered the war in the same way.

Although African-American veterans succeeded with their comrades, their effect on the broader nonveteran community is more difficult to gauge; however, these posts were invited to a number of important celebrations where their presence must have been noticed by white Americans. This stands in stark contrast to social practices in antebellum Pennsylvania. Susan G. Davis's study of parades in Jacksonian era Philadelphia demonstrates that African Americans were neither welcome in mixed race processions nor allowed to organize their own parades. When they marched, white Philadelphians rioted and attacked African Americans and their property. A similar proscription against black veterans would have been impossible because of their membership in the Grand Army of the Republic and therefore Posts 27 and 80 marched in the national 1876 Centennial Parade in Philadelphia. The "City of Brotherly Love's" 1882 bicentennial parade included a number of black posts. Outside Philadelphia, Scranton welcomed the Keith Post of Wilkes-Barre to its 1885 Fourth of July parade. The participation of all-black posts in commemorative parades allowed these organizations to fulfill their role as sites of memory for Pennsylvanians who were not members of the GAR.[38]

In 1894 the national encampment came to Pittsburgh, providing Pennsylvania's black veterans with a national audience. The extent to which white Americans noticed African-American GAR members attending this meeting would be difficult to measure. If the souvenir edition of the *Pittsburgh Press* is any indication, however, black GAR men were highly visible. For example, the Press's souvenir edition included special articles on each GAR post in Pittsburgh. The paper described the Shaw Post as "our colored post, . . . an organization of which the city is proud." This article included a history of this post, a list of founding members, and a sketch of Post 206's commander and other prominent black GAR men. The Shaw Post was accorded the exact same treatment as the all-white GAR posts in this edition. Although it is impossible to discern the motivation of newspaper editors who lived more than one hundred years ago, these men must have either viewed the Shaw Post as the equal of other Pittsburgh posts or were afraid to incur the GAR's displeasure by slighting this organization.[39]

Not content with merely describing the Shaw Post, this special edition included an accurate account of African-American Civil War service. Entitled "The Colored Veterans," this article portrayed the unique difficulties faced by black soldiers during the war because of racial discrimination, for example, the race-based Union army pay scale: "This discrimination caused a great deal of discontent among colored troops. Despite these difficulties, they proved their great value in aiding to crush the rebellion." This edition described and illustrated the Fort Pillow massacre when black and white soldiers were massacred by Confederate soldiers under General Nathan Bedford Forrest. Such Confederate atrocities meant that "each soldier . . . knew he was not to go forth to meet his opponents in arms merely, it was a struggle for freedom, a fight for life." This souvenir edition highlighted critical engagements involving African-American regiments. "The assault on Ft. Wagner," the *Press* declared, "was one of the most heroic of the whole four years of war." Pittsburgh residents and visiting veterans would have also been reminded of the African-American heroism in the 1864 battles around Petersburg, Virginia. During one of these clashes, a group of black soldiers who had never been under fire were sent forward, "troops [that] had been slaves. They now came face to face with their former oppressors." When "the order was given to go forward, as they advanced they received a volley of canister and musketry. A hundred of them were laid low; the living took their places. Shells crashed through their ranks, but as they went up the hill at a full run the rebels retreated." These former slaves, the writer explained, had "proved their manhood and in the future no fears were expressed as to the fighting elements of the colored soldiers." The prominence of black veterans in this newspaper coverage underscores contemporary Americans' awareness of the military service of African Americans.[40]

The *Press*'s article concluded by describing one of the first demands made by a black soldier to define the meaning of their Civil War service: African Americans fighting in a struggle for the freedom of their race. A wounded African-American soldier and a senior officer met at the end of the Petersburg battles. The officer tells this young black amputee, "My dear fellow you seemed to have lost a leg for glory." The colored soldier replied, "No, . . . not for Glory, but for the elevation of my race." This young soldier's assertion, apocryphal or not, demonstrates that the mainstream press was aware of black veterans' struggle to define the meaning of their service and sacrifice. Ironically, one of the most effective sites of memory for the African-American Civil War experience created in the modern era was a movie that defined the black military experience in one word, *Glory*.[41]

The same year the national encampment met in Pittsburgh, the torch began to pass to a new generation in Pennsylvania—men and women who would forget the African-American experience in the Civil War. In Carlisle, the 1894 Memorial Day ceremonies were different. According to the local newspaper, for the "first time Sons of Veterans conducted the service" because "most of the members of the posts are growing old, some are very old." As the century came to a close, communities all over Pennsylvania modified the traditional Memorial Day observances because of aging veterans. For example, in Washington, where black and white veterans had always marched together the veterans in 1899 took cars to separate cemeteries, because as a local newspaper explained, the day had "gone by when these veterans can all march even a few squares." In cities and towns where black and white GAR men had always observed Memorial Day together, they now separated. As more veterans joined the ranks of those whose graves were decorated, fewer, more feeble, veterans remained behind to adorn these final resting places. Elderly veterans expended less energy on parades and ceremonies and more time strewing flowers over the graves of the ever-growing ranks of the army of the dead.[42]

As death thinned the ranks of GAR members, African-American veterans were not spared. In 1903 two longtime black GAR men died. They were given an unusual honor: the state records included memorials to these men. These

COMMANDER EDWARD F. HARRIS,
John W. Jackson Post, No. 27,
Department Aid and Assistant Secretary Committee on United
States Colored Troops.

Fig. 7.3   Edward Harris, commander of Post 27, was
eulogized by his GAR comrades in 1903. Courtesy of Daniel
A. P. Murray Collection, Library of Congress.

comrades were the only GAR members who had not been senior officials so
honored. This distinction demonstrated the status of African-American
comrades in this organization. According to these memorials, Edward Harris
(see Fig. 7.3), was "at the time of his death . . . in his seventh consecutive year
as [Post 27] Commander. As a comrade and a citizen, he was respected by all
with whom he came in contact." The record described Samuel Jones, of Post
80, as "the embodiment of an affable and genial Comrade; as a soldier and a
citizen, his record was unimpeachable. His example was one that will be ever
cherished." Jones died in Reading and was buried there by the local white
post. Black GAR posts and their members meet Nora's criteria as they, like all
old soldiers, fade away. Nora argued that veterans' associations as *lieux de
mémoire* are transitory because they tend "to disappear along with those who
shared" these wartime experiences.[43]

As the Civil War generation passed into history, the memory of the conflict for its successor generation was replaced by more recent events, such as
the Spanish-American War. A Memorial Day editorial in a Lancaster paper
explained the difference between how the Civil War generation remembered
the war and what he called "true Americans." The editorial writer imagined
what different generations recollected as they watched the Memorial Day

parade. He speculated that the older generation observed the Memorial Day parade and remembered the "power . . . of *Uncle Tom's Cabin*, the uncompromising fierceness of Horace Greeley's *Tribune*, . . . Thaddeus Stevens, the great debate of Lincoln and Douglas, 'squatter sovereignty,' the Christiana Riots, the Harpers Ferry Raid, and all the fearful storm of the anti-slavery movement." However, the editor explained a "true American" viewed the procession differently and understood that "the [Civil] war made each section respect the bravery of the other; that the tombs and cemeteries of both armies are perpetual monuments to American Bravery, and, finally that the day came when the Sons of Confederates and Federals . . . stormed the hill of San Juan and thundered their guns at Santiago and at Manila Bay." The editor implicitly argued that a "true American" forgot about slavery and freedom as the cause and consequence of the war. The Spanish-American War was one of the most important milestones on the road to reunion. Gaines Foster, historian of the "Lost Cause," argued that the war was so critical to Southern rehabilitation and sectional reconciliation that "the nation might have staged it if the Spanish-American war had not come along when it did."[44]

The dead and the aged veterans of the Civil War may have lost the battle for Civil War memory when the younger generation had a new use for this mythology, inspiring a new generation of Southern and Northern youth to serve and die. A Memorial Day address by Thomas Stewart, deputy superintendent of the Harrisburg Public Schools, explained how the memory of the Civil War could inspire military ardor among the nation's youth: "It is necessary that the rising generation have instilled into their minds the memory of the sacrifices made by their fathers that in a similar crisis their patriotism would call them forth to die bravely fighting for the honor of our reunited nation." The Spanish-American War marked the debut of the United States on the world stage, and the foreign entanglements inherent in this new role would require, at least for the first three-quarters of a century, a number of new generations of American soldiers.[45]

Inspired by the courage of their fathers and grandfathers, the next generation of American youth fought a battle to make the world safe for democracy while Southern states disenfranchised and segregated African Americans. A veteran of the first war to end all wars suggested in a speech to the Pennsylvania GAR in 1919 that a new day had dawned for a new generation of African-American veterans. Captain William C. Rehm, 109th Machine Gun Battalion, told a story about black soldiers in France. He described a "colored soldier who was engaged in repairing the roads in the rear." The

African-American soldier had not been to the front and was startled when he heard a shell. A lieutenant explained that the shell was made of TNT. The captain related the black soldier's response. "I know what TNT means; it means—travel, nigger, travel—and I am going to travel." This appears to be the only time "nigger" was ever published in the Pennsylvania records, and it may have been the first time it was ever used on the encampment floor. The relegation of most, but not all, black soldiers to support roles may partially explain Rehm's failure to embrace his African-American comrades. White Americans ignored African-American heroism in France, particularly when it was acclaimed by French military officials. Rehm's generation remembered only the African-American road repair crews, not the predominantly black 92nd and 93rd combat divisions.[46]

Scholars' world-war era evaluation of African-Americans' Civil War achievements reinforced Captain Rehm's belief that black Americans were cowards. Historians depicted a Civil War in which black Americans as "faithful slaves" played only a passive role in an all-white "brothers' war." James F. Rhodes, the dean of Civil War historians in 1917, argued that "one of the strange things in this [the Civil War's] eventful history is the peaceful labor of three and one-half million negro slaves whose presence in the South was the cause of the war and whose freedom was fought for after September, 1862, by Northern Soldiers." Only when Northern soldiers, black and white, faded into history could this version of the Civil War be fully accepted by white Americans.[47]

Although black Pennsylvanians were successful in impressing the memory of their deeds upon their contemporaries in the black and white community, they were less successful with the generation of Rehm and Rhodes. But African-American former soldiers may have experienced only a temporary setback in their campaign. The same black-owned newspaper that covered the African-American posts in Wilkes-Barre, Pittsburgh, and Philadelphia recounted the triumphs of W. E. B. Du Bois, a young African-American scholar. Du Bois came of age in a world where black GAR men created sites of memory for the African-American experience in the Civil War. Du Bois's *Black Reconstruction* would help fulfill the hopes of the all-black Shaw Post's members, recorded in their personal war sketches, that their "Children and [their] Children's Children . . . cherish the memories of those comrades names which are written in this book when the great cause for which they Suffered and Died will be known only in history." Returning African Americans to the Civil War's center stage allows those black Pennsylvanians who marched in that Washington parade, so very long ago, to claim their final victory.[48]

"A DISGRACE THAT CAN NEVER BE WASHED OUT"

Gettysburg and the Lingering Stigma of 1863

J i m   W e e k s

On the fortieth anniversary of the battle of Gettysburg, townspeople mounted a celebration of the hostilities that had transfigured their town. Seven committees promoted and managed the festivities, which included parades, speeches, band music, fireworks, a planned reenactment of Pickett's charge (which failed to materialize), and unveiling a monument to John Burns. The Burns statue, reminiscent of the Daniel Chester French Minuteman monument at Concord Bridge, memorialized a Gettysburg septuagenarian who had fought with Union troops on the battle's first day. Alongside a pantheon of lapidary heroes at this shrine of national salvation, the Burns figure advances toward the enemy dressed in rustic yeoman's garb. A stalwart visage of republican virtue, the monument fixed in bronze the legend of John Burns as a solitary Gettysburg hero. Bret Harte's poem "John Burns of Gettysburg," read at the monument dedication, cultivated this image of Burns as "The only man who didn't back down/When the Rebels rode through his native town." Ironically, while the statue evoked a memory of selflessness and civic duty as opposed to self-seeking gain, it also added permanence to Burns's value as a tourist attraction. The town committees sponsoring the 1903 anniversary festival, in fact, advertised the dedication to draw more tourists. Yet some citizens felt annoyed with Burns's aggrandizement at their expense, in spite of the town's ultimate economic gain. One townsperson, apparently without approval from the committees, printed a pamphlet that included a parody of Harte's poem reading, "Among the people here 'tis a conviction/ Half the tale is fact, the other is fiction."[1]

The paradoxical situation mixing conflicting memories with commerce stretched back to the shrine's founding event forty years earlier. For Gettysburg and Adams County residents in 1863, the front that shifted their way brought balm as well as bitterness. Although the campaign that culminated at Gettysburg left damaged property, crops, and detritus, it also attracted a mobile market of consumers. Sensing a lucrative opportunity, enterprising citizens profited by selling food, drink, firewood, and other vendibles to troops on both sides. Regardless of the prevalence of such entrepreneurial activity, press reports that locals had exploited Union soldiers brought censure that became an enduring, self-perpetuating stigma for Gettysburg.

The town's dilemma points to the problems of shrines created in modern industrial societies. Placed in an inescapable position by the vagaries of war and subsequent popularity of the battlefield, the people of Gettysburg helped build a shrine celebrating national rebirth that resulted from suffering, valor, and selflessness. Yet the reborn America accelerated the triumph of a consumer economy emphasizing mass consumption and leisure over the work-and-save ethic of an older producer nation. Pilgrims arriving at Gettysburg are tourists who consume goods and such services as transportation, orientation, food, drink, lodging, souvenirs, and entertainment. These same consumers, however, often condemn the town's purveyors as exploitative if not a desecrating influence on the shrine. Moreover, commercial cultural trends influence the way the battlefield is presented and consumed. In the twentieth century, the shrine's appearance often has not matched consumer expectations, which has generated censure of the town. Although commemorating the republican sacrifice and self-denial of an earlier day, Gettysburg has been driven in large measure by a self-indulgent consumer nation demanding satisfaction from the leisure experiences it purchases.

The argument advanced in this chapter builds on the work of many social, cultural, and religious historians. Together, these scholars provide a foundation for inquiry into the apparent paradox of Gettysburg as a sacred American icon simultaneously entwined with the marketplace. Perhaps the most significant of these works is Daniel Boorstin's pathbreaking book *The Image*. Boorstin suggests that the graphic revolution beginning before the Civil War launched a society that has progressively thrived on illusions rather than reality. Tourists, Boorstin argues, experience what he termed the "pseudo-event" from publicity and staging of tourist attractions. Much travel to places bandied about in commercial culture—sights "well-known for their well-knownness" as Boorstin terms them—is prompted by a desire to see if they live up to their images. Since the aftermath of the battle the Gettysburg image has been progressively disembodied from the carnage of the original event, disseminated as a special place set apart from the quotidian for the interaction of commemoration and tourism.[2]

Two seminal studies of nineteenth-century tourism also informed the writing of this chapter. John F. Sears's *Sacred Places: American Tourist Attractions in the Nineteenth Century* examines how the tourist industry in the mid-nineteenth century catered to the market of genteel, middle-class travelers seeking the sublime in nature. As Sears points out, in a young nation devoid of antiquities, natural wonders such as Niagara Falls or landscaped areas such as rural cemeteries were considered "sacred places" that helped Americans define themselves. Similarly, Dona Brown in her study *Inventing New England* shows how a combined effort among transportation companies, travel writers, poets, and artists created Boorstin's "image" that whetted the genteel tourist's appetite to see New England scenery. Both of these works provide the context for Gettysburg's development as a shrine: they show how commerce provides the venue for consumption of sacred space that appears to transcend the marketplace.

American religious histories, including Colleen McDannell's *Material Christianity* and R. Laurence Moore's *Selling God*, also offered useful analyses. McDannell explores the way tangibles tied to the marketplace aid religious practice even though in theory they are eschewed by Protestant America. Moore shows how American religion adopted the ways of the marketplace to succeed, arguing that its success depended on collaboration with commercial culture. Leigh Eric Schmidt's *Consumer Rites* supplied another key work for constructing this chapter. Schmidt examines how the marketplace revived, standardized, promoted, and transformed old festivals like Christmas and Easter into national holidays in the latter half of the nineteenth century. During the commercial celebration of the nation that occurred at this time, Gettysburg similarly was publicized by a variety of commercial sources as America's Mecca.[3]

The stigma that lingered at Gettysburg started in mid-July 1863 when bad publicity as well as enormous material and human wreckage burdened Gettysburg and Adams County citizens. In spite of the heroic efforts of citizens to succor thousands of wounded soldiers, war correspondents and other outsiders labeled Gettysburg residents as selfish, disloyal, and cruel to the Federal troops who had defended them. Suddenly jolted from the wings to center stage in the civil strife bleeding the nation, Gettysburg citizens were thrust into the national limelight. Postbattle critiques of reprehensible behavior appearing especially in New York papers seemed to confirm editorials published before the battle in the Knickerbocker press about apathy for the war in Pennsylvania.[4]

One of the first and most vitriolic of the damning accounts appeared July 9 in the *New York Times*, a strong supporter of Northern war aims. Written by war correspondent Lorenzo Livingston Crounse, the news story described "only a few specimens of the sordid meanness and unpatriotic spirit manifested by these people," including levying excessive charges on soldiers for bread, milk, and bandages. More, Crounse conflated extortion with cowardice, claiming the menfolk "mostly ran away" and presented bills for losses to Federal authorities as soon as they returned. Crounse wrote, "The conduct of the majority of male citizens of Gettysburg, and the surrounding county of Adams, is such as to stamp them with dishonor and craven-hearted meanness." Crounse and others applied the term "mean" to Gettysburg as a synonym for "stingy."[5]

Other papers with wide circulation corroborated Crounse's statements. The day after Crounse's article rolled off the press, two correspondents from the rival *New York Herald* contributed more odious examples in their accounts. One, J. H. Vosberg, related that "the most substantial citizens of the town and vicinity" not only charged soldiers for food and drink, but also locked their pumps to prevent thirsty soldiers from obtaining water. The other *Herald* correspondent concluded, "The meanness of some of the citizens of Pennsylvania is literally disgusting." He cited soldiers' being charged exorbitant rates for eggs, bread, and ham, and farmers demanding reimbursement for the pettiest losses. The correspondent singled out two citizens who demanded more than two dollars from a wounded soldier for a ride to the hospital. "A few in Pennsylvania are good and kind," the correspondent wrote, "but a majority are worse than the secessionists." *Harper's Weekly* trailed with a sharp jab the next day that graphically illustrated this censure. A cartoon depicted a Pennsylvania farmer selling a fatigued New York soldier "Susquehanna water" for six cents a glass.[6]

One might dismiss the observations of the Knickerbocker press corps as disparagement about Pennsylvanians for isolated mistreatment of New York troops. But in his bitter July 9 article, Crounse claimed he simply echoed "the unanimous sentiments of the whole army—an army which now feels that the doors from which they drove a host of robbers, thieves, and cut-throats, were not worthy of being defended." Crounse may have exaggerated with the phrase "unanimous sentiment." A Gettysburg resident remembered selling hard liquor to cavalry troopers before the battle opened, although that hucksterism appears to have generated no complaints from the ranks.[7]

Plenty of condemnation against greedy and apathetic Gettysburg and Adams County residents did emanate from soldiers, however. In a letter written July 12, Charles Francis Adams Jr., of the 11th Massachusetts Cavalry claimed that Pennsylvanians ran away, protected their property by aiding the Confederates, and, "after the battle, turned to with all their souls to make money out of their defenders by selling soldiers bread at twenty-five cents a loaf and milk at fifteen cents a canteen." Sarcastically, he gibed: "They are a great people." Provost Marshall of the Army of the Potomac Marsena Patrick added that townspeople not only appeared disloyal, but profited from the battle by stealing government property. "I am thoroughly disgusted with the whole Copperhead fraternity of Gettysburg and the county about," Patrick wrote in his diary July 5, "as they came in swarms to sweep and plunder the battle grounds." An officer in the quartermaster corps echoed Patrick's sentiment in a letter to Quartermaster General Montgomery Meigs, singling out an example of greed that repelled him. He saw a farmer demand a soldier's overcoat in exchange for a loaf of bread, and the officer told the farmer "he ought to be ashamed to rob a soldier who had come here to fight for him."[8]

Some officers vented their anger with even greater vitriol. One remembered farmers locking pumps, charging outrageous prices for food, and in one case demanding rent from an exhausted Union regiment that camped overnight in a field. "The meanest man I ever met anywhere was in that county," the officer recalled of the incident. Similarly, Colonel Charles Wainwright wrote that Pennsylvanians "fully maintain their reputation for meanness." Wainwright repeated the litany of contemptible behavior, including selling goods for inflated prices, insisting on payment for small damages, and charging wounded soldiers for rides. Two days after the battle ended he noted in his journal that the townsmen who fled before the battle had returned, "great strong able looking fellows most of them, but not one had courage enough to take a musket in hand for defense of his own home." Incensed by what he had seen, Wainwright wrote of Gettysburg, "its inhabitants have damned themselves with a disgrace that can never be washed out."[9]

Others besides Union officers and war correspondents shared disdain for the behavior of locals. Georgeanna Woolsey, a nurse with the U.S. Sanitary

Commission, could not shake the image of Pennsylvania farmers charging the wounded for rides to the hospital or railroad station. In her account of the battle's aftermath, she praised the kindness of Gettysburg women but added, "Few good things can be said of the Gettysburg farmers, and I only use scripture language in calling them 'evil beasts.'" She reserved special animosity for Pennsylvania Germans, illustrated in a sardonic anecdote about one "old Dutchman" who arrived at Sanitary Commission headquarters asking to see Confederate soldiers in the flesh. A woman volunteer ushered the yeoman into a large tent full of recuperating Confederates. "Boys," she announced to the wounded, "this gentleman has never seen a Rebel soldier before and wants to see one." Hoots and guffaws erupted in the tent as the farmer stiffened with mouth agape. According to Woolsey, the woman volunteer then asked him, "Why weren't you there helping to drive them off our soil?"[10]

Even the enemy, staggered by the abundance of southern Pennsylvania, found the behavior of its citizens remarkable. Some Confederates expressed amazement at the number of military-age male citizens laboring on farms or lounging on streets. "It gave us a realizing sense of the strength of the enemy," a Confederate remembered, "to see that they could have so large armies in the field and leave so many lusty men in peace at home." Chatting with Confederate officers, a Gettysburg woman recalled "what seemed to dishearten them more than anything else was the fact that on the farms and in the towns there seemed to be so many able-bodied men left for service in any emergency, whereas they knew with them all their men, young and old, were long ago in the ranks, with no reserves left." Lieutenant Colonel Arthur James Fremantle, a British observer who hobnobbed with Confederate brass hats, found the behavior of southern Pennsylvanians shocking despite his Southern bias. "They are the most unpatriotic people I ever saw," Fremantle penned in his diary, "and openly state that they don't care which side wins, provided they are left alone." While Fremantle reserved his censure for "the Dutch," or as he explained, "the descendants of Germans, who speak an unintelligible language," Colonel Edward Porter Alexander seemed bemused by them. Alexander recounted that a farmer paid for lodging and feeding Confederate soldiers exclaimed, "By Jiminy! Ain't dis war big luck for some peoples!"[11]

Some Federal soldiers despaired over profits wrung from the crisis and pointed to the larger issue at hand. A Union enlisted man marching through southern Pennsylvania informed readers of the *Lancaster Daily Express*, "Woe, woe I say unto the soldier who falls among his friends, if these are our friends." He noted how Pennsylvania farmers would "laugh at their cunning" by selling tobacco and writing paper to the wounded at outrageous prices. "It seems that many of the professed patriots of today have no God but gold—no duty but what is paid for—no end to secure but their own aggrandizement," he despaired. More than those who used ethnicity to explain perfidy, this soldier addressed the crux of the problem. For decades, cultural leaders had raised the question of whether abundance, prosperity, and pursuit of lucre would sap civic spirit. Their concern reflected a lingering republican ideology that made the maintenance of self-government understandable for the revolutionary generation. According to republicanism, frugal and industrious producers formed the bedrock of society. Only a virtuous citizenry free of corrupting influences could maintain the vigilance and civic responsibility essential to self-government. "Republican notions insinuate themselves into all the ideas, opinions, and habits of the Americans," Alexis de Tocqueville wrote in *Democracy in America*.[12]

Ever since the market revolution, many Americans had puzzled over the toll that self-seeking gain and the accumulation of wealth might exact on virtue. Acquisitiveness and greed sapped virtue just as abundance and luxury endangered public welfare. "Will you tell me how to prevent riches from producing luxury?" John Adams wrote to Thomas Jefferson in 1819. "Will you tell me how to prevent luxury from producing effeminacy, intoxication, extravagance, Vice and folly?" As Northerners saw it, the slave power's drive to wring profits from slavery created a life of decadent luxury that blinded them to civic responsibility. Selfishness and lust for money had not only condoned the immoral practice of slavery, but had torn apart the republic itself.[13]

Although a middle-class ethic emerging from the market revolution eclipsed republican theory by the mid-nineteenth century, the Civil War stirred and brought to the surface republican notions. Because the middle-class ethic stressed industry and self-monitoring as well as ambition and refinement, the war forced Northerners into a self-examination process. Northerners fretted whether a society of frenetic acquisitiveness and individual striving could subordinate self-interest to a great collective effort. They questioned whether they possessed the wherewithal to preserve the American experiment in self-government. "We are yet a nation of over-grown babies," a surgeon in a Connecticut regiment wrote on the eve of Gettysburg. "We have had too much comfort and luxury and too little hard work and self-denial." Indeed, some religious leaders and intellectuals believed that the war represented divine punishment for material abundance and self-absorption.[14]

Because the Confederate incursion into Pennsylvania represented not only the Union's nadir but also the first clash of great armies in the Northeast, the campaign raised questions about the moral stamina of Northerners. As the war had ground on, and war profiteering and festivity increased, many sensed an overall lack of commitment to saving the republic. Ralph Waldo Emerson, for example, noted the ascendancy of commerce and frivolity during the war, joking that perhaps prosecution of the war should be turned over to a business enterprise. It seemed the virtue essential for victory had been transformed into self-serving greed and love of luxury. Northerners thus eyed the Confederate incursion into Pennsylvania during 1863 with anxiety. A resident of Mercersburg, Pennsylvania, wrote in his journal on June 26, "The darkest hour of the American republic and the cause of the Union seems to be approaching."[15]

Unfortunately in this unparalleled emergency, reports from the front indicated that the virtue of civilians had been tested and found wanting. Although some accounts held the "Dutch," or Pennsylvania German Americans responsible, the issue was larger than both Germans and Pennsylvania. After all, regardless of their ethnicity, Northerners grown fat from abundance had cracked under the iron hammer of war. The seamy behavior of some Gettysburg residents may have been a mirror into which other Northerners looked nervously for their own reflection. Perhaps this examination process jolted many Northerners with the realization that a new structure of values and motivations gripped industrializing America. It appeared that the older ideology had been resuscitated to provide a veneer of security during the national crisis.

Eight months after the battle, a writer visiting Gettysburg remarked, "This people, it is true, have been repeatedly accused of apathy and a stupid acquiescence in the perils of their position." Although the entire North might have behaved similarly were it subjected to the same pressure, the citizens of Gettysburg assumed the burden for the region's perceived moral weakness. As the identifiable population center of Adams County, Gettysburg received much censure rightfully placed elsewhere. No matter that Gettysburg consistently met its quota for recruits without a draft, or remained Republican in a Democratic county, or that its citizens had received praise for their attention to the wounded, it continued to bear the ignominy of 1863 for decades after the war. This blemish, which persisted despite repeated rebuttals, denials, and explanations by Gettysburg officials, resulted from a number of sources related to Gettysburg's growth as a national shrine. To many who visited

Gettysburg during the decades near the turn of the century, citizens continued to fleece pilgrims to the shrine just as they gouged those who earlier saved the nation.[16]

Gettysburg's two homegrown heroes mythologized by the press as moral exemplars made their fellow citizens appear ignoble by comparison. According to the news accounts and their embellishments, John Burns and Jennie Wade were virtuous republicans who rose above the marketplace. Burns, a septuagenarian who received three wounds as a volunteer yeoman fighting for the republican cause, became a popular hero immediately. Featured on the cover of *Harper's Weekly* a month after the battle, Burns received praise from the accompanying article as "the only citizen of Gettysburg who shouldered his rifle and went out to do battle in the Union ranks against the enemies of his country. . . . Honor to his name!" Invited to Philadelphia in fall 1863 and presented with a commemorative gun, Burns also accepted a gold-headed cane from the city council of Pittsburgh and several thousand dollars in contributions. A visitor to Gettysburg in 1865 found Burns's picture being sold as a souvenir while the old man sat in the town square, displaying "evident delight in the celebrity he enjoys." On the occasion of Major General Winfield Scott Hancock's visit to the town in 1866, the crowd assembled to hear Hancock speak started chanting "Burns! Burns! Burns!" When he died in 1872, the *Gettysburg Star and Sentinel* stated that Burns, "known abroad as the Hero of Gettysburg . . . found himself suddenly raised to world-wide notoriety, being lionized wherever he went, and his heroism celebrated in song and story." Apparently all did not condone the popular plaudits for this people's hero, however. In 1903 the *Philadelphia Public Ledger* found the erection of a monument to the "wandering village free shooter" appalling. A vulgar intrusion on a battlefield memorializing true warriors, the Burns statue was "symbolic of the multitude of cheap reputations that have been coming into existence since the real heroes have been dying off."[17]

Jennie Wade's reputation did not rise in popular culture as rapidly as Burns's, but the press quickly identified her as a virtuous republican maid. The accounts stressed that she had been shot dead by a Confederate bullet while baking bread for Union soldiers, though not, one might suppose, to sell for a dollar a loaf. For some, Wade represented the selfless virgin who sacrificed herself to save the nation. One newspaper reported in 1863, "While she was busily engaged in her patriotic work, a minie ball pierced her pure heart and she fell a holy sacrifice in her country's cause." *Harper's New Monthly Magazine* termed Wade's death "genuine heroism." Several months after the battle, the *Harrisburg Telegraph* explained that "Innocent Jenny Wade was the only sacrifice which the people of that locality had to offer on the shrine of their country." The article added, "Let a monument rise to greet the skies in token of [her] virtue, daring, and nobleness." In 1901 the Grand Army of the Republic (GAR) affiliate Women's Relief Corps of Iowa did erect statuary over her grave resembling the virgin and went so far as to pour water over the monument as part of the ceremony. By the time of her monument's dedication, the house where Wade received her fatal wound had been opened as a museum. The shop sold miniature wooden dough trays and clay canteens featuring Wade's picture as souvenirs. After being shown around by the museum owner, a visitor reported, "When he illustrates how and where she was shot tears run down the cheeks, and when he solemnly buries her in the yard, all gospel truth, even the hard hearted visitor buys an extra dose of relics and souvenirs and tip toes out."[18]

As Gettysburg's stature swelled, the shrine featured Burns and Wade as saints of the celestial circle. More than simple human interest stories, the couple reflected the way common people transcended self-interest in the national crisis. Yet like Gettysburg itself, they also were images disseminated by endless circulation and recirculation in the service of commerce. Whether sold as tiny icons or their residences highlighted on battlefield tours, market exchange spread and reinforced the legends. In 1901 a visitor returning to Gettysburg for the first time since 1863 remarked, "Jenny Wade and John Burns were then unknown beyond the confines of the little hamlet, now so conspicuous in the world's history; but their names and 'what they did here' are inseparably linked with that momentous struggle." Both Burns and Wade were foreground figures in the Gettysburg shadowbox of tourism, with other townspeople gathered in the background as a bland silhouette. Burns's fame rested on the fact that only he among his fellow townsmen shouldered a musket in the republican cause. Wade's story emphasized that her life represented a gift to the republic just as the bread she baked represented a gift to sustain the nation's warriors. The mythical stature of virtue attained by both heroes did nothing to refurbish the shabby reputation of fellow townspeople accused of apathy and avarice. If any human characters are counterpoised to virile courage, it is old men and young women. Heroes made out of a seventy-year-old man and a twenty-year-old girl symbolized nothing if not a poke at the town's manhood.[19]

Whenever the opportunity presented itself, townspeople tried to explain to outsiders the inaccuracies of the Burns and Wade stories. Five months after the battle, the *Adams Sentinel* indignantly refuted "the incidents of the heroine and hero of Gettysburg . . . going the rounds of the press." What the paper found particularly irritating was not the "beautifully touching, noble and sublime" publicity about Burns and Wade, but the "malicious slander" that Burns represented the town's only hero and Wade its only sacrifice. With remarkable prescience, the paper feared that if no attempt were made to correct the stories "their continued repetition, uncontradicted, may carry with them some semblance of truth." A few weeks later, the paper discredited the Burns account by noting "another who went out to meet the Rebels when here," Phineas A. Branson. Although such an individual did serve with the cowed 26th Pennsylvania Emergency Militia, no other source has ever surfaced suggesting that Branson fought in the battle. The *Adams Sentinel,* however, asserted that Branson "behaved valiantly" but because he was not wounded he "did not receive the notice that our old friend Burns did."[20]

Townspeople apparently enjoyed debunking the Burns legend for tourists. In 1865, a visitor talked to Gettysburg residents who called Burns "a perfect humbug." As late as 1900, a veteran of the Iron Brigade returning to Gettysburg for the first time since the battle reported that townspeople termed Burns "a myth and a fraud." Citizens found the line in Bret Harte's poem stating that Burns was "the only man who didn't back down when all his townfolk ran away" especially galling. Time and again the local press berated the poem's accuracy, criticizing it as "fanciful throughout," or "there is scarcely a line that is correct as to the details presented." The dispute revived again when the state legislature appropriated money for the Burns statue on the battlefield. At the 1903 Burns monument dedication, a local speaker, the Reverend E. J. Wolf, acknowledged Burns as "a lion-hearted and fiery patriot." But he underscored the fact that "Burns was not the only citizen to help repel the rebels" and emphasized that the war had siphoned off other townsmen who otherwise would have taken up arms with Burns. As for Wade, rumors circulated questioning her virtue. In 1869 a *New York Tribune* correspondent gathering material in Gettysburg labeled her "a girl of the crudest material out of which to make martyrdom." Most corrections of the Wade story, however, explained the activities of other heroic women in Gettysburg who unselfishly fed troops and cared for the wounded.[21]

The legend of Burns and Wade grew in proportion to the emergence of Gettysburg as both a tourist site and a sacred place. Just as the old man and maiden served as a continual if distorted reminder of other townspeople's avarice, so too did Gettysburg's growth as a national shrine encourage that image. Establishing shrines in modern capitalist societies requires ritualistic but also commercial activity that promotes the special site and offers services to consumers. If, as observers claimed, Gettysburg citizens exploited Union soldiers at the time of the battle, the town in time transformed this temporary economic opportunity into the permanent bonanza of tourism.

At the time of the battle, America's tourist industry consisted of railroads, travel writers, printmakers, and poets packaging scenery and other edifying attractions for middle-class travelers. These genteel, romantically inspired tourists sought spiritual and physical rejuvenation from sublime natural settings that displayed divine handiwork. Gettysburg, with its amphitheater-like views, dramatic terrain, and sacred associations as a site of national salvation fit squarely into this itinerary. Described in newspaper battle accounts as if it were a grand romantic painting, the place became an instant sensation, attracting throngs of curiosity seekers and inspiring such marketable commemorative items as maps, prints, stationery, sheet music, and stereographs. Just a month after the battle, a local Gettysburg attorney and town booster named David McConaughy founded the Gettysburg Battlefield Memorial Association (GBMA), which the state legislature incorporated in 1864. McConaughy quickly acquired battlefield land possessing the most scenic vistas, dramatic terrain, and evidence of fierce combat. Thus, a local booster took the first step of creating both a shrine and a tourist site appropriate for genteel Victorian tourists. Eventually the GBMA improved the gaze for tourists by mounting cannon, erecting signs, and rebuilding lunettes that had deteriorated.[22]

Less than a year after the battle, the *Adams Sentinel* reported that the GBMA boasted title to seventy acres, and "it will not be long before historic shafts and memorial columns, works of art and taste, will rise upon these grounds to commemorate in all time the great deeds of valor and patriotism, which render this Battle-field ever memorable." By describing a future of "historic shafts and memorial columns, works of art and taste," the paper referred to a favorite haunt of middle-class touring, the rural cemetery. Two decades passed before Gettysburg began resembling a rural cemetery with its multifarious monuments and carriage avenues inviting pensive meandering. Still, a steady stream of tourists continued arriving, prompting a *New York Times* correspondent to write in 1865, "The battle is proving a great source of benefit to Gettysburg," and predict "it will become one of the most popular places of resort, that is, if the means of getting there are improved."[23]

Urged by local leaders, a new town industry emerged to enhance the experience of visitors. Locals responded to the steady stream of tourists with guide services and hack rentals, although a *Philadelphia Inquirer* correspondent in 1869 claimed the guides had "many cock and bull stories to relate." Townspeople at all levels of the social hierarchy sensed that memory of the battle possessed value. They knew their town had acquired "sudden and world-wide fame," as the *Gettysburg Compiler* commented in 1863, and that the epochal landscape in their backyard was as marketable as eggs or cordwood. Locals capitalized on the rage for Gettysburg relics, although in a few years relic scarcity prompted cottage manufacture of surrogate canes, miniature cannon, and other bric-a-brac. Some citizens advertised their properties' historic value and desirability as a summer boarding house. Many whose property had the misfortune of being defaced by gunfire carefully preserved these scars and zestfully pointed them out to visitors. Two years after the battle a writer for the *Atlantic Monthly*, J. T. Trowbridge, reported that on registering at the town's Globe Inn, the innkeeper "with proud satisfaction" informed him he stood on the battlefield at that very moment. To prove it, the proprietor escorted him outside and pointed to a Confederate shell embedded in a brick wall. With some sarcasm, Trowbridge added, "The battle-field was put into the bill."[24]

But the battlefield proved to be only the first lucrative opportunity for Gettysburg to create a genteel touring site. In 1865 the owner of a Gettysburg spring promoted the medicinal value of the water, with which wounded Confederates purportedly healed their wounds. The springs received widespread attention in Philadelphia and New York, as according to scientific examination they contained a coveted therapeutic substance known as "lithia." People with infirmities began drifting into town in search of the water's miraculous healing powers. An article appearing in the *Gettysburg Star* declared the springs' "marvelous properties" attributable only to "supernatural agency, and for providential purpose." It seemed providence had destined Gettysburg not only as a shrine of national sacrifice, but as a place for miraculous healing as well. Publicity about the water affirmed its potential to cure gout, rheumatism, kidney stones, constipation, impotence, bronchitis, and other ailments. Prominent Gettysburg citizens, including McConaughy and David Wills, formed a corporation that by 1870 constructed a bottling works, baths, and a hotel with a cupola for viewing the battlefield. The *New York Times* in 1869 claimed that Gettysburg, "famous in the national annals as a field of glory, promises to rival Saratoga as a watering place."[25]

For a time Gettysburg flourished as a middle-class resort boasting a spa, cemetery, cultural institutions, and scenery with historic associations. That Gettysburg early on served as a quintessential genteel touring site is evidenced in Appleton's 1867 traveler's guide, which described the town's "extensive views" and suggested that travelers allow one day to tour the battlefield and two days for visiting the springs and other "objects of attraction in and around the village." McConaughy and other boosters had transformed war so hideous into edifying pleasure, but the effort to combine memory of the battle with touring standards paid off. "Ever since the battle of Gettysburg," the *Gettysburg Star and Sentinel* boasted in 1871, "the Town has been growing and improving."[26]

Yet it was precisely the effort of Gettysburg citizens to forge both a shrine and a tourist site that perpetuated stories about disloyalty and avarice. In a sense, Gettysburg continued its role as host of the decisive struggle for national life. Whether it wanted to or not, circumstances forced responsibility on the town to serve as steward of a national memory. As McConaughy demonstrated, however, townspeople could control their own destiny by shaping the site for tourists. Promoted by a progressive press and enterprising boosters, tourism succeeded as Gettysburg's chief industry. But the commercial activity necessary for supplying the services and experiences expected by modern pilgrims at the shrine drew fire. For example, in 1869 McConaughy hosted a publicized reunion of Union and Confederate officers at the Gettysburg Springs Hotel. Between evenings of conviviality at the hotel, the officers were supposed to point out their positions during the battle for subsequent placement of monuments. The press saw through the event as a promotional gimmick, however. A *New York Herald* correspondent called it "an enduring first-class advertisement to the Gettysburg springs as a summer resort." The *New York Tribune* reporter wrote that the event "will probably be the last inflated effort to lengthen out the mercantile uses of this battlefield which should hereafter be left as the nation intended it, a pleasant cemetery to many brave dead, but not a perennial fair ground made ludicrous by failures such as this which I have noticed beyond its due."[27]

But the 1869 reunion represented only the beginning and not the last of the battlefield celebrations. In the 1880s and 1890s, Gettysburg's popularity skyrocketed with a fascination for the nation's past, increasing leisure for Americans, and a new railroad into town that both eased access and advertised extensively. During the furious pace of change that nationalized American culture, Gettysburg provided stability as a shrine to a mythic era of American valor and patriotism. At the same time, the shrine owed its popularity to an increasingly commercial culture's latest communication technologies and marketing techniques. In a nation devoid of state religion and ancient sacred places, Gettysburg's byname "Mecca of the Patriot" seemed incompatible with the dollars and cents of tourist services. Although the moniker's allusions of pilgrimage to a sacred city had been used by McConaughy in the 1860s, it became common parlance near the turn of the century through continual use by railroads and veterans.[28]

By the 1890s, Gettysburg catered to new types of visitors who shared the battlefield with the genteel Victorian tourist. Throngs of day-trippers, encouraged by vigorous railroad promotion, arrived during the summer. An 1886 history of Adams County termed Gettysburg "one of the most inviting places to the tourist and the oppressed in the great cities." The new visitors were more peripatetic, more carefree, and more interested in amusement than their genteel counterparts. Entrepreneurs accommodated their tastes with dance halls, picnic pavilions, and an electric trolley. Thousands of veterans also poured into town for reunions and to erect memorials to their sacrifices at Gettysburg, bringing to fruition McConaughy's dream of a genteel pleasure ground. "The visiting veterans and their friends are the goose that lays the golden egg for our town," the *Gettysburg Star and Sentinel* stated in 1886. With its frequent reunions, anniversaries, and encampments drawing thousands of spectators, Gettysburg became a permanent seasonal display of national might lubricated by the marketplace. "The better the celebration the larger the crowd and the more money will be left in the town," the *Gettysburg Compiler* observed before the battle's fortieth reunion.[29]

The festivities invited media coverage as well as hucksters hoping to cash in on the crowds. Gettysburg's celebrations lured fakirs, hawkers, and impresarios who clustered so thickly at the 1878 GAR encampment that the *Gettysburg Star and Sentinel* commented, "Even the monkey and fat woman show was on hand." Locals grew so accustomed to street vending that the *Gettysburg Compiler* remarked, "It is not a question but a fact that Gettysburg has developed the most skilled fakirs to be found among native-born Americans." The press went so far in one case to term Gettysburg "a community of beggars living off the pilgrims of patriotism who make it their Mecca." Complaints raged about inflated hotel, hack rental, and guide services as well as such alleged penny-pinching as selling water to veterans. Even if these were infrequent acts by catch-penny opportunists, they appeared in print enough to besmirch the town. At the twenty-fifth anniversary of the battle, the *New York Times* remarked that Gettysburg "appears to be one of the very few communities in the United States that participate in patriotic celebrations from mercenary motives." In another column about the anniversary a week later, the reporter commented, "Nowhere else in the wide world is the art of squeezing so thoroughly understood and so highly practiced as at Gettysburg." The correspondent stated that Gettysburg citizens demanded money from New York national guardsmen for drinking water and for camping in a field. Of course, he took the opportunity to connect this story of avarice with the hackneyed tale that Gettysburg citizens charged soldiers for water during the battle.[30]

The simple fact that Gettysburg attracted the press meant that stories about the town during the battle received constant recirculation. Although their metaphorical meaning grew fainter, tales of the geriatric Burns as "the only man who didn't back down," the maiden Wade's free bread and sacrifice, and the sheepishness of citizens were recirculated periodically. Writing from Gettysburg in 1885, a correspondent for the veterans' newspaper *National Tribune* remembered "those hot July days of '63, when half the people took to the woods and the other half sought refuge in cellars and wells from bullet and screaming shell." A story in the *Philadelphia Inquirer* about Gettysburg recalled for readers how residents of "this overgrown Pennsylvania village . . . lived in their cellars like moles in their burrows during the three days' fighting." Another reporter added that hiding during the battle "had a depressing effect" on townspeople, as they now had no greater ambition than "to live off the people who come here."[31]

Veterans of the battle who reported on their visits to the battlefield sometimes commented on shameless avarice. "A town is guiding and finding and photographing and fleecing the perpetual tourist," a visiting veteran commented. A Philadelphia veteran hoped to see at least a patriotic display of American flags and bunting among the huckstering. "Thus show that your patriotism has not been crushed by avarice," he wrote. Following a trip to Gettysburg for the Irish Brigade's monument dedication, a veteran complained "we paid $32, *a la* Gettysburg, to the irresponsible swine who are suffered to infest the place." Other former soldiers repeated the old stories but churned them in with new stories about extortion. A veteran of the 14th Indiana declared, "If ever a soldier received so much as a crust of bread while in the state without paying four or five times its value, I never heard of it." At the twenty-fifth anniversary, General Martin McMahon purportedly said to a *New*

York World reporter, "They [citizens of Gettysburg] charged us ten cents a glass during the battle, and I presume they imagine the soldiers are better prepared to pay now than they were then."[32]

Thus, Gettysburg faced a problem whose solution was denied by circumstances. Successive civic and business organizations over the years promoted tourism and spectacles, which attracted media attention. The media repeated embarrassing old stories about the town or else linked old stories to excesses in the tourist business. Townspeople tried to refute the charges through the press or by other means. Just days after the battle, a group of Pennsylvania clergymen wrote a letter to the *New York Times* complaining about the unfairness of L. L. Crounse's damning column. When Crounse himself reappeared in town in 1865, a mob formed and threatened to lynch him, but he escaped by fleeing to a prominent citizen's home. A correspondent commented that the people of Gettysburg "expected to show they were a liberal and hospitable people by lynching a writer who had stated the contrary." The *New York Times* refused to provide details of the incident "which would only add to a load of odium already too great for the people of the locality to bear." If efforts to amend the record did not backfire, they proved ineffective as rebuttals were confined to the Gettysburg press. An irritated townsman's letter to the *Gettysburg Star and Sentinel* in 1885 complained of newspaper "misrepresentations" about citizens "who bore at the time of the battle all the intensity of suffering incident to it . . . and no compensation even at this late date has been made. Yet these citizens have to hear and bear all the vituperation it may suit the whim of any outsider to inflict."[33]

Yet townspeople also considered another method to counter outside criticism. In 1862 David McConaughy proposed erecting a monument to Adams County's war dead in the local Evergreen Cemetery. Three years after the battle, the project was revived, but with the intent of placing the monument in the town square. With a stream of outsiders arriving to view the cemetery and battlefield, the proposal intended "to erect a memorial upon this great battle-field, of such character and proportions as shall be creditable to the county." McConaughy's GBMA took up the work again in 1875, seeking donations for a "Memorial Column" in the square. This time, the proposal intended to dedicate the monument to Adams County's unknown dead as well as to the charity work of the U.S. Christian and Sanitary Commissions. Again the project stalled, and another ten years passed before the local GAR post reintroduced a scheme to erect "a stately column or obelisk [*sic*] to be seen from nearly every elevation in the county—to be a credit to its citizens and meet the public judgment in ages to come." J. Howard Wert, a Harrisburg school principal and battlefield guidebook author, wrote to the *Gettysburg Star and Sentinel* praising such a monument "especially in view of the yearly increasing importance of Gettysburg as an American Mecca for all patriots." Two years later, however, although receiving the imprimatur of the Gettysburg town council, the GAR monument project still faltered for want of contributions. Again the dedicatory intent had changed, adding to Adams County's soldier sacrifice an inscription to "the *liberality* (italics added) of the patriotic citizens of Adams County" during the battle. Thus as Gettysburg became an ever more popular tourist attraction and wartime obloquies were recycled, some bristling townspeople sought to construct a symbol of the town's wartime loyalty as a countermeasure. At any rate, the project for the public square monument languished.[34]

As veterans died out along with the rest of the generation that fought the Civil War, the old stories about avarice and poltroonery faded. But new versions of Gettysburg's mercenary assault on national ideals surfaced when the town shifted from the railroad to the automobile touring market. Living with the continual fear that tourism might decline, the chamber of commerce and later a travel council marketed Gettysburg to automobile tourists. The post–World War II boom in family touring brought a reconfiguration of tourist services in Gettysburg. Entrepreneurs established family tourist attractions, gas stations, and restaurants along the spokes of highways leading to town. With the public increasingly turning to history for its leisure, Gettysburg offended those who saw its rejuvenating role for Americans threatened by tokens of commercial culture.[35]

As early as 1946, the executive director of the Pennsylvania State Planning Board told the Gettysburg Rotary Club that the plethora of signs in town was simply bad business. The "rash of signs," he said, "gives the appearance of the midway at Coney Island rather than a historical center." By the end of the next decade, *Parade Magazine* and the comedian Cliff Arquette (who, paradoxically, owned a commercial museum at Gettysburg) launched popular appeals to save Gettysburg. *Parade Magazine* editor Jess Gorkin fretted that "the shrine is in danger" by "the march of commercialism," and Arquette asked for "a buck to save Gettysburg" on the *Jack Paar Show*. Civil War activists formed an organization, the Gettysburg Battlefield Preservation Association, to save battlefield land from commercial encroachment and respond to condemnation by the media. The press focused attention on Gettysburg for its "gaudy eyesore of commercial tourism," as the *New York Daily News* complained. A flurry of articles termed "the second battle of Gettysburg" by the press culminated with the construction of a 307-foot observation tower in 1974, which the Gettysburg Travel Council and town boosters supported as a boon for the tourism. "In another few years," the *Philadelphia Inquirer* remarked as the tower rose, Gettysburg "will have become a neon-winking, honky-tonk, cheap, tawdry monument to American materialism." Reminiscent of its position of more than a century before, Gettysburg faced widespread censure for its self-interested response to a sacred enterprise. As his earlier counterpart may have remarked, Borough Manager Charles Kuhn said of the tower: "We are not exploiting anything. We didn't ask for the Civil War." Through its own bungled stewardship of the national shrine, Gettysburg appeared to have engendered the disgrace that could not be washed out.[36]

But by the end of the twentieth century, the vestiges of republicanism had long since disappeared. The consumer nation aborning since before the Civil War had finally triumphed over the producer nation emphasizing industry, frugality, and independence from the market. Now, rather than a society of independent producers, democracy meant a marketplace where all were free to desire the same goods. Consuming rather than producing became the path to self-fulfillment. Americans sought the good life in luxury, not self-denial. Those who attacked Gettysburg for avarice or apathy were now criticizing Gettysburg from inside the marketplace instead of outside. In other words, the same marketplace that supported Gettysburg's establishment as a tourist site and shrine also helped censure those involved in catering to the tourists who inevitably arrived.[37]

Even in the late 1990s struggle over a new visitors' center and quixotic National Park Service plans to return the battlefield to its 1863 appearance reflected the lucrative contemporary vogue for heritage tourism. Heritage tourism attempts to plunge visitors into a simulacrum of the past through costume drama spectacles and simulated environments. No longer will monuments symbolizing a present obligation to the past suffice. Unlike past generations, contemporary Americans are unsure of the nation's destiny, preferring the security of a tangible, re-created past over the uncertainty of a national future. Heritage tourism is more popular than history, notes historian David Lowenthal, because of its visual power and sensitivity to the public's zeitgeist. "It combines moral certainty and emotion with 'truth,'" he writes.[38]

Restoring the battlefield to its 1863 appearance is as much a part of the cultural marketplace as cemeteries were a century ago. It is useful to note that heritage tourism is big business, and that even Disney's most recent efforts have created simulations of African savannas and 1940s boardwalks. Rather than preservation, the real struggle defends the "viewshed"—that ugly neologism—against visual intrusion that offends consumer preferences for simulacra. A *Pittsburgh Post-Gazette* news release on August 4, 1998, reported that park officials believe the new visitors' center and "rehabilitating fences, wood lots, orchards and other small-scale landscape elements" will "heighten Gettysburg's attractiveness, thus increasing visitation from 1.65 million to nearly 2 million people annually, and boosting spending on food, lodging, transportation, retail and amusements from $112 million to nearly $146 million annually." Progress toward restoring a period look came with the tower's demolition in 2000. Unlike the nineteenth century's ambition to manipulate public spaces for uplift, today's public space is staged for entertainment as if it were all a studio's big back lot. Sacred space of the nineteenth century, whether nature, a battlefield, or museum, has transmogrified into commercial entertainment, while commercial entertainment is contemporary culture's state of grace.

There are other ironies connected with this story aside from the fact that the bludgeon used against Gettysburg has emerged from the marketplace itself. One is the fact that although Gettysburg in the late nineteenth century served as a tangible link to America's republican past, it pushed Americans to adopt a consumer ethic through its packaging of commercial leisure. A second irony is that although John Burns and Jennie Wade were advanced as popular heroes who transcended the self-interest of their townsmen, their legends grew through market transactions. Both Burns and Wade became part of the commercial culture of Gettysburg, continually reaffirmed through guide services, souvenirs, postcards, guidebooks, and museums. And third, the monument to Adams County's patriotism proposed for the public square never came to fruition as planned. In 1891, however, the local GAR post erected a monument to Adams County's wartime sacrifices in front of the post hall. In an exercise of apparent parsimony for which townspeople had established a reputation, the monument was chiseled from a stone rejected by the 2nd New York Cavalry monument association.[39] Dr. Robert Fortenbaugh of Gettysburg College wrote that Gettysburg suffered losses from the battle for which it never received fair compensation, but that "the fame and consequent benefits which have accrued to this whole area because of the events of '63 have long since far outweighed the original loss and damage." One might wonder about this conclusion considering the censure heaped on residents as a result of the battle and their behavior afterward. Much like a company town, Gettysburg's self-determination was limited to responses undertaken as host of a national shrine whose pilgrims are consumers. Indeed, responsibility for the tourist industry placed the mark of Cain on Gettysburg. Gettysburg served as the custodian of a national memory; but it also had to deal with its own memory shaped by outsiders after the battle. The tourist industry, which made it appear that the town was exploiting a national treasure, made escape from the stigma impossible. As it both shaped a shrine and sold experiences to tourists, Gettysburg could not help but suffer censure from these often clashing aims.

Nearly a century old now, the Burns monument is a permanent symbol of America's earlier producer culture of self-denial as well as civic virtue. In contrast, the twenty-first century's monument will be "restoring" the battlefield to its 1863 appearance, a memorial to a self-indulgent consumer society. Because Americans need to feel that certain tangibles transcend the marketplace, we have been too intoxicated by our own smug preservationism to admit that we are the consumers of Gettysburg demanding that we experience the place a certain way. We prefer not to acknowledge how the sacred and profane have entwined at Gettysburg, and that the market has been a key force in creating Gettysburg from the very beginning. Perhaps rather than conjuring an illusion of the battlefield's 1863 appearance, we should recognize our commercial culture's ancestry in the successive generations of consumers who have shaped Gettysburg, beginning with the troops who arrived in July 1863.[40]

"MAGNIFICENCE AND TERRIBLE TRUTHFULNESS"

Peter F. Rothermel's *The Battle of Gettysburg*

Mark Thistlethwaite

In his dramatic eyewitness account of the climactic moment of the battle of Gettysburg, Union Lieutenant Frank A. Haskell wrote: "The color sergeant of the 72nd Pennsylvania, grasping the stump of the severed lance in both his hands, waved the flag above his head and rushed towards the wall. . . . The line springs—the crest of solid ground with a great roar heaves forward its maddened load, men, arms, smoke, fire, a fighting mass. It rolls to the wall—flash meets flash, the wall is crossed—a moment ensues of thrusts, yells, blows, shots, and undistinguishable conflict, followed by a shout universal that makes the welkin ring again, and the last and bloodiest fight of the great battle of Gettysburg is ended and won."[1]

In spite of the evocative nature of his own words, Haskell believed that "many things cannot be described by pen or pencil—such a fight is one. . . . A full account of *the battle as it was* will never, can never be made. Who could sketch the changes, the constant shifting of the bloody panorama? It is not possible."[2] Possible or not, hundreds of writers and painters have been inspired to record and interpret this epic struggle.

Some of the largest pictures exhibited in nineteenth-century America took Gettysburg as their subject. These included James Walker's 7 1/2 x 20 feet *The Battle of Gettysburg: Repulse of Longstreet's Assault* (1868, private collection) and Paul Philippoteaux's colossal 1883 *Gettysburg Cyclorama*, measuring 50 x 400 feet. The most notable and often reproduced of these gigantic

Fig. 9.1 Peter F. Rothermel, *The Battle of Gettysburg: Pickett's Charge*, 1870, oil on canvas. The State Museum of Pennsylvania, Pennsylvania Historical and Museum Commission, Harrisburg.

compositions is Peter Frederick Rothermel's 16 x 32 feet *The Battle of Gettys-burg: Pickett's Charge* (1870, State Museum of Pennsylvania; Fig. 9.1).[3] Although frequently used to illustrate accounts of the battle, Rothermel's painting has little concerned scholars, particularly art historians.[4] The reasons for this vary, but they revolve around a twentieth-century prejudice against nineteenth-century history painting. The most thorough discussion of the picture appeared forty years ago, when historian Edwin B. Coddington chronicled in admirable detail the commissioning of the painting and assessed its historical veracity. While necessarily and unavoidably rehearsing some of Coddington's information and points, this chapter complements his article through an expanded analysis of the painting's composition, context, and critical reception.[5] As a major Civil War painting and significant example of nineteenth-century public art patronage, *The Battle of Gettysburg* (to use the abbreviated title favored by its contemporaries) merits close examination.

Fought from July 1 through July 3, 1863, the Battle of Gettysburg has long been considered a turning point of the Civil War. Here the Army of the Potomac under Major General George G. Meade defeated General Robert E. Lee's Army of Northern Virginia in the last major Confederate invasion of the North. The most intense and bloodiest episode of the battle occurred in the afternoon of July 3, when Confederate Major General George E. Pickett led close to 15,000 Southern troops in what has become the most famous charge in United States military history. Under intense artillery bombardment and rifle fire, Pickett's men managed to reach the Union line—and briefly puncture it—but ultimately could not break through. Pickett's charge symbolized for many the high-water mark of the Confederacy and, in historian James M. McPherson's apt assessment, it "represented the Confederate war effort in microcosm: matchless valor, apparent initial success, and ultimate disaster."[6] The dramatic moment of this epic confrontation—when "flash meets flash," in Haskell's words—provided the subject for Rothermel's monumental painting.

When viewing the painting one is initially overwhelmed by the immense size and scale of one of the largest framed canvases ever created in this country. The topographic sweep of the battle scene is matched by the panoramic range of human action and reaction, as faces and gestures register and express fear, shock, resignation, determination, and aggression (see Fig. 9.2). Rothermel shows soldiers shooting and shot, attacking and repulsing, standing their ground and fleeing, and living, dying, and dead. With its "full length" character, the raging conflict presents itself less as a painted representation and

Fig. 9.2 Detail of *The Battle of Gettysburg*. Photo: author.

more as a virtual reenactment. The composition engulfs the viewer, fills peripheral vision, and pulls one into its field. The sensation of being part of the action is enhanced today by its installation at the State Museum of Pennsylvania, where the immense painting does not hang as pictures typically do, but actually rests on the floor. This arrangement puts the battle literally at the viewer's feet.

The crowded scene, teeming with expressive figures and episodes of conflict, stimulates the spectator's eye to bounce around the composition in a manner paralleling the frantic, chaotic action of battle itself. Nevertheless, the picture ultimately centers, in terms of both form and content, on the musket-clubbing Federal soldier identified in the key to the painting as Private Sills (see Fig. 9.3).[7] This figure straddles the stone wall that dynamically cuts into the composition from the lower center and leads directly to him. The large figures grouped in the lower corners also funnel the viewer's attention to the center. Drawn here, the eye is arrested by Sills's furious action and by the dense packing of soldiers across the middle zone of the composition. Sills's raised musket carries the viewer to the left side of the picture, while his body's orientation leads to the right. The eye sweeps side to side, as it tries to absorb the intensity of the scene. Beyond this middle zone, the battlefield opens up to evoke the physical and symbolic greatness of the battle and provide a vast space that both relieves and reinforces the claustrophobic confrontation in the middleground. The centrally placed flag, the copse of trees, and the towering plumes of smoke return the eye to Private Sills, who personifies the determination and "valor of the rank and file" of the Union troops.[8]

While various compositional lines direct the viewer to the picture's center, along the way one's attention is captured by striking individual figures and groups, which read like vignettes or chapters in a book. Indeed, the painting's episodic and narrative quality defines it as eminently "literary." At the lower left, a muscular figure loads one of the cannons of Arnold's battery as dead and wounded men lie about him. Above him, on horseback, Lieutenant Frank A. Haskell reports to General Meade and his son, Captain George Meade. Behind them can be seen the artillery and rearing steeds of Lieutenant Gulian V. Weir's battery. Moving toward the composition's center, the eye rests upon a fallen drummer boy, "a pathetic incident of the battle," observed one contemporary.[9] Just behind, a litter bears Colonel Dennis O'Kane off the field. Under the American flag the color sergeant of the 72nd Pennsylvania struggles to hold it aloft, while beyond the flag Major General Winfield Scott Hancock can be seen on horseback. Below him, General Alexander S. Webb urges his men forward, with sword raised. Planted at the center is the

Fig. 9.3 Detail of *The Battle of Gettysburg.* Photo: author.

composition's linchpin, Private Sills. Next to him, Federal and Confederate troops dramatically cross bayonets. Moving farther right, one encounters the mortally wounded General Lewis A. Armistead, still waving his sword with his hat pierced on its tip. Nearby a Rebel runs for cover, while above and to the right a Confederate officer who had mounted one of the guns of Lieutentant Alonzo H. Cushing's battery is blown back. Codori's farm appears in the distance. At the far right and to the left of the top of the Confederate flag, General George Pickett steadies a rearing horse. The viewer's eye, when not sweeping through the composition, lingers over and reads these and other elements comprising the immense visual narrative.

Among the many objects broken, discarded, and strewn across the battle-field is the provocative inclusion in the lower center of an abandoned rifle leaning against the stone wall. The silenced gun poignantly symbolizes the loss of human life. Below the weapon and at an angle paralleling it, the artist inscribed his name in bloody red paint (see Fig. 9.4). The color of the signa-ture is typically Rothermel, but its prominent central placement is not, for the artist usually signed his work in one of its lower corners. Its conspicuous location foregrounds the picture's creator, suggesting a certain pride, and inserts him into a struggle in which, in fact, he did not participate. Being forty-nine and father of three when the conflict broke out, Rothermel did not serve in the Civil War. But the artist, who had to negotiate his way through what he described as the "contradiction and confusion in the various reports of Officers, eye witnesses and writers," may have felt that the painting's execu-tion was itself a battle.[10] Others did specifically link the artistic and militaristic. Reverend William Suddards equated "the work of Art to the work of Arms," while General Meade recalled he had told the artist "that I thought he had almost as hard a task as I had to win the battle."[11] The juxtaposition of the weapon and the signature not only opens the possibility of the artistic-militaristic metaphor, but provides fodder for a host of other interpretations (including Rothermel's vicarious soldiering and guilt over not serving). As allusive as the meaning of the juxtaposition may be, its intentionality is certain. In con-structing such a complex painterly machine as *The Battle of Gettysburg*, the artist would have left nothing to chance. The production of a picture intended to be equally inspiring, instructive, and visually arresting required thorough research and calculated compositional planning.

During the four and a half years he worked on the picture, Rothermel increased his knowledge of the battle by traveling to the battlefield, gather-ing information, and interviewing participants on both sides.[12] Rothermel

Fig. 9.4 Detail of *The Battle of Gettysburg*. Photo: author.

compared and weighed the significance and validity of often contrasting recollections "with the allowances necessary to be made for the excitement and natural confusion of memory in details."[13] The varying and contradictory responses came, however, to frustrate the artist. Rothermel also sifted through published accounts of the engagement, as well as reading the then-unpublished narrative of Frank Haskell.[14] The artist accumulated images of the participants, rendering some portraits from life and obtaining photographic likenesses of others. Comparing recently found drawings of Charles F. Carpenter, Elijah Cundy, James Mellor, and James R. Wilson, and an oil sketch of Major Samuel Roberts to the painting shows Rothermel's success in conveying individual likenesses.[15] Recognition of his thoroughness and expertise is evident when John Watts Depeyster, who authored pamphlets on the battles at Gettysburg and Antietam, told Rothermel that he would be happy to hear "your opinion of their correctness."[16] The painter was pleased by First Army Corps Colonel Edmund L. Dana's remark praising his judicial examination of sources.[17] Rothermel, confident in the truthfulness of his visualization, felt that the only incident he could not fully verify was that of the fallen drummer boy. Unlike the realism of many of the other figures, the boy's features were idealized from the face of a young girl.[18] The validity of the motif's inclusion was, however, affirmed by J. Hyatt Smith, a clergyman who had tended survivors of the battle. Smith informed Rothermel that he had spoken to a wounded drummer boy, "a news-boy of glorious old Philadelphia," and so the figure has "a right to a place in your wonderful painting."[19] Although the drummer received historical legitimacy, two other figures proved more problematic.

General Meade, who like most soldiers lauded the painting, pointed out that he was not on the battlefield at the moment the picture depicts. Major W. G. Mitchell took the artist to task for showing Lieutenant Haskell, not Mitchell himself, delivering the official word of victory to Meade.[20] Who actually announced the news to the major general generated conflicting views. Meade himself recalled Haskell, not Mitchell, telling him. Based on what he considered convincing historical evidence, Rothermel elected to show Haskell. The inaccurate inclusion of Meade in the scene, however, would have been a decision effected more by political and artistic concerns. It made political sense to include Meade, a native Pennsylvanian and commander of the Union forces, in a work commissioned by the Commonwealth. Even Hancock concurred that "there doubtless is propriety" in including Meade because he commanded the army whose deeds the picture chronicles.[21] Adding Meade's commanding presence expanded the visual interest of the narrative painting and reminds us that Rothermel was rendering his artistic interpretation of the event and that an inspiring pictorial image ultimately mattered more to him than the precise facts of history.

Paralleling his military research, Rothermel would have sought out examples of battle paintings for compositional models and sources of inspiration. Such artistic research formed part of his academic approach to painting. Rothermel's embrace of the academic tradition accounted for his building a picture by tempering realism with idealization. For example, the convincing details of individual likenesses, topography, and military equipment were subsumed by an idealized compositional framework that ennobled form and elevated content. Still, a powerful sense of realism, stronger than in his earlier work, abounds in *The Battle of Gettysburg*, and the painting garnered praise for its believability and being "a marvel of force and fidelity."[22] The artist proudly recalled hearing of two ladies viewing the picture who had been convinced that he must have witnessed the battle because his rendering looked "so natural."[23] Ultimately, however, the realistic details are secondary to the picture's overall grand and dramatic effect. The scene looked "so natural" because of Rothermel's intelligent, artistic orchestration of pictorial elements. In typically academic fashion, Rothermel would appropriate figures from other artists' compositions, as well as his own. For instance, the running—almost flying—form of the figure identified as Sergeant Cunningham recalls one of the avenging angels in Raphael's *The Expulsion of Heliodorus* (1512, Vatican, Rome). As an artist perpetuating the idealization and high drama of the academic style known as the Grand Manner, Rothermel would naturally look to works by the leading artists of that tradition, especially his American "ancestors": Benjamin West, John Trumbull, and Washington Allston.

Although Rothermel did not appropriate specific motifs from these artists' works, their art served as paradigms. For instance, Washington Allston's *The Dead Man Restored to Life by Touching the Bones of the Prophet Elisha* (1813, Museum of American Art of the Pennsylvania Academy of the Fine Arts) features large, expressive, and agitated figures similar to those that populate the foreground corners of Rothermel's composition. This work, belonging to the Pennsylvania Academy of the Fine Arts since 1816, would have been well known to Rothermel, who directed and played other roles at this academy. Rothermel would have been familiar with an engraving after John Trumbull's *The Death of General Warren at the Battle of Bunker's Hill, June 17, 1775* (1786, Yale University Art Gallery), which shows a soldier using his weapon as a club near the composition's focal point. The one work that probably offered greatest inspiration to Rothermel was Benjamin West's *Death on a Pale Horse* (1817, Museum of American Art of the Pennsylvania Academy of the Fine Arts). Like the Allston, this large work (measuring more than 14 x 25 feet) hung in the Pennsylvania Academy of the Fine Arts at the time of the Civil War. With its expressionistic melange of suffering figures, furious action, and smoky sublimity, *Death on a Pale Horse* provided a fitting model for Rothermel's composition. A direct (though negative) connection between the two paintings was made in 1879 by a writer who, detesting "broadcast monuments and similar grand productions," suggested that West's "art by the acre" be removed from the Pennsylvania Academy to Fairmount Park, where it could be hung with *The Battle of Gettysburg*.[24] Another large West painting available for Rothermel's study was *William Penn's Treaty with the Indians* (1771, Museum of American Art of the Pennsylvania Academy of the Fine Arts).[25] This composition, though nearly opposite in content to the Gettysburg subject, features two sides centrally arranged and enclosed by figural groups in the lower corners. These examples of Grand Manner pictures indicate a few of the works that may well have inspired Rothermel as he grappled with his composition of epic dimensions and heroic subject matter.

Rothermel undoubtedly looked also to the plethora of contemporary prints and illustrations of the Civil War.[26] The striking delineation of Private Sills, for example, resembles numerous musket-clubbing soldiers who populated the pages of *Harper's Weekly, Frank Leslie's Illustrated Newspaper*, and other popular journals. The ubiquity of ferocious battle images was noted disapprovingly by the *Army and Navy Journal* in 1864: "If all the terrific hand-to-hand encounters which we have seen for two or three years displayed in the pages of our popular weeklies had actually occurred, the combatants on each side would long ago have mutually annihilated each other."[27] Such popular depictions, however, would have appealed to Rothermel because hand-to-hand combat and the use of muskets as clubs did occur at Gettysburg. The rendering of Sills, who personifies the valor of the anonymous soldier caught in the "whirlpool of slaughter," is historically acceptable and fits easily into the visual culture of the day.[28] His stance and actions suggest a further level of meaning derived from popular imagery.

The figure's pose resonates with that of Abraham Lincoln enthusiastically attacking the Confederacy, as portrayed in illustrations and cartoons. In these popular images, Lincoln and those under his direction wield axes or rail-splitters' mauls as they cut down or smash the rebellion. *Lincoln's Last Warning*, from *Harper's Weekly*, shows the president chopping down the tree

Fig. 9.5 Frank Bellew, *Lincoln's Last Warning*, from *Harper's Weekly*, October 11, 1862, p. 656.

of slavery (Fig. 9.5). A Currier and Ives print pictures Lincoln overseeing Generals Halleck and McCellan "breaking the backbone" of rebellion. The motif appeared in at least one painting: David Gilmour Blythe's *Lincoln Crushing the Dragon of Rebellion* (1862, Museum of Fine Arts, Boston). Blythe's determinedly aggressive Lincoln anticipates the look and action of Rothermel's Private Sills. It is, however, unlikely Rothermel knew this painting. The similarity between the two figures results from both artists playing off the same motif and sharing an expressionistic style (until recently, a Civil War scene by Rothermel in the Boston museum was attributed to Blythe). In *Lincoln Crushing the Dragon of Rebellion*, the enraged president attacks the beast with a maul, which closely resembles a cannon swab of the kind seen in the lower left portion of Rothermel's painting.[29] Familiarity with images of the aggressive Lincoln would have reinforced the contemporary reading of Rothermel's Private Sills as personifying not only the anonymous soldier, but also the Union itself. Rothermel scrutinized, evaluated, and drew upon a wealth of information—military and artistic—during the four and a half years he worked on the picture.

Most accounts, including Rothermel's, state that the actual painting process took eighteen months. Thomas Eakins, who frequently dropped in on Rothermel as he worked on the picture, reported that its execution took even longer.[30] Rothermel apparently began the picture in a studio in the Western Market House (on Market Street, near Sixteenth Street in Philadelphia) but finished it in another space (on Market between Fifteenth and Merrick [now Broad] Streets). In the latter building, the second floor had to be removed in order to accommodate the picture's great dimensions.[31] As was his practice, Rothermel executed preparatory drawings and oil sketches; one report cites a ten-foot-long study.[32] Of probably dozens of studies, only a few survive. The most interesting and informative is a highly developed compositional study (see Fig. 9.6).

The general layout and action of the study closely resemble those of the completed painting, although Rothermel did make significant changes in the composition when moving from one work to the other. In the preliminary work, a wooden fence cuts into the immediate foreground. This does not appear in the final composition. The lower corners also include elements not found in the final version, including the officer on the galloping horse vaulting over a fallen horse (this motif may owe something to the pale horse in West's 1817 painting).[33] Most important, Rothermel altered the scene's center. In the study, Private Sills appears less prominently than in the completed work because of his slightly diminished scale and dark jacket (instead of the eye-catching white shirt). Also, a greater number of Union flags, raised higher, visually compete with Sills as the focal point. In moving from sketch to painting, Rothermel modified the composition to emphasize the central figure.

The point of view that Rothermel presents in *The Battle of Gettysburg* is the same as in the study. The copse of trees appears just right of center, the

Fig. 9.6 Study for *The Battle of Gettysburg*, oil on canvas, 1866–70. Museum of American Art of the Pennsylvania Academy of Fine Arts. Lent by Peter F. Rothermel Jr.

Codori farm farther to the right, while Little Round Top and Big Round Top are visible to the left. Rothermel situates the scene at the edge of the Angle: the rebellion's high-water mark. Here, on the third day of the battle of Gettysburg, the North held its ground during intense fighting and won one of the great battles of the Civil War. On the battlefield today, this area contains monuments to the 71st and 72nd Pennsylvania Regiments. The latter memorial features a sculpted figure whose stance is clearly based on Rothermel's Private Sills (see Fig. 9.7). Rothermel places the viewer not precisely at the Angle, but several yards away. The stone wall that Private Sills straddles divides the painting and the two armies. The wall makes a ninety-degree turn (stones are visible to the right of Sills) and continues to the Angle proper. Standing on the portion of the battleground that Rothermel assigns his picture's viewer, one recognizes the veracity and fiction of the artist's rendering of the terrain (see Fig. 9.8). The Round Tops and copse of trees cohere to what is seen in the picture, but the Codori farm in reality lies much farther to the right. The expansive *The Battle of Gettysburg* actually compresses space to achieve its panoramic effect.

Rothermel would have experimented with a number of points of view before selecting the one he thought most compositionally effective and thematically appropriate. We normally read pictures, especially narrative ones, left to right. Rothermel takes advantage of this tendency to reinforce the focus on Private Sills. At the left edge of the composition both Meade and the cannoneer direct our gaze into the middle of the work. The surging Federal troops, especially the running Sergeant Cunningham, further carry our vision to the center. Here the eye stops to focus on the musket-wielding private staving off the charging Rebels, with their fixed bayonets. The dividing element of the wall helps halt and anchor the viewer's eye movement. After this pause, the left-to-right reading continues, generated by the Confederate soldier who has turned to flee. The picture's composition effectively exploits the way we read paintings in order to take the viewer to the core of the painting and the heart of the battle. Further, Rothermel organizes the work so that the spectator views the field of action from the north. Compositionally, this allows the visual narrative to flow through a space marked by recognizable Gettysburg topographical features (the Round Tops, copse of trees, farm, and stone wall). This angle of vision also serves well the painting's content. Looking at the battle scene from the north means that the viewer assumes, metaphorically, a Northern perspective. Symbolically, this reinforces the source of the artist's patronage and the battle as a Union victory.

Fig. 9.7   Reed and Stephens, Monument to the 72nd Pennsylvania Infantry, dedicated 1891. Gettysburg National Military Park. Photo: author.

Fig. 9.8 View near Arnold's battery and the Angle. Gettysburg National Military Park. Photo: author.

Although Rothermel was careful not to diminish the Confederates' valiant efforts, the Northern perspective does reflect his own sympathies. In 1863 he had been a founding member of the Union League of Philadelphia, an organization dedicated to defending the Union and begun by gentlemen "disgusted with the pro-Southern sentiments."[34] Rothermel believed that an important reason Union troops prevailed at Gettysburg was because "the North had the great advantage of Justice of Liberty to all."[35] His picture aimed to impart this inspiring sentiment as well as to celebrate the superior forces and resources that helped achieve the Federal victory. The Northern perspective from which Rothermel renders his scene serves, then, a dual purpose: it facilitates a convincing representation of topography and military action; it symbolically identifies the artist and spectator with the army that prevailed in this crucial battle.

Not surprisingly, Rothermel's Northern bias conditioned the four additional paintings he executed, as part of the commission, depicting other aspects of the three-day battle. All take a Union viewpoint except for *The Pennsylvania*

Reserves Charging at Plum Run, which shows the scene from the Confederate viewpoint. Rothermel later "corrected" this anomaly by painting the same theme but from the Federal lines. The introduction here of the companion paintings to *The Battle of Gettysburg* brings us to a consideration of the commission itself.

In his annual message to the legislature in January 1866, Pennsylvania Governor Andrew G. Curtin recommended that a historical painting be commissioned for the state capitol commemorating the battle at Gettysburg. The famous engagement was not only "a glorious victory" but also "the beginning of the end of the war, and occurred on the soil of the Commonwealth." A select, joint committee of three state representatives (James N. Kerns, A. W. Markley, H. Allen) and senators (George Cormell, David McConaughy, A. Heistand Glatz) soon formed, and word went out for artists to submit studies. After consulting with the governor, Generals Meade, Hancock, and Samuel W. Crawford, and "a large number of artists and other gentlemen," the committee tendered its report. The document did not name any of artists interviewed and cited but one "gentleman": Philadelphia manufacturer and art collector Joseph H. Harrison Jr. The committee visited his private art gallery, one of the finest in the country, and considered his "suggestions and judgments" very helpful.[36] After its conversations with Harrison and others, the committee realized that because the "subject embraces not merely a single battle but the battles of Gettysburg, involving the grand martial conflict of three distinct days, each of which takes rank with the first battles of the world, the proper and successful execution of the work may require three paintings, so as to embody a theme from some grand epoch of the struggle of each day."[37]

In June Peter F. Rothermel and another artist, James Walker, traversed the battlefield with the committee and General Hancock. Throughout the commission, Hancock took an active role. Initially he encouraged Emanuel Leutze to submit studies for the committee's consideration (it is not known if the painter did). Hancock also wrote several letters of battle information to Rothermel, and he apparently visited the artist's studio to examine the work in progress.[38] James Walker was to produce an immense painting of the engagement, titled *The Battle of Gettysburg: Repulse of Longstreet's Assault, July 3, 1863* (1868, private collection). Finished before Rothermel's version, Walker's painting similarly shows a vastly populated, panoramic battle scene. Both artists drew upon the battleground studies and maps of John B. Bachelder. With its figures dispersed across the vast field of action, the Walker composition lacks the heroic focus of the Rothermel: "about as moving as a blueprint" is how Coddington aptly describes the Walker painting.[39] Given the immensity of each canvas and its representation of the same subject, comparisons between the two would be expected. Virtually none exist, however. One writer did mention the two when observing the limited number of Civil War battle paintings.[40] A hint of comparison, and rivalry, does occur in Bachelder's 1870 descriptive key to Walker's painting. Bachelder declared that the Walker image aimed to avoid the stereotypical battle scene "taught us in our earliest school-books and other illustrated works, and kept up during the war by the illustrated papers and not unfrequently indulged in even now by some would-be battle-scene painters of the present day." Rothermel may have been one such "would-be" painter in Bachelder's opinion. His next sentence may also allude to Rothermel, who was well known for his dramatically charged historical subjects, including those drawn from the medieval past: "Such pictures and paintings, in which giants struggle in fierce hand-to-hand conflicts, bayoneting, or dashing each other's brains out, may possibly resemble the conflicts of the middle ages; certainly they do not illustrate the general features of modern battles."[41] Without naming Rothermel, Bachelder implicitly diminished his work, and for good reason. Bachelder, whom Congress had appointed official historian of the battle, was heavily invested in the success of Walker's painting.[42] General Hancock noted that Walker had come to the battleground to meet with the committee that June "in the interest of Mr. Bachelder."[43] It was Bachelder who instigated Walker's undertaking soon after the battle. He supplied the artist with extensive historical and visual information and took credit for "historically arranging" the composition.[44] Bachelder also held the copyright for the engraving after the painting. Knowing that Walker's painting had chronological priority and convinced of its greater historical accuracy, Bachelder promoted his own interests by implicitly belittling Rothermel's commission. Bachelder was also likely disappointed that Rothermel, not Walker, received patronage from the Commonwealth.

In a memorandum of July 13, 1866, the select committee contracted with Rothermel to fulfill the state's $25,000 commission. Although one diarist seemed stunned—"Rothermel is engaged by the Legislature to paint 'The Battle of Gettysburg' for $25,000!!! *Rothermel*!!!"—the selection should not have been surprising, for this Philadelphia artist was recognized as one of America's leading history painters.[45]

Beginning in the early 1840s, Rothermel established himself as a major history painter specializing in colorfully painted large compositions of grand drama. Rothermel was enamored of scenes highlighting intense confrontation.

Among his best-known works were *Patrick Henry in the Virginia House of Burgesses, Delivering His Celebrated Speech Against the Stamp Act* (1851, Patrick Henry National Memorial Shrine, Brookheal, Virginia), *King Lear* (1858, Dayton Art Institute), and *Christian Martyrs in the Coliseum* (1863, unlocated). Based on his artistic reputation, he was the logical choice for the Gettysburg commission. Undoubtedly, his selection was bolstered by support from his friend and patron Joseph H. Harrison Jr. Both men participated in the Union League of Philadelphia and had worked together on Philadelphia's 1864 Great Central Fair, held in support of relief efforts for Union troops. When committee members visited Harrison's impressive art collection, they would have seen Rothermel's *Patrick Henry* and *King Lear* in the company of Benjamin West's *William Penn's Treaty with the Indians* and *Christ Rejected* (c. 1814, Museum of American Art of the Pennsylvania Academy of the Fine Arts), among other American and European works. Rothermel's affiliation with the prestigious Harrison, his high reputation as a history painter, and his status as a native son, all worked to his advantage in clinching the commission.

The 1866 memorandum also delineated the requirements and expectations of the commission. The painting was to be no less than 15 x 30 feet, "embracing a Landscape View, with Battle Scene in large figures, embodying some great epoch in said battle."[46] The picture was to include a three-foot-wide border containing the battle's "great conflicts" and "such interesting episodes as shall be determined by the Committee" in consultation with the artist.[47] The state was to receive the work by 1869.

The completed picture actually measured 16 x 32 feet, included no border images, was not finished until 1870, and not delivered until 1894. In lieu of the painted border, Rothermel completed four separate compositions, referred to by Coddington as the "side series": *Death of General Reynolds, Repulse of the Louisiana Tigers, Charge of the Pennsylvania Reserves at Plum Run,* and *Repulse of General Johnson's Division by General Geary's White Star Division.* These pictures, which I prefer calling pendants or companion paintings, were not executed until after the completion of the large painting and thus date from 1871 to 1872. All are nearly identical in size, each being approximately 36 x 67 inches.

Rothermel informed the Commonwealth that *The Battle of Gettysburg* and its pendants would be ready for delivery on or before Washington's Birthday 1872. This was the date designated by the state for the final payment of the commission.[48] Even though it had been known for years that no government building in Harrisburg was sufficiently large to accommodate the colossal canvas and its companion paintings, the situation had not been remedied by the time the pictures were completed. Consequently, they remained in Philadelphia until 1894, when they were finally installed in the capitol. Because of the lack of space in the capitol, the official unveiling of the large picture had been permitted to occur in Philadelphia at the Academy of Music on December 20, 1870.

The picture's ceremonial unveiling came under the auspices of the Pennsylvania Academy of the Fine Arts. Joseph H. Harrison Jr., had suggested this sponsorship as a means to "keep the Academy before the public, and do away with the idea that the Institution was entirely inactive."[49] At this time, the Pennsylvania Academy of the Fine Arts had sold its building, and its new home would not open until 1876. The academy's sponsorship was also an entirely appropriate way to honor Peter F. Rothermel, who had been actively involved in the institution for many years, serving as a director, president of the Council of Pennsylvania Academicians, member of several committees, and instructor. The organizers of the festivities must have grown panicky as the event drew near since they did not actually receive permission from the Commonwealth to host the ceremonies until December 17 and because the artist was making changes to the composition until the last minute.[50] Invitations for the December 20 event were sent only on December 2, which probably accounted for so many distinguished invitees (among them, Hamilton Fish, Joshua Chamberlain, Samuel F. B. Morse, and Henry Longfellow) having to decline attending. Nonetheless, the auditorium was packed "from parquet to dome." Present were many Union officers, including General Meade, Major General William T. Sherman, John L. Burns (the civilian "hero of Gettysburg"), legislators, and artists—most notably artist Albert Bierstadt.[51] Interest in the event ran high as invitees requested additional tickets (each was allotted two). One wrote: "Since I was personally engaged in some of the fiercest scenes of that great national battle, it is naturally my desire to give my family, consisting of four members, an opportunity, to enjoy that masterpiece that will give them a more correct idea of the great event in which they have become so deeply interested."[52] Interspersed throughout the evening's program was stirring music played by Hassler's Grand Military Band and Drum Corps. The honor of addressing the audience following the unveiling and the playing of the "Marche aux Flambeaux" fell, not surprisingly, to Harrison. After linking the artist's work to that of Raphael, Leonardo, and Michelangelo, the speaker broached an issue that would arise when *The Battle of Gettysburg* appeared in the 1876 Centennial Art Exhibition: the propriety of the subject. "It is not well to foster, or to keep alive too strongly, even in art, the bitterness engendered in the first years of the last decade. But if any theme in this eventful history appeals to us more strongly for remembrance than any other, it is the Battle of Gettysburg. It is no partial picture. Union and Confederate soldiers alike, have had full justice done them. Like two sturdy athletes, well-matched, the contending hosts met, and the best man won."[53] Harrison continued: "I will prophecy that, so long as this canvas holds together, and these colors remain unfaded, our countrymen, North and South, East and West, will have a just pride in this picture."

Although a Union bias certainly underlay the commissioning and execution of the picture, Harrison and others asserted the painting's American character. "This is not a Picture only—it is an epic—a national struggle, a national record," declared Colonel William McMichael, who spoke after Harrison.[54] The painting was heralded as a strong lesson against "the evil and horror of war" by General Meade, who had risen to speak in response to the enthusiastic urgings of the audience.[55] The crowd then called upon Sherman, who concurred with Meade "that many good lessons could be gathered from such a painting, especially to the young, chief among which was a lesson about the evils of war."[56] These public declarations of the painting's inspiring, didactic character paralleled more privately voiced words. For instance, Reverend Suddards penned a letter in which he hoped that the picture would be a harbinger of "a continuous peace."[57] The high estimations of and expectations for the painting offered in the full flush of the celebratory unveiling were to give way, however, to more negative assessments within just a few years.

One can well imagine the excitement and awe that attended the presentation of Rothermel's huge composition, in "all its magnificence and terrible truthfulness."[58] For an audience whose image of the Civil War was conditioned primarily by small, black and white illustrations, engravings, and photographs, the gigantic painting powerfully conjured up the noise, fury, and frenzy of battle. Its colossal scope and scale made the work more than a mere picture and would have struck the spectator as a dramatic reenactment of the battle. The work's theatricality—its highly expressive figures, cast of thousands, and panoramic sweep—was heightened by its placement on the Academy of Music stage: "The canvas was stretched behind the curtain on the stage, brilliantly lighted up by a multitude of gas jets in the flies and wings, stretched in such a way and position to be distinctly seen from every portion of the house. When the curtain rolled up, displaying the painting, the applause was unbounded, wild for a minute and then the thronged audience subsided into a deathlike stillness, every eye devouring the picture in its entirety and in its details."[59] The perception of the huge canvas as a theatrical spectacle was reinforced by the recommendation that viewers bring opera glasses to better examine it.[60]

After the unveiling ceremonies, Rothermel was allowed to exhibit the picture publicly, charge admission, and keep any proceeds. This arrangement provoked controversy—neither "Mr. Rothermel nor no one else should be permitted to peddle around this picture," editorialized the *Harrisburg Patriot.*[61] Nevertheless, the painting opened to public view on December 24, 1870, in a temporary building constructed on a vacant lot at Tenth and Chestnut Streets.[62] Over the next several months, "thousands of people went to see it" as "it touched the mystic chords of memory."[63] Later in 1871, the painting traveled for exhibition in Boston, Chicago, and Pittsburgh. It was in Chicago at the time of the Great Fire and had to be cut from its frame to be saved.[64] Neither scorched nor burned, it did tear and needed to be relined in Pittsburgh. When the composition was back in Philadelphia and stored in a bank, the artist joked about the Commonwealth's dilemma concerning the painting's monumental size: "It has an elephant on its hands and no available stablery for it."[65] He indicated that it would gratify him were it to remain permanently in Philadelphia. For many years, it looked as though it might.

In 1873, the Pennsylvania Legislature granted permission to the Fairmount Park Commission to care for Rothermel's entire series of Civil War paintings. The works had supplied the motivation for and primary attraction of a new fireproof gallery in the park.[66] Three years later, the big picture moved to Memorial Hall as part of the Centennial Art Exhibition. There it remained for nearly two decades, except for inclusion along with its companion paintings in an American art exhibition in London. The Pennsylvania Legislature passed an act allowing the travel overseas.[67] *The Battle of Gettysburg* was insured for $30,000 and photographs taken so that the artist could execute a replica should the original be damaged or destroyed. Finally in 1894, all five paintings were installed in the new Executive and Library Building in Harrisburg.

By this time, *The Battle of Gettysburg* was a familiar fixture in Philadelphia, where "thousands stood before [it] each week."[68] The painting served as a reminder of the heroic role played by residents of the Quaker City in securing the victory at Gettysburg. Most of the Union troops depicted in the picture's foreground and middleground represent men of Brigadier General Alexander S. Webb's Second Brigade. Known as the Philadelphia Brigade, this was the only brigade in the war that bore a city's name.[69] When the picture left the city for Harrisburg in 1894, Philadelphians regarded its new home as dulling the painting's luster: "Those who looked often upon the picture in its favorable position in [Memorial Hall] will regret that the immense canvas filled with figures in the full significance of battle cannot be seen so well in Harrisburg. It does not show there to advantage."[70] While this observation implicitly advocated that *The Battle of Gettysburg* remain in Philadelphia, this desire had been expressed more explicitly years before.

At the unveiling ceremonies, Colonel McMichael asserted that the work should reside where the nation could appropriately study it "in the shadow of old Independence Hall."[71] Before the unveiling, the *Evening Telegraph* urged that the picture be retained by the city, arguing that no proper place existed for it in Harrisburg and that it would be "a pity to bury such a work of art in a country town, where comparatively few persons would have an opportunity to inspect it."[72] When promoting his scheme for a free art gallery in Fairmount Park, Harrison had argued that such a venue would allow the painting to be preserved permanently in the city.[73] By 1894 Philadelphians felt they held proprietary rights to the painting. The city's identification with the picture was so strong that a Philadelphia guide published as late as 1901 listed the colossal battle painting as an "object of popular interest here"![74]

The Quaker City's favorable disposition toward *The Battle of Gettysburg* had begun as soon as the painting was completed in 1870. The *Evening Telegraph* deemed it Rothermel's magnum opus and assessed that "simply as a piece of painting it is superb." It declared "he has produced a picture that is an admirable representation of the great battle it commemorates, that is not only a credit to American art, but is without exaggeration the greatest pictorial work of art ever executed on this side of the Atlantic." After describing the battle as a "splendid display of valor on both sides," the newspaper praised the painting for focusing on the heroics of the common soldier: "Gettysburg was emphatically a soldiers' battle, and while all honor and credit are due to the officers who aided in winning the victory, Mr. Rothermel's picture more truly represents the true character of the battle."[75] Even the *Harrisburg Patriot*, which objected to Rothermel exhibiting the work on his own, considered it "worthy of the great scenes which it commemorates, as well as the genius of this distinguished artist."[76] Philadelphia's *Press* praised the work's accuracy, while noting that "one does not look for beauty in a battle scene, but Mr. Rothermel has produced a sky and clouds in this Picture so poetic and so full of nature's attractiveness, that they go far toward compensating for the horrors depicted below."[77] The *Evening Telegraph* agreed by deeming the sky "a beautiful piece of painting" and the landscape "treated admirably."[78] This initial, positive reception of the painting gave way, however, during the Centennial celebration to a more hostile response.

Both the form and content of the picture received negative criticism. John Sears found *The Battle of Gettysburg* too theatrical: "It is a fearful and wonderful production, about the size and shape of a drop-curtain and of the same order of merit."[79] Clarence Cook, art critic for the *New York Tribune*, fiercely attacked the painting before the Centennial officially opened. Calling it "a Centennial Blunder," Cook fumed that he had it on good authority that Rothermel's *The Battle of Gettysburg* would have the place of honor in the art building, and he strenuously objected not only to this, but also to it being exhibited at all. He believed that a viewer could choose to pass over Rothermel's other five paintings in the exhibition, but because the huge picture was to be centrally placed, it could not be ignored. The painting entirely covered one end of the American gallery in Memorial Hall. Cook, who disliked Rothermel's art in general, particularly lambasted the painting's subject: "For the picture is not a picture of heroism. It is a picture of blood and fury, of men—of brother—men, of fellow citizens—murdering one another in the heat of hate; of soldiers, brave men of South and North, in the spasms of mortal agony; of dead men with blue faces and swollen hands—horrors piled on horrors for a central show-piece at the Centennial feast of peace and good-will!"[80]

In a similar vein, critic Susan Carter objected to the character of the picture: "a work of art can never afford to be repulsive or disgusting. Rothermel seems in this painting to have taken almost fiendish delight in bringing forward, almost to the feet of the spectator, multitudes of the bodies, bloody and wounded, of dead men; and when the eye, sickened with the confusion and turmoil of the fight in the distance, drops upon the near images, it is caught and horrified by the sight of so much death, which would not be appalling if it were not painted so weakly. It is the life and not the death of battle with which art can legitimately concern itself."[81] Author Joacquin Miller charged that Rothermel "went so far out of his way for horrors as to paint an utterly impossible scene, only for the sake of blood and butchery."[82]

These criticisms reproaching the picture's grotesque display of blood are intriguing because it in fact shows remarkably little blood, especially considering its subject. Rothermel, known as "the American colorist" and famous for his vivid colors, especially an orange red, elected to tone down his palette for *The Battle of Gettysburg*.[83] It is one of his least colorful paintings, though one writer argued that only a colorist of genius could render such a wonderful harmony of tints.[84] Rothermel likely muted his palette for two reasons. First, it enabled him to concentrate on the articulation of the figures and their actions. Large amounts of intense color, especially in a canvas so vast, would have visually competed, if not overpowered, the narrative. Second, he did not need intense, expressive colors for a subject so tremendously emotion-laden for contemporaries. Critics who decried the depiction's bloodiness spoke more from their associating glowing colors with Rothermel's art and their knowledge of the battle's carnage than from what they could actually see in the painting. The perception of blood obscured the critics' vision. Where in 1870, the picture had received praise for its "correctness and fidelity," its vividly inspiring recording of a "national struggle," its offering a positive lesson on the horrors of war, and its artistic treatment, by 1876 it was vilified as too sensational.[85]

This change in attitude exemplifies the context-bound nature of interpretation. Even without specifically chronicling the many historical changes that occurred between 1870 and 1876, common sense realizes that a context just five years after war's end differed from one not only eleven years after the event, but also conditioned by a Centennial celebration that emphasized mutual prosperity and sectional harmony. Works of art do read differently at different times. I have found this to be true in my own reading of *The Battle of Gettysburg*. In 1988, I evaluated it negatively, describing it as exemplifying "herculean reportage" and failing "to convey effectively any quality of high-minded purpose or value."[86] Since then, as I have more closely examined the composition and investigated its subject—deepened my context of understanding as it were—I have come to hold it in higher regard and appreciate its heroic ambitions.

Along with exemplifying how interpretations fluctuate, the shift in the reception of *The Battle of Gettysburg* raises the still vexing issue of appropriateness in exhibiting historical imagery. Both Carter and Cook argued that the big painting would "sow ill-will, add discord, and reopen wounds once closed" and "be an unsuitable reminder, at this Centennial time of discords that are past and troubles which will be scarcely renewed."[87] Another critic, John Sears, was troubled over Civil War images "stirring up unhappy memories."[88] The argument over appropriateness and potential fractiousness was also made, comically, in a popular book on the Centennial (see Fig. 9.9). Here the painting triggers the wrangling of "two one-legged relics of the late war"—hardly Harrison's "sturdy athletes."[89] Each points out evidence in the canvas to support his position, and their agitation, the author humorously

BEFORE THE GREAT PICTURE OF THE BATTLE OF GETTYSBURG.—FIGHTING THE BATTLE OVER AGAIN.

Fig. 9.9 "Before the great picture of the Battle of Gettysburg. Fighting the battle over again," from *Going to the Centennial* (New York: Collin and Small, 1876), p. 32.

claims, "shows that the painting has some merit." Acknowledging that Rothermel's painting "has created the greatest amount of controversy," the writer assesses that "to my thinking it is terrible enough to prevent any nation from going to war."[90] Although the image and text assume a tongue-in-cheek character, they do reinforce the worries of Cook, Carter, and Sears.

Aware of concerns over the suitability of Civil War subjects, the organizers of the Centennial Art Exhibition adopted a policy prohibiting such scenes.[91] John Sartain, chief of the Art Bureau, recognized that the Centennial's director general, A. T. Goshorn, had "a decided objection to all that class of pictures that were calculated to awaken ill feeling in our Southern visitors, such as the Battle of Gettysburg."[92] How then did Rothermel's immense and ferocious battle scene not only get into the exhibition, but also come to occupy the main focus of the American art gallery? The answer undoubtedly revolves around Sartain, a longtime friend of Rothermel who had contracted with the artist to produce a large engraving of the painting.

Sartain likely decided to feature Rothermel's picture in order to generate sales for his print, a motive suggested by Clarence Cook.[93] However, when Sartain realized that he could not complete the engraving by the Centennial's opening, he probably saw the painting's inclusion as a way to appease a disappointed and angry Rothermel and to whet the public's appetite for a future print. In any case, the prospect of an engraving played a role in the painting's Centennial appearance.

The picture's inclusion surely related also to Rothermel serving as a member of Sartain's advisory board. Partly because of the responsibility he saw attached to this position, John Sears scolded the artist for allowing *The Battle of Gettysburg* to be hung in the exhibition. He even scripted what Rothermel should have said: "Under any circumstances I should regret wounding the sensibilities of my compatriots; being a member of the Art Bureau, it becomes impossible that I should incur the risk of doing so."[94] Sears rebuked both Rothermel for failing to say anything like this and his fellow Art Bureau members for supporting the inclusion of the work.

The painting did have some defenders. A writer for the *Independent* took issue with Clarence Cook: "We do not see wherein the insult to them [Southern brethren] lies. If they can bear up under the infliction which our Union soldiers put upon them at Gettysburgh [*sic*], they will not be such imbeciles as to feel any annoyance at Mr. Rothermel's 'bloody daub.' If nations are to be prohibited from the preservation of painted representations of their conquest in war, lest they give offence to their vanquished foes, one of the most efficient means of encouraging art will be destroyed."[95] The writer then asserted that no work of art in the gallery had a better claim to be there than *The Battle of Gettysburg*, since the artist was a Pennsylvanian and the most distinguished artist in Philadelphia, the work was commissioned by the Commonwealth, the battle was the greatest of the Civil War, it took place in Pennsylvania, and the victorious general was a native son.[96] Another author found Cook "to be the only person" who saw the picture as brutalizing Southerners and deemed the picture "a powerful treatment of a very difficult subject, and the best art judges have long ago decided in its favor."[97] Its "Veronese-study of grays" received praise from one critic.[98] Most people admired the picture, for although it was "sharply criticized," it "found favor with the masses that daily thronged around it."[99] Voicing sentiments probably shared by many, William Dean Howells sensibly wrote: "To be sure Mr. Rothermel does not spare a huge slaughter of Rebels in his Battle of Gettysburg, but I heard it said that this picture was not a work of art. I do not know about such things myself. I had a horrific interest in the spectacle, almost as large as the canvas, which covers the whole end of one room; and I thought the rebels were fighting hard, and, if they were dying, were dying bravely."[100]

Following the Centennial, commentary about *The Battle of Gettysburg* quieted down. The painting engaged writers again only at Rothermel's death in 1895. No obituary was complete without mentioning the canvas as his most famous work. Calling it his greatest achievement, the *Weekly Reading Eagle* hyperbolized: "The picture touched the popular chord and aroused an interest, such as no American production had done before or since."[101] Another account claimed that "critics have pronounced it the greatest battle piece of the nineteenth century."[102] In these accounts, as in earlier ones, the pendants received scant notice. The immensity of *The Battle of Gettysburg* and its being the focus of the commission understandably overshadowed the companion paintings. Yet, as part of the state's commission, the other works warrant attention.

Rothermel's four pendants were executed 1871–72 and take nearly identical dimensions (about 36 x 67 inches). All display a greater sketchiness in the delineation of figures and other compositional forms than seen in the big canvas. They are also more loosely painted than a smaller, earlier work, *Sharpshooters at Round Top* (1867, Pennsylvania State Museum), which was not part of the commissioned series.[103] More than the large painting, the pendants exhibit the coloristic effects so closely associated with Rothermel's art. The four companion paintings portray battles leading to the culminating engagement on July 3 and highlight the heroics of Pennsylvanians. The artist produced small, sequentially numbered delineations of the compositions, with accompanying keys identifying figures and topography.[104]

The work labeled first of the pendants is *The Death of General Reynolds*. In the central foreground of the composition soldiers carry off their leader, who was shot during the first day of the three-day conflict. John Reynolds, a Pennsylvanian, was regarded as the beau ideal of the Union officer and as perhaps the best general in the army. His death was a great tragedy.[105] Although Rothermel features Reynolds in the lower center of the composition, he represents this tragic incident rather prosaically and emphasizes instead the immensity and confusion of the battlefield. As with figures in the large picture, the representation of Reynolds being carried off the field suggests Rothermel's familiarity with both high and popular art, for example, Nicolas Poussin's *The Burial of Phocion* (1648, Louvre) and an illustration of the Army of the Cumberland in *Harper's Weekly* (December 19, 1863). With small-scale soldiers, horses, and batteries rushing around in all directions at once, *The*

Death of Reynolds lacks, however, the focus and grandness of the large canvas. But this arguably makes the pendant a more believably realistic view of war. J. William Hofmann, who had led the 56th Pennsylvania on this opening day of the battle at Gettysburg, praised Rothermel's composition: "Your efforts to reproduce on canvas the operation on this part of the field have been, in my opinion, eminently successful. I believe that the survivors will all concur in this opinion."[106] Here, as in the other companion paintings, Rothermel attended more to the landscape than he had in the larger picture, resulting in some fine passages of nature.

Rothermel designated *Repulse of the Louisiana Tigers* the second of the pendants, even though it shows an engagement that occurred after that depicted in the third companion painting. The viewer is placed close behind the 5th Maine Battery firing upon the Confederate assault of Cemetery Hill at dusk on July 2. A recently discovered oil study for this painting demonstrates again the process of change that occurred as Rothermel worked on a particular subject. The study, belonging to Gettysburg College, closely approximates the final composition.[107] Some differences are apparent, however. The study includes a mounted officer at the lower left and the gatehouse to Evergreen Cemetery is clearly visible at the top of the hill. Also, the study conveys a greater sense of the Confederates swarming over the hill. The finished painting, of a larger size, shifts the line of cannons slightly, features more smoke, and includes Colonel Samuel S. Carroll's brigade charging in double quick from the left.

The third pendant is *The Charge of the Pennsylvania Reserves at Plum Run.* Unlike in the other paintings, Rothermel sets the viewer behind Confederate lines. The extended line of Brigadier General Samuel W. Crawford's troops charge from below Little and Big Round Top toward the Rebel forces stationed behind rocks. Crawford, who told Rothermel that he was very pleased by the reception of the large picture, provided the artist with battle information.[108] Apparently a question arose concerning Crawford's participation in the charge at Plum Run and "certain of Genl Crawford's subordinate officers are making an effort to exclude him from Mr. Rothermel's representation."[109] Rothermel had written to various individuals, as he did throughout the commission, soliciting information and asking questions. One question he asked about this particular engagement was: "Did you see Genl. Crawford take the colors from Corpl. Swope and carry them across Plum run in the front of the 1st regt to or near the stonewall occupied by the rebs?"[110] The painting shows Crawford bearing the Union flag, which surely pleased the general. He inquired if the artist had made a study and, if so, he would like the privilege of purchasing it.[111] The general appears more prominently, still holding the flag, in Rothermel's second version of the subject. In 1880 the artist proposed the same subject for the adjutant general's office in Harrisburg.[112] Larger (47 x 70 inches) than the pendant, the work renders the battle from the Federal side. A wonderfully animated sketch of the composition is found in the Peter F. Rothermel Papers (see Fig. 9.10).

The fourth pendant, *Repulse of General Johnson's Division by General Geary's White Star Division*, captures action on the morning of July 3 on Culp's Hill. The incident allowed Rothermel to move from depicting the open landscape, characteristic of the other pendants, to representing a tight space enclosed by tall trees. Strikingly painted, the trees display to the fullest Rothermel's ability to render nature. The composition includes the anecdotal incident of a dog belonging to the 1st Maryland scampering ahead of the charging Rebels. Union General Thomas L. Kane informed the artist that the dog licked someone's hand "after being perfectly riddled. Regarding him as the only Christian minded being on either side, I ordered him to be honorably buried."[113] Barely visible at the far right stands General Geary who at the time Rothermel painted this work served as governor of Pennsylvania.

The companion paintings to *The Battle of Gettysburg* afforded the artist an opportunity to represent the multifaceted and temporal nature of the three-day battle. Still, these pictures clearly played a secondary role in the commission, being overwhelmed by the grand scale and focused intensity of the huge canvas. It was the larger picture that generated interest in the commission and came to embody the Commonwealth's patronage. It was, also, the scene of Pickett's charge, not any of the others, that was printed as an engraving.

Rothermel copyrighted his battle painting in 1872, probably with the idea of having it engraved.[114] Two years later, he approached his friend, the eminent engraver John Sartain about producing an engraving and, in 1875, the men agreed to a contract. The engraver was to work from a four-piece photographic image of the big canvas. As indicated, Rothermel intended the engraving to be ready for purchase at the Centennial Exposition the following year. Sartain expressed some concerns about meeting the deadline, but he regarded the project as a "first rate opportunity," not to be passed up.[115] Rothermel likewise worried about Sartain meeting the deadline and urged him to refuse the contract if he was not confident of completing the work on time. The painter's misgivings escalated when Sartain was named chief of the Art Bureau of the Centennial. Rothermel wrote Sartain complimenting him

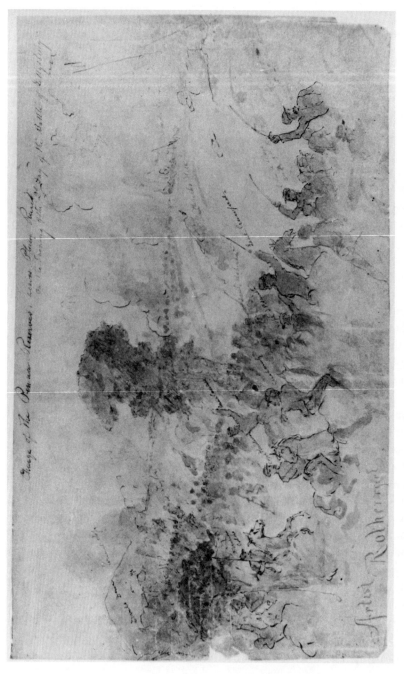

Fig. 9.10 Study for *Charge of the Pennsylvania Reserves at Plum Run*, 1880–81, pen, ink, and wash on paper. Peter F. Rothermel Papers, Pennsylvania State Archives, Harrisburg.

on his appointment but also relaying his fears that the plate would not be ready on time. Sartain assured him it would.[116] Sartain's Centennial involvement, however, did indeed preclude finishing the work on schedule, much to the bitter disappointment of Rothermel: "The hankering after prominence proved too much for his honesty . . . his word of honor worthless," Rothermel acrimoniously asserted.[117] The contract was eventually renegotiated, and the large engraving (24 7/8 x 38 1/4 inches) was delivered in 1879.

The following year Rothermel was approached by John M. Jewell of the War Department's Engineer Bureau about including *The Battle of Gettysburg* in his "Stereo Panopticon" exhibition of the war. Jewell explained that a photograph of the engraving would be turned into a transparency on glass. This would be projected on an eighteen-foot-square canvas by means of a stereo panopticon illuminated by oxyhydrogen or calcium light. Rothermel's composition would be the sole illustration of Gettysburg in this Civil War display and would always be identified as "From Rothermel's great painting of that Battle, painted for the State of Pennsylvania by order of the Legislature of that State." Rothermel accepted the proposal but emphasized that he did so only under the condition that no stereoscopic views, photographs, engravings, or other reproductions of the work would be made. No record of an exhibition featuring Jewell's intriguing "entertaining" illustrations can be found.[118]

With the completion of the second version of *The Charge of the Pennsylvania Reserves at Plum Run* in 1881, Rothermel's Gettysburg subjects came to an end. For fifteen years, Peter F. Rothermel had concerned himself with representing the battle at Gettysburg. The focus of this involvement was the commission and execution of the colossal *The Battle of Gettysburg*. This major commission afforded the painter the opportunity to direct his considerable talents in picturing history to the rendering of the present. Although differing from his other history paintings in chronicling the contemporary, *The Battle of Gettysburg* exemplifies in grand fashion the artist's proclivity for creating highly charged, theatrically dramatic scenes centering on episodes of intense confrontation. *The Battle of Gettysburg* represents the artist's historical interpretation and painterly expression of what happened on that celebrated battlefield. Rothermel translated a momentous event in the history of the United States into a dynamic visual image that was, and is, simultaneously didactic, inspiring, and artistically striking.

THE BROTHERS' WAR

Gettysburg the Movie and American Memory

William Blair

Today, the battlefield is peaceful. Cornfields and apple orchards surround the town of Gettysburg, creating a pleasant scene that belies the grim harvest of 1863. On these selfsame pastoral fields in south-central Pennsylvania, men expended great energy trying to kill each other. And they succeeded awfully well. Generations have read the accounts of the corpses piled around the fields, viewed the photographs of dead snipers in Devil's Den, marveled at the estimates that the wagon train of Confederate wounded stretched for seventeen miles, and recalled the butcher's bill of more than 50,000 total casualties. Yet despite this grisly history, the battlefield that places Pennsylvania on the Civil War map wears a benign face in American memory, as familiar and comfortable as today's rural landscape that covers the scars beneath. One of the war's biggest bloodbaths ironically has become a symbol of reunion—a means of diminishing sectional discord through heroic images of valiant Americans paying the ultimate sacrifice so that this nation might live.

One need look no further for the meaning that Gettysburg holds in our national memory than the movie of the same name. Produced by Ted Turner, *Gettysburg* opened to acclaim in theaters during fall 1993. Directors consulted, and used, a host of Civil War reenactors to represent the period and tactics as faithfully as possible. The filmmakers also closely followed Michael Shaara's Pulitzer prize-winning novel on which the action was based, *Killer Angels.* For all of the painstaking efforts to ensure accuracy to both the period and the book, the movie reveals arguably as much about the present as the past—perhaps more. It highlights an interpretation of the conflict that I call the "brothers' war," an idealized memory of the war that celebrates the heroic attributes of all the soldiers. It also reaffirms the mythology of the battle of Gettysburg as *the* turning point in the war, the battle that saved the Union and lost the war for the Confederacy.

Although "brothers' war" can serve simply as the shorthand for a civil war—that people from the same national family fought each other—the term carries additional baggage in popular thought. "Brothers' war" conveys the meaning that the Civil War occurred between two very similar people. They were siblings caught in a tragic family quarrel that, once resolved, could be smoothed over with a handshake. Brothers may fight hard, but they can make up easily because they come from the same family and have few fundamental differences. Both would accept the verdict of armed contest. An interpretation of the conflict based on the "brothers' war" minimizes the problems of reunification by playing down the sources of friction, especially racial strife, hatred of each other, or serious differences of any kind between the sections. Instead, enemies confront each other only because they have to, out of a sense of duty rather than true acrimony. While the war resulted in the destruction of slavery, Southerners in this interpretation do not fight for preservation of the institution but for state rights. Although historian Eric Foner did not use the term "brothers' war," he came close to capturing my meaning for the term when he observed that Ken Burns's PBS series on the Civil War portrayed "a family quarrel among whites, whose fundamental accomplishment was the preservation of the Union and in which the destruction of slavery was a side issue and African Americans little more than a problem confronting white society."[1]

The movie *Gettysburg* depicts the Civil War squarely within this framework, making it easy to revere the conflict while overlooking less tidy complexities. The reasons for fighting, the sentimental attachment between the two armies, the heroism of the soldiers, and the treatment of the battle as the victory that saved the Union all strike deep mythological chords within the American soul. Categorizing these elements as myth does not mean that they had no validity or basis in actual events. Men at times fought heroically. Friendships between opposing generals sometimes existed. Some Southerners fought for reasons other than to protect slavery. The mythology, however, overlooks how men often killed each other without a shadow of remorse. It also mutes the conflicts within each region, especially dissent over war aims or whether governments treated rich and poor alike when it came to military service.

Finally, seeing the war as a brothers' war limits the role of slavery in Southern life, as well as the widespread prejudice among nineteenth-century Northerners against black people.

This becomes evident in four areas of the film: the reasons that soldiers fight, the common sympathy between enemies, the reinforcement of Gettysburg as the ultimate turning point of the conflict, and the romantic portrayal of combat. It should be noted, though, that a critical look at the movie *Gettysburg* says less about the filmmakers' limitations than about the way in which significant portions of Americans choose to remember the war as the forge of a particular kind of nationhood, minus complications between the races or dissent among white people

The film's portrayal of why soldiers fought contains considerable irony. In *Gettysburg* Northern soldiers battle to end the institution of slavery, which the Southern characters claim they are not fighting to protect. (No one asks why the South does not just give up the institution that seems so peripheral to them.) The Northern characters thus fight for freedom while Southerners battle either to protect states' rights or to have the Yankees leave them alone.

The Union side of the story is told within the first fifteen minutes of the film as Colonel Joshua Chamberlain of the 20th Maine reasons with men from another Maine regiment who want out of the conflict altogether and have been held under guard for mutiny. The soldiers have demonstrated bravery in battle but believe they have been mistreated. To get them to join with his regiment, Chamberlain reminds the men why they enlisted in the first place: some out of boredom and others because it seemed the right thing to do at the time. He then warms to the task, telling the men that this is a different kind of army. Men are not fighting for land, power, or money. "We are an army out to set men free," he states, adding that by doing so it will prove that Americans have to bow to no one. "We all have value." It is a moving speech that scores heavily with the men. All but a few pick up their muskets.

Later in the movie the character of Sergeant Kilrain offers the reasons for fighting from the common man's perspective, which prove to be more populist in nature. An Irishman who speaks in brogue, the practical Kilrain serves as a foil to Chamberlain who is from the upper crust and an idealist. Kilrain has gone to war to prove that a democratic society can function. He also hopes to break the back of the Southern aristocracy. The common soldier explains that he fights for the right to prove that he is a better man than planters. He damns gentlemen of all kinds, whether European or Southern. "I'll be treated as I deserve," he tells Chamberlain, adding, "not as my father deserved." For that reason—and not because he is convinced about the innate equality of black and white people—he supports freeing the slaves.

To the movie's credit, the sentiment among Northerners about black people is somewhat ambiguous although still not totally consistent with nineteenth-century American attitudes. Chamberlain represents the quintessential abolitionist who sees no differences between the races. He remains credible because of his reaction to a wounded runaway slave found by Kilrain in the bushes near camp. Despite his feelings about equality, Chamberlain displays some queasiness about this person. He has not seen many black people in his life. The runaway raises considerable curiosity within the colonel who seems a little shocked at his rough speech and demeanor. (The book, by the way, gets this across much better than the movie.) But Chamberlain makes it clear that he remains firmly committed to equality. Kilrain is less supportive of black people. He does not believe that the races are equal, but neither does he support oppression or the right of some men to lord themselves over others no matter the race or country. Populism informs his white supremacy.

Although it is laudable that the Northern characters are not simplistic in their racial beliefs, the movie avoids the outright racism that made emancipation a difficult issue. It took eighteen months before the progress of the war pushed President Lincoln to a stand that contained enormous political risks. Emancipation created controversy within the army and the home front. The Union states of Kentucky, Maryland, and Missouri still clung to the peculiar institution. The Democratic Party gained momentum as an opposition party to Lincoln and the Republicans because of the Emancipation Proclamation. In New York City just a couple of weeks after the battle of Gettysburg, disenchanted people from the working class—many of them Irish like Kilrain—conducted a five-day orgy of violence in protest of the draft. Black people formed a primary target for the protesters. Several Midwestern states still barred free black people from emigrating and Pennsylvania, in 1863, experienced a movement in the legislature, albeit an unsuccessful one, to create a similar ban. African Americans in Philadelphia protested to end segregation on streetcars and in other public accommodations. The movie lacks this less sanguine view of the North. It also does not reveal that many Union soldiers did not at first believe in a war to destroy slavery but converted to emancipation less for black rights than as a means of eliminating the source of power for planters, of bringing the war to a close, or of punishing the South.[2]

The Southern side of this story comes in two scenes in particular. In one, Confederate officers confer around a campfire after the opening day of battle. Represented are Lieutenant General James Longstreet and the principal officers under his command. James Kemper, a general in the army who became a governor of Virginia after the war, vigorously denies that slavery forms a basis for the Southern cause. According to Kemper, the South fights for freedom from power. It resisted encroachment by Northern politicians in its affairs. "Virginia, by God, Sir, is going to be run by Virginians," Kemper thunders, adding that the state will not be dictated to by money-grubbing Yankees. Thick-headed Northerners just do not get the message. They seem to Kemper far too obsessed with "the darkies." A similar message echoes from the ranks as the brother of Joshua Chamberlain talks with a Confederate prisoner about the reasons for fighting. Tom Chamberlain indicates that the Union army hopes to free slaves and preserve the Union. The Confederate private, meanwhile, claims to be fighting for his rights, not for "darkies." The soldier adds, "Let us live the way we do."

Both scenes distance Southerners from slavery; in fact, nowhere in the film does a Southerner admit to fighting for the peculiar institution or even concede that slavery forms more than an unfortunate circumstance in their lives. "Let us live the way we do" perpetuates the belief that the war was not about slavery because most Southerners did not own slaves. It does not indicate that roughly one-third of all Southerners lived in households that used slave labor and that most white people had become committed to the institution for a variety of reasons. They may have aspired to become a planter or hired slaves during crucial times when labor was needed on the farm.

This does not mean that every Confederate soldier should be shown as a die-hard, proslavery ideologue. That, too, would be inaccurate. Defense of homeland provided cause enough for many a Confederate soldier to train his musket on a Northerner. Historian James McPherson has conducted the most recent study of soldier motivations, finding that most Southerners did not even mention slavery in letters home. But he does not see this as indicating that little support existed for slavery among common folk, many of whom would have favored the system out of racial views that elevated all white people. McPherson, instead, argues that the peculiar institution was part of the way of life that Southerners tacitly accepted. Few references to it appeared in letters because it needed no justification from any internal controversy. Most people, as other historians have noted, tend to accept the world into which they are born.[3]

Michael Shaara must have believed that the reference to rights included the right to take slaves into the western territories. Shaara's version of the meeting between Tom Chamberlain and the Confederate prisoner in *Killer Angels*, which he authored, differs significantly from the movie. In the book, readers do not actually experience the incident, but learn of it when Tom Chamberlain runs up to his brother chuckling over the ignorance of the farmer he has just encountered. After hearing the Confederate soldier proclaim that he fought for rights, the Union officer adds, "Then after that I asked this fella what rights he had that we were offendin', and he said, well, he didn't know, but he must have some rights he didn't know nothin' about. Now, aint that something?"[4] In the eyes of Shaara, Tom Chamberlain understood that the right to own slaves formed at least one part of Southern concerns—a possibility the movie avoids.

In spite of the use of the term "Yankees," the enemies who oppose each other in Gettysburg do so with little rancor. Instead, they share a tragic awareness of their common bonds, either from prior relationships or through the experience of combat. From the officer corps through the enlisted men runs a healthy respect for the enemy. The officers in particular understand that devotion to state or family caused the unfortunate circumstance in which former friends have become foes. No one has made the decision to support either side very happily. We are left to admire the sense of duty that it took to enter the conflict and perform the job of reluctant killers for respective nations.

The friendship between Confederate Lewis Armistead and Union Winfield Scott Hancock provides the quintessential expression of this sentiment. Both men had been friends in the old army, serving in Mexico and other posts on the western frontier. Armistead was a Virginian; Hancock hailed from Pennsylvania. When the war opened, they chose opposite sides, although Armistead and other men who became Confederates—such as George Pickett and Richard B. Garnett—all had sought Hancock's advice. He supported the Union firmly but the Southerners felt compelled to support their states. All were aware of the special poignancy surrounding the party on the night of their farewell from assignment in California. Mrs. Hancock described Armistead as the most dejected of all. He apparently placed hands on Hancock's shoulders and said: "Hancock, good-bye; you can never know what this has cost me, and I hope God will strike me dead if I am ever induced to leave my native soil, should worse come to worst."[5]

Fate ensured that the worst came. The armies that arrived at Gettysburg contained Armistead and Hancock. They never quite met, but Armistead on the third day of the battle led a portion of the assault that became known as Pickett's charge, which attempted to puncture the position held by Hancock's command. Armistead led his men on foot with a black hat held on sword point. The story has become a central part of Gettysburg lore, with millions of visitors to the battlefield becoming acquainted with it through the circular painting of Pickett's charge in the Cyclorama. Both men were wounded in this final assault; Armistead died while Hancock lived not only to see the end of the war but to run unsuccessfully as president. The dying Confederate general sent to his former friend a watch and other valuables. For years, Northern journals perpetuated an apocryphal story that Armistead had repudiated the cause for which he fought while on his deathbed. Even in the late nineteenth century, the friendship between the two men provided a means for healing the country's wounds and affirming the primacy of the nation.[6]

In *Gettysburg*, Richard Jordan plays the role of Armistead to the maudlin hilt, captured best in a scene in Longstreet's tent on the night before the final day of the engagement. Plagued by the possibility that he might face his former friend, Armistead asks his superior officer if he could avoid the conflict by relinquishing his command. Recalling the night in California when the friends last parted, Armistead tells Longstreet that he promised his friend: "If I ever raise my hand against you, God strike me dead." Teary-eyed, he gulps for breath. Longstreet of course cannot grant his subordinate's request to be relieved. On the morrow the two friends will fight, perhaps against each other. Hancock has been going through his own torture about the possibility of meeting his friend. At Federal headquarters on the night after the first day of battle he learns that Armistead, known to his friends as Lo, is with the enemy. Hancock wonders how his friend is doing and confesses to being unsettled because Lo is just over the ridge. On the final day of battle, Hancock asks if there is a story about friends who find themselves on opposing ends of the battlefield. Although Longstreet will not relieve Armistead from command, it is not because the general cannot understand his subordinate's view of the enemy. At one point when Longstreet confers with Lee, the former remembers service in the Mexican War with many of the generals on the opposing side. "Those men in blue never seem to be an enemy," he tells Lee.

The scene with brother Tom and a Southern captive indicates that men in the ranks could form these bonds even if they had not known each other before the war. They could find common ground through suffering similar experiences as soldiers. Just after proclaiming that he fought only to protect his rights, the Confederate private suggests the common tragedy that both sides have experienced. He proclaims that a lot of men have been lost so far. Some wore blue and some wore gray. "I seen enough of this war," he tells Tom Chamberlain, echoing sentiments of a soldier from the 2nd Maine who wanted out of the conflict. The conversation ends with the prisoner mouthing, "See you in hell, Yank." But this statement contains no acrimony. Instead, it conveys the sense that the two men may share the same ultimate fate.

Throughout the movie the only hint of bitterness between the two armies comes at the end of Pickett's charge. As the surviving Confederate soldiers pick their way through a grisly field to return to their lines some Union soldiers stand up and chant, "Fredericksburg, Fredericksburg." The reference is to a series of assaults made by the Army of the Potomac against a well-entrenched enemy on December 13, 1862. Union soldiers sustained roughly 13,000 casualties in the debacle, for which it took the Union army approximately seven months to win vengeance.

Yet even this harassment by Union soldiers is mild and lacks the range of emotions that characterized wartime relations. Like all mythologies there is some truth to the portrayal. Scholarly works on soldiers often have stressed the similarities between the two sides and how soldiers conducted informal trade in tobacco, food, and other goods when officers looked the other way. But this was not the whole story. This comfortable portrait hides the times in which soldiers relished shooting an opponent or, at the least, coldly went about their business.

A number of examples contrast with the images of Gettysburg. The first concerns the battlefield. E. Porter Alexander, a top artillerist in the Army of Northern Virginia, offered an anecdote about the battle of Fredericksburg during which he had witnessed Union soldiers cut to pieces by a side shot from an artillery piece. Alexander indicated that this was the bloodiest round that he had ever witnessed, killing or wounding as many as twenty men. Writing a number of decades after the war—when presumably the passions of the conflict had cooled—he still remembered: "The sight of the shot excited me so that I felt bound to have some share," indicating that he then sent forty more rounds down on the position. Alexander also remembered a time at Petersburg in 1864 when he spotted a Union soldier walking about 800 yards away. "Lend me a gun & let me try him," Alexander had yelled to nearby soldiers and then fired a round. "The man fell & the men around me, looking over [the] parapet gave a little hurrah at the shot."[7] Again, there is no sense of regret or a second thought even though this was written years after the event.

Alexander can be forgiven for having done only what hundreds of thousands of men did and, in fact, were encouraged to do. It was his duty to kill, especially on the field of battle. But the war also featured atrocities that reveal the ugly side of human nature and a less comfortable glimpse of our own past. Guerrilla warfare existed. Reprisal hangings occurred under the command of Philip Sheridan in the Shenandoah Valley in 1864 over this kind of warfare. Civilians could be caught in the cross fire. In western North Carolina near the Tennessee border, thirteen prisoners herded together as suspected bushwhackers were summarily executed by members of a Confederate militia unit. The victims ranged from age thirteen to fifty-nine. The community of Shelton Laurel in the Appalachians remembers this still.[8] In eastern North Carolina at Kinston in 1864, George Pickett presided over the executions of twenty-two suspected Unionists. Not only were the prisoners treated without compassion, but officials also showed little respect for the corpses, tossing unclaimed bodies into a mass grave at the foot of the gallows and allegedly using some for "experimenting surgery." The incident almost led to Pickett's being tried for war crimes after the conflict.[9]

Finally, the war and its aftermath created animosity that prevented a true reunion of the heart for at least a decade after the war and, arguably, not until the Spanish-American War in 1898. One of the best testimonies to this is a song first published in New Orleans in 1867. "I'm a Good Old Rebel" contains the diatribe of a recalcitrant Confederate who makes no bones about the hatred that he still harbored against the Yankee nation. The narrator only wishes he could have killed more of the enemy. One stanza in particular expresses this desire:

> Three hundred thousand Yankees
> Is stiff in Southern dust;
> We got three hundred thousand
> Before they conquered us;
> They died of Southern fever
> And Southern steel and shot,
> I wish they was three million
> Instead of what we got.[10]

The common respect exemplified in the film did exist among some people. A number of soldiers played by the rules, confining their killing to combat. But the unseemly side of war is missing in the movie, which represents the more heroic images that allow Americans to remember the conflict in a way that accentuates reunion and respect for both sides.

Even the most casual student of the war approaches Gettysburg with some awe. Among its attractions is its status as the high-water mark of the Confederacy—the battle that turned back the Southern tide and ensured victory for the Union. No less than a Nobel Prize winner in literature has judged it so. William Faulkner's novel *Intruder in the Dust* alleges that for every Southern boy there comes a time when it is just before one o'clock on July 3, the cannonade has not yet begun, and once it does life will never be the same.[11] That sense of a missed opportunity for the Confederacy has dominated perceptions about the battle of Gettysburg. On these three days of accidental combat, so the mythology goes, turned the life of the nation as we know it.

The movie perpetuates this belief, beginning with Robert E. Lee. He considers Gettysburg the decisive conflict that might end the war. As the general rocks in a chair reflecting on the action on the first day, a voice-over says, "Tomorrow or the next day will determine the war." Emerging from their consultation with the general, Major General John Bell Hood tells Longstreet that if Lee has set the right battle plan in place, "then the war's over by sundown." It thus frustrates Lee to no end that the second day of fighting results in a close call but without the dramatic victory he had wanted. "I could see a clear road all the way to Washington," he says. Other officers share this sentiment. Major General Richard Garnett, who will lose his life in Pickett's charge, says before the tragic march, "Maybe we'll win today and today will be the last day. Maybe today." Longstreet falls into line with the rest when he says, "I do believe this attack will decide the fate of our country." The Confederate command stakes a great deal on the contest, especially the final doomed assault against the Federal center.

For the Union, the battle is no less important. To motivate the members of the 2nd Maine to fight, Joshua Chamberlain reminds them of the importance of defeating Lee in the North. After going through the passionate speech that lists the reasons why Northerners have volunteered to fight, the colonel pulls out his final trump card to convince the men to pick up arms instead of facing courts-martial: "I do believe this attack will decide the fate of our country," he intones. The meaning is clear. Lose this battle and the

Union loses the war. Fortunately for the colonel, most of the men heed the warning.

In 1863 the public viewed the battle more ambivalently than we do today. Northerners, of course, were ecstatic with the repulse of the Army of Northern Virginia from Pennsylvania. But they were equally happy with the fall of Vicksburg. Coupled with the capture of Port Hudson, the western campaign had opened the Mississippi to the Union, split the Confederacy in two, and turned 30,000 Southerners into prisoners of war. These were achievements that no one could dispute. No matter how welcome, the defeat of Lee was not as complete. It had been an important battle for turning back the Confederate offensive, but it lacked the decisiveness of Vicksburg. Both armies returned to positions in Virginia that they had held the previous winter. Lincoln was frustrated—unrealistically so—that Major General George G. Meade who commanded the Army of the Potomac had not dealt a fatal blow by cutting the retreating army to pieces. No one at the time could know if the North, and not the South, had missed the greater opportunity. As war ground on through 1864, Northern morale would sag once more as the conflict consumed more men with final victory seemingly proving elusive.[12]

Meanwhile, the battle confused then disheartened the Southern public. People understood that tremendous losses had occurred but many believed at first that Lee had won a victory. Rains swelled the Potomac. For eight days Lee's army could not cross. Nor could communications go to the newspapers in Richmond. As word came of the retreat, hearts fell. But like their counterparts in the North, Confederates did not greet the news of Gettysburg in isolation. They were well aware of Vicksburg, too. Southern fortunes had turned, and people realized it at the time. But even then, the citizenry steeled itself for the longer conflict. In a letter to Jefferson Davis that August, Lee proclaimed himself satisfied with the campaign. Despite the casualties, he had achieved his goals to relieve Virginia from the Union army and delay any offensive until the following spring. By that time, a number of factors actually would raise Southern hopes, including a temporary increase in provisions. And the war continued.[13]

Only later, when the true significance of the victory could be assessed, did the battle gain the prominence we assign it today. Lincoln helped the cause by dedicating the cemetery at the battlefield in a speech on November 19, 1863, that stands as one of the greatest in American history. The president's inspired oration has become evidence of a shift from thinking of the United States as a conglomeration of states to a single nation. But for a while after the Southern surrender, Gettysburg remained a divisive issue as men from both sections attempted to write their version of history. Beginning in the late 1870s, the Southern Historical Association consciously used the engagement as the decisive battle on which Confederate fortunes turned. In their accounts, the association's writers chose Longstreet as the scapegoat, placing on his shoulders the entire burden for defeat. But by the late nineteenth century, the battlefield had become a symbol of reunion and a place to honor the valor of the men who had fought there. Veterans from both sides returned to commemorate the war and help place monuments to regiments in the positions that the men had occupied at the time. One of the greater symbols of sectional reconciliation came on the fiftieth anniversary of the battle, which featured a reunion of Confederate and Union veterans at Gettysburg. By this time, participants remembered the war's greatest achievement as the consolidation of the nation and that soldiers on both sides fought equally nobly for their ideals.[14]

For a variety of reasons Gettysburg's status as the great divide of the war has come under reassessment—at least among historians. Antietam, for one, has joined the list of candidates as the most prominent battle of the war. Fought in 1862, that conflict between Lee and McClellan arguably resulted in the greatest consequences of the war for it gave Lincoln the victory he needed to issue the Emancipation Proclamation. Changing the war to one that proclaimed freedom for slaves helped keep Europe from recognizing the Confederacy and brought a fresh pool of soldiers—African Americans—into the Union army. Fall 1862 also was the last time that the Confederate nation mounted an offensive in the two major theaters of war, with profound consequences possible. Southerners still hoped that victories would bring Kentucky and Maryland into the Confederate fold. These areas also promised more than spiritual resources. Even if volunteers did not rush to the colors, the Southern army would benefit from access to more supplies.

More recently, scholars have come around to seeing the war's outcome as resulting from a series of events and not just one battle. Some cite as many as seven turning points, but recent work settles on four: summer 1862 when Confederates turned back the Union army on the Peninsula and began twin offensives; fall 1862 when Federal soldiers turned back the Southern advances; summer 1863 when Vicksburg fell and the South lost at Gettysburg; and summer 1864 when it appeared that Lincoln might not win re-election.[15] In this interpretation, Gettysburg still remains an important victory. It was the bloodiest engagement of the war, blunting Lee's march and bleeding the

Army of Northern Virginia so much that it could not mount an effective offensive again. Yet one cannot diminish the importance of Vicksburg in bringing about Southern defeat. Nor is it wise to ignore that the war lasted nearly two more years, with one of the darkest times for the Union occurring in July and August of 1864 as the offensives planned by Ulysses S. Grant either failed or turned into sieges at Atlanta and Petersburg. Lincoln believed then that he would lose the election. For a brief moment he toyed with the idea of trading emancipation as a bargaining chip for peace. Without the victories of Mobile Bay, Atlanta, and the Shenandoah Valley from August through October, the Confederacy may well have existed as an independent nation and Gettysburg would have survived as an epic struggle but without the reputation it now enjoys.

As Chamberlain and the 20th Maine fight for their lives on Little Round Top, the camera pans down the line, shooting head-on so that viewers peer into the rifle barrels from the perspective of the oncoming Confederates. Men do not fire until within camera view. Each soldier seems posed. The scene moves slowly, languidly, and without fury or frenzy within the combatants. Even the sound of firing is muted. The scene proceeds less like a moving picture than a series of paintings that collectors order from the advertisements in Civil War magazines. Much of the movie is shot in this style as *Gettysburg* provides romantic images with little of the horrors of war. Overall the cinematography paints lush pictures that sanitize combat.

Two scenes in particular borrow from paintings that represent twentieth-century depictions of the battle. When Union Major General John Reynolds dies on the first day of battle, the men gather around the body. The scene freezes for a moment with no one moving. Men are arranged nicely so that the eye flows to the body at the center. Some of the men hold hands over hearts. It would be easy to forget that a battle rages around them. Later in the movie a similar scene unfolds with Union Major General Hancock receiving the blessing of Irish troops before they head into battle. Once again, movement stops as the men align themselves as if posed by an artist. Uniforms remain clean; few of the men look as if they have slept on open ground or marched under a summer sun in wool uniforms they have worn for months.

Combat scenes are similarly pristine. The most shocking image comes as Confederate troops advancing during Pickett's charge face a point-blank shot from an artillery piece that belches a column of smoke, sending the men reeling backward. This may be the most memorable fighting scene of the movie. For the most part, though, we encounter wounds similar to those found in John Wayne movies in which heroes wear a bandage around the head or friends swab the shoulder of a comrade. No limbs are severed or heads crushed by cannonball. No one shrieks or becomes crazed in a blood lust. No one runs from the enemy or shows any fear. All perform their duty unflinchingly. When they fall, as Kilrain does, they have time to reassure friends that they die honorably and for a good cause. Even the hospitals are remarkably clean. As Longstreet visits the wounded John Bell Hood it is a peaceful place, orderly and without confusion of any kind.

Other movies have remembered a different side of war. Although it featured no combat and is guilty of perpetuating racist stereotypes of the Old South, *Gone with the Wind* presented war's horrible face more vividly than *Gettysburg* and without resorting to buckets of gore. In one shot famous in film history, the camera pulls back to reveal the yard full of wounded men writhing and moaning in the hot Atlanta sun. The makeshift hospital inside also contrasts markedly from the one in *Gettysburg*. Viewers gag along with Scarlett O'Hara as she witnesses a doctor amputate a leg. We never see the operation but feel it through her reaction. Later in the same movie the Confederate soldiers who retreat from Atlanta appear bedraggled and worn, in far worse shape than the men in the more recent film. A still more recent movie, *Glory*, also reveals a harsher war. Near the beginning of the film as Union soldiers march on Confederates at Antietam, a cannon shot splatters the head of an officer and we see a man crawling across the ground with blood spurting from the stump of a leg freshly shorn. In combat the men grimace and scream, become carried away, get stabbed or shot in the back by desperate enemies. Neither of these movies is perfect, but they indicate that there are ways to hint of war's nature without being X-rated for violent content.

Reasons probably vary why *Gettysburg* displays combat in its romantic fashion. For one thing, the project began production with a television audience in mind, and producers in midstream decided to open the film in theaters. Television images must be more tidy for its family audience. Also, the novel *Killer Angels* points filmmakers in this direction. Yet the producers and director must have chosen this way to tell the story. It is no accident that the pace of combat moves slowly or that characters pose portraitlike while bathed in romantic light. The entire package reaffirms the notions of the brothers' war—a view that has dominated mainstream America for so long and perhaps unwittingly influenced the movie's making.

Of course the brothers' war does not hold currency with everyone. Scholars for the past twenty years have been unearthing evidence of the conflicts within Northern and Southern societies and restoring the role of black people in their liberation. Similarly, movies other than *Glory* present different sides to the conflict. More recently, *Pharaoh's Army* has captured the war from a smaller perspective—a handful of Union soldiers who run into problems trying to strip food from a western farm where the main provider has enlisted in the Confederate army. Issued in 1995 by Orion Home Video, this movie highlights how the Union officer and the Confederate woman found they had more in common than they may have thought. But they also remain enemies, and the empathy inevitably dissolves into violence. Hatred never fully disappears.

Competing visions of the war are not only reflected in film but also in the popular culture as a whole, especially in the commemorations of the war and also in a renewed interest in preserving slavery in our national memory. Throughout the country, reenactment groups have surged in popularity and Southern heritage groups have constructed Web pages on the Internet to protect Confederate traditions, such as the battle flag that bears the St. Andrew's Cross. Similarly, African-American interest in the war has increased. Reenactment groups have formed and a memorial has been dedicated to U.S. Colored Troops in Washington, D.C. Controversy still erupts over these issues, especially taking the Confederate flag from the capitol at Columbia, South Carolina, or including it on vanity license plates in Maryland. Others found distasteful the re-creation of a slave auction at Williamsburg.

One thing seems reasonably certain: we live in a time when American memory itself is changing. Cultural artifacts today reflect this split personality within our own society. *Gettysburg* and *Glory* describe different ways to remember the conflict: the first the more traditional brothers' war and the second a more recent focus on the centrality of slaves and free blacks to the conflict. *Gettysburg* provides more comforting images that ennoble the participants, eliminate potentially divisive issues, celebrate the survival of the nation, and highlight the heroic nature of the combatants. *Glory* is no less nationalistic, but it includes African Americans in the equation, gives a more cogent look at racial problems, and presents perhaps the most realistic combat footage of any Civil War movie yet made.[16] The jury is still out whether the memories of war represented in *Gettysburg* and *Glory* can come together or will remain parallel, attracting different publics—whether the war continues or peace finally comes.

NOTES

INTRODUCTION

1. W. Wayne Smith, "Pennsylvania and the American Civil War," in *A Guide to The History of Pennsylvania*, ed. Dennis B. Downey and Francis J. Bremer (Westport, Conn.: Greenwood Press, 1993), 215. Smith provides a nice overview of the Civil War studies involving the Keystone State. Antislavery studies have been prevalent, as well as biographies of key military and political figures. Pennsylvania also appears frequently as an important piece in broader political studies. For military studies, the best overview of the state's signature battle remains Edwin B. Coddington, *The Gettysburg Campaign: A Study in Command* (New York: Charles Scribner's Sons, 1968). Books of note that have appeared recently on the subject include Harry W. Pfanz, *Gettysburg: The Second Day* (Chapel Hill: University of North Carolina Press, 1987) and his *Gettysburg—Culp's Hill and Cemetery Hill* (Chapel Hill: University of North Carolina Press, 1993); Gabor S. Boritt, ed., *The Gettysburg No One Knows* (New York: Oxford University Press, 1997); Carol Reardon, *Pickett's Charge in History and Memory* (Chapel Hill: University of North Carolina Press, 1997); and Gary W. Gallagher, ed., *Three Days at Gettysburg: Essays on Confederate and Union Leadership* (Kent, Ohio: Kent State University Press, 1999).

2. Arnold Shankman, *The Pennsylvania Anti-War Movement, 1861–1865* (Cranbury, N.J.: Associated University Presses, 1980); Grace Palladino, *Another Civil War: Labor, Capital, and the State in the Anthracite Regions of Pennsylvania, 1840–68* (Urbana: University of Illinois Press, 1990); William J. Miller, *The Training of an Army: Camp Curtin and the North's Civil War* (Shippensburg, Pa.: White Main Publishing, 1990); Michael F. Holt, *Forging a Majority: The Formation of the Republican Party in Pittsburgh, 1848–1860* (New Haven: Yale University Press, 1969); J. Matthew Gallman, *Mastering Wartime: A Social History of Philadelphia During the Civil War* (New York: Cambridge University Press, 1990).

3. Maris A. Vinovskis, *Toward a Social History of the American Civil War: Exploratory Essays* (Cambridge: Cambridge University Press, 1990); James M. McPherson and William J. Cooper, Jr., eds., *Writing the Civil War: The Quest to Understand* (Columbia: University of South Carolina Press, 1998); William Blair, "The Quest for Understanding the Civil War," *Reviews in American History* 27, no. 3 (September 1999): 422, 427.

4. Phillip Shaw Paludan, *"A People's Contest": The Union and Civil War 1861–1865* (New York: Harper and Row, 1988); J. Matthew Gallman, *The North Fights the Civil War: The Home Front, American Ways Series* (Chicago: Ivan R. Dee, 1994); Phillip Shaw Paludan, "What Did the Winners Win? The Social and Economic History of the North During the Civil War," in *Writing the Civil War*, ed. McPherson and Cooper, 186–87.

5. James M. McPherson, *Abraham Lincoln and the Second American Revolution* (New York: Oxford University Press, 1990); Stanley Engerman and J. Matthew Gallman, "The Civil War Economy: A Modern View," in *On the Road to Total War: The American Civil War and the German Wars of Unification, 1861–1871*, ed. Stig Förster and Jörg Nagler (Cambridge: Cambridge University Press, 1997), 222–44. For expansion of the central state, see Richard Franklin Bensel, *Yankee Leviathan: The Origins of Central State Authority in America, 1859–1877* (Cambridge: Cambridge University Press, 1990).

6. Jörg Nagler, "Loyalty and Dissent: The Home Front in the American Civil War," in *On the Road to Total War*, ed. Förster and Nagler, 329–55.

7. James M. McPherson, *For Cause and Comrades: Why Men Fought in the Civil War* (New York: Oxford University Press, 1997); Reid Mitchell, *Civil War Soldiers: Their Expectations and Their Experiences* (New York: Viking, 1988); Earl J. Hess, *Liberty, Virtue, and Progress: Northerners and Their War for Union* (New York: New York University Press, 1988). For an example of the earlier argument, see Bell Irvin Wiley, *The Life of Johnny Reb: The Common Soldier of the Confederacy* (Indianapolis: Charter Books, 1943), 309; Wiley, *The Life of Billy Yank: The Common Soldier of the Union* (Indianapolis: Charter Books, 1952) 39–40.

8. David M. Potter, *The South and the Sectional Conflict* (Baton Rouge: Louisiana State University Press, 1968), 60–63; Kenneth H. Wheeler, "Local Autonomy and Civil War Draft Resistance: Holmes County, Ohio," *Civil War History: A Journal of the Middle Period* 45, no. 2 (June 1999): 147–59; James M. McPherson, *Battle Cry of Freedom: The Civil War Era* (New York: Oxford University Press, 1988), 859.

9. Gerald G. Eggert, *Harrisburg Industrializes: The Coming of Factories to an American Community* (University Park: The Pennsylvania State University Press, 1993).

10. Ella Lonn, *Desertion During the Civil War* (1928; repr. Lincoln: University of Nebraska Press, 1988), 205.

11. Amy J. Kinsel, "From Turning Point to Peace Memorial: A Cultural Legacy," in *Gettysburg No One Knows*, ed. Boritt, 203–22; Reardon, *Pickett's Charge in History and Memory*.

12. Drew Faust, "'Ours as Well as That of the Men': Women and Gender in the Civil War," in *Writing the Civil War*, ed. McPherson and Cooper, 228–40.

13. For a similar work involving the letters from the Virginia front by a correspondent for a Philadelphia newspaper, see R. J. M. Blackett, ed., *Thomas Morris Chester: Black Civil War Correspondent* (Baton Rouge: Louisiana State University Press, 1989).

CHAPTER 1. KEYSTONE CONFEDERATES

1. W. G. Bean, "The Unusual War Experience of Lieutenant George G. Junkin, C.S.A.," *Virginia Magazine of History and Biography* 76 (May 1968): 181–90.

2. Quoted in the letter Junkin wrote to Jackson, in ibid., 188–89.

3. For purposes of this chapter, "Pennsylvanians" are defined as persons either born in Pennsylvania or those who lived there more than twenty years before the war. After reviewing more than forty Virginia regimental rosters in the "Virginia Regimental Series" published by H. E. Howard, a very conservative estimate of Pennsylvanians who fought for the Confederacy would fall around 2,000. This number is based on the discovery of at least two or three soldiers in each Virginia regiment I checked who listed their state of birth as Pennsylvania (a more detailed discussion of the tabulation methodology follows).

4. Kenneth M. Stampp, *And the War Came: The North and the Secession Crisis, 1860–1861* (Baton Rouge: Louisiana State University Press, 1970), 126–27.

5. Arnold M. Shankman, *The Pennsylvania Anti-War Movement, 1861–1865* (Cranbury, N.J.: Associated University Presses, 1980), 38–40; J. Matthew Gallman, *Mastering Wartime: A Social History of Philadelphia During the Civil War* (New York: Cambridge University Press, 1990).

6. Quoted in Shankman, *Pennsylvania Anti-War Movement*, 55–56, 67.

7. Ibid., 56–57.

8. Atwood, White and Co., Dry Goods Merchants, to D. L. Hopkins, February 1, 1861, Lewis Leigh Collection, book C-1, Archives of the U.S. Army Military History Institute, Carlisle Barracks, Pa. (hereafter USAMHI).

9. Ibid. For an excellent pamphlet that captures the border mentality during secession, see John Pendleton Kennedy, "The Border States: Their Power and Duty in the Present Disordered Condition of the Country," in *Southern Pamphlets on Secession: November 1860–April 1861,* ed. Jon L. Wakelyn (Chapel Hill: University of North Carolina Press, 1996), 217–46.

10. John Bell was the candidate of the Constitutional Union Party, whose supporters hailed mainly from Virginia, Tennessee, Kentucky, and Maryland. His platform offered a peaceful solution to the sectional crisis based on adherence to the Constitution and the rejection of radical measures proposed by either Southern secessionists and Northern Republicans. Atwood, White and Co., Dry Good Merchants, to D. L. Hopkins, February 1, 1861, Lewis Leigh Collection, book C-1, USAMHI. The "Mr. Mason and Hunter" referred to here were James Mason and Senator R. M. T. Hunter, ardent Virginia secessionists who would later become prominent Confederate politicians.

11. Quoted in Arnold Shankman, "William B. Reed and the Civil War," *Pennsylvania History* 39 (October 1972): 455–68, 460.

12. William C. Wright, *The Secession Movement in the Middle Atlantic States* (Cranbury, N.J.: Associated University Presses, 1973), 134–35. Wright analyzes Buchanan's statements regarding the secession crisis and finds him guilty only of a strict constructionist interpretation of the Constitution: "Buchanan advocated allowing those states that so desired to leave the Union in peace and not permitting the use of force to hold them in the Union, provided that they did not attack United States property. This was a de facto recognition of secession" (p. 133). He further argues that Buchanan's and Lincoln's views on the constitutionality of secession "divided on the question of de facto secession. Buchanan did not recognize the right of secession nor the right of the United States to force a state to stay within the Union" (p. 132). Traditionally, Buchanan is vilified by historians as a "doughface" president under the sway of Southern interests who did nothing to prevent secession from occurring. Wright would argue that Buchanan was simply upholding the law as he understood it. For another supportive study of Buchanan, see Philip Shriver Klein, *President James Buchanan: A Biography* (University Park: The Pennsylvania State University Press, 1962).

13. The final tally of votes in Cumberland County in the 1860 election, for instance, revealed that in Carlisle, Lincoln had edged out John C. Breckenridge, the Southern Rights candidate from Kentucky, by only nineteen votes (425 to 406), and in the county by only 386 votes (3,593 to 3,207). Information taken from Merkel Landis, "Civil War Times in Carlisle," an address delivered at the Hamilton Library, Carlisle, Pa., on February 12, 1931, copy at the Cumberland County Historical Society, Carlisle, Pa. (hereafter CCHS). Carlisle may have had a larger percentage of Democratic voters than most other southern Pennsylvania towns because of the presence of the Carlisle Barracks, at which were stationed Southern-born officers and their families. Some of these officers retired in the area. Intermarriage with the local families probably created a greater sense of community with the South than in other towns.

14. Wright, *Secession Movement*, 147.

15. *Harrisburg Patriot and Union*, April 9, 1861.

16. *Bedford Gazette,* March 8, 1861. Other newspapers quoted in Wright, *Secession Movement,* 148, 152.

17. Wright, *Secession Movement,* 136.

18. *The Congressional Globe,* pt. 1, 36th Cong., 2nd sess., p. 48. Bigler believed that Kentucky Senator Crittenden's last-ditch attempt at compromise between the two sections was the best remedy for the secession crisis. Crittenden's plan proposed allowing slavery into the territories below the old Missouri Compromise line of 36'30" and a guarantee by the federal government that it would not challenge that right in the future. After the failure of the Crittenden Compromise, Bigler advocated allowing the seceded states to leave the Union in peace rather than risk civil war.

19. Letter by anonymous Southerner "BU" to "Friend Joe," May 16, 1861, Lewis Leigh Collection, book 66, USAMHI.

20. Bell Irvin Wiley, *The Life of Johnny Reb: The Common Soldier of the Confederacy* (1943; repr. Baton Rouge: Louisiana State University Press, 1994), 322; Shankman, *Pennsylvania Anti-War Movement,* 59. Wiley goes into no further discussion of the topic of Northerners who fought for the Confederacy.

21. The largest problem to overcome in recounting the story of these unusual Confederates is the elusiveness of source material. Few Pennsylvania towns would have welcomed back a wayward son after the war, and even fewer of those who fought for Dixie returned. There is precious little mention of them in county histories and records, and thus the search for them must concentrate on Southern sources. The regimental rosters of Confederate units, when complete, often provide enough information to create a brief character sketch. A few monographs of well-known Pennsylvania Confederates, such as Pemberton, assist in explaining why they fought, and such reference guides as Robert K. Krick's *Lee's Colonels* (Dayton, Ohio: Morningside House, 1992) and Ezra J. Warner's *Generals in Gray* (Baton Rouge: Louisiana State University Press, 1959) give good biographical information on some of the lesser-known field-grade officers of Pennsylvanian birth in Confederate service.

22. This result is achieved by multiplying the number of reviewed Virginia rosters (40) by 2 (= 80) or 3 (= 120). Since there (conservatively) were at least 80 different Virginia regiments if artillery, cavalry, and infantry units are combined, the above numbers (80 or 120) should be doubled and averaged. The result, 200, is a conservative estimation of Pennsylvanians in Virginia's service considering that several regiments I reviewed had well over two to three soldiers of Pennsylvanian birth. The Rockbridge Artillery, for instance, had five.

23. James M. McPherson, *What They Fought For, 1861–1865* (Baton Rouge: Louisiana State University Press, 1994) and *For Cause and Comrades* (New York: Oxford University Press, 1997); Reid Mitchell, *Civil War Soldiers* (New York: Viking Press, 1988). Both McPherson and Mitchell include other motivational factors along with ideology in their discussions of why Southern soldiers fought, and they agree that often ideology and kinship ties, for example, together dictated Confederate loyalties. Although I concur with these conclusions, I believe both authors ignore the possibility of Northern men fighting for the Confederacy and downplay economic and marital motivations. The factors influencing these expatriate soldiers were frequently complex and included much emphasis on economics and marital allegiance along with ideology. As will be shown, marital allegiance in itself became ideological for some Pennsylvania Confederates.

24. Quoted in Bean, "Unusual War Experience of Lieutenant George G. Junkin," 184.

25. Lee A. Wallace Jr., *The Fifth Virginia Infantry* (Lynchburg, Va.: H. E. Howard, 1988), 97.

26. Shankman, *Pennsylvania Anti-War Movement,* 67, 80.

27. See the card catalog of family names at the CCHS.

28. John Kennedy Hitner to "My good friend Miss Grattan," July 31, 1863, no. 6830-B, box cf 1862–64, Alderman Library Special Collections, University of Virginia, Charlottesville, Va.

29. Robert J. Driver, Jr., *The First and Second Rockbridge Artillery* (Lynchburg, Va.: H. E. Howard, 1987), 68. The Virginia Historical Society in Richmond holds other letters by Hitner. One of them, dated December 9, 1904, to Robert E. Lee, Jr., mentions a compliment paid Hitner by Robert E. Lee at Malvern Hill for retrieving fallen comrades under fire (file no. Mss1L51g108). Hitner also wrote in this letter about the diary he kept during the war. One scholar cited it as part of the collections of the Virginia Historical Society, but close scrutiny of the society's archives reveals, unfortunately, no such document. One other possible reference to Hitner may be found in a letter Mrs. R. K. Hitner of Carlisle wrote to her "dear friend" Mrs. David Hastings on July 6, 1863, just after the retreat of the rebels from Pennsylvania. She mentions news of one brother fighting in the Army of the Potomac and then adds, almost as an afterthought, "For our other poor brother we feel in various ways more than words can express—we have heard a great deal of him that I will tell you when we meet." Is this a reference to John Kennedy Hitner? If so, it indicates that his family in Pennsylvania was torn emotionally by his Confederate service. See Mrs. R. K. Hitner to Mrs. David Hastings, July 6, 1863, Carlisle Barracks Collection, USAMHI.

30. Peter J. Meaney, O.S.B., "Valiant Chaplain of the Bloody Tenth," *Tennessee Historical Quarterly* 41 (March 1982): 37–47.

31. Wesley Culp File, Gettysburg National Military Park Library, Gettysburg, Pa. (hereafter GNMPL). See esp. the unmarked article in the *Pittsburgh Gazette* of November 9, 1913, contained in the file. Harry W. Pfanz, *Gettysburg—Culp's Hill and Cemetery Hill* (Chapel Hill: University of North Carolina Press, 1993), 328, and Henry Kyd Douglas, *I Rode with Stonewall* (Chapel Hill: University of North Carolina Press, 1983), 242. Culp was also the only soldier from the 2nd Virginia killed in the battle of Gettysburg.

32. David A. Welker, ed., *A Keystone Rebel: The Civil War Diary of Joseph Garey, Hudson's Battery, Mississippi Volunteers* (Gettysburg, Pa.: Thomas Publications, 1996), 103.

33. Marion B. Lucas, "The Civil War Career of Colonel George Washington Scott," *Florida Historical Quarterly* 58 (June 1979): 129–49.

34. Driver, *First and Second Rockbridge Artillery*, 71; Wallace, *Fifth Virginia Infantry*, 146; Dennis E. Frye, *The Second Virginia Infantry*, 2nd ed. (Lynchburg, Va.: H. E. Howard, 1984), 94; Robert K. Krick, *Lee's Colonels: A Biographical Register of the Field Officers of the Army of Northern Virginia*, 4th ed., rev. (Dayton, Ohio: Morningside House, 1992), 238–39, 286.

35. Ezra J. Warner, *Generals in Gray: Lives of the Confederate Commanders* (Baton Rouge: Louisiana State University Press, 1959), 198–99. Warner's biographical reference sketches the careers of several Pennsylvanians who were general officers in the Confederate army. In the interest of space, only some are outlined here, but a cursory review reveals six names: Josiah Gorgas, John C. Pemberton, Johnson Kelly Duncan, William McComb, Richard Griffith, and William S. Walker. New York, Ohio, and Massachusetts also contributed at least three generals each.

36. Frank E. Vandiver, ed., *The Civil War Diary of General Josiah Gorgas* (University: University of Alabama Press, 1947), xi. Also see Vandiver, *Ploughshares into Swords: Josiah Gorgas and Confederate Ordnance* (Austin: University of Texas Press, 1952). Both books recount the almost miraculous growth and maintenance of the Ordnance Department under Gorgas's leadership.

37. Quoted in Sarah Woolfolk Wiggens, ed., *The Journals of Josiah Gorgas, 1857–1878* (Tuscaloosa: University of Alabama Press, 1995), 37. Wiggens's book is more comprehensive than Vandiver's collection, including more pre- and postwar material from Gorgas's diary.

38. Vandiver, *Ploughshares into Swords*, 53.

39. Ibid.

40. Michael J. Strong, *Keystone Confederate: The Life and Times of General Johnson Kelly Duncan, CSA* (York, Pa.: Historical Society of York County, 1994), 23–27, 31. See also Duncan's biographical sketch in Warner, *Generals in Gray*, 77–78.

41. Strong, *Keystone Confederate*, 35, 46. For a good analysis of the bureaucratic troubles Duncan faced in preparing for the Federal onslaught and an in-depth description of the battle between the forts and Farragut's fleet, see Chester G. Hearn, *The Capture of New Orleans, 1862* (Baton Rouge: Louisiana State University Press, 1995).

42. Quoted in Strong, *Keystone Confederate*, 53.

43. Michael B. Ballard, "Disaster and Disgrace: The John C. Pemberton Story," *Alabama Heritage* 27 (winter 1993): 6–18.

44. Michael B. Ballard, *Pemberton, A Biography* (Jackson: University Press of Mississippi, 1991), 83–86. Ballard takes a revisionist stand on Pemberton, arguing that his administrative talents were not properly recognized by the Confederate leadership, and that he could have contributed more positively to the Southern cause if they had been. Pemberton emerges from this interpretation a soldier who was promoted too rapidly and whose real skills were rendered almost useless in assignments not suited to them.

45. Ibid., 86.

CHAPTER 2. AVENUE OF DREAMS

1. "The Lesson of the Fairs and the War," *The Canteen* 11 (March 4, 1864).

2. Charles Stillé, *Memorial of the Great Central Fair for the U.S. Sanitary Commission* (Philadelphia: for the Commission, 1864), 33.

3. The first general history of the sanitary fair movement was Frank Goodrich, *The Tribute Book* (New York: Derby and Miller, 1865). The first modern account is William Y. Thompson, "The Sanitary Fairs of the Civil War," *Civil War History* 4 (March 1958): 51–67, and William Quentin Maxwell mentions the fairs in *Lincoln's Fifth Wheel: The Political History of the United States Sanitary Commission* (New York: Longmans, Green, 1956). See J. Matthew Gallman, *Mastering Wartime: A Social History of Philadelphia During the Civil War* (New York: Cambridge University Press, 1990); his chapter on the Great Central Sanitary Fair in Maris Vinovskis, ed., *Toward a Social History of the American Civil War: Exploratory Essays* (Cambridge: Cambridge University Press, 1990), 93–116; and Beverly Gordon, *Bazaars and Fair Ladies: The History of the American Fundraising Fair* (Knoxville: University of Tennessee Press, 1998). See also Rejean Attie "'A Swindling Concern': The United States Sanitary Commission and the Northern Female Public, 1861–1865" (Ph.D. diss., Columbia University, 1987) for an account of New York's Metropolitan Sanitary Fair.

4. Tony Bennett, "The Exhibitionary Complex," *New Formations* 4 (spring 1988): 72–73, reprinted in *The Birth of the Museum* (London: Routledge, 1995), 59–88. In his study of the American world's fairs, Robert Rydell borrowed the term "symbolic universe" from sociologists Peter Berger and Thomas Luckman to characterize the world's fairs as structures of legitimation-explanatory blueprints of social experience. Although Rydell notes the sanitary fair precedent, he dates the creation of such consciously hegemonic spaces to the period of Reconstruction and after. There is strong evidence, however, that successful efforts to create such "symbolic universes" were well under way more than a decade before the Centennial. Robert Rydell, *All the World's a Fair* (Chicago: University of Chicago Press, 1984), 10.

5. Bennett, "Exhibitionary Complex," 76.

6. Ibid., 99.

7. Ibid., 81.

8. Blackwell had made her call for a central organization to consolidate the burgeoning relief effort at the first meeting of the Women's Central Relief Association in New York in April.

Rejean Attie has reconstructed the important role played by Blackwell and other women in the creation and achievements of the Sanitary Commission, a role ignored or belittled by subsequent historians. See "'Swindling Concern,'" 45–54 and passim.

9. The title of the commission was borrowed from the British Sanitary Commission created in 1855 during the Crimean War to investigate and correct the deplorable conditions and quality of care in army hospitals. See Charles Stillé, *History of the United States Sanitary Commission* (Philadelphia: J. B. Lippincott, 1866), 63. During its existence, the United States Sanitary Commission issued numerous publications, most notably bulletins reporting new medical procedures and policies. The first "official" history of the commission may have been Katharine Prescott Wormsley's *The United States Sanitary Commission: A Sketch of Its Purpose and Its Work*, published to aid the Boston Sanitary Fair of 1863. See also "An American Citizen," *The Philanthropic Results of the War in America* (New York: Sheldon, 1864). It was not until almost a century later that two modern histories of the Sanitary Commission appeared almost simultaneously with William Y. Thompson's "The U.S. Sanitary Commission," *Civil War History* 2 (June 1956): 41–63, and Maxwell's *Lincoln's Fifth Wheel*.

10. Prompted by a Sanitary Commission report on the squalid conditions of military hospitals in Washington, construction of new temporary hospital complexes in the capital had started by fall 1861. The innovative barrack-pavilion designs recommended by Florence Nightingale in her 1859 volume *Notes on Hospitals* were adopted by builders in both the North and the South, notably at Chimborazo Hospital in Richmond and at the Mower Hospital in Chestnut Hill, a suburb of Philadelphia. See John D. Thompson and Grace Goldin, *The Hospital: A Social and Architectural History* (New Haven: Yale University Press, 1975), 155–75. It is not insignificant that the secretary of the Sanitary Commission during the first two years of its existence was Frederick Law Olmsted, the designer of Central Park. For the impact of the Civil War on changing attitudes to hospitalization, see Charles E. Rosenberg, *The Care of Strangers: The Rise of America's Hospital System* (New York: Basic Books, 1987), 97–99 and passim.

11. [William Cullen Bryant?], "How Can We Best Help Our Camps and Hospitals?" (New York: W. C. Bryant, 1863). For an assessment of the significance of the Sanitary Commission, see George M. Fredrickson, *The Inner Civil War* (New York: Harper and Row, 1965), 98–112.

12. Those in charge of the Sanitary Commission on a national level were all leading members of the East Coast elite, including New York diarist George Templeton Strong, Boston physician Samuel Gridley Howe, landscape architect Frederick Law Olmsted, and Alexander Dallas Bache. Philadelphians who served on the commission during the war included the venerable attorney Horace Binney, noted engineer and University of Pennsylvania professor Fairman Rogers, and attorney Charles Stillé, later provost of the University of Pennsylvania, who wrote a history of the commission at war's end.

13. To coordinate the activities of the commission throughout the North, branch offices were established in several cities, including Boston, Pittsburgh, Cleveland, and Cincinnati. A semi-independent northwestern branch operated in Chicago, while in Saint Louis, the Sanitary Commission maintained a delicate partnership with the independent Western Sanitary Commission. Philadelphians had been involved in the activities of the Sanitary Commission on both the national and local levels since its founding. The Philadelphia branch of the Sanitary Commission operated from its headquarters at 1307 Chestnut Street: the branch executive committee included commission members Horace Binney, Charles Stillé, and Fairman Rogers, as well as such civic leaders as Matthias Baldwin, Thomas Tasker, and Caleb Cope. See Maxwell, *Lincoln's Fifth Wheel*.

14. Planning for the fair began at a meeting of women delegates from northwestern states, held in Chicago on the September 1 and 2, 1863. See Mary Livermore, *My Story of the War* (Hartford: A. D. Worthington, 1888), 411; Attie, "'Swindling Concern,'" 284–89, and Gordon,

Bazaars and Fair Ladies, 58–93. The first event to be called a "sanitary fair" was organized at Lowell, Massachusetts, in February 1863, but this was a small gathering and because it was not widely promoted, it was not as influential as the Chicago fair. See Goodrich, *Tribute Book*, 28.

15. Charity fairs were put to wartime use in the South as well. Diarist Mary Chesnut reports that she contributed a string of pearls to be raffled at a Columbia, South Carolina, fair that raised "bushels of money" for the purchase of a gunboat. Quoted in Robert H. Bremner, *The Public Good: Philanthropy and Welfare in the Civil War Era* (New York: Alfred A. Knopf, 1980), 62. Nor were sanitary fairs the only charity fairs produced in the North during the war, as Gordon discusses in *Bazaars and Fair Ladies*, 94–115.

16. Only New York's Metropolitan Sanitary Fair was officially sponsored by the Sanitary Commission. See Bremner, *Public Good*, 62–65. Competition among cities sponsoring these fairs was fierce. In December 1863 committees from Manhattan and Brooklyn came together to plan a joint fair for New York City, to open on Washington's birthday. But when the Manhattan fair committee fell behind in its planning, Brooklyn's committee "seceded" from the joint project and went out on its own, "the first great act of self-assertion ever made" by the "City of Churches." See *History of the Brooklyn and Long Island Fair* (Brooklyn: "The Union" Steam Presses, 1864), 1.

17. The Women's Pennsylvania Branch of the Sanitary Commission had formed in 1863 to coordinate the collection of supplies from more than 350 subsidiary aid societies in Pennsylvania, Delaware, and western New Jersey. Among the leaders of the women's branch were Mrs. William H. Furness, Mrs. Bloomfield Moore, and Mrs. R. M. Lewis, as well as the wives of many of the executive committee members, including Mrs. Caleb Cope and Mrs. Charles Stillé. The women were inspired to organize a fair by Sarah Hoge, one of the organizers of the Chicago fair, who delivered a spirited report on the success of that event at a meeting on January 25, 1864. See Stillé, *Memorial of the Great Central Fair*, 14, and Minutes of the Executive Committee, Philadelphia branch, United States Sanitary Commission, Historical Society of Pennsylvania, Philadelphia, Pa. (hereafter HSP).

18. Other members of the thirty-two-man committee included A. E. Borie, N. B. Browne, Frederick Fraley, John Cresson, Joseph Harrison, and George Whitney. Stillé, *Memorial of the Great Central Fair*, 19–21.

19. Gallman, *Mastering Wartime*, 146–69.

20. Bennett, "Exhibitionary Complex," 80. For a history of the American Manufactures Institute fairs, see Bruce Sinclair, *Philadelphia's Philosopher Mechanics: A History of the Franklin Institute, 1824–1865* (Baltimore: Johns Hopkins University Press, 1974), 85–103, 295–98.

21. In New York, for example, the female organizers petitioned the mayor for permission to construct a temporary exhibition hall in Union Square to supplement the Fourteenth Street Armory. See Attie, "'Swindling Concern,'" 292.

22. "The Great Central Fair: Description of the Buildings," *Philadelphia Daily Evening Bulletin*, June 4, 1864, p. 1. The production of a "fair" in Philadelphia held unique historical resonance because traditional fairs had been banned in the city for many decades. In his *Annals of Philadelphia*, John Fanning Watson noted: "We have all heard of Fairs once held in our markets before the Revolution, but few of the present generation have any proper judgement of what manner of things they were." According to Watson, during the seventeenth and eighteenth centuries fairs were held in May and November and continued for three days. There one could purchase "every description of dry goods and millinery . . . cakes, toys and confectioneries etc. The stalls were fancifully decorated, and inclosed [*sic*] with well made patchwork coverlets. The place was always thronged, and your ears were perpetually saluted with toy trumpets, hautboys, fiddles and whistles." These events were discontinued by an act of the legislature in the late 1780s. "It is really surprising they should ever have been adopted in any country where regular stores and business is ordinarily found sufficient for all purposes of trade!" Watson concluded.

John F. Watson, *Annals of Philadelphia and Pennsylvania*, 3 vols. (1857; rev. ed., Philadelphia: Edwin S. Stuart, 1898), 1:364.

23. Logan Square had been an unnamed potter's field until 1825 when the city named the site for William Penn's secretary, James Logan. Thereafter, development of the square accelerated. In 1846 construction of the imposing Roman Catholic Cathedral of Saints Peter and Paul was started on the east side of the square. Religious services were first held in the cathedral in spring 1862; it was consecrated in fall 1864. By this date several hospitals and benevolent institutions also were located in the immediate vicinity of the square, and trolley service had been established.

24. This gesture recalled the similar preservation of several large trees in London's Hyde Park around which Joseph Paxton designed and constructed the Crystal Palace. "The Great Central Fair" (editorial), *Philadelphia Daily Evening Bulletin,* June 3, 1864, p. 4.

25. Stillé, *Memorial of the Great Central Fair*, 21–22.

26. For an account of the opening day ceremonies, see Gallman, *Mastering Wartime*, 148–50.

27. The American mechanics' institute fairs were in turn modeled on European trade fairs, the oldest of which were the annual exhibitions of the Royal Society of Arts in London, which dated from the 1750s. We must not discount the influence of more recent developments in Europe, specifically the mammoth international world's fairs initiated in 1851 with the Crystal Palace Exhibition in London—an event that many wealthier Americans visited, including members of the Sanitary Commission, most notably Henry Bellows, who delivered a sermon on exhibitions to his New York congregation, later published as "The Moral Significance of the Crystal Palace: A Sermon . . . ," *North American Review* 164 (July 1854): 1–30.

28. "The Proceedings and Progress of the Great Central Fair," undated clipping, John Welsh Scrapbook, HSP.

29. "Our Own Great Central Fair," *Our Daily Fare*, no. 2 (June 9, 1864): 13.

30. "The Great Central Fair," *Philadelphia Daily Evening Bulletin,* June 4, 1864, p. 1, and "The Great Central Fair," *Philadelphia Daily Evening Bulletin,* June 9, 1864, p. 3. Similar "kitchens" and period rooms filled with historic artifacts had been featured at other sanitary fairs—including the "Laclede Tavern" at the Mississippi Valley Sanitary Fair in Saint Louis and the "Knickerbocker Tavern" in New York. See Karal Ann Marling, *George Washington Slept Here: Colonial Revivals and American Culture, 1876–1986* (Cambridge: Harvard University Press, 1988), 38–42.

31. See *Memorial of the William Penn Parlor* (Philadelphia: published for the Benefit of the Fair, James Rodgers, Printers, 1864).

32. See "Our Own Great Central Fair," *Our Daily Fare*, no. 12 (June 21, 1864): 94. For a history of the cult of Washington, see Marling, *George Washington Slept Here.*

33. "Our Own Great Central Fair," *Our Daily Fare*, no. 10 (June 18, 1864): 77–78. Several contributors were members of the Pennsylvania Horticultural Society, founded in 1827 and based in Philadelphia, that had sponsored horticultural exhibitions since 1829. Some visitors to the Floral Department were unimpressed nonetheless. "I saw no plants worthy of special mention," George Fahnestock recorded. "We have a much better horticultural display at home any day." George Fahnestock Diary, June 13, 1864, HSP. Similar displays were featured at other sanitary fairs. See Gordon, *Bazaars and Fair Ladies*, 86–90.

34. For a general discussion of art galleries at the various fairs in different cities, see Gordon, *Bazaars and Fair Ladies*, 81–86.

35. Harrison also opened the art gallery in his house on Rittenhouse Square to the public for the duration of the fair (admission was fifty cents) as did Henry C. Carey.

36. An album was compiled at the request of Mrs. Bloomfield Moore for presentation to the actress Charlotte Cushman in appreciation of the several benefit performances she gave for

the Sanitary Commission. Noted in the Minutes of the Fine Arts Committee of the Great Central Fair, April, 9, 1864, Sartain Papers, HSP.

37. See Minutes of the Fine Arts Committee of the Great Central Fair, passim, Sartain Papers, HSP.

38. Ibid., June 4, 1864. Curiously, though Harrison kept up with business correspondence on site for the duration of the fair, using special stationery with an Art Gallery letterhead, he never recorded his personal impressions of the exhibition. See Joseph Harrison Papers, HSP.

39. This evocative pairing is discussed by John Peters-Campbell in "The Big Picture and the Epic American Landscape" (Ph.D. diss., Cornell University, 1989), 240–50. Peters-Campbell points out that Chimborazo, the Andean volcano depicted by Church, was also the name of one of Richmond, Virginia's "seven hills" and the site of a military hospital during the Civil War. At Philadelphia, W. S. Stewart loaned a view of Chimborazo by the Southern-born artist Louis Remy Mignot.

40. "A Wounded Soldier" and "Recollections of the Fair in New York," *Our Daily Fare*, no. 3 (June 10, 1864): 18.

41. George Fahnestock Diary, June 13, 1864, HSP. For Fahnestock's biography, see *The Biographical Encyclopedia of Pennsylvania of the Nineteenth Century* (Philadelphia: Galaxy Publishing, 1874), 192.

42. "The Art Gallery," *Philadelphia Forney's War Press*, June 11, 1864, p. 4. Predictably, the strongest showing was from Philadelphia artists, including Thomas Moran, William Trost Richards, George Cochran Lambdin, James Hamilton, and Christian Schussele. The popularity of the works of former city resident Emanuel Leutze, nine of whose pictures were shown at the Metropolitan Sanitary Fair, was further confirmed at Philadelphia where eleven of his pictures were on view. But Leutze ran second to Peter Rothermel, a member of the Fine Arts Committee, who was represented by twenty paintings. These were lent by such leading private collectors as William Wilstach, Cephas Childs, and Henry Gibson, who shared Rothermel's Republican politics and support for the fair effort.

43. "Art Gallery," p. 1.

44. Mark Thistlethwaite, *Painting in the Grand Manner: The Art of Peter Frederick Rothermel (1812–95)* (Chadds Ford: Brandywine River Museum, 1995), 88–90. Significantly, Deborah Norris, on whose eyewitness account Rothermel based his picture, married George Logan, a descendant of the man for whom Logan Square was named. For an account of the incident, see Thompson Westcott, *The Historic Mansions and Buildings of Philadelphia, with Some Notice of Their Owners and Occupants* (Philadelphia: Porter and Coates, 1877), 120–21.

45. "Art Gallery," p. 5. Beverly Gordon is incorrect when she states that Church's *Heart of the Andes* also was exhibited at Philadelphia. See *Bazaars and Fair Ladies*, 84.

46. "The Great Central Fair," *Philadelphia North American and United States Gazette*, June 14, 1864, p. 1.

47. "Fine Art Gallery," *Philadelphia North American and United States Gazette*, June 25, 1864, p. 2.

48. "City Affairs: The Great Central Fair," *Philadelphia North American and United States Gazette*, June 17, 1864, p. 1. Most other local newspapers also printed the texts of the addresses delivered by Everett and Lincoln on this occasion.

49. "Art Gallery," p. 2.

50. "The Beauty of the Fair" (editorial), *Philadelphia Daily Evening Bulletin*, June 18, 1864, p. 4.

51. "An Evening at the Fair," *Philadelphia Daily Evening Bulletin*, June 10, 1864. Touring the fair could be painful. During their first day at the fair, the Fahnestock family "wandered for a mile along galleries, all decorated profusely with American flags and containing every imaginable

article for sale," then ate lunch at the restaurant, attended a dance performance at the Indian Exhibition and visited the old curiosity department. "Tired out, we came home at 2:30," George Fahnestock recorded, "daughter was so exhausted that she went to bed quite sick." George Fahnestock Diary, June 13, 1864, HSP.

52. "The Transept," *Illustrated Exhibitor* 1 (June 7, 1851): 9.

53. Bennett, "Exhibitionary Complex," 95. "Introduction," *Illustrated Exhibitor* 1 (June 7, 1851): 2.

54. Gordon, *Bazaars and Fair Ladies*, 81–82.

55. Net receipts for the fair amounted to $1,043,539.35, falling just short of the record set at New York. Total attendance was 442,658; the highest number admitted on one day was 33,080. There were surprisingly few reports of any disturbances—probably because the civilian and military police in Philadelphia had three years' experience in controlling the tens of thousands of soldiers who had passed through the city since 1861. Final accounting of monies raised by the various committees is published in Stillé's history.

56. Attie, "'Swindling Concern,'" 295, and Gordon, *Bazaars and Fair Ladies*, 84.

57. Marling, *George Washington Slept Here*, 38–39.

58. William Forten and Ebenezer Bassett to John Welsh, April 23, 1864; Welsh to Forten and Bassett, April 24, 1864, Furness Papers, HSP. Quoted in Gallman, *Mastering Wartime*, 156–57, though with no mention that Forten and Bassett were African American.

59. Broadsides advertising both events are preserved at The Library Company of Philadelphia. My thanks to Phil Lapsansky for bringing these to my attention.

60. *The Age*, a radical Democratic newspaper, suggested that restrictions on the number of African Americans admitted to the fair were removed on June 20, 1864, because admission receipts had dipped sharply. See "The Great Central Fair," *The Age*, June 21, 1864, p. 1.

61. Stillé, *Memorial of the Great Central Fair*, 58. In April 1864 John Welsh had written Albert Bierstadt, who supervised the Native American performers at New York's Metropolitan Fair, to ask that he hire performers for Philadelphia. Bierstadt in turn referred Welsh to Chief Peter Wilson, a member of the Council of the Six Nations. Furness Papers, HSP. There is no record of how Barclay came to be hired to manage the troupe.

62. "The Close of the Fair," *Philadelphia Daily Evening Bulletin*, June 25, 1864, p. 4.

63. Executive Committee Resolution, July 5, 1864, Furness Papers, HSP.

64. Stillé, *Memorial of the Great Central Fair*, 146–50.

65. One editor proclaimed that "the splendor and variety" of the American sanitary fairs "excelled that of the great 'Expositions' held a few years ago in Europe." "The Great Central Fair" (editorial), *Philadelphia Daily Evening Bulletin*, June 8, 1864, p. 10.

66. Gallman also notes the important differences between the two events, notably that the Central Fair was produced wholly by private citizen-volunteers, whereas the Centennial received funding from federal, state, and local as well as foreign governments. See Gallman, *Mastering Wartime*, 335–38.

67. See Lee L. Schreiber, "Bluebloods and Local Societies: A Philadelphia Microcosm," *Pennsylvania History* 48 (1981): 251–66.

68. J. Thomas Scharf and Thompson Westcott, *History of Philadelphia, 1609–1884*, 3 vols. (Philadelphia: L. H. Everts, 1884), 3:1773–74.

69. The Franklin Institute ultimately did move to Logan Square but not until after the turn of the century. The new building designed by John T. Windrim at the southeast corner of Logan Square, now Logan Circle thanks to construction of the Benjamin Franklin Parkway, opened in 1934. By this time the central branch of the Free Library of Philadelphia (designed by Horace Trumbauer and opened in 1927) stood at the northwest corner of the circle and construction had begun on the Municipal Court (designed by John Windrim and W. R.

Morton Keast and dedicated in 1941) at the northeast corner. See David B. Brownlee, *Building the City Beautiful: The Benjamin Franklin Parkway and the Philadelphia Museum of Art* (Philadelphia: Philadelphia Museum of Art, 1989), 89–94. For the Pennsylvania Academy, see Frank H. Goodyear, Jr., "A History of the Pennsylvania Academy of the Fine Arts, 1805–1976," in *In This Academy: The Pennsylvania Academy of the Fine Arts, 1805–1976*, ed. Frank H. Goodyear, Jr. (Philadelphia: Pennsylvania Academy of the Fine Arts, 1976), 29–31.

70. *Acts of Assembly Relating to Fairmount Park* (Philadelphia: King and Baird, 1870), 4. For the early history of Fairmount Park, see Elizabeth Milroy, "Assembling Fairmount Park," in *Philadelphia's Cultural Landscape: The Sartain Family Legacy, 1830–1930* (Philadelphia: Temple University Press, 2001).

71. Beverly Gordon argues persuasively for a connection between the design and popularity of the horticultural or floral departments at several sanitary fairs and the growing urban park movement. *Bazaars and Fair Ladies*, 87–90.

72. *Third Annual Report of the Commissioners of Fairmount Park* (Philadelphia: King and Baird, 1871), 79–80.

73. William Cullen Bryant, *Prose Writings* (New York: D. Appleton, 1884), 262.

74. Recent studies of the changing role of the American upper class in the running of art museums and other cultural institutions after the Civil War have tended to focus on the elites of Boston and New York. See Neil Harris, "The Gilded Age Revisited: Boston and the Museum Movement," *American Quarterly* 14 (winter 1962): 545–66; Paul DiMaggio, "Cultural Entrepreneurship in Nineteenth-Century Boston: The Creation of an Organizational Base for High Culture in America," and "Cultural Entrepreneurship in Nineteenth-Century Boston, Part II: The Classification and Framing of American Art," *Media, Culture and Society* 4 (1982): 33–50, 303–22; Lawrence Levine, *Highbrow, Lowbrow: The Emergence of Cultural Hierarchy in America* (Cambridge: Harvard University Press, 1988), 146–60. A noteworthy new addition to this literature that includes discussion of Philadelphia's cultural institutions is Steven Conn, *Museums and American Intellectual Life, 1876–1926* (Chicago: University of Chicago Press, 1998).

75. Gallman, *Mastering Wartime*, 334. See also Peter McCaffrey, *When Bosses Ruled Philadelphia: The Emergence of the Republican Machine, 1867–1933* (University Park: The Pennsylvania State University Press, 1993), 2–16.

76. "Art Museum," in *Third Annual Report*, 25–27.

77. The letter was read at the September 11, 1875, meeting of the Fairmount Park Commission. A transcript is contained in appendix 74 of the commission minutes for that year. City of Philadelphia, City Archives, record group 149.

CHAPTER 3. "WE WERE ENLISTED FOR THE WAR"

1. Jennie P. Sellers Diary, April 15, 17, 18, 30, 1861, Chester County Historical Society, West Chester, Pa. (hereafter CCHS).

2. Susan Trautwine MacManus Diary, May 15, 1862, Historical Society of Pennsylvania, Philadelphia, Pa. (hereafter HSP).

3. MacManus Diary, April 13, 1861.

4. MacManus Diary, April 15, 1861.

5. MacManus Diary, May 6, 1861.

6. Meshler was probably older than Trautwine. There is no reference to Meshler's age, but her father turned 74 on January 12, 1860. Amanda L. Meshen memorandum book, 1860–63,

HSP. Note that the memorandum book is catalogued under the name "Meshen," but I believe this is a mistake; the name as I read it is Meshler.

7. Meshen memorandum book, 1860–63.

8. An area for further research is the political affiliations of women who did and did not join ladies' aid societies. Sellers's, Meshler's, and Trautwine's journals reveal, to a varying degree, their political leanings—Sellers was unabashedly a Democrat and Meshler undoubtedly Republican, while Trautwine's partisan affiliation was unclear, but she supported the war effort. Did Jennie's Democratic leanings affect her decision to join a debate society instead of a ladies' aid society? It is my belief that most women who joined ladies' aid societies had Republican leanings, but more work needs to be done in this area.

9. Lori D. Ginzberg, *Women and the Work of Benevolence: Morality, Politics, and Class in the Nineteenth-Century United States* (New Haven: Yale University Press, 1990), 69.

10. Sara Evans, "Women's History and Political Theory: Toward a Feminist Approach to Public Life," in *Visible Women: New Essays in American Activism*, ed. Nancy A. Hewitt and Suzanne Lebsock (Urbana: University of Illinois Press, 1993), 128–29.

11. Other historians have examined ladies' aid societies. Anne Firor Scott describes the evolution of ladies' aid societies as part of the history of women's voluntary efforts in *Natural Allies: Women's Associations in American History* (Urbana: University of Illinois Press, 1993), chap. 3. Mary Elizabeth Massey celebrates women's contributions through ladies' aid societies but provides little analysis of their political nature. Mary Elizabeth Massey, *Women in the Civil War* (Lincoln: University of Nebraska Press, 1996). Rejean Attie's work does an excellent job of drawing out the intricate and complicated relationship between women in local aid societies and the United States Sanitary Commission. Rejean Attie, *Patriotic Toil: Northern Women and the American Civil War* (Ithaca: Cornell University Press, 1998). Lori Ginzberg also studies the United States Sanitary Commission and women's local efforts to support it in her study *Women and the Work of Benevolence*. Some scholars have questioned the extent to which the ladies' aid societies had an impact on women's status. Wendy Hamand Venet notes: "Women had long been accepted as nurses and seamstresses and charity organizers. Their Civil War work in these areas, while significant, was not pathbreaking." She argues that by contrast the "petitioning, public speaking, and political organizing that Northern women performed during the war helped to gain new acceptance for women in the public sphere after the war." Similarly, J. Matthew Gallman suggests that while women's benevolent work "won the nation's gratitude," it "did not typically yield increased powers" for women. George Rable argues that when Southern women sewed bandages and banners to support the Confederacy, their actions "kept them on the fringes of politics" and "nurtured conventional ideas about [women's] own place and character." Wendy Hamand Venet, *Neither Ballots nor Bullets: Women Abolitionists and the Civil War* (Charlottesville: University Press of Virginia, 1991), 161; J. Matthew Gallman, *Mastering Wartime: A Social History of Philadelphia During the Civil War* (New York: Cambridge University Press, 1990), 10; George C. Rable, *Civil Wars: Women and the Crisis of Southern Nationalism* (Urbana: University of Illinois Press, 1989), 45, 121.

12. It has been estimated that between 7,000 and 20,000 ladies' aid societies existed. See Scott, *Natural Allies*, 205n19. For the density of soldiers' aid societies in one Pennsylvania county, see Anna M. Holstein, "Women of Montgomery County in War Time," *Historical Sketches: A Collection of Papers Prepared for the Historical Society of Montgomery County, Pennsylvania*, 7 vols. (Norristown, Pa.: The Society, 1895–1925), 1:219–31. She lists groups in Norristown, Upper Merion, Gwynedd, Plymouth, Conshohocken, Bridgeport, Pottstown, and Whitpain. She does not list the group in Weldon, Abington Township. Little evidence survives of black women's aid societies during the war. In Pittsburgh, Susan Paul Vashon organized a sanitary fair to benefit

black refugees in the Ohio Valley (see Scott, *Natural Allies*, 67). In 1865, when the Pennsylvania state legislature ratified the Thirteenth Amendment to the Constitution, abolishing slavery, the Colored People's Union League Association sponsored a "grand demonstration" at a concert hall. At the "entertainment" a "Committee of the Ladies of the Sanitary Committee of St. Thomas' Church" planned to present the president of the Union League Association with a testimonial. ("GRAND DEMONSTRATION . . . March 2, 1865." Leon Gardiner Collection, box 1g, folder 5, HSP.) Black women formed at least one auxiliary society to the state union league, called the Ladies' Union Association of Philadelphia. They are listed with auxiliary associations represented in the state league. See Pennsylvania Abolition Society Papers, microfilm, HSP. Other black women were members of the Office of the Colored Soldiers and Sailors' Orphans Committee and helped set up a boarding school for children of black soldiers in Bucks County. See "To the Widows and Orphans of the Colored Soldiers and Sailors of Pennsylvania," broadside, Leon Gardiner Collection, box 13, folder 1, HSP.

The four ladies' aid societies discussed in this chapter (the Spring Garden Hospital Aid Society, the Weldon Ladies' Aid Society, the Richmond [Mansfield] Ladies' Aid Association, and the Philadelphia Ladies' Aid Society) represent those societies in Pennsylvania with the most complete extant records of which I am aware. Whereas three of these were among the better-organized groups in the state, the Spring Garden group represents the more temporary type of organization that was probably most common. In the records of the others, moreover, there is significant information on other societies in their areas.

13. Often women joined ladies' aid societies with their mothers, sisters, and in-laws. In the Weldon society membership lists, for instance, there are four women with the surname Bradfield, four with Tyson, four with Luken, and five with Kirk. Membership list, Second Year of the Ladies' Aid Association of Weldon, October, 1863, Ladies' Aid Association of Weldon Papers, Historical Society of Pennsylvania, Philadelphia, Pa. (hereafter LAAW).

14. Mary Browne to Robert Browne, December 18, 1862, Robert Browne Letters, Civil War Miscellaneous Collection, U.S. Army Military History Institute, Carlisle Barracks, Carlisle, Pa. (hereafter USAMHI). Reid Mitchell has demonstrated that the exchange of information between home and front was extremely important to the soldiers as well as to their families. He argues that the transferal of community values to the men both undercut army discipline and motivated the men to keep fighting. See Reid Mitchell, "The Northern Soldier and His Community," in *Toward a Social History of the American Civil War: Exploratory Essays*, ed. Maris Vinovskis (New York: Cambridge University Press, 1990), 78–92.

15. James C. Mohr, ed., *The Cormany Diaries: A Northern Family in the Civil War* (Pittsburgh: University of Pittsburgh Press, 1982), 443, 378.

16. Ibid., 441.

17. Ibid., 281.

18. Catherine Fair to William Fair, April 13, 1865, Fair Family Papers, Harrisburg Civil War Round Table Collection, USAMHI.

19. Mohr, *Cormany Diaries*, 401.

20. Ibid., 369.

21. Ibid., 444–45.

22. Ibid., 448.

23. Margaret Lipplinger Deposition, February 5, 1861, Addison Files, Letters Received, 1861, Adjutant General's Office, record group 94, National Archives, Washington, D.C. (hereafter NA).

24. Thankful Hipwell, September 4, 1863, Enlisted Branch, Letters Received, 1863, Adjutant General's Office, record group 94, NA.

25. Quarter Sessions Dockets, August 16, 1865, Chester County Archives, West Chester, Pa.

26. During the war women were often called upon to share information not only with each other, but also about each other. Women's close relationships with their neighbors provided many opportunities for them to perform the roles of both witness for and informant against each other. As Christine Stansell has shown for antebellum New York City, urban working-class streets often served as informal courts, trying the behavior of the residents against the neighborhood's moral standards. During the Civil War tensions ran high, money was often scarce, and women and families were under considerable stress. As in New York City, neighborhood arguments in smaller towns often turned violent, and participants were sometimes hauled into court during the Quarter Sessions to settle differences. The records for the Chester County Quarter Sessions reveal that women were no strangers to the courts and appeared often as witnesses, complainants, and as defendants. Their experiences reveal some of the tensions underlying daily life during the Civil War and belie romanticized exaggerations of women's cooperation. See Chester County Quarters Sessions Dockets, Chester County Archives, West Chester, Pa.

27. Sarah Murphy to Brother [B]ert, July 6, 1863, Sarah A. Murphy, Civilian Letters, Civil War Miscellaneous Collection, USAMHI.

28. Mohr, *Cormany Diaries*, 334.

29. Ibid., 337.

30. Of the nine husbands of Weldon and Richmond ladies' aid society members I located in manuscript census data, six were farmers, and their wives were therefore likely responsible for much household production.

31. Richmond Ladies' Aid Society Records, Pennsylvania State Historical Commission, Harrisburg, Pa. (hereafter RLAS), October 23, 1861.

32. Scott, *Natural Allies*, 58.

33. LAAW, January 14, 1864.

34. LAAW, January 28, 1864.

35. LAAW, December 1, 1864.

36. Drew Faust has argued that in the South, the war's death toll "dictated the emergence of yet another dimension of female responsibility," that of celebrating and sanctifying the martyrdom of others. "Through rituals of public grief, personal loss could be redefined as transcendent communal gain." Yet in the Weldon example, these Northern women "deplore" this death, demarcating it as a "public loss," not a communal gain. Faust, "Altars of Sacrifice: Confederate Women and the Narratives of War," in *Divided Houses: Gender and the Civil War*, ed. Catharine Clinton and Nina Silber (New York: Oxford University Press, 1992), 184.

37. "First Report of the Mansfield Soldiers' Aid Society," RLAS, October 28, 1863. Note that at some point the group changed its name, substituting "Mansfield" for Richmond. Richmond was the township, Mansfield the county. It is unclear whether the change resulted from widening membership throughout the county or because of the negative associations with the name "Richmond."

38. LAAW, September 30, 1863.

39. Meshen memorandum book, March 7, 1862, HSP.

40. RLAS, October 9, 1861. See Scott's description of similar activities by the Northern Ohio Soldiers' Aid Society in *Natural Allies*, 60–61.

41. Fannie Dyer to Mrs. Morris, RLAS, November 9, 1863.

42. Evans, "Women's History and Political Theory," 128.

43. LAAW, February 25, 1863.

44. This is most certainly Gail Hamilton (Mary Abigail Dodge's pseudonym), "A Call to My Countrywomen," *Atlantic Monthly* (March 1863). For an insightful reading of this and other essays published by women during the war, see Lyde Cullen Sizer, "'Tis Women's Part of Glory': Northern Women Essayists During the American Civil War," *Retrospection* 1 (1992): 37–49.

45. LAAW, March 25, 1863.
46. LAAW, June 17, 1863, and June 24, 1863.
47. Venet, *Neither Ballots nor Bullets*, 103.
48. LAAW, August 12, 1863.
49. Venet, *Neither Ballots nor Bullets*, 121.
50. As Scott notes, many ladies' aid societies were established before the Sanitary Commission was organized. For the relationship between the Sanitary Commission and local ladies' aid societies, see Attie, "'Swindling Concern.'" Attie convincingly argues that although the Sanitary Commission publicly described its mission as concerned solely with supplying the soldiers and the hospitals as efficiently as possible, there were other goals embedded in its actions. Henry Bellows, Frederick Olmstead, and George Templeton Strong saw in women's benevolent work a chance to channel women's patriotic energies into a new type of nationalism. By getting women to accept a centrally directed institution to oversee their local aid societies, these men hoped to train women to accept an extension of federal power more generally.
51. Attie, "'Swindling Concern,'" 194.
52. Ibid., 202.
53. Printed circular, "The Duties of an Associate Manager," RLAS, Correspondence.
54. RLAS, January 20, 1864.
55. LAAW, November 11, 1863.
56. Mrs. Russell Smith to Mrs. M. B. Grier, December 2, 1863, LAAW, Correspondence.
57. See, for instance, the records of donations received to the Richmond Ladies' Aid Society on July 11, 1863, and July 31, 1863, and sent to the United States Sanitary Commission. RLAS, July 11 and 31, 1863.
58. J. L. Merrill to Ellen Orbison Harris, December 9, 1861, Ellen Matilda Orbison Harris Papers, subgroup III of the Orbison Family Papers, 1750–1902, manuscript group 98. Pennsylvania Historical and Museum Commission, Harrisburg (hereafter PHMC).
59. Elizabeth Varon, "Tippecanoe and the Ladies Too: White Women and Party Politics in Antebellum Virginia," *Journal of American History* 82 (September 1995): 494–521.
60. Abiding by middle-class rules of propriety, the women did not address the soldiers directly but enlisted Mr. King, a soldier from the War of 1812, to present on their behalf.
61. RLAS, October 16, 1861, October 23, 1861. In March 1862, for instance, it was "quite satisfactory" to them that the Tioga Mountaineers had "resolved to keep the flag with them during their campaign," especially since they had understood that the flag had been lost.
62. Mary P. Ryan, *Women in Public: Between Banners and Ballots, 1825–1880* (Baltimore: Johns Hopkins University Press, 1990), 142.
63. Russell Smith was listed in the census as a "landscape painter," with real estate worth $7,000 and personal property worth $10,000. Next to him lived Ellwood Tyson, a farmer, who owned $9,000 worth of real estate and $14,000 personal property. Jacob Tyson had no occupation listed but owned $15,000 worth of real estate and $8,000 worth of personal property. Eighth Census of the United States, 1860, Pennsylvania, vol. 44, Montgomery County I, 1–1037. Clearly, ladies' aid societies served political purposes for the women who joined them. More surprising, perhaps, is the possibility that these societies also played a political role for men. Eligible men who stayed at home rather than joining the army may have found protection from charges of lukewarm patriotism through their participation in ladies' aid societies. In addition, older or disabled men may have found in them a productive way to get involved in the war effort. While women ran ladies' aid societies and completed the great bulk of their labor, men did play a role in the workings of these groups, specifically in collecting and distributing supplies. The Richmond Ladies' Aid Society was meeting in a schoolroom when Mr. Wilson brought in a basket of crab apples and Robert Bailey presented a bushel of

plums for the women to make into preserves. In February 1863 a Weldon committee packed enormous boxes with food and clothing to be sent to Acquia Creek. Ellwood Tyson, Jonathon Bradfield, and Edward Ivins—male relatives of several members—joined the women at the hall and, according to the secretary, rendered "essential service in the work." Ivins also took the boxes to Philadelphia the next day. In June of that year Abner Bradfield and Ivins "gave very important assistance by closing the boxes, furnishing gratuitously the nails and iron hoops for the purpose. Mr. Ivins gave further aid by marking them, and kindly volunteered to take them to the Baltimore Rail Road Depot in the city." Men also contributed money to the women's associations. The Richmond Ladies' Aid Society set up a committee to obtain a monthly sum of twenty-five cents from gentlemen in the vicinity. In Weldon, a few days after the battles at Gettysburg, Abner Bradfield sent the secretary a letter he had just received from his son Thomas, who was in the army. The young soldier made "an enthusiastic appeal" to his father to urge the men of Weldon and the vicinity for "a liberal donation" to the ladies' aid association. The money, he thought, should be used "for the purpose of purchasing further supply of delicacies to alleviate the sufferings of the thousands" of soldiers who had been wounded in the horrible fighting. Thomas Bradfield made it clear that while he assumed women controlled the outlay of funds, men could and should participate in raising them. Helping with the work of a ladies' aid society may have been a way for men on the home front to signal to their neighbors their loyalty and willingness to sacrifice. RLAS, September 1863; LAAW, June 10, 1863, July 8, 1863. I have been unable to locate the ages of these men and do not know, therefore, whether they were eligible to fight or not. If they were not, then their service to the societies may have provided them with a way to channel their patriotic energies, functioning for them in much the same way it did for women. Lori Ginzberg's *Women and the Work of Benevolence* discusses the ways in which the interaction of men and women in antebellum benevolent work disproves the notion of wholly separate worlds in which men and women did not interact. Men and women, in fact, she notes, performed many of the exact same tasks in benevolent societies.

64. The Weldon group elected a board of managers for the hall, which included among others the secretary Mrs. Smith, the president Emeline M. Tyson, the treasurer Hannah Ann Tyson, and Mary B. Tyson. The board met with Willett Comly, who had offered to donate a lot of land "adjacent to his own buildings" for the hall. The women wanted to find out whether he would give them the ground "free from any reserve claim, this being thought the only way in which it could possibly be accepted by the Society." However, it turned out that Comly wanted to have the privilege of using the hall whenever he wanted, "for the use of a company or dancing party too large to be accommodated in his own house." The managers could not accept this, and "Mr. Comly being equally firm it was found necessary to look elsewhere." On March 2, 1864, they purchased a half-acre lot for $225.00. There was a long and rancorous debate over the society's name, the reasons for which are unclear.

65. Lori Ginzberg notes that in the antebellum period, corporate charters were granted easily to "benevolent societies run by prosperous women whose goals conformed to a traditional, charitable framework and whose organizational needs included protecting significant financial resources." She also points out that elite women could exchange financial contributions to political campaigns and their influence with a "certain class of citizens" and contacts within their social circle for material and legal benefits to their organizations. She notes that the women who incorporated their societies were "among the most influential in their communities, and their organizations were financially and culturally significant institutions." The Weldon case supports this finding for the wartime period as well. See *Women and the Work of Benevolence*, 52, 53, 77.

66. LAAW, March 9, 1864.

67. Mrs. Russell Smith to Mr. Thomas Cochran, copied in minutes of the LAAW, in report made to the president on March 9, 1864.

68. LAAW, October 12 and 19, 1864.

69. LAAW, November 22, 1865.

70. LAAW, November 9, 1864.

71. LAAW, January 25, 1865. As the war wound down, the women's benevolent activities turned more and more toward the freedpeople, and they may therefore have felt less competition with whoever was making these requests. The women also formed a relationship with Colonel Wagner of Camp William Penn, a military camp for black soldiers outside of Philadelphia. A band from the camp often played for the fairs and fund-raising activities the aid society sponsored, and the women had given a Thanksgiving dinner to the soldiers there. Perhaps their continuing interaction with the African-American soldiers and their commander heightened their awareness of the needs of the freedmen and made them more interested in aiding that cause.

72. Meshen memorandum book, April 7, 1865.

73. Attie, "'Swindling Concern,'" 363.

74. Mrs. Thomas W. James to Mrs. Russell Smith, July 5, 1865, LAAW, Correspondence.

75. LAAW, August 16, 1865.

76. LAAW, March 3, 1869.

77. Ladies' Aid Society of Philadelphia, *Fourth Semi-Annual Report* (Philadelphia: C. Sherman, Son, 1863), 5. Anne Scott points out that their work had real economic and military significance and that, ironically, if they had not produced so much for the armies, the war may have ended sooner.

78. LAAW, Minutes, vol. 1, front cover. Smith added, "Therefore, I would suggest (although I have no right to interfere) that when the Society breaks up (which may happen) these journals be deposited in the State Library or one of those lasting public ones in Philadelphia."

79. Elizabeth Cady Stanton and others, *History of Woman Suffrage*, 6 vols. (1881–1922; repr., New York: Arno Press and the New York Times, 1969), 2:88.

80. RLAS, "First Report," unpub., October 26, 1863.

CHAPTER 4. "THE WORLD WILL LITTLE NOTE NOR LONG REMEMBER"

1. Cindy L. Small, *The Jennie Wade Story: A True and Complete Account of the Only Civilian Killed During the Battle of Gettysburg* (Gettysburg, Pa.: Thomas Publications, 1991), 30.

2. Examples included the poems "The Maid of Gettysburg" by R. Stewart Gibbs and the anonymously penned "Jennie Wade." Both in Ann Brophy, *The Story of Jennie Wade: The Only Civilian Casualty at the Battle of Gettysburg* (Fairfield, Conn.: by the author, 1988), 27–31.

3. Bret Harte, "John Burns of Gettysburg," in *Bret Harte: Representative Selections, with Introduction, Bibliography, and Notes*, ed. Joseph B. Harrison (New York: American Book Company, 1941), 48–51.

4. James M. McPherson, *Battle Cry of Freedom: The Civil War Era* (New York: Oxford University Press, 1988), 584. For an example of the debate surrounding the attributes of "loyal" womanhood and their appropriate display, see "A Few Words in Behalf of the Loyal Women of the United States by One of Themselves (Loyal Publication Society No. 10)," in *Union Pamphlets of the Civil War, 1861–1865*, 2 vols., ed. Frank Freidel (Cambridge: Harvard University Press, Belknap Press, 1967), 2:766–86.

5. I use the term "separate spheres" to refer to the historically specific nineteenth-century ideology that imposed a set of boundaries, with regard to socially acceptable behavior, on both women and men. For a discussion of the multiple uses (and abuses) of this term by historians, see Linda K. Kerber's essay, "Separate Spheres, Female Worlds, Woman's Place: The Rhetoric of Women's History," *Journal of American History* 75 (June 1988): 9–39.

6. Recent scholarship has questioned the utility of accepting separate spheres as the metalanguage of nineteenth-century gender relations. Such studies as Deborah Gray White's *Ar'n't I a Woman?: Female Slaves in the Plantation South* (New York: W. W. Norton, 1985) and Christine Stansell's *City of Women: Sex and Class in New York, 1789–1860* (New York: Alfred A. Knopf, 1986) reveal that separate spheres ideology spoke only to some groups of nineteenth-century women (primarily white, native-born, middle-class Protestants) and was, in many cases, more prescription than reality. Such books as Wendy Venet's *Neither Ballots nor Bullets: Women Abolitionists and the Civil War* (Charlottesville: University Press of Virginia, 1991) and Lori Ginzberg's *Women and the Work of Benevolence: Morality, Politics and Class in the Nineteenth-Century United States* (New Haven: Yale University Press, 1990), however, show that separate spheres ideals (and corresponding notions of boundaries) did persist for white middle-class women involved in mid-nineteenth-century abolition and benevolent organizations. It is therefore reasonable to conclude that separate spheres ideology retained its hold over socially acceptable behavior for the men and women of Gettysburg, Pennsylvania, a town with all the aspirations of white middle-class America in the mid-nineteenth century.

7. For a detailed account of the fighting, see Edwin B. Coddington, *The Gettysburg Campaign: A Study in Command* (New York: Charles Scribner's Sons, 1968).

8. Sarah Sites Rodgers, *The Ties of the Past: The Gettysburg Diaries of Salome Myers Stewart, 1854–1922* (Gettysburg, Pa.: Thomas Publications, 1996), 161.

9. Coddington, *Gettysburg Campaign*, 167–68.

10. Sallie Myers used "In Rebeldom" as the dateline for her Friday, June 26, 1863, diary entry and described Confederate campfires "in the Mountains" three days later. See Rodgers, *Ties of the Past*, 161, 162.

11. Sarah M. Broadhead, *The Diary of a Lady of Gettysburg, Pennsylvania: From June 15 to July 15, 1863* (1864; repr., Hershey, Pa.: Gary T. Hawbaker, 1990), 15 (page references are to reprint edition).

12. The Gettysburg women did share one common characteristic: all were white. No eyewitness account of the battle of Gettysburg by an African-American woman has yet come to light.

13. Sarah Broadhead's story has been widely retold and often offered as the "woman's" version of the battle of Gettysburg. A recent example is its inclusion in Ken Burns's immensely popular PBS documentary "The Civil War."

14. This was unusual. None of the women listed as a schoolteacher in the 1860 census was a wife and mother. In fact, Sarah Broadhead was not listed as a teacher on the 1860 census. This probably was because her daughter Mary was only seven months old at the time. 1860 census, Adams County Historical Society, Gettysburg, Pa. (hereafter ACHS).

15. Broadhead, *Diary of a Lady of Gettysburg.*

16. William Frassanito offers excellent discussions of the physical location of structures in 1863 Gettysburg in his two photographic histories of the battle and the town: *Gettysburg: A Journey in Time* (New York: Charles Scribner's Sons, 1975), and *Early Photography at Gettysburg* (Gettysburg, Pa.: Thomas Publications, 1995).

17. There is no indication that Mary McAllister had help from either John or Martha Scott in the day-to-day operation of the store. The 1860 census lists John as a merchant and Martha as a wife. 1860 census, ACHS.

18. Mary McAllister, *Philadelphia Inquirer,* July 26–29, 1938 (transcribed by Robert L. Brake, July 1974), file 8–11: Mary McAllister account, Gettysburg National Military Park Library (hereafter GNMPL).

19. Broadhead, *Diary of a Lady of Gettysburg,* 16.

20. [Elizabeth Salome Myers], "How a Gettysburg Schoolteacher Spent Her Vacation in 1863," *San Francisco Sunday Call,* August 16, 1903 (transcribed by Robert L. Brake), file 8–13: Elizabeth "Sallie" Myers account, West High Street, GNMPL; Clifton Johnson, "The School Teacher," in *Battleground Adventures* (Boston: Houghton Mifflin, 1915), 176–82. Sallie Myers's diaries have more recently been collected by her great-great-granddaughter Sarah Sites Rodgers and published as *The Ties of the Past.*

21. Sallie's younger sister Sue also left an account of the battle. [Sue Myers], "Some Battle Experience as Remembered by a Young School Girl," *Gettysburg Compiler,* April 24, 1907 (transcribed [n.d.]), file 8–2, Battlefield Adventures: Civilian Accounts, GNMPL.

22. The *Gettysburg Compiler,* July 1, 1903, reported an encore performance given by these same "girls" some forty years later. According to the article, "The idea originated with Mrs. Sallie M[yers] Stewart and immediately took hold with the other women who encouraged the soldiers with their sweet melodies."

23. Tillie was a naïve young girl caught up in the romance of the moment. She prepared bouquets of flowers to give to the men as they marched by, but in her excitement promptly forgot about them. She remembered them sitting on the kitchen table where she had left them only after the men had passed by and the battle had begun. Mrs. Tillie (Pierce) Alleman, *At Gettysburg: Or What a Girl Saw and Heard of the Battle* (1889; repr., Baltimore, Md.: Butternut and Blue, 1987), 33–35.

24. Fannie J. Buehler, *Recollections of the Rebel Invasion and One Woman's Experience During the Battle of Gettysburg* (1896; repr., Hershey, Pa.: Gary T. Hawbaker, n.d.).

25. Ibid., 10.

26. Parts of this letter were subsequently published as newspaper articles. [Jennie McCreary], "A Letter Written July 1863," *Gettysburg Compiler,* July 1, 1903; [Jennie McCreary], "Girl Saw Streets Filled with Dead and Wounded at Gettysburg," *Philadelphia Evening Bulletin,* July 2, 1938. Copies of both newspaper clippings in Battle Eyewitness Accounts Compilation, eleven loose-leaf binder volumes (hereafter BEAC), ACHS.

27. [Sarah Barrett King], "Battle Days in 1863," *Gettysburg Compiler,* July 4, 1906, p. 2.

28. "It would be a surprising thing," wrote King, "if I could name the different articles the bosom of my dress contained." Ibid.

29. Mrs. Jacob A. Clutz [Liberty Augusta Hollinger], "The Battle of Gettysburg," ed. Elsie Singmaster, *Pennsylvania History* 5 (July 1938): 166–78.

30. [Harriet Hamilton Bayly], *Gettysburg Star and Sentinel,* September 25, 1888, p. 1, copy of newspaper clipping in BEAC, ACHS; [Harriet Hamilton Bayly], "Mrs. Joseph Bayly's Story of the Battle: Mother of William Hamilton Bayly," *Gettysburg Compiler Scrapbook* (n.d.) (transcribed by William Ridinger, October 30, 1939), file 8–5: Mrs. Joseph Bayly account, GNMPL.

31. Peter Thorn was mustered in to Company B of the 138th Pennsylvania Volunteers on August 16, 1862. He spent the Gettysburg Campaign at Harpers Ferry and Washington, D.C. File 8–15: Elizabeth Thorn account Evergreen Cemetery Gatehouse, GNMPL; and Eileen Conklin, *Women at Gettysburg 1863* (Gettysburg, Pa.: Thomas Publications, 1993), 166.

32. Elizabeth gave birth to a girl in early October 1863. She named the child Rosa Meade Thorn in honor of the commander of the Army of the Potomac, Major General George Gordon Meade.

33. Mrs. Peter [Elizabeth] Thorn, "Experience During Battle," *Gettysburg Compiler,* July 26, 1905, p. 2, copy of newspaper clipping in BEAC, ACHS; and [Elizabeth Thorn], "Mrs. Thorn's War Story," *Gettysburg Times,* July 2, 1938.

34. This includes men who were absent for part of the time but were not gone for the duration of the battle. For example, Harriet Hamilton Bayly's husband was gone on an errand to a neighbor's when the Confederates arrived at her farm. Also, Sarah Broadhead's husband was back in town before the battle although he had been a member of a party that hoped to halt the Confederate advance by felling trees in their path.

35. Bayly, *Gettysburg Compiler Scrapbook* account, 1.

36. Three war scares occurred in Gettysburg during the Civil War: April 1861, July and August 1862, and June 1863. Charles H. Glatfelter, "The Gettysburg Community in 1863," unpub. paper, file 9-G1b: History of Gettysburg, General Information folder #2, GNMPL.

37. King, "Battle Days," 2, 3.

38. Examples include Broadhead, *Diary of a Lady of Gettysburg*, 7, 8; Hollinger account, 169; and Myers, *Battleground Adventures*, 176.

39. Bayly, *Star and Sentinel* account, n.p.

40. Reid Mitchell found that many Confederates were proud of their restraint in the invasion of Pennsylvania. See his *Civil War Soldiers: Their Expectations and Experiences* (New York: Simon and Schuster, 1988), 152–54.

41. Lorenzo L. Crounse, "Further Details of the Battle of Gettysburgh—Characteristics of the People of the Town—Interesting Incidents, & c.," *New York Times*, July 9, 1863. In fact, one of the few townspeople who escaped Crounse's wrath was John Burns. By instinctively fighting to protect his home—without regard for age, infirmity, or the niceties of military organization—Burns, it seemed, had set himself apart from the majority of men in and around Gettysburg. Bret Harte's ode to John Burns echoed this sentiment: "He was the fellow who won renown/The only man who didn't back down/When the Rebels rode through his native town/But held his own in the fight next day/When all his townsfolk ran away." Harte quoted from Harrison, ed., *Bret Harte*, 48.

42. *Adams Sentinel*, July 14, 1863. For a more recent treatment of this debate, see Timothy Smith, "'Those Were Days of Horror': The Gettysburg Civilians," *Unsung Heroes of Gettysburg: Programs of the Fifth Annual Gettysburg Seminar* (Gettysburg, Pa.: National Park Service, 1996), 81–89.

43. McAllister account, 5; King, "Battle Days," 2; Buehler account, 19.

44. Broadhead, *Diary of a Lady of Gettysburg*, 16. Mary McAllister also recalled how "we thought we were safe" when the Union troops arrived on July 1. McAllister account, 1.

45. Thorn, *Compiler* account, 2; Hollinger account, 168; McCreary, *Evening Bulletin* and *Compiler* accounts, n.p.

46. General Orders Number 73, as cited in *The Wartime Papers of R. E. Lee*, ed. Clifford Dowdey (Boston: Little, Brown, 1961), 533–34. For a discussion of these orders, especially how and why they were later disregarded by Brigadier General John McCausland in 1864, see Everard H. Smith, "Chambersburg: Anatomy of a Confederate Reprisal," *American Historical Review* 96, no. 2 (April 1991): 432–55.

47. The Confederates occupied a large portion of the town from the evening of July 1 to the early morning of July 4. Thus, despite Lee's exhortations in General Orders Number 73, the guards were apparently protecting the townswomen from the unruly element within their own army.

48. King, "Battle Days," 3; McAllister account, 5.

49. On Southern women confronting Union troops in the occupied South, see Stephen V. Ash, *When the Yankees Came: Conflict and Chaos in the Occupied South, 1861–1865* (Chapel Hill: University of North Carolina Press, 1995), esp. 42–44. It is tempting to view the women of Gettysburg as analogous to Southern women because of their firsthand experience of invasion and battle. One should be wary, however, of making too many connections between the

experiences of Southern women and their Northern counterparts—even those who experienced physical hardships as the result of an enemy invasion—because of the wide disparity of material circumstances between the two groups. On Southern women and the Civil War, see Drew Gilpin Faust, *Mothers of Invention: Women of the Slaveholding South in the American Civil War* (Chapel Hill: University of North Carolina Press, 1996); George Rable, *Civil Wars: Women and the Crisis of Southern Nationalism* (Urbana: University of Illinois Press, 1989); Lee Ann Whites, *The Civil War as a Crisis in Gender: Augusta, Georgia, 1860–1890* (Athens: University of Georgia Press, 1995); and various essays included in Catherine Clinton and Nina Silber, eds., *Divided Houses: Gender and the Civil War* (New York: Oxford University Press, 1992).

50. Thorn, *Compiler* account, 2; Broadhead, *Diary of a Lady of Gettysburg*, 18.

51. King, "Battle Days," 3; Bayly, *Star and Sentinel* account, n.p.; McAllister account, 4.

52. McAllister account, 3; Broadhead, *Diary of a Lady of Gettysburg*, 18; Myers, *Sunday Call* account, 2.

53. Broadhead, *Diary of a Lady of Gettysburg*, 19–20.

54. For further discussion of this dismissive attitude, as well as a trenchant analysis of the subsequent demand for recognition of women's labor donations to the Northern war effort, see Jeanie Attie, "Warwork and the Crisis of Domesticity in the North," in *Divided Houses*, ed., Clinton and Silber, 247–59. Elizabeth D. Leonard also focuses on women war workers' struggles for recognition in *Yankee Women: Gender Battles in the Civil War* (New York: W. W. Norton, 1994).

55. But Jennie Wade's mother did. She applied for and was awarded a mother's pension for Jennie's service during the battle. This is significant because the most traditional service rendered by a woman during the battle resulted in one of the most nontraditional demands. Her request was so unusual that the mother's pension form that Mary Wade filled out had to be modified: in every instance the word "son" was neatly crossed out and "daughter" put in its place. Copy of application in Wade Family file, ACHS.

56. These findings are consistent with J. Matthew Gallman's recent study of Gettysburg, which argues that although the exigencies of the Civil War created "a world in flux" for the men and women of Gettysburg, "the larger story is one of broad continuities." See J. Matthew Gallman with Susan Baker, "Gettysburg's Gettysburg: What the Battle Did to the Borough," in *The Gettysburg Nobody Knows*, ed. Gabor S. Boritt (New York: Oxford University Press, 1997), 147.

57. Thorn recalled, "For all the work of burying the soldiers we never received any extra pay from the cemetery nor from any other source, only the monthly salary of $13." Her responsibilities may have multiplied, but her remuneration had not. Thorn, *Compiler* account, 2.

58. Myers, *Sunday Call* account, 3; McCreary, *Compiler* account, n.p.; Broadhead, *Diary of a Lady of Gettysburg*, 19.

59. Buehler account, 22.

60. Myers, *Sunday Call* account, 3.

61. Camp Letterman was named for the medical director of the Army of the Potomac, Jonathan Letterman. For a detailed examination of the field hospitals in and around Gettysburg after the battle, see Gregory Coco, *A Vast Sea of Misery: A History and Guide to the Union and Confederate Field Hospitals at Gettysburg July 1–November 20, 1863* (Gettysburg, Pa.: Thomas Publications, 1988).

62. Here I refer to Stephen B. Oates's description of Clara Barton "seizing" the opportunity that nursing in the Civil War brought to her in *A Woman of Valor: Clara Barton and the Civil War* (New York: Free Press, 1994).

63. David McConaughy (Elizabeth Thorn's boss) and David Wills were the two local men most instrumental in establishing the GBMA. The organization was very localized in character until 1880, when veterans of the Grand Army of the Republic were able to dominate the board of directors. For more information on the GBMA, see John Mitchell Vanderslice, *Gettysburg: A*

History of the Gettysburg Battle-field Memorial Association (Philadelphia: The Memorial Association, 1897), and Gerald R. Bennett, *Days of "Uncertainty and Dread": The Ordeal Endured by the Citizens at Gettysburg* (Littlestown, Pa.: by the author, 1994), 87–90.

64. In her application for a mother's pension filed August 4, 1882, Mary Wade claimed that she had been dependent on Jennie since her husband had died. This is interesting, considering that James Wade was still alive in the Adams County Poor House when Jennie was killed in 1863. Was this merely a reluctance to acknowledge unsavory family secrets, or did Mary Wade intentionally exploit the popular image of her daughter as the selfless heroine of Gettysburg for her own economic gain? Evidence suggests the latter. In 1882 Mary Wade still had two healthy sons, Samuel and Harry, who could have been expected to support her, yet she applied for the mother's pension. And although the Wade family had not been wealthy, they were not altogether destitute. The 1860 census listed Mary Wade as a tailoress with $250 in real estate and $50 in personal estate. When Jennie's sister, Georgia Anna (who had been listed as a milliner), left this household to marry John Louis McClellan in 1862, no doubt Jennie had become a vital contributor to the household's economy. However, a claim that Jennie had totally supported her mother at the time of her death must be treated as highly suspect. A copy of the act of the U.S. Congress granting Mary Wade a mother's pension is in Wade Family file, ACHS.

65. For more information on the intricacies of Jennie Wade's local "scandals," see John S. Patterson, "John Burns and Jennie Wade: The Hero and Heroine of Gettysburg?" unpub. paper presented to the American Folklore Society meeting, Philadelphia, October 19, 1989, in file 8–28 (John Burns: July 1st), GNMPL, 11, and Frassanito, *Early Photography at Gettysburg*, 119–28.

66. Letter from Frank Moore to John Burns, January 17, 1866, in John Burns Family file, ACHS. Moore's book was eventually published as *Women of the War: Their Heroism and Self-Sacrifice* (Hartford, Conn.: S. S. Scranton, 1866).

67. Burns was elected constable in 1855, appointed in 1856, and elected in 1857. He ran again in 1860 but was defeated. File 8–28 (John Burns: July 1st), GNMPL. It is relevant that in Burns's obituary, the local press insisted on placing the word hero in quotation marks. *Gettysburg Star and Sentinel*, February 9, 1872, as cited in Patterson, "Hero and Heroine of Gettysburg?" 8.

68. "Although many years ago, somewhat free in his habits as to drinking, he has for some twenty years past been a strictly temperate man, not having tasted liquor during that time." Copy of report of the United States Senate in John Burns Family file, ACHS. Burns was awarded a pension of eight dollars a month for his service at Gettysburg—an amount equal to that later awarded to Mary Wade for the service of Jennie.

69. Mrs. Burns's reaction was recorded by Gettysburg resident Henry Dustman. His account was reprinted in the *Gettysburg Times*, December 5, 1946, copy of clipping in BEAC, ACHS.

CHAPTER 5. THE AVERY MONUMENT

1. The only twentieth-century writings on the Avery Monument are found in Pittsburgh area newspapers and a mention in the short biography of Charles Avery by Stanton Balfour, "Charles Avery: Early Pittsburgh Philanthropist," *Western Pennsylvania Historical Magazine* 43, no. 1 (March 1960): 19–22. The monument is identified as the earliest depiction of African Americans in public sculpture by Kirk Savage in *Standing Soldiers, Kneeling Slaves: Race, War, and Monument in Nineteenth-Century America* (Princeton: Princeton University Press, 1997), 70–72.

2. On rural cemeteries, see David Charles Sloane, *The Last Great Necessity: Cemeteries in American History* (Baltimore: Johns Hopkins University Press, 1991), 1–98, which builds upon the

brief observations of Frederic A. Scharf, "The Garden Cemetery and American Sculpture: Mount Auburn," *Art Quarterly* 24, no. 1 (spring 1961): 80–88. French and British influences are discussed by Richard A. Etlin, *The Architecture of Death: The Transformation of the Cemetery in Eighteenth-Century Paris* (Cambridge: MIT Press, 1984), 358–68, and by Blanche Linden-Ward, "Putting the Past Under Grass: History as Death and Cemetery Commemoration," *Prospects* 10 (1985): 279–314. For an example of interracial uses of cemeteries for recreational purposes, see Annie Parker, "Rural Cemeteries," *Frederick Douglass' Paper* (August 13, 1852). For Pittsburgh's rural cemetery, see Walter C. Kidney, *Allegheny Cemetery: A Romantic Landscape in Pittsburgh* (Pittsburgh: Pittsburgh History and Landmarks Foundation, 1990), and Roy Lubove, "Pittsburgh's Allegheny Cemetery and the Victorian Garden of the Dead," *Pittsburgh History* 75, no. 3 (fall 1992): 148–56.

3. For the monument to Bowditch, see Blanche Linden-Ward, *Silent City on a Hill: Landscapes of Memory and Boston's Mount Auburn Cemetery* (Columbus: Ohio State University Press, 1989), 236–38 and 282–83.

4. The Avery Monument does not fit well into either of two recent attempts at establishing a typology of grave markers in major American cemeteries. See Kenneth L. Ames, "Ideologies in Stone: Meanings in Victorian Gravestones," *Journal of Popular Culture* 4, no. 4 (spring 1981): 641–56, and Peggy McDowell and Richard E. Meyer, *The Revival Styles in American Memorial Art* (Bowling Green: Bowling Green State University Popular Press, 1994).

5. The first published biography of Charles Avery was written by the popular journalist James Parton: "Charles Avery," in his *People's Book of Biography; or, Short Lives of the Most Interesting Persons of All Ages and Countries* (Hartford: A. S. Hale, 1868), 122–27. It was apparently written during Parton's 1867 tour of Midwestern cities that also produced the profile of Pittsburgh for *Atlantic Monthly*, in which he coined the phrase "Hell with the lid off" to describe the nation's center for heavy industry: Milton E. Flower, *James Parton* (Durham: Duke University Press, 1951), 78–91. Parton's tribute to Avery opened with a description of the monument and returned to the grave site at its conclusion. This narrative device was imitated by subsequent biographers: "Rev. Charles Avery," *People's Monthly* 1, no. 2 (July 1871): 17–18, which contained the most hyperbolic praise of the monument, and *History of Allegheny County Pennsylvania*, 2 vols. (Chicago: A. Warner, 1889), 1: s.v. "Avery." These last two biographies were commissioned by the executors of Avery's estate. See "3rd and Final Account of Josiah King surviving executor of . . . ," City of Pittsburgh, Orphan's Court, #84, June term, 1879, Allegheny County, Register of Wills, Pittsburgh, Pennsylvania (hereafter Allegheny County). The contents of these two commissioned biographies were repeated in most subsequent biographies.

6. The Avery project seems to be one of four surviving sculptures by Louis Verhaegen. His full-length portrait, *Daniel Webster*, is owned by the St. Louis Mercantile Library Association. It was a gift from Henry D. Bacon acquired between 1846 and 1859. See *A Guide to the Sculpture, Paintings, and Other Objects of Art, in the Halls of the St. Louis Mercantile Library Association, December, 1859* (St. Louis: George Knapp, 1859), cat. #3. This Webster portrait is the only one of Verhaegen's extant works that predates the Avery commission. While completing the Avery project, Verhaegen began a monument for John Scudder, a missionary from New Jersey who worked in India on behalf of the Dutch Reformed Church and who died at the Cape of Good Hope in 1855. Fundraising for his monument began in 1859. By mid-1860 Verhaegen had been commissioned and the fund-raising committee requested that the Scudder Monument be placed in Brooklyn's Greenwood Cemetery, but this idea was rejected by the church's governing board. Instead the sculpture was erected near Hertzog Hall, at Seminary Place, in New Brunswick and was moved to its current location, in the yard of the First Reformed Church of that city, in 1862. A relief panel on the front of this monument has similarities to the relief in the Avery Monument—a portrait of the deceased holding a Bible and gesturing, in this case as if preaching to South Asians in loin

cloths gathered at both sides to listen. Badly worn indications of architecture, presumably Indian, are discernible behind the group. See the Inventory of American Sculpture Database maintained by the National Museum of American Art, and Meredith Arms Bzdak and Douglas Petersen, *Public Sculpture in New Jersey: Monuments to Collective Identity* (New Brunswick: Rutgers University Press, 1999). The dates related to Scudder's monument can be determined from *The Acts and Proceedings of the General Synod of the Reformed Protestant Dutch Church in North America* (New York: Board of Publication of the Reformed Protestant Dutch Church, for 1859, 1860, and 1861) and two letters from Thomas C. Doremus, chairman of the monument committee, held in the papers of the Reformed Church in America, Board of Foreign Missions, at the New Brunswick Theological Seminary Library. (I am grateful to Russell Gasero, archivist of the Reformed Church in America, for helping to establish the dates of the Scudder Monument.)

For Verhaegen's Lytle Monument in Cincinnati's Spring Grove Cemetery, see McDowell and Meyer, *Revival Styles*, 77, and Blanche M. G. Linden, *Spring Grove: Celebrating 150 Years* (Cincinnati: Cincinnati Historical Society, 1995), 77–78. Like Verhaegen's other extant works, the Lytle Monument was carved of marble, apparently shortly after the war. It deteriorated so badly that it was remade of granite in 1915. It contains a relief panel of the battle of Chickamauga that Linden believes may have been a separate work by Randolph Rogers. The bibliography on Verhaegen (also seen as "Verhagen") is scant: George C. Groce and David H. Wallace, *New-York Historical Society's Dictionary of Artists in America, 1564–1860* (New Haven: Yale University Press, 1957), 648, reports that Verhaegen was listed with a partner (Peeiffer or Pfeiffer) in the *New York City Business Directory* in 1851, that Verhaegen was listed alone in directories from 1851 through 1860, and that he exhibited a "marble bust" of Daniel Webster and a plaster figure of Tom Thumb at the American Institute in 1856. The Webster won a bronze medal at the American Institute for "best marble bust." It could be the same work now owned by the St. Louis Mercantile Library Association or perhaps another version of it. The plaster *Tom Thumb* might well have been a fanciful conceit, a common type exemplified by Harriet Hosmer's *Puck* and described in William H. Gerdts, *American Neo-Classic Sculpture: The Marble Resurrection* (New York: Viking, 1973), 136–37. But *Tom Thumb* could also have been a portrait of the popular circus midget. The American Institute exhibits were trade and patent shows in which the arts played a minor role: *Transactions of the American Institute, of the City of New York* (Albany: The Legislature, 1857), 142. Verhaegen also contributed a sculpture or a painting (or both) entitled *Union* to the auction and exhibition held for the Metropolitan Sanitary Fair in New York in 1864. See James Yarnall et al., *The National Museum of American Art's Index to American Art Exhibition Catalogues from the Beginning Through the 1876 Centennial Year*, 6 vols. (Boston: G. K. Hall, 1986), 6:3704.

7. "The Avery Monument and Statue," *Scientific American*, n.s., 1, no. 23 (December 3, 1859): 364.

8. Avery's business dealings must be pieced together from disparate sources. Before the 1830s these were mostly recollections of acquaintants. During the late 1830s his investments were of a scale that they were sometimes mentioned in the newspapers. Many of the newspaper items are cited in Erasmus Wilson, *Standard History of Pittsburg Pennsylvania* (Chicago: H. R. Cornell, 1898). Wilson was a Pittsburgh newspaper journalist and his extensive chronicle serves as a partial index to Pittsburgh's nineteenth-century news media. Avery made the transition from comfortable wealth to remarkable wealth by his investment in copper mining. See Donald Chaput, *The Cliff Mine: America's First Great Copper Mine* (Kalamazoo: Sequoia Press, 1971), 19–77.

9. On Avery's patronage of Duncanson, see Joseph D. Ketner, *The Emergence of the African-American Artist: Robert S. Duncanson, 1821–1872* (Columbia: University of Missouri Press, 1993), 25–45, and cat. #16 and #38. The *Garden of Eden* was the only object in Avery's home that was bequeathed separately: "I give to Wm. M. Shinn, as a testimonial of my appreciation of his active

interest in the education and elevation of the colored race inhabiting this country, my large picture representing the Garden of Eden, painted by Duncanson, a colored artist of the City of Cincinnati." City of Pittsburgh, Orphan's Court, Will Books, vol. 9, p. 11, 1858, Allegheny County. In the inventory of his household it was valued at $250, a sum greater than any other item within the well-furnished house. The twenty-two other prints and paintings listed, mostly portraits of Methodist leaders or family members, were appraised at a total of $228. See City of Pittsburgh, Orphan's Court, "Schedule of Household Furniture & Etc. . . . Rev. Charles Avery," 1858, Allegheny County.

10. The scholarship at Oberlin was endowed in January 1849. It was used to pay tuition and other expenses for an African American from Pittsburgh named Amelia Freeman. Afterward it was to be assigned to another African-American student by the faculty or by Avery. See Treasurer's Journal, #14, p. 303; and Secretary's Office, Catalog and Record of Colored Students, Archives of Oberlin College, Oberlin, Ohio (hereafter Oberlin). John Peck, a wig maker who was active in the region's early black conventions, has been credited with the idea that Avery should start a college. See Ann G. Wilmoth, "Pittsburgh and the Blacks: A Short History, 1780–1875" (Ph.D. diss., University Park: The Pennsylvania State University, 1975), 183, and Joe W. Trotter, Jr., *River Jordan: African-American Urban Life in the Ohio Valley* (Lexington: University of Kentucky Press, 1998), 40, 45. Peck was also considered a leader in establishing Pittsburgh's African Methodist Episcopal Church. See Benjamin T. Tanner, *An Apology for African Methodism* (Baltimore: n.p., n.d.), 289–93. For Martin Delany's assertion that the editorials in his Pittsburgh newspaper, the *Mystery*, inspired Avery's college, see Frank A. Rollin, *Life and Public Services of Martin R. Delany* (Boston: Lee and Shepard, 1868), 50. Avery was active in the Pittsburgh Anti-Slavery Society, along with Delany and several other leaders of the black community. In the 1830s that organization proposed, but did not realize, a school. See Wilmoth, "Pittsburgh and the Blacks," 71–74.

11. On this denomination and Avery's role in it, see Wallace Guy Smeltzer, *Methodism on the Headwaters of the Ohio, the History of the Pittsburgh Conference of the Methodist Church* (Nashville: Parthenon, 1951), 137–50; T. H. Colhouer, *Sketches of the Founders of the Methodist Protestant Church* (Pittsburgh: Methodist Protestant Book Concern, 1880), 420–27; and George Brown, *Recollections of Itinerant Life* (Cincinnati: R. W. Carroll, 1866), 168–70, 206–18. Avery's earliest activities as a preacher were recorded in the diaries of John Wrenshall, the first ordained circuit rider assigned to the Pittsburgh area. He welcomed Avery's willingness to help him with his preaching duties in 1814 because Wrenshall's sideline of trading in banned British goods was requiring increasing amounts of his time. See John Wrenshall, Mss. Journal, vol. 3, pp. 112–15, Historical Society of Western Pennsylvania, Pittsburgh, Pennsylvania (hereafter HSWP). Later glimpses of Avery's preaching are found in John Scott, *Recollections of Fifty Years in the Ministry* (Pittsburgh: Methodist Protestant Board of Publication, 1898), 87–94.

12. The well-known split in the Methodist Episcopal Church into northern and southern denominations occurred in 1844. The less famous schism over slavery in Avery's Methodist Protestant Church took place throughout the 1850s, culminating in the north-south division of that denomination in 1857. See Ancel H. Bassett, *A Concise History of the Methodist Protestant Church* (Pittsburgh: James Robinson, 1877), 156–61. Even before the official split, Avery was involved in pro- and antislavery tensions in his denomination such as those surrounding the effort to establish a seminary in Uniontown, Pennsylvania. See W. Harrison Daniel, "Madison College, 1851–1858: A Methodist Protestant School," *Methodist History* 17, no. 2 (January 1979): 90–105.

13. Colhouer, *Sketches*, 427.

14. "Rev. Charles Avery," *Pittsburgh Gazette*, January 19, 1858; "Will of the Late Rev. Charles Avery," *Pittsburgh Gazette*, January 25, 1858.

15. Hugh Honour, *The Image of the Black in Western Art*, vol. 4, *From the American Revolution to World War I* (Cambridge: Menil Foundation, 1989), pt. 1, 170.

16. City of Pittsburgh, Orphan's Court, Will Books, vol. 9, pp. 9–15, 1858, Allegheny County. The will and a complex group of documents related to the dispersal of the estate were recorded in Allegheny County's "Register for the Probate of Wills" (now the Office of the Register of Wills) between March 1857 and June 1879. These include the will, three codicils, an inventory of the estate (including the books and artwork in the household), some records of a challenge to the will, and accounts of the executor's disbursement of funds.

17. The Republican contest for governor began behind the scenes at least one full year before the February 1860 state party convention. See John F. Coleman, *The Disruption of the Pennsylvania Democracy, 1848–1860* (Harrisburg: Pennsylvania Historical and Museum Commission, 1975), 130. The reason for starting early was that the gubernatorial election was seen as the major effort by both the Democratic and Republican Parties since the presidential outcome was predictable in the region. See Michael F. Holt, *Forging a Majority: The Formation of the Republican Party in Pittsburgh, 1848–1860* (New Haven: Yale University Press, 1969), 272–73. A biography of Howe claims that his friends urged him toward this nomination "when the memorable gubernatorial campaign of 1859 and '60 dawned on the view." See Seelye A. Willson, "The Growth of Pittsburgh Iron and Steel," *Magazine of Western History* 2, no. 6 (October 1885): 552. So it is likely that Howe's considerations about running for governor would have predated the commissioning of the monument. Biographical information on Thomas M. Howe can be found in *Biographical Encyclopedia of Pennsylvania of the Nineteenth Century* (Philadelphia: Galaxy Publishing, 1874), 662–63; Willson, "Growth of Pittsburgh Iron," 550–56; *History of Allegheny County*, 1:239, 2:262–63; Wilson, *Standard History of Pittsburgh*, 1004–5; *Encyclopaedia of Contemporary Biography of Pennsylvania*, 3 vols. (New York: Atlantic Publishing and Engraving, 1898), 1:74–76; and *History of Pittsburgh and Environs*, 5 vols. (New York: American Historical Society, 1922), 3:851–53.

18. *Biographical Encyclopedia*, 645; Wilson, *Standard History of Pittsburgh*, 132, 339, 789, 830; and "Meeting of the Republican County Convention," *Pittsburgh Daily True Press*, January 5, 1860. The Henry King Siebeneck Collection, HSWP, contains some family letters to and from King regarding his respect for his mother's religious teachings. During the 1860s Howe and King became active in founding the Allegheny Observatory. See Wallace R. Beardsley, "The Allegheny Observatory During the Era of the Telescope Association, 1859–1867," *Western Pennsylvania Historical Magazine* 64, no. 3 (June 1981): 213–36.

19. Charles C. Arensberg, "Evergreen Hamlet," *Western Pennsylvania Historical Magazine* 38, nos. 3–4 (fall–winter 1955): 117–23; Wilson, *Standard History of Pittsburgh*, 238, 387, 783, 787, 790, 795, 813–14, 822, 827; *Pittsburgh Saturday Visitor*, July 27, 1853; death notice in the *Pittsburgh Gazette*, August 31, 1865.

20. R. J. M. Blackett, "Freedom, or the Martyr's Grave: Black Pittsburgh's Aid to the Fugitive Slave," *Western Pennsylvania Historical Magazine* 61, no. 2 (April 1978): 127–28, notes that Howe's stance on the Fugitive Slave Act was somewhat slippery.

21. Joseph P. Gazzam [to an officer of Oberlin College], February 9, 1858, Secretary's Office, Trustee Records, Avery Fund, Oberlin. Dr. Gazzam served with Shinn and others on the board of the Avery Institute. He was active in the Pittsburgh chapter of the Anti-Slavery Society.

22. For the suit and its resolution, see City of Pittsburgh, Orphan's Court, #55, March term, 1858, Allegheny County, and William Shinn, "The Will of Mr. Avery," *Pittsburgh Gazette*, February 15, 1858. Martha Avery finally relinquished her claims to one-half of the personal property and one-third of the real estate in exchange for a sum of $80,000.

23. In addition to being large, the monument was costly. "The Further Account of Thomas M. Howe and Josiah King surviving executors . . . ," City of Pittsburgh, Orphan's Court,

#7, September term, 1866, Allegheny County, contains a record of payments made between February 1859 and May 1866, but not individually dated. Among them is:

Expenses of Monument as follow to wit:

L. Verhagen	For Monument	$ 10,047.73
Ino Chislett	Services	500
	disbursements in c/o foundation	148.95
Miller & Gordon	fencing lot	1033.70
Schuchman	lithograph of College Building	11
J. Cochran & Bro	Gate to fence	81
putting name of Mr. Avery		
on vault doors		25
		$ 11,847.38

For an engraving illustrating the monument before its fence was removed, see *People's Monthly* 1, no. 2 (July 1871): 20. The fence was well designed and at the four corners repeated the decorative motif of inverted torches from the four corners of the monument. The purpose of a lithograph, presumably of the Avery Institute, in relation to the monument is unclear.

24. William M. Shinn to George Whipple, May 6, 1858, American Missionary Association Archives, Amistad Research Center, Fisk University, Nashville, Tenn. (hereafter AMA).

25. William M. Shinn to George Whipple, May 27, 1858, AMA.

26. Shinn's letter to Whipple of May 6 opened by acknowledging a letter from Mr. Whipple of April 30, in which some general statement recognizing the need for an appropriate monument must have been conveyed on behalf of the American Missionary Association. Most of the remainder of Shinn's letter consisted of an effusive justification in the style of a sermon. In the final sentence Shinn mentioned, apparently for the first time, his large estimate of the cost of a proper memorial. Whipple responded promptly on May 15—apparently not as wholeheartedly in favor of the idea after seeing the price tag. Shinn wrote again on May 27, this time in language more suitable to the courtroom than the pulpit. He acknowledged that Whipple had presented "some good arguments and cogent reasons against our views," but he "did not propose to answer them, although not convinced by them" because they had been expressed too late: "Before its date [Whipple's May 15 letter] however we had already entered into a contract for the chief feature of the Avery monument a full length statue—conformable to our judgt. of what was becoming and proper, as foreshadowed in my letter to you of the 6th incl. Shortly after that date Mr. Vaerhagen [*sic*] of your city (who had executed a bust of Mr. A. for his niece Mrs. Doremus also of New York) came here, not upon our invitation however, for the express purpose of submitting some plans and drawings for the monument for our inspection and to solicit a contract from us. With him we made a contract for the statue, for which he has already procured the marble and commenced the work." William M. Shinn to George Whipple, May 27, 1858, AMA.

27. William M. Shinn to George Whipple, May 6, 1858, AMA. In this letter Shinn expressed attitudes about ambition and good citizenship similar to those in William M. Shinn, *Inaugural Address Delivered Before Philological Institute* (Pittsburgh: Philological Institute, 1839).

28. For a discussion of associating "the other" with nature, see Peter Mason, *Deconstructing America: Representations of the Other* (London: Routledge, 1990), 43–50. For this theme's role in the origins of racism in the United States, see Winthrop D. Jordan, *White Over Black: American Attitudes Toward the Negro, 1550–1812* (Chapel Hill: University of North Carolina Press, 1968), 216–311. Musings on the relation between the agricultural conquest of nature and domination of race or gender are supplied by Jim Mason, *An Unnatural Order: Uncovering the Roots of Our Domination of Nature and Each Other* (New York: Simon and Schuster, 1993).

29. Frederick J. Blue, *The Free Soilers: Third Party Politics, 1848–1854* (Urbana: University of Illinois Press, 1973); Eric Foner, *Free Soil, Free Labor, Free Men: The Ideology of the Republican Party Before the Civil War* (New York: Oxford University Press, 1970); John Mayfield, *Rehearsal for Republicanism: Free Soil and the Politics of Antislavery* (Port Washington: National University Publications and Kennikat Press, 1980).

30. For the early years of Allegheny Cemetery, consult *First Report of the Managers of the Allegheny Cemetery* . . . (Pittsburgh: Johnston and Stocking, 1849); *Second Report of the Managers of the Allegheny Cemetery* . . . (Pittsburgh: W. S. Haven, 1857); *Allegheny Cemetery: Historical Account of Incidents and Events* . . . (Pittsburgh: Blakewell and Marthens, 1873); *Annual Proceedings: Corporators of Allegheny Cemetery, June 29, 1889* . . . (Pittsburgh: Press of the East Ender, 1890); *The Allegheny Cemetery, Pittsburgh, Pennsylvania: Its Origin and Early History* . . . (Pittsburgh: n.p., 1910). Charles Avery was a charter member of the corporation and also on the board of managers until 1847. When Avery died, William M. Shinn took his place on the corporation. Howe was a corporator from the outset. Josiah King resigned from the corporation in June 1845, shortly after the Great Fire.

31. For the interment of Avery and the expansion of the cemetery lot, see Day Book, April 1, 1851–May 30, 1863, Allegheny Cemetery, entries January 18, 1858, and January 20, 1859; for the establishment of Tour Avenue, see Minutes of the Board of Managers meetings, May 1845–June 1866, Allegheny Cemetery, entry February 19, 1859. (I am grateful to Thomas G. Roberts, general manager, and his staff at Allegheny Cemetery for permitting me to examine these documents.)

32. *Allegheny Cemetery: Historical Account*, 32.

33. The photo, by Seth Voss Albee, was published in *Allegheny Cemetery: Historical Account*, facing p. 73. It is apparently an albumen print, a process that often fades rapidly.

34. "Avery Monument and Statue," *Scientific American*, 364; "The Avery Monument and Statue," *Pittsburgh Evening Chronicle*, December 2, 1859; "The Avery Monument," *Pittsburgh Daily True Press*, December 3, 1859; "The Avery Monument and Statue," *Pittsburgh Saturday Dollar Chronicle*, December 10, 1859. Only a fraction of the sword remains, where it attaches above Charity's right knee.

35. "A Visit to Avery's Tomb," *Christian Recorder*, January 16, 1869.

36. Hiram Powers's proposed figure of Liberty for the U.S. Capitol (1848–50) met with some resistance because his inclusion of the Phrygian cap was considered a provocative reference to abolition. See Jean Fagan Yellin, "Caps and Chains: Hiram Powers' Statue of 'Liberty,'" *American Quarterly* 38, no. 5 (1986): 798–826. For a broader study of the changing representation of liberty in the nineteenth century, see Michael Kammen, *Spheres of Liberty: Changing Perceptions of Liberty in American Culture* (Madison: University of Wisconsin Press, 1986), 65–126.

37. Parton interpreted Avery's departure from the white lead business as an example of unusual integrity in business because most manufacturers diluted this material to increase profits. "If I cannot sell a good article, I will give up the business." This quote was repeated by subsequent biographers. See Parton, *People's Book*, 123. William Shinn in a letter to the *Gazette* defending the will against Martha Avery's suit, took offense in the use of the word "injustice" in a previous news article. "Injustice," he responded, "is a word never applied to Mr. Avery in his lifetime and cannot, and will not, be used in reference to the final closing up of his earthly affairs." *Pittsburgh Gazette*, February 15, 1858.

38. Blackett, "'Freedom,'" 127–28; *Pittsburgh Gazette*, September 30, 1850.

39. Rollin, *Life and Public Services*, 75–76.

40. *The Lawyer's Dream* (cat. #132), *Courtroom Scene* (cat. # 172), *The Higher Law* (cat. #181), *Justice* (cat. #186), and *Trial Scene* (cat. #205)—all in Bruce W. Chambers, *The World of David Gilmour Blythe (1815–1865)* (Washington: Smithsonian Institution Press, 1980). The description of the scales in *The Lawyer's Dream* is quoted by Chambers (p. 71) from an undated clipping.

41. Cruikshank's illustrations were produced for an 1852 London edition of *Uncle Tom's Cabin*. (I am grateful to Janet McCall for bringing this illustration to my attention.) An inventory of the contents of Charles Avery's household listed this title in his library, but the edition was not specified.

42. For some time, historians have interpreted the schisms in Protestant churches over slavery as contributing to the coming of the Civil War. See Richard J. Carwardine, *Evangelical Politics in Antebellum America* (New Haven: Yale University Press, 1993). For Mitchell Snay's assessment of the relationship as more symbiotic, with political situations and philosophies sometimes encouraging denominational splits, see his *Gospel of Disunion: Religion and Separatism in the Antebellum South* (Cambridge: Cambridge University Press, 1993), 113–50, and a supportive Rick Nutt, "'The Advantages of Liberty': Democratic Thought in the Formation of the Methodist Protestant Church," *Methodist History* 31, no. 1 (October 1992): 16–25.

43. Charles Avery to Lewis Tappan, May 15, 1854, AMA.

44. William E. Gienapp, *The Origins of the Republican Party, 1852–1856* (New York: Oxford University Press, 1987). Because of Avery's apparent focus upon moral issues, he might be categorized as a political pietist, a faction that has been traced from the "Conscious Whigs" through the Free Soil Party to Republicans by Mayfield, *Rehearsal for Republicanism*, 34–59.

45. The memorial to DeWitt Clinton is described in Wayne Craven, "Henry Kirke Brown: His Search for an American Art in the 1840s," *American Art Journal* 4 (November 1972): 55–58. For Clinton's identity with public works, see Craig R. Hanyan, "DeWitt Clinton and Partisanship: The Development of Clintonianism from 1811 to 1820," *New-York Historical Society Quarterly* 56, no. 2 (1972): 108–31. The memorial to DeWitt Clinton would have been known to New York sculptors not only because of its prominent site and size, but because it was the first large bronze statue of any quality that had been cast in the United States.

46. Owners of the seven cotton mills banded together to close down in protest of the ten-hour law. The workers, almost all girls and young women, focused their demonstration on the Penn Mill in Allegheny, which was not owned by Avery. Prominent Democrats supported the workers at rallies and in the party newspapers. Monte A. Calvert, "The Allegheny City Cotton Mill Riot of 1848," *Western Pennsylvania Historical Magazine* 46, no. 2 (April 1963): 97–133. (Calvert incorrectly states that Avery's interest in the Eagle Mill was sold in 1846. This did not happen until well after his death. See Thomas Howe to George Whipple, January 19, 1866, AMA.) John E. Parke, *Recollections of Seventy Years and Historical Gleanings of Allegheny, Pennsylvania* (Boston: Rand, Avery, 1886), 80, indicates that a subsequent riot occurred at the Eagle Mill, the one in which Avery was a partner, on July 7, 1850, but I have not been able to corroborate that date in newspaper accounts.

Joe Trotter notes the fascinating irony of a moral abolitionist like Charles Avery building his fortune largely on the purchase and use of Southern cotton. See Trotter, *River*, 48. During the 1830s and 1840s, Avery seems to have been an anomaly in this regard. In Massachusetts, a center for both cotton manufactures and abolitionist activities, industrialists were often described as "Cotton Whigs" or "Conscience Whigs"—cloth and thread makers remaining exclusively in the former category. But after the Fugitive Slave Act and the Kansas-Nebraska Act, more exceptions could be found to these categories, the most obvious being Amos Adams Lawrence who became a leader in the effort to make Kansas a free state. See Richard H. Abbott, *Cotton and Capital: Boston Businessmen and Antislavery Reform 1854–1868* (Amherst: University of Massachusetts Press, 1991), 23–64; Thomas O'Connor, *Lords of the Loom: The Cotton Whigs and the Coming of the Civil War* (New York: Charles Scribner's Sons, 1968), 93–113; James Brewer Stewart, "Boston, Abolition, and the Atlantic World, 1820–1861," in *Courage and Conscience: Black and White Abolitionists in Boston*, ed. Donald M. Jacobs (Bloomington: Indiana University Press, 1993), 101–25; Mayfield, *Rehearsal for Republicanism*, 34–59.

47. Holt, *Forging a Majority*, 220–303.

48. Honour, *Image of the Black*, vol. 4, pt. 1, 25–258, and Dwight Lowell Dumond, *Antislavery: The Crusade for Freedom in America* (Ann Arbor: University of Michigan Press, 1961), treat abolitionist imagery. Kenneth M. Stampp, *America in 1857: A Nation on the Brink* (New York: Oxford University Press, 1990), 135–43, describes this Republican strategy.

49. *Christian Recorder*, January 16, 1869. The relief panel measures 26 1/2 inches tall and 46 inches wide.

50. For the 1873 photo of Avery presenting a Bible and gesturing toward the ship, see *Allegheny Cemetery: Historical Account*, facing p. 73. For a halftone reproduction of another photograph published in 1910 in which the same details can be seen from another angle, see *The Allegheny Cemetery . . . Origin and Early History . . .*, n.p.

51. Wilberforce, near Xenia, Ohio, was destroyed by fire in 1865, the same day that President Lincoln was assassinated. Rebuilding was nearly finished in 1871 with the help of funds from the Avery estate. See M. B. Goodwin, "Legal Status of the Colored Population in Respect to Schools and Education in the Different States," in Department of Education, *Special Report of the Commissioner of Education on the Condition and Improvement of Public Schools in the District of Columbia* (Washington, D.C.: GPO, 1871), 373. For two gifts made to Wilberforce College by the executors of the Avery estate, see "1st and Final Account of one half of the residuary estate . . ." City of Pittsburgh, Orphan's Court, #42, March term, 1880, Allegheny County.

52. The lantern tower was apparently cropped by the frame of the relief sculpture for compositional reasons. An article on the facility, published shortly after it opened, described the interiors as partitioned with separate male and female entrances and areas. The top floor was for use by an African Methodist Episcopal Church congregation. Its ceiling and walls were "ornamented with fresco" by "Mr. Mitchell, a German artist." See "Colored Institute," *Pittsburgh Gazette*, January 23, 1850. Bernard Morris, "Avery College: Symbol Worth Preserving," *Carnegie Magazine* 43, no. 1 (January 1969): 23, is one of several recent writers who accept the notion that the school's basement was used as a station in the Underground Railroad. Although plausible, it seems impossible to prove. For Pittsburgh's participation in the Underground Railroad, see Blackett, "'Freedom,'" 116–34.

53. William M. Shinn to Lewis Tappan, Jan. 19, 1860, AMA.

54. Howard Jones, *Mutiny on the Amistad* (New York: Oxford University Press, 1987); Clara Merritt DeBoer, *Be Jubilant My Feet: African-American Abolitionists in the American Missionary Association, 1839–1861* (New York: Garland Publishing, 1994), 3–112. The earliest known letter from Avery to the American Missionary Association is October 7, 1847, AMA. It suggests that he had been following events at the Mende Mission for some time because he lamented the series of deaths of missionaries there. The portrait of Cinque on the *American Missionary* masthead was based upon a painting by Nathaniel Jocylyn. See Eleanor Alexander, "A Portrait of Cinque," *Connecticut Historical Society Bulletin* 49, no. 1 (winter 1984): 30–51.

55. Margru was known as Sarah Kinson by the Amistad Committee and Sarah Green after her marriage. See Ellen NicKenzie Lawson and Marlene D. Merrill, *The Three Sarahs: Documents of Antebellum Black College Women* (New York: Edwin Mellen Press, 1984), 3–45, and DeBoer, *Be Jubilant*, 110–12. The dates of Margru's study at Oberlin are reported variously in the secondary sources, but all accounts place her at Oberlin with funding between 1841 and 1850. Lawson and Merrill seem to base the dates 1846 to 1849 on clues in correspondences. Those attributing her education to the American Missionary Association include Robert Samuel Fletcher, *History of Oberlin College: From Its Foundations Through the Civil War*, 2 vols. (Oberlin: Oberlin College, 1943), 1:260, and Jones, *Mutiny on the Amistad*, 255n27. For historians of Methodism who name Avery as her benefactor, see Bassett, *Concise History*, 389–90; Colhouer, *Sketches*, 425–26; J. C. Broomfield, "Our Obedience," 91–92; Smeltzer, *Methodism on the Headwaters*, 309. Oberlin's records name

only the American Missionary Association. For the protracted publicizing of Margru and the other Amistad celebrities, see "Death of an Amistad," *American Missionary* 2, no. 1 (January 1858): 1–2.

56.   George Thompson, *Thompson in Africa: or, an Account of the Missionary Labors, Sufferings, Travels, and Observations . . .*, 2nd ed. (New York: by the author, 1852), and City of Pittsburgh, Orphan's Court, "Schedule of Household Furniture & Etc. . . . Rev. Charles Avery," 1858, Allegheny County.

57.   The letter was dated January 28, 1854, published in the *Pittsburgh Gazette* and reprinted as "The Amistad Captives," *American Missionary* (December 1854): 13.

58.   Charles Avery to Lewis Tappan, May 15, 1854, AMA.

59.   "Amistad Captives," 13.

60.   Charles Avery to an unknown officer of the American Missionary Association, October 7, 1847, AMA.

61.   On unsuccessful efforts to find African Americans to accompany the Amistad victims home, see DeBoer, *Be Jubilant*, 29–35. In 1834 the Methodist Protestant Church formed its board of foreign missions and three years later sent a black missionary named "James" to Liberia, an effort supported partly by Avery but which apparently did not succeed. His attention then turned to the Mende Mission and the Amistad victims. See J. C. Broomfield, "Our Obedience to the Great Command" in *Centennial Anniversary of the Methodist Protestant Church, 1928*, 91–92.

62.   Bassett, *Concise History*, 389, identified Margru and her husband in the relief panel: "these two were ultimately married, and were sent out by a Missionary Association, to the Mendi Mission, at the expense of Mr. Avery, who subsequently provided for their support, as missionaries, while he lived. He also did largely in the maintenance of the mission, to the end of his life. The scene of Mr. Avery sending these missionaries to Africa is beautifully represented in sculpture on his monument."

63.   For the estimate that only 5 percent of slaves could read in 1860, see Bruce Levine, *Half Slave and Half Free: The Roots of Civil War* (New York: Hill and Wang, 1992), 164–66.

64.   For the slow advances in Pittsburgh public education for African Americans and Avery's efforts, see Ann G. Wilmoth, "Nineteenth-Century Education in Pittsburgh, Allegheny City: Path Toward Equality?" in *Blacks in Pennsylvania History: Research and Educational Perspectives*, ed. David McBride (Harrisburg: Pennsylvania Historical and Museum Commission, 1983), 3–17.

65.   The African-American debate on practical or classical education is recounted in Tunde Adeleke, "Martin R. Delany's Philosophy of Education: A Neglected Aspect of African-American Liberation Thought," *Journal of Negro Education* 63, no. 2 (1994): 221–36. George Vashon, president of the Avery Institute from 1863 to 1867, wrote an early history of Avery's College in Goodwin, "Legal Status," 380–82. Wilmoth, "Nineteenth-Century Education in Pittsburgh," 13–15, describes the curriculum as both classical and manual training, which is true for most of the school's history, but not from its inception. The articles of incorporation declared "for the education of colored Americans in the various branches of Science, Literature, and Ancient and Modern Languages." See Catherine M. Hanchet, "George Boyer Vashon, 1824–1878: Black Educator, Poet, Fighter for Equal Rights, Part Two," *Western Pennsylvania Historical Magazine* 68, no. 4 (October 1985): 334.

66. $1,500 was awarded to Avery College. Its neighbor in Pittsburgh, the Western University of Pennsylvania, was granted $25,000: "1st and Final Account of one half of the residuary estate . . . ," City of Pittsburgh, Orphan's Court, #42, March term, 1880. Of course, before his death Avery had endowed his own college with $25,000 to maintain its small faculty and other expenses. Goodwin, "Legal Status," 381. His institute may also have received some state funds from its inception: Blackett, "Freedom," 120. For the admission that the institute "has not been as generally patronized by our colored citizens as was anticipated," see "Commencement at

Avery College," *Pittsburgh Gazette*, July 12, 1855, and John Peck's defense of the segregation policy in *Frederick Douglass' Paper*, January 27, 1854.

67. Dewey F. Mosby et al., *Henry Ossawa Tanner* (New York: Rizzoli, 1991), 23–24.

68. Amelia Freeman, the first beneficiary of the scholarship for blacks established at Oberlin by Avery in 1849, studied at Oberlin and then became an instructor of music and drawing at the Avery Institute. Sarah Elizabeth Miller, who became Benjamin Tanner's wife, was also an Avery student. Emma Woodson was a student and later administrative assistant. For these, see respectively *Frederick Douglass' Paper*, January 27, 1854; Mosby et al., *Henry Ossawa Tanner*, 23–24; Goodwin, "Legal Status," 381. Two other students E. L. Waters of Erie and Caroline Woodson are mentioned in "Commencement at Avery College," *Pittsburgh Gazette*, July 12, 1855.

69. "Amistad Captives," 13.

70. Edward D. C. Campbell, Jr., and Kym S. Rice, eds., *Before Freedom Came: African-American Life in the Antebellum South* (Richmond: Museum of the Confederacy, 1991), reproduces dozens of photos and illustrations of slaves in normal work clothing and the frequency of figures posed seated on the ground is striking. On the "Am I Not a Man and a Brother?" emblem, see Honour, *Image of the Black*, pt. 1, 62–64.

71. Honour, *Image of the Black*, pt. 1, fig. 65; Jeffrey Weidman et al., *William Rimmer: A Yankee Michelangelo* (Hanover, N.H.: University Press of New England, 1985), cat. #2.

72. Foner, *Free Soil*, 14–16, 23–29, and throughout; Gienapp, *Origins*, 353–58.

73. Wilson, *Standard History of Pittsburgh*, 822; Gienapp, *Origins*, 354–55; Mayfield, *Rehearsal for Republicanism*, 84–117. For Pittsburgh Democrats raising the specter of amalgamation in the 1859–60 campaigns, see Holt, *Forging a Majority*, 281–82.

74. On Delany's prewar interest in colonization, see Victor Ullman, *Martin R. Delany: The Beginnings of Black Nationalism* (Boston: Beacon Press, 1971), and Robert S. Levine, *Martin Delany, Frederick Douglass, and the Politics of Representative Identity* (Chapel Hill: University of North Carolina Press, 1997), 57–98. Levine observes (p. 57) that Delany's first hint of interest in African emigration was in his article describing his meeting with Margru while she was at Oberlin. On the responses to colonization among African Americans, see Kwando M. Kinshasa, *Emigration vs. Assimilation: The Debate in the African-American Press, 1827–1861* (Jefferson: McFarland, 1988), and DeBoer, *Be Jubilant*, 58–59. For the American Colonization Society, see P. J. Staudenraus, *The African Colonization Movement 1816–1865* (New York: Octagon Books, 1980).

75. Republican interest in colonization was encouraged in 1857 by the *Dred Scott* decision because it suggested that black people, no matter where they were born, were not citizens of the United States. See Staudenraus, *African Colonization Movement*, 245–48; Foner, *Free Soil*, 267–80; Stampp, *America in 1857*, 135–43.

76. "Dr. Reed's Mission Among Us," *Pittsburgh Gazette*, January 18, 1860; Staudenraus, *African Colonization Movement*, 243–44; "For Liberia," *Pittsburgh Gazette*, December 6, 1859. Concurrent endorsements of Howe include *Pittsburgh Gazette*, December 17, December 24, December 30, 1859. At the Allegheny County Republican Convention that winter, a resolution supporting Howe for governor was presented by Russell Errett, the editor of the *Gazette*. See "Meeting of the Republican County Convention . . . ," *Pittsburgh Daily True Press*, January 5, 1860. The *Pittsburgh Evening Dollar Chronicle* and *Saturday Dollar Chronicle* also carried procolonization letters and news during these months, including inflated reports of Martin Delany's travels in Africa: "A Colored Doctor in Luck," *Pittsburgh Saturday Dollar Chronicle*, March 10, 1860. Despite the exaggerated publicity, very few African Americans went to Africa. See Trotter, *River Jordan*, 50–51, and Wilmoth, "Pittsburgh and the Blacks," 124–39.

77. "Avery Monument and Statue," *Scientific American*, 364.

78. Many antislavery activists supported colonization early in the century but grew to oppose it during the 1830s. Avery was among them and his conversion was such good news to the American Anti-Slavery Society that it was reported in their journal. See "Extract of a Letter from Dr. J. P. Gazzam of Pittsburgh, Pa.," *The Emancipator*, n.s., 2 (September 1835): 1. For William Shinn's activity in colonization organizations in the 1830s, see Wilson, *Standard History*, 813–14.

79. These are cited in note 34, above. In spite of their dates, the sequence in which the articles appeared can be determined from *Pittsburgh Evening Chronicle*, December 2, 1859, and William Shinn to Lewis Tappan, January 19, 1860.

80. William Shinn to Lewis Tappan, January 19, 1860.

81. "The Avery Monument," *Pittsburgh Dispatch*, December 6, 1859. The *Dispatch* generally opposed colonization. See "If Senator Trumbull Be Correctly Reported," *Pittsburgh Dispatch*, December 10, 1859; Holt, *Forging a Majority*, 392; "Now Let Us Be Reasonable," *Pittsburgh Dispatch*, December 8, 1859. The correction about Avery also mentions that John Chislett, Pittsburgh's most prominent architect, had corrected the *Pittsburgh Evening Chronicle*, apparently for attributing the design of the monument to him. See *Pittsburgh Saturday Dollar Chronicle*, December 10, 1859.

82. Clyde S. Kilby, *Minority of One: The Biography of Jonathan Blanchard* (Grand Rapids: Eerdmans Publishing, 1959). The debate between Blanchard and J. B. Pinney, former governor of Liberia, took place in the Methodist Protestant Church and was summarized, in a partisan manner, in "Colonization Debate," *The Emancipator* 2, no. 29 (November 16, 1837): 111–12, and 2, no. 30 (November 23, 1837): 116.

83. On Edmund Blanchard, see *Commemorative Biographical Record of Central Pennsylvania* (Chicago: J. H. Beers, 1898).

84. Many of the limbs and heads show signs of breakage worn smooth with age. As early as 1867 the estate expenditures recorded payments for cleaning, and a few years later "repairing and cleaning," and in 1878 "restoring and repairing." See "3rd and Final Account of Josiah King surviving executor of," City of Pittsburgh, Orphan's Court, #84, June term, 1879.

85. Parton, *People's Book*, 122, 127.

86. John Peck, Martin H. Freeman, and George Boyer Vashon began printing and distributing a circular in May 1858, with which they solicited "the advice of colored men" on how the estate might best be used "for the advancement of us as a people." Shinn was unaware of this effort until mid-July: William Shinn to George Whipple, July 12, 1858, AMA; Wilmoth, "Pittsburgh and the Blacks," 54–55.

87. Savage, *Standing Soldiers*, 18.

88. William Shinn to George Whipple, May 27, 1858.

CHAPTER 6. THE CIVIL WAR LETTERS OF QUARTERMASTER SERGEANT JOHN C. BROCK

1. Among the essential works of Pennsylvania historiography that do not cite any letters from African-American soldiers are the following: Frederick M. Binder, "Pennsylvania Negro Regiments in the Civil War," *Journal of Negro History* 37 (1952): 383–417; George L. Davis, "Pittsburgh's Negro Troops in the Civil War," *Western Pennsylvania Historical Magazine* 36 (1953): 101–13; Jeffry D. Wert, "Camp William Penn and the Black Soldier," *Pennsylvania History* 46 (October 1979): 335–46; Sanford W. Higginbotham, William A. Hunter, and Donald H. Kent, *Pennsylvania and the Civil War: A Handbook* (Harrisburg: Pennsylvania Historical and Museum Commission, 1961); J. Matthew Gallman, *Mastering Wartime: A Social History of Philadelphia During the Civil War* (New York: Cambridge University Press, 1990).

2. Philip S. Klein and Ari Hoogenboom, *A History of Pennsylvania* (New York: McGraw-Hill, 1973).

3. Herbert Aptheker, *Documentary of the Negro People in the United States* (New York: Citadel, 1951); James M. McPherson, *The Negro's Civil War: How Black Americans Felt and Acted During the War for Union* (1965; repr., New York: Ballantine Books, 1991); Ira Berlin et al., eds., *The Black Military Experience* (Cambridge: Cambridge University Press, 1982), reissued in shorter version by the same press in 1998; James Henry Gooding, *On the Altar of Freedom: A Black Soldier's Civil War Letters from the Front*, ed. Virginia M. Adams (Amherst: University of Massachusetts Press, 1991); *A Grand Army of Black Men: Letters from African American Soldiers in the Union Army, 1861–1865* (Cambridge: Cambridge University Press, 1992); Noah Andre Trudeau, *Like Men of War: Black Troops in the Civil War, 1862–1865* (Boston: Little, Brown, 1998).

4. Roy P. Basler, ed., *The Collected Works of Abraham Lincoln*, 8 vols. (New Brunswick: Rutgers University Press, 1953), 5:388.

5. Alfred M. Green, *Letters and Discussions on the Formation of Colored Regiments and the Duty of the Colored People in Regard to the Great Slaveholders' Rebellion in the United States of America* (Philadelphia: Ringwalt and Brown, 1862), 5.

6. Captain Samuel Sanders to Brigadier General James S. Neeley, reprinted in the *Pittsburgh Gazette*, April 18, 1861; George L. Davis, "Pittsburgh's Negro Troops," *Western Pennsylvania Historical Magazine* 56 (June 1953): 104, 112.

7. There is some confusion over the precise number of black Philadelphia regiments. Quarles says there were two while Dusinberre says there were three. Unfortunately, neither historian gives proof for their claim. See Benjamin Quarles, *Lincoln and the Negro* (1962; repr., New York: DaCapo Press, 1991), 67; William Dusinberre, *Civil War Issues in Philadelphia, 1856–1861* (Philadelphia: University of Pennsylvania Press, 1965), 161.

8. U.S. War Department, *The War of the Rebellion: A Compilation of the Official Records of the Union and Confederate Armies*, 127 vols. (Washington: GPO, 1880–1901), Union Correspondence, etc., ser. 3, vol. 3, 16, 20–21, 38–39 (hereafter *OR*); Berlin et al., eds., *Black Military Experience*, 9.

9. "The Proclamation and a Negro Army," February 6, 1863, in *The Frederick Douglass Papers*, series 1: *Speeches, Debates, and Interviews*, 3 vols., ed. John W. Blassingame (New Haven: Yale University Press, 1979–1992), 3:566. A search of both the Frederick Douglass Papers at the Library of Congress and the Curtin Papers [record group 26] at the Pennsylvania State Archives revealed no extant correspondence between Curtin and Douglass.

10. Frank Taylor, *Philadelphia in the Civil War* (Philadelphia: Published by the City, 1913), 188; *OR*, ser. 1, vol. 27, pt. 3, 203; Harry C. Silcox, "Nineteenth Century Philadelphia Black Militant: Octavius V. Catto (1839–1871)," *Pennsylvania History* 44, no. 1 (January 1977): 60–61; Frederick M. Binder, "Pennsylvania Negro Regiments in the Civil War," *Journal of Negro History* 37, no. 4 (October 1952): 390. Among those white Pennsylvania volunteer and militia companies serving three months in 1861 were the 17th, 18th, 20th, 21st, 22nd, 23rd, 24th Infantry, Commonwealth Artillery, First Troop Philadelphia City Cavalry, and the McMullen Rangers.

11. C. W. Foster to Thomas Webster, June 22, 1863, *OR*, ser. 3, 3:404–5.

12. Steve Conrad, "Cheltenham Township and the Civil War: Camp William Penn," undated essay, courtesy of Perry Triplett and Citizens for the Restoration of Historical La Mott.

13. Taylor, *Philadelphia in the Civil War*, 188. See the records of the "Free Military School for Applicants to Command Colored Troops" at the Historical Society of Pennsylvania, Philadelphia.

14. Thomas Webster to Edwin M. Stanton, July 30, 1863, W-68, 1863, Letters Received, series 360, Colored Troops Division, record group 94 [B-46], National Archives, Washington, D.C. (hereafter NA); see also Berlin et al., eds., *Black Military Experience*, 97–98.

15. Heather Doughty and Mary Margaret Geis, comps., *Medal of Honor Recipients, Commonwealth of Pennsylvania Commemorative Edition, 10 November 1994* (Harrisburg: Office of the Cultural Adviser, Commonwealth of Pennsylvania, 1994), 25, 28, 30, 44–45.

16. *Harrisburg Daily Telegraph,* June 25, 1863.

17. *Harrisburg Daily Telegraph,* June 26, 1863; *Harrisburg Patriot and Union,* June 29, 1863.

18. R. J. M. Blackett, ed., *Thomas Morris Chester, Black Civil War Correspondent: His Dispatches from the Virginia Front* (1989; repr., New York: DaCapo Press, 1991), 35. Chester later claimed that his men were the first blacks mustered in as U.S. Colored Troops: "I not only urged the colored men of this city to rally around the standard of the Union, but placing myself at the head of a company of one hundred men, we had the honor of being the first Negroes armed by the state of Pennsylvania, the very first to whom the authorities of this Commonwealth entrusted swords." *Harrisburg Telegraph,* October 7, 1870.

19. Birth certificate of John C. Brock. Obituary of John C. Brock, *West Chester Village Record,* August 22, 1901.

20. United States Census of 1850, Pennsylvania, Cumberland County, Carlisle, microfilm 432, roll 773, frame 379, Pennsylvania State Archives (hereafter PSA).

21. United States Census of 1860, Pennsylvania, Cumberland County, Carlisle, microfilm 653, roll 110, frames 126–27, PSA.

22. J. C. Brock, "Annual Report of the A.M.E. Sabbath School of Carlisle," *Christian Recorder,* April 25, 1863, p. 1.

23. Military record of John C. Brock: "Field and Staff Muster-Out Rolls," John C. Brock, 43rd Regiment, USCT; Pension record of John C. Brock, Department of the Interior, Bureau of Pensions, NA.

24. "Declaration for Widow's Pension," Lucinda J. Brock, Pension record of John C. Brock, NA.

25. United States Census of 1870, Pennsylvania, Cumberland County, Carlisle, West Ward, microfilm 593, roll 1332, frame 327, PSA.

26. Obituary of John C. Brock.

27. United States Census of 1880, Pennsylvania, Chester County, West Chester, PSA. See also Pension record of John C. Brock, NA.

28. Catherine Quillman, "When Black Businesses Thrived in West Chester," *Philadelphia Inquirer,* February 26, 1995.

29. Brock was ordained an elder in June 1881. See Alexander W. Wayman, *Cyclopedia of African Methodism* (Baltimore: Methodist Apostolate Book Depository, 1882), 26. Brock's obituary suggests that he was ordained a minister but it does not say when.

30. Pension record of John C. Brock, NA. Obituary of John C. Brock.

31. Frederick H. Dyer, *A Compendium of the War of the Rebellion,* 3 vols. (New York: T. Yoseloff, 1959), 3:250, 1731.

32. Originally printed in the *Christian Recorder,* April 30, 1864.

33. Chelton Hill is the vicinity of present-day La Mott, Cheltenham Township, Montgomery County where Camp William Penn was located. As early as the Revolutionary War period Quakers settled the region, of whom abolitionist Lucretia Coffin Mott (1793–1880) was the most famous locally. Her son-in-law Edward Davis, owned an estate called Oak Farm where a training camp for more than 11,000 black soldiers was in operation from 1863 to 1865. The village of La Mott is named for the La Mott family.

34. Ambrose E. Burnside (1824–81) was a career army man who also manufactured a breech-loading weapon known as the Burnside carbine, thought to be the first American military gun to use metallic cartridges. Lincoln named Burnside a brigadier general after the

first battle at Bull Run and later made him commander of the Army of the Potomac. He also served as head of the Department of the Ohio.

35. First printed in the *Christian Recorder*, June 25, 1864.

36. Brock is mistaken here about the commander's name. It was Joshua K. Sigfried, colonel of the 48th Pennsylvania Infantry. Sigfried was white. He commanded the First Brigade, Fourth Division, Ninth Corps of the Army of the Potomac. See Dyer, *Compendium*, 1:317; Joseph Gould, *The Story of the Forty-Eighth: A Record of the Campaigns of the Forty-Eighth Regiment Pennsylvania Veteran Volunteer Infantry* (Mount Carmel, Pa.: Regimental Association, 1908), 22–23.

37. Fredericksburg, Virginia, was the scene of major Civil War events, notably battles on December 13, 1862, and May 3–4, 1863, as well as a military campaign from November to December 1862.

38. I have been unable to trace the source of this alleged quote by Robert E. Lee.

39. First printed in the *Christian Recorder*, June 18, 1864.

40. White House Landing, Virginia, was a military depot for Union troops and witnessed military action on June 21, 1864, which involved the Pennsylvania 1st, 2nd, 4th, 8th, 13th, 16th, and 17th Cavalry. Union losses were ten killed, fifty-one wounded, and twenty-two missing.

41. I failed to find anyone named Sterritt listed as a chaplain in the 36th Regiment USCT. I wonder if Brock is really referring to Reverend David Stevens of Harrisburg who is recorded as chaplain of the 36th. See *Official Army Register of the Volunteer Force of the United States Army for the Years, 1861, '62, '63, '64, '65*, 9 vols. (1867; repr., Gaithersburg, Md.: Ron R. Van Sickle Military Books, 1987), 8:207; and John W. Blassingame, "Negro Chaplains in the Civil War," *Negro History Bulletin* 27, no. 1 (October 1963): 23. The reference to Morgan is that of First Sergeant John R. V. Morgan, Company C, 43rd Regiment, USCT. See Samuel P. Bates, *History of Pennsylvania Volunteers 1861–65*, 5 vols. (Harrisburg: B. Singerly, 1871), 5:1089.

42. Originally printed in the *Christian Recorder*, July 30, 1864.

43. Roughly twenty miles or so from Washington in northern Virginia, Manassas Junction was an important rail center that on July 21, 1861, featured the first major battle of the war, otherwise known as Bull Run. On August 10, 1862, various Pennsylvania units—including the Pennsylvania First Cavalry, the First Light Artillery, and the Pennsylvania Reserve Infantry—fought a small engagement there as a prelude to the more major battle of Second Manassas (or Second Bull Run) on August 29–30, 1862.

44. Prior to Brock's present letter, at least twenty-six military skirmishes and events had taken place in and around Fairfax Court House, Virginia.

45. References to Lieutenant Colonel H. Seymour Hall and Adjutant James O'Brien of the 43rd Regiment, United States Colored Troops. Brock mistakenly refers to O'Brien as "C. Bryan."

46. Major General Irvin McDowell (1818–85) commanded the Union army in the battle of First Bull Run in July 1861.

47. Originally printed in the *Christian Recorder*, August 6, 1864.

48. Corporal James Brewster was mustered in at Philadelphia on March 17, 1864, and discharged on surgeon's certificate on January 6, 1865. Bates, *Pennsylvania Volunteers*, 5:1089.

49. Reverend James Underdue, chaplain, 39th Regiment, USCT. See Blassingame, "Negro Chaplains," 24; *Official Army Register*, 8:212.

50. Joseph P. Cullen, "The Siege of Petersburg," in *Battle Chronicles of the Civil War 1864*, 6 vols., ed. James M. McPherson (New York: Macmillan, 1989), 4:59.

51. "Scenes in the Crater at Petersburg," *Christian Recorder*, August 13, 1864.

52. For the Congressional investigation of the battle, see United States Congress, *Report of the Committee on the Attack on Petersburg, on the 30th day of July 1864*. 38th Cong., 2nd sess., Sen. Rep. Com. no. 114. (Washington, D.C.: GPO, 1865).

53. Originally printed in the *Christian Recorder*, August 20, 1864.

54. "While white troops were paid $13 per month plus $3.50 for clothing and one ration per day, troops in the black regiments were paid $10 per month and one ration, less $3 for clothing." Hondon B. Hargrove, *Black Union Soldiers in the Civil War* (Jefferson, N.C.: McFarland, 1988), 50–51. Congress on June 15, 1864, enacted legislation that granted African-American soldiers equal pay. According to historian James M. McPherson, "It was made retroactive to January 1, 1864, for all black soldiers, and retroactive to the time of enlistment for those Negroes who had been free on April 19, 1861." See his *Negro's Civil War*, 206.

55. Originally printed in the *Christian Recorder*, September 10, 1864.

56. A quote from the poem "Verses Supposed to Be Written by Alexander Selkirk During His Solitary Abode on the Island of Juan Fernandez," by the British poet William Cowper (1731–1800).

57. Originally printed in the *Christian Recorder*, November 12, 1864.

58. J. M. Mickley to Adjutant General U.S.A., 31 January 1865, M-296 1865, Letters Received, series 12, Colored Troops Division, record group 94 [K-525], "Endorsements," NA.

59. Originally printed in the *Christian Recorder*, March 18, 1865.

CHAPTER 7. SITES OF MEMORY, SITES OF GLORY

1. "Keystone Veterans," *Washington Post*, September 21, 1892.

2. Stuart McConnell, *Glorious Contentment: The Grand Army of the Republic, 1865–1900* (Chapel Hill: University of North Carolina Press, 1992), 7–8, 71. For an influential study of African Americans in the GAR written when historians minimized the importance of African Americans' Civil War experience, see Wallace A. Davies, "The Problem of Race Segregation in the Grand Army of the Republic," *Journal of Southern History* 13 (August 1947): 354–72. Davies's article is incorporated into a larger work in which he examines the GAR and other patriotic organizations, *Patriotism on Parade: The Story of Veterans and Hereditary Organizations in America, 1783–1900* (Cambridge: Harvard University Press, 1955). The most recent examination of African Americans in the GAR, Donald R. Shaffer's unpublished dissertation, asserts that the existence of separate black posts and anecdotal evidence of white veterans' negative attitudes toward their African-American comrades demonstrates that black veterans faced "condescension, apathy, and hostility" within the GAR. Although Shaffer believes that black GAR men were treated poorly, he concludes that "it was no small victory that black veterans could expect white Union veterans to call them comrade." See his "Marching On: African-American Civil War Veterans in Postbellum America, 1865–1951" (Ph.D. diss., University of Maryland, 1996), ii, 245, 251–52, 245–90, 291–300. Another dissertation that deals briefly with black and white GAR men is Earl F. Mulderlink III, "'We Want a Country': African-American Citizenship and Irish-American Community Life in New Bedford, Massachusetts, During the Civil War Era" (Ph.D. diss., University of Wisconsin, 1995). Mulderlink recognizes the importance of the all-black Robert Gould Shaw Post to the African-American community. For a recent work on nineteenth-century patriotism that includes a section on African Americans in the GAR, see Celia O'Leary, *To Die For: The Paradox of American Patriotism* (Princeton: Princeton University Press, 1999), 63–69. Black veterans also marched in the 1892 parade as members of racially mixed posts. The *Washington Post*'s report described the Major Howe Post, number 47, of Haverhill, Massachusetts, as "noted for the several colored veterans in its ranks." See "Gen. Butler in Line," *Washington Post*, September 21, 1892.

3. Rayford W. Logan, *The Betrayal of the Negro: From Rutherford B. Hayes to Woodrow Wilson* (1954; repr., New York: DaCapo Press, 1997).

4. Gaines M. Foster, *Ghosts of the Confederacy: Defeat, The Lost Cause, and The Emergence of the New South, 1865–1913* (New York: Oxford University Press, 1987); Charles Reagan Wilson, *Baptized in Blood: The Religion of the Lost Cause, 1865–1920* (Athens: University of Georgia Press, 1980); Thomas L. Connelly and Barbara L. Bellows, *God and General Longstreet: The Lost Cause and the Southern Mind* (Baton Rouge: Louisiana State University Press, 1982).

5. David Blight, *Frederick Douglass' Civil War: Keeping Faith in Jubilee* (Baton Rouge: Louisiana State University Press, 1989), 221, and Kirk Savage, *Standing Soldiers, Kneeling Slaves: Race, War, and Monument in Nineteenth-Century America* (Princeton: Princeton University Press, 1997).

6. Geneviève Fabre and Robert O'Meally, eds., *History and Memory in African American Culture* (New York: Oxford University Press, 1994), 7, 8, 12, 289, 299; Pierre Nora, *Realms of Memory: Rethinking the French Past*, trans. Arthur Goldhammer (New York: Columbia University Press, 1996). For an overview of the topic, see David P. Thelen, ed., *Memory and American History* (Bloomington: Indiana University Press, 1989).

7. W. E. B. Du Bois, *Black Reconstruction in America, 1860–1880* (1935; repr., New York: Touchstone, 1995); Fabre and O'Meally, eds., *History and Memory*, 45–71, 289.

8. While black men formed separate "colored" veterans' organizations in the postwar era, these former soldiers created longer lasting organizations when they affiliated with the predominantly white GAR. For a discussion of the other types of all-black veterans' organizations, see Shaffer, "Marching On," 245–49.

9. Mary Ann Clawson, *Constructing Brotherhood: Class, Gender, and Fraternalism* (Princeton: Princeton University Press, 1989), 131–32, 133–35.

10. Grand Army of the Republic, Department of Pennsylvania, *Proceedings of the Encampments January 16th 1867 to January 24th 1872, Inclusive* (Pottsville: Rannan and Ramsey, Journal Steam Press, 1872), 110, vii.

11. Grand Army of the Republic, Department of Pennsylvania, *Proceedings of the Forty-eighth Annual Encampment* (Harrisburg, Pa.: William Stanley Ray, State Printer, 1914), 32; *Proceedings of the Forty-ninth Annual Encampment* (Harrisburg, Pa.: William Stanley Ray, State Printer, 1915), 36. The Pennsylvania GAR held semiannual encampments until 1895; after that the organization met once a year. Because of this change, encampment records are sometimes listed as covering two encampments and in other years as one encampment.

12. Barbara A. Gannon, "'Colored Comrades': African Americans in the Grand Army of the Republic and the Construction of Interracial Veteranhood," paper presented at the annual meeting of the Southern Historical Association, Fort Worth, Texas, November 1999.

13. Grand Army of the Republic, *Grand Army Blue Book* (Philadelphia: Burk and McFetridge Printers, 1884), 21; and *Grand Army Blue Book* (Philadelphia: J. B. Lippincott, 1904), 33. The Ezra Scranton Post appeared to be racially mixed based on the death records of the Pennsylvania GAR. Correspondence with the historian of this post, Mr. Joseph Long, revealed that at least nine African-American veterans belonged to this predominantly white post.

14. *Proceedings of the Thirty-sixth and Thirty-seventh Encampments* (Philadelphia; n.p., 1885), 260–61.

15. Gary B. Nash, *Forging Freedom: The Formation of Philadelphia's Black Community, 1720–1840* (Cambridge: Harvard University Press, 1988), 6, 247, and James and Louise Horton, *In Hope of Liberty: Culture, Community, and Protest Among Northern Free Blacks, 1700–1860* (New York: Oxford University Press, 1997).

16. Although this analysis included the examination of all published Pennsylvania departmental records from 1867 to 1931, the identification of black posts was facilitated by three separate reports made by the assistant adjutant general that identified all-black posts in various years. *Proceedings of the Thirty-fourth and Thirty-fifth Encampments* (Philadelphia: n.p., 1884), 134; *Proceedings of the Thirty-eighth and Thirty-ninth Encampments* (Philadelphia: Town Print, 1886), 172;

Proceedings of the Fortieth and Forty-first Encampments (Philadelphia: Town Print, 1887), 168. The identity of Post 80 in West Chester was revealed by the membership of a black veteran, Levi M. Hood, who spoke at a Pennsylvania GAR event. *Proceedings of the Encampments January 16th 1867 to January 24th 1872, Inclusive* (Pottsville: Rannan and Ramsey, Journal Steam Press, 1872), viii, ix, 59. For the activities of the all-black Post 535 in Brownsville, see "Our Colored G.A.R. Post," *Brownsville Clipper,* June 2, 1892. Once black GAR posts were identified, Pennsylvania encampment records were examined to identify their names, location, memberships, year in which these posts were chartered, and the date these units disbanded. See Department of Pennsylvania, *Proceedings of the Annual Encampments,* 1867–1876, 1878–1931.

17. "Colored Veterans Organizing," *Wilkes-Barre Record,* June 26, 1884; "The Grand Army of the Republic in Lancaster County," *Journal of the Historical Society of Lancaster* 97, no. 3 (1995): 98–103.

18. Grand Army of the Republic, Department of Pennsylvania, Robert Gould Shaw Post, *Personal War Sketches,* unpaged preface (Archives of Industrial Society, University of Pittsburgh); "G.A.R. Notes," *Philadelphia Inquirer,* June 16, 1883.

19. The records of the 1931 encampment, which published information on the status of GAR posts in 1930, did not have membership figures for Post 487, though it was not listed as disbanded in that year. Twenty-five black GAR members represents the total number of veterans in the other four surviving posts.

20. A study of local newspapers preserved at the Pennsylvania State Library in Harrisburg revealed the Memorial Day activities of all-black posts. All extant papers for towns and cities hosting an African-American post were examined for the period surrounding Memorial Day. This review began the year in which an African-American post was established in any given location. The examination ended when local newspapers provided only limited information on the local GAR posts' Memorial Day observances; generally, this occurred early in the twentieth century.

21. "Sermon to the Colored GAR Post," *Carlisle Evening Sentinel,* May 29, 1899; and "A Colored Preacher's Eloquence," *Wilkes-Barre Record,* May 25, 1886.

22. "Memorial Day," *Philadelphia Public Ledger,* May 31, 1890; "Secret Societies," *Pittsburgh Press,* May 26, 1895; and "All About Steelton," *Harrisburg Patriot,* May 30, 1891.

23. *Proceedings of the Fifty-fourth and Fifty-fifth Encampments* (n.p., 1894), 186–202; "Afternoon Exercises," *Lancaster Daily Examiner,* May 30, 1896. For more information on African-American women in the Women's Relief Corps of the GAR, see O'Leary, *To Die For,* 82–90. The Shaw Post in Pittsburgh had three separate ladies' auxiliaries, one Women's Relief Corps unit and two Ladies of the Grand Army of the Republic organizations, another type of GAR auxiliary. Research has not yet revealed any other post, white or black, with as many associated women's organizations. Grand Army of the Republic, Department of Pennsylvania, Robert Gould Shaw Post, Minutes, June 15, 1897–September 17, 1904, 66. Committee on U.S. Colored Troops, *Souvenir Handbook and Guide, Complimentary to the Colored Veterans, Grand Army of the Republic, 33rd Reunion and Encampment, Philadelphia, 1899* (Philadelphia: n.p., 1899).

24. "Memorial Day," *Carlisle Daily Evening Sentinel,* May 25, 1887; and "Will Attend Two Services," *Washington (Pa.) Reporter,* May 25, 1895; "It Was Grand Army Sunday," *Washington (Pa.) Reporter,* May 30, 1898.

25. "How Sleep the Brave," *Washington (Pa.) Reporter,* May 23, 1893; and "Our Patriot Dead," *Chester Times,* May 31, 1890.

26. "Mounds and Memories," *Pittsburgh Press,* May 29, 1892; and "Memorial Day," *Philadelphia Public Ledger,* May 31, 1890.

27. "Editorial Notes," *Uniontown Genius of Liberty,* June 2, 1898; "GAR Program," *Uniontown Genius of Liberty,* May 25, 1899; "Memorial Day," *Uniontown Republican Standard,* May 29, 1890; "The Dead Defenders," *Uniontown Republican Standard,* June 1, 1893.

28. "The Brave Who Slept," *York Gazette*, May 31, 1888; "Our Labor of Love," *Williamsport Daily Sun and Banner*, May 30, 1887; "Memorial Day," *Williamsport Daily Sun and Banner*, May 28, 1889; "Memorial Day," *Williamsport Sun*, May 29, 1891; "Decoration Day" and "Honoring the Dead," *Washington (Pa.) Reporter*, June 2, 1893.

29. "At the Grave of Thaddeus Stevens," *Lancaster Daily Examiner*, May 31, 1886; "Our Fallen Braves," *Lancaster Daily Examiner*, May 26, 1891.

30. *Proceedings of the Encampments January 16th 1867 to January 24th 1872, Inclusive* (Pottsville: Rannan and Ramsey, Journal Steam Press, 1872), viii–ix.

31. *Proceedings of the Thirty-fourth and Thirty-fifth Encampment* (n.p., 1885), 266; *Proceedings of the Twenty-sixth and Twenty-seventh Encampments* (Philadelphia: Town Printers, 1880), 144; and "G.A.R. Notes," *Philadelphia Inquirer*, June 16, 1883. Hector spoke at many different types of GAR gatherings. For example, in 1885, he was the Memorial Day speaker at a predominantly white post in Manheim. "The Day in Manheim," *Lancaster Daily Examiner*, June 1, 1885. For an examination of GAR campfires, see McConnell, *Glorious Contentment*, 174–80.

32. "Keith Post," *New York Freeman*, May 30, 1885; "A Bad Candidate," *New York Freeman*, October 17, 1885; and "A Worthy General," *New York Freeman*, January 30, 1886.

33. *Proceedings of the Forty-sixth and Forty-seventh Encampments* (n.p., 1890), 249–50.

34. *Proceedings of the Forty-second and Forty-third Encampments* (Philadelphia: Town Print, 1888), 285–86.

35. *Proceedings of the Thirty-sixth and Thirty-seventh Encampments* (Philadelphia, n.p., 1885), 295; and *Proceedings of the Fortieth and Forty-first Encampments* (Philadelphia: Town Print, 1887), 288–89.

36. *Proceedings of the Thirty-sixth Annual Encampment* (Harrisburg: William Stanley Ray, State Printer, 1902), 55–56; and *Proceedings of the Thirty-fifth Annual Encampment* (Harrisburg: William Stanley Ray, State Printer, 1901), 61, 64.

37. *Proceedings of the Fourteenth and Fifteenth Encampments* (Philadelphia: Press of Merrihew and Son, 1874), 51; *Proceedings of the Thirty-fifth Annual Encampment* (Harrisburg: William Stanley Ray, State Printer, 1901), 268; *Proceedings of the Forty-sixth and Forty-seventh Encampments* (n.p., 1890), 252.

38. Susan G. Davis, *Parades and Power: Street Theater in Nineteenth Century Philadelphia* (Philadelphia: Temple University Press, 1986), 4, 46–47; *Proceedings of the Twentieth and Twenty-first Encampments* (n.p., 1877), 15; "Bicentennial Celebration," *Philadelphia Public Ledger*, October 28, 1882; "Indignant Excursionists," *New York Freeman*, July 11, 1885; Shane White, "'It Was a Proud Day': African Americans, Festivals, and Parades in the North, 1741–1834," *Journal of American History* 81, no. 1 (1994): 13–50. Mitch Kachun, "Before the Eyes of All Nations: African-American Identity and Historical Memory at the Centennial Exposition of 1876," *Pennsylvania History* 65, no. 3 (1998): 300–323.

39. "Our Colored Post," *Pittsburgh Press*, September 9, 1894.

40. "The Colored Veterans," "The Fort Pillow Massacre," *Pittsburgh Press*, September 9, 1894.

41. "The Colored Veterans."

42. "Our Honored Dead," *Carlisle Evening Sentinel*, May 31, 1894; and "Memorial Day at Washington," *Washington (Pa.) Reporter*, June 2, 1899.

43. *Proceedings of the Thirty-seventh Annual Encampment* (Harrisburg: William Stanley Ray, State Printer, 1903), 49.

44. "Memorial Day," *Lancaster Daily Examiner*, May 30, 1900; Foster, *Ghosts of the Confederacy*, 144, 145–59; and Nina Silber, *The Romance of Reunion: Northerners and the South 1865–1900* (Chapel Hill: University of North Carolina Press, 1993), 178–85.

45. "Beautiful Memorial Day," *Harrisburg Patriot*, May 31, 1898.

46. *Proceedings of the Fifty-third Annual Encampment* (Harrisburg: J. L. L. Kuhn, Printer to the Commonwealth, 1919), 36; and Arthur E. Barbeau and Florette Henri, *The Unknown Soldiers: Black American Troops in World War I* (Philadelphia: Temple University Press, 1974).

47. James F. Rhodes, *History of the Civil War, 1861–1865* (1917; repr. New York: Frederick Ungar, 1961), 380-81.

48. "Memorial Day in Boston," *New York Age*, May 31, 1891; "Pittsburgh Notes," *New York Freeman*, July 11, 1885; "New Churches to Be Built," *New York Age*, June 8, 1889. The *New York Age* was the same paper as the *Freeman* under different ownership. Shaw, *Personal War Sketches*, unpaged preface.

CHAPTER 8. "A DISGRACE THAT CAN NEVER BE WASHED OUT"

1. *Gettysburg Star and Sentinel*, April 17, 1903, May 20, 1903, June 24, 1903; July 8, 1903; unattributed pamphlet dated 1903, Gettysburg National Military Park Library (hereafter GNMPL) clipping file, vol. 4, p. 138.

2. Daniel J. Boorstin, *The Image: A Guide to Pseudo-Events in America* (New York: Vintage Books, 1992), 77–117.

3. John F. Sears, *Sacred Places: American Tourist Attractions in the Nineteenth Century* (New York: Oxford University Press, 1989); Dona Brown, *Inventing New England: Regional Tourism in the Nineteenth Century* (Washington, D.C.: Smithsonian Institution Press, 1995), 1–74; Colleen McDannell, *Material Christianity: Religion and Popular Culture in America* (New Haven: Yale University Press, 1995); R. Laurence Moore, *Selling God: American Religion in the Marketplace of Culture* (New York: Oxford University Press, 1994); Leigh Eric Schmidt, *Consumer Rites: The Buying and Selling of American Holidays* (Princeton: Princeton University Press, 1995).

4. J. Cutler Andrews, *The North Reports the Civil War* (Pittsburgh: University of Pittsburgh Press, 1955), 436.

5. *New York Times*, July 9, 1863.

6. *New York Herald*, July 11, 1863; *Harper's Weekly* 7 (July 11, 1863): 448.

7. Robert L. Bloom, *A History of Adams County, Pennsylvania, 1900–1990* (Gettysburg, Pa.: Adams County Historical Society, 1992), 200.

8. C. Worthington Ford, ed., *A Cycle of Adams Letters, 1861–1865*, 2 vols. (Boston: Houghton Mifflin, 1920), 2:45; Marsena R. Patrick, *Inside Lincoln's Army: The Diary of Marsena Rudolph Patrick, Provost Marshall General, Army of the Potomac*, ed. David Sparks (New York: Thomas Yoseloff, 1964), 268; Captain W. Willard Smith to Brigadier General Montgomery Meigs, July 23, 1863, box 48, folder 1862–3, Edward McPherson Papers, Library of Congress, Manuscript Division.

9. Senator Joseph W. Fisher, April 4, 1867, in George Bergner, *The Legislative Record: Containing the Debates and Proceedings of the Legislature for the Session of 1867* (Harrisburg: Harrisburg Telegraph, 1867), 910–11; Charles S. Wainwright, *A Diary of Battle: The Personal Journals of Colonel Charles S. Wainwright, 1861–1865*, ed. Allan Nevins (New York: Harcourt, Brace and World, 1962), 230, 254.

10. [Georgeanna Woolsey], *Three Weeks at Gettysburg* (New York: Anson D. F. Randolph, 1863), 13.

11. Francis Dawson cited in Reid Mitchell, *Civil War Soldiers* (New York: Simon and Schuster, 1988), 151–52; Liberty Augusta Hollinger Clutz, *Some Personal Recollections of the Battle of Gettysburg* (n.p., [1925?]), 8; Gary Gallagher, ed., *Two Witnesses at Gettysburg: The Personal Accounts*

of Whitelaw Reid and A. J. L. Fremantle (New York: Brandywine Press, 1994), 108; Gary Gallagher, ed., *Fighting for the Confederacy: The Personal Recollections of General Edward Porter Alexander* (Chapel Hill: University of North Carolina Press, 1989), 229–30.

12. *Lancaster Daily Express,* July 13, 1863; Sean Wilentz, *Chants Democratic: New York City and the Rise of the American Working Class, 1788–1850* (New York: Oxford University Press, 1984), 14–15, 61–63; Alexis de Tocqueville, *Democracy in America,* 2 vols. (New York: Vintage Books, 1945), 1:436.

13. Stephen Innes, *Creating the Commonwealth: The Economic Culture of Puritan New England* (New York: W. W. Norton, 1995), 26; Earl J. Hess, *Liberty, Virtue, and Progress: Northerners and Their War for the Union* (New York: New York University Press, 1988), 10, 19, 24–25.

14. Charles Sellers, *The Market Revolution: Jacksonian America, 1815–1846* (New York: Oxford University Press, 1991), 237–39; Burton J. Bledstein, *The Culture of Professionalism: The Middle Class and the Development of Higher Education in America* (New York: W. W. Norton, 1978), 4–7; Paul E. Johnson, *A Shopkeeper's Millennium: Society and Revivals in Rochester, New York, 1815–1837,* American Century Series (New York: Hill and Wang, 1978), 4–8; Richard L. Bushman, *The Refinement of America: Persons, Houses, Cities* (New York: Vintage Books, 1992), xii–xvi, 208–9, 232–37. These scholars point to the middle class as a cultural category characterized not only by occupational expertise and aspiration, but by moral conviction, social status, and refinement through the acquisition of certain manners and goods. "Pulpit, schoolroom, and a rising tide of print," notes Sellers, "dinned in middle-class myth and ethic" (239). Hess, *Liberty, Virtue, and Progress,* 8–9, 56–57; Phillip Shaw Paludan, *"A People's Contest": The Union and Civil War* (New York: Harper and Row, 1988), 342–43. The quote by Robert Hubbard is from a letter he wrote to Nellie, May 24, 1863, Hubbard Papers, U.S. Military History Institute, cited in Hess, p. 69.

15. Hess, *Liberty, Virtue, and Progress,* 69–70; Philip Schaff, "The Gettysburg Week," *Scribner's Magazine* 16 (July 1894): 21.

16. "Four Days at Gettysburg," *Harper's New Monthly Magazine* 28 (February 1864): 387; J. Matthew Gallman and Susan Baker, "Gettysburg's Gettysburg: What the Battle Did to the Borough," in *The Gettysburg Nobody Knows,* ed. Gabor Borritt (New York: Oxford University Press, 1997), 166.

17. *Harper's Weekly* 7 (August 22, 1863): 529; *Gettysburg Compiler,* July 1, 1916; J. T. Trowbridge, "The Field of Gettysburg," *Atlantic Monthly* 16 (November 1865): 616–17; see Tyson Brothers advertisement for card photographs of "the old hero" John Burns in the *Gettysburg Compiler,* April 11, 1864; *Gettysburg Star and Sentinel,* February 9, 1872; *Philadelphia Public Ledger,* July 3, 1903.

18. Undated newspaper clipping, box 98, "Gettysburg Scrapbook," Edward McPherson Papers, Library of Congress, Manuscript Division; "Four Days at Gettysburg," 388; *Harrisburg Telegraph,* November 21, 1863; *Gettysburg Star and Sentinel,* September 11, 1901; *Gettysburg Compiler,* March 7, 1906.

19. *Gettysburg Star and Sentinel,* November 6, 1901.

20. *Adams Sentinel,* December 1, 1863, December 29, 1863; William A. Frassanito, *Early Photography at Gettysburg* (Gettysburg, Pa.: Thomas Publications, 1995), 90–91.

21. Trowbridge, "Field of Gettysburg," 622; Robert Beecham, *As If It Were Glory: Robert Beecham's Civil War from the Iron Brigade to the Black Regiments,* ed. Michael E. Stevens (Madison, Wis.: Madison House, 1998), 115. For refutations of the Harte poem, see *Gettysburg Star and Sentinel,* March 8, 1872, May 3, 1882, January 23, 1901; *Gettysburg Compiler,* August 31, 1886; for the Burns monument, see *Gettysburg Star and Sentinel,* January 23, 1901, July 8, 1903; *New York Tribune,* August 27, 1869. For accounts of other women heroines, see *Gettysburg Compiler,* July 29, 1863; Woolsey, *Three Weeks at Gettysburg,* 8; *Gettysburg Star and Sentinel,* May 19, 1885, July 6, 1886, May 10, 1887; "A Woman's Courage at Gettysburg," *The Veteran* (Worcester, Mass.) 3 (August 1893): 8; Clutz, *Some Personal Recollections,* 10.

22. *Adams Sentinel,* August 4, October 13, 20, 1863; *Gettysburg Star and Sentinel,* April 9, 1897; John Bachelder, *The Bachelder Papers,* ed. David L. and Audrey J. Ladd, 3 vols. (Dayton, Ohio: Morningside Bookshop, 1994), 1:10, 43; David McConaughy to Rev. Dr. D. P. Krauth and Others, August 14, 1863, David McConaughy Papers, Special Collections, Gettysburg College; *Adams Sentinel,* September 8, 1863.

23. *Adams Sentinel,* May 17, 1864; *New York Times,* July 10, 1865; David Charles Sloane, *The Last Great Necessity: Cemeteries in American History* (Baltimore: Johns Hopkins University Press, 1991), 44–95.

24. *Gettysburg Compiler,* November 16, 1863; *Philadelphia Inquirer,* August 8, 1869; Trowbridge, "Field of Gettysburg," 616–17.

25. *The Gettysburg Katalysine Water, Reports of Physicians and the People of Its Wonderful Cures: History of the Spring* (New York: Gettysburg Spring Company, 1868), 4, 5–19. The *New York Times* of June 2, 1868, reported that the wounded of the battle who used the springs "recovered with great rapidity." *Adams Sentinel,* December 26, 1865; *Gettysburg Star* clipping is undated and is attached to January 26, 1866, letter to Edward McPherson from E. Harmon, Edward McPherson Papers, box 6, Library of Congress, Manuscript Division; *Gettysburg Compiler,* November 27, 1865, April 30, 1866; Bergner, *Legislative Record,* 369, 444, 662, 755; *New York Times,* June 26, 1869.

26. *New York Times,* June 26, 1869; *Gettysburg Star and Sentinel,* August 25, 1871, November 4, 1870, August 7, 1879; *Appleton's Hand Book of American Travel,* 9th ed. (New York: D. Appleton, 1867), 169; *Gettysburg Star and Sentinel,* December 24, 1871.

27. *New York Herald,* August 24, 1869; *New York Tribune,* August 27, 1869.

28. See, e.g., Gettysburg and Harrisburg Railroad Company, *The Battle-field of Gettysburg* (Harrisburg: by the company, 1886), 15; *History of Cumberland and Adams Counties, Pennsylvania, Containing History of the Counties* (Chicago: Warner and Beers, 1886), 203; *Gettysburg Compiler,* July 18, 1899, cited *The Story of the 116th Regiment Pennsylvania Infantry* by General St. Clair Mulholland (commander of the regiment during the battle) that "the field is fast becoming a National Mecca, and year after year the number of visitors to the ground increases, until tens of thousands of Americans annually make a pilgrimage to the holy ground and worship at the shrine where so many noble men laid down their lives."

29. *History of Cumberland and Adams Counties,* 203; *Gettysburg Star and Sentinel,* June 23, 1886; *Gettysburg Compiler,* May 27, 1903.

30. *Gettysburg Star and Sentinel,* July 25, 1878, August 3, 1881; *Gettysburg Compiler,* January 16, 1907; *Chambersburg Public Opinion,* n.d., clipping file, vol. 2, GNMPL; *New York Times,* July 5, 1888, July 16, 1888. The *Gettysburg Star and Sentinel,* September 19, 1900, reprinted a story from the *Punxsutawney Spirit* about selling water to veterans.

31. *National Tribune,* May 14, 1885, July, 5, 1888; *Philadelphia Inquirer,* October 16, 1898.

32. "Old Soldier" in *Gettysburg Compiler,* October 7, 1903; letter signed "Post 2, GAR, Philadelphia Lancers," *Gettysburg Star and Sentinel,* July 21, 1885; *Grand Army Review* 4 (August 1888): 875; *Gettysburg Star and Sentinel,* citing the December 4, 1882, *Indianapolis Journal,* December 29, 1882.

33. The *New York Times* did not print the letter from the clergymen, but it appeared in the *Adams Sentinel,* July 14, 1863, and in the *New York Tribune,* July 24, 1863. The *Gettysburg Compiler,* August 21, 1888, recounts the threatened lynching incident; *New York Herald,* July 6, 1865; *Gettysburg Star and Sentinel,* May 8, 1894.

34. *Gettysburg Compiler,* May 14, 1866; *Gettysburg Compiler,* July 4, 1875; *Gettysburg Star and Sentinel,* March 24, 1885; *Gettysburg Compiler,* March 22, 1887; *Gettysburg Star and Sentinel,* March 8, 1887, March 22, 1887. McConaughy's original monument proposal appeared in the *Adams Sentinel,* June 24, 1862.

35. John A. Jakle, *The Tourist: Travel in Twentieth-Century North America* (Lincoln: University of Nebraska Press), 185–98; Michael Kammen, *Mystic Chords of Memory: The Transformation of*

Tradition in American Culture (New York: Alfred A. Knopf, 1991), 673–74; John Bodnar, *Remaking America: Public Memory, Commemoration, and Patriotism in the Twentieth Century* (Princeton: Princeton University Press, 1992), 169–73.

36. *Gettysburg Star and Sentinel,* April 6, 1946; *Parade Magazine,* May 17, 1959; *Gettysburg Times,* December 21, 1959. The *Gettysburg Times* reported that the GBPA was founded on September 13, 1959. *Philadelphia Inquirer,* May 24, 1974; Bloom, *History of Adams County,* 397; *Harrisburg Evening News,* July 10, 1973.

37. Daniel J. Boorstin, *The Americans: The Democratic Experience* (New York: Random House, 1973), 89–90; Joseph Haroutunian, *Lust for Power* (New York: Macmillan, 1949), 55–60; William Leach, *Land of Desire: Merchants, Power, and the Rise of a New American Culture* (New York: Vintage Books, 1993), 3–4, 4–8.

38. John Harvey, *The Condition of Postmodernity* (Cambridge, Mass.: Blackwell, 1990), 54, 59; David Lowenthal, *Possessed by the Past: The Heritage Crusade and the Spoils of History* (New York: Free Press, 1996), 1–2, 97–99, 170.

39. *Gettysburg Compiler,* October 6, 1891; conversation with Senior Gettysburg National Military Park Historian Kathleen Georg Harrison, August 7, 1998.

40. Bloom, *History of Adams County,* 219.

CHAPTER 9.
"MAGNIFICENCE AND TERRIBLE TRUTHFULNESS"

1. Frank A. Haskell, *The Battle of Gettysburg,* ed. Bruce Catton (Boston: Houghton Mifflin, 1958), 112–13.

2. Ibid., 113, 156.

3. Over the years, the work has been cited with varying dimensions. The Pennsylvania State Museum recently measured it as 16 3/4 x 32 1/6 feet. Contemporary accounts generally described the picture as being 16 x 32 feet; I have used these rounded off dimensions.

4. Notable exceptions are Edwin B. Coddington, "Rothermel's Paintings of the Battle of Gettysburg," *Pennsylvania History* 27 (January 1960): 1–27; Donald A. Winer, "Rothermel's Battle of Gettysburg: A Victorian's Heroic View of the Civil War," *Nineteenth Century* 1 (winter 1975): 6–10; Kent Ahrens, "Painting for Peer, Patron and Public," *Pennsylvania Heritage* 18 (spring 1992): 24–31.

5. This chapter includes, revises, and expands material previously published in William H. Gerdts and Mark Thistlethwaite, *Grand Illusions* (Fort Worth: Amon Carter Museum, 1988); Mark Thistlethwaite, "A Fall from Grace: The Critical Reception of History Painting, 1875–1925," in *Picturing History,* ed. William H. Ayres (New York: Rizzoli, 1993), 177–99; Mark Thistlethwaite, *Painting in the Grand Manner: The Art of Peter Frederick Rothermel (1812–1895)* (Chadds Ford: Brandywine River Museum, 1995), 21–22, 102–11. My work on this chapter was facilitated by the assistance of Mary Snare of the State Museum of Pennsylvania and Michael Sherbon of the Pennsylvania State Archives.

6. James M. McPherson, *Battle Cry of Freedom: The Civil War Era* (New York: Oxford University Press, 1988), 662.

7. The key, published in *Picture of the Battle of Gettysburg, Painted by P. F. Rothermel* (Philadelphia: Dunk, Longacre, 1871), names fifty-six individuals. Other than this source, Sills's identity remains a mystery, as does how Rothermel came to include him. No Union roster I have consulted lists a Private Sills. Intriguingly, a good friend, earlier supporter, and patron of the artist had been Joseph Sill.

8. "The Fine Arts: Rothermel's Painting of 'The Battle of Gettysburg,'" *Evening Telegraph,* December 17, 1870, p. 1, unpaginated clipping in the Peter F. Rothermel Papers, MO-108, Pennsylvania State Archives (hereafter PFR Papers). Coddington refers to this as a Harrisburg newspaper. While both Harrisburg and Philadelphia had newspapers with this name in 1870, this article is from the Philadelphia publication. Rothermel reinforces Sills's role as the personification of the rank and file by eschewing any specific uniform accoutrements, such as insignias.

9. Ibid.

10. Peter F. Rothermel manuscript, 1879, unpaginated, PFR Papers.

11. Reverend William Suddards to the Committee of the Pennsylvania Academy of the Fine Arts, December 7, 1870, PFR Papers; *Picture of the Battle of Gettysburg,* 21.

12. The Peter F. Rothermel Papers in the Pennsylvania State Archives contain letters from officers responding to the artist's questions about their involvement in the three-day conflict. Several included maps of the battlefield, indicating troop placement and movement; General Webb's correspondence, for example, contains a diagram of the Angle.

13. Rothermel manuscript, PFR Papers.

14. Coddington, "Rothermel's Paintings of the Battle of Gettysburg," 7.

15. Paul W. Worman kindly brought these and other Rothermel drawings to my attention. The portraits (with the exception of the Mellor one), and a drawing for Weir's battery, now belong to the State Museum of Pennsylvania, the Museum and Historical Commission. Mary Snare, of the museum, confirmed that Carpenter, Roberts, and Wilson are listed in the "Key to Rothermel's Battle of Gettysburg," as numbers 55, 64, and 54. Elijah Cundy, who is not listed in the key, appears to be the soldier to the left of Wilson. The study of James Mellor closely resembles the figure on the front line, fourth to the right of Sills.

16. John Watts Depeyster to P. F. Rothermel, March 30, 1868, PFR Papers. The two pamphlets appeared under the title *The Decisive Conflicts of the Late Civil War, or Slaveholder's Rebellion* (New York: Macdonald, 1867).

17. "A Venerable Artist," *Philadelphia Public Ledger,* March 19, 1890, p. 3.

18. Ibid.

19. J. Hyatt Smith to P. F. Rothermel, December 12, 1870, PFR Papers. Smith was pastor of the Lee Avenue Baptist Church, Brooklyn.

20. A disgruntled Mitchell wrote Rothermel, reminding the artist that showing Haskell as the messenger "was not at all your intention when I last saw you, and sat next to you, in Philadelphia in the Spring of 1869." W. G. Mitchell to P. F. Rothermel, December 19, 1870, PFR Papers.

21. W. S. Hancock to P. F. Rothermel, December 13, 1870, PFR Papers.

22. "Gettysburg," *Philadelphia Press,* December 21, 1870, quoted in *Picture of the Battle of Gettysburg,* 15.

23. "Venerable Artist," p. 3.

24. John V. Sears, "Art in Philadelphia.—The Academy," *Aldine* 9 (1878–79): 108.

25. During the time Rothermel executed *The Battle of Gettysburg,* the West painting belonged to the collection of Joseph H. Harrison, Jr.

26. The "flying" figure of Sargent Cunningham, for instance, relates not only to high art, but also to an illustration of a running Zouave in Benson J. Lossing, *Pictorial Field Book of the Civil War in the United States of America,* 3 vols. (New York: T. Belknap, 1868), 2:177.

27. Joshua Emmett Brown, "'Frank Leslie's Illustrated Newspaper': The Pictorial Press and the Representations of America, 1855–1889" (Ph.D. diss., Columbia University, 1993), 81.

28. John Watts Depeyster to P. F. Rothermel, March 30, 1868, PFR Papers.

29. Donald D. Keyes and Lisa Taft, "David G. Blythe's Civil War Paintings," *Antiques* 108 (November 1975): 997n3.

30. "Hovenden and Rothermel," *Philadelphia Press,* August 17, 1895, p. 4.

31. Joseph Jackson, *Encyclopedia of Philadelphia* (Harrisburg: National Historical Association, 1931–33), 1056.

32. "Books and Art in Philadelphia," *New-York Daily Tribune*, December 14, 1870, p. 6. It may be this large study that is listed as *Battle of Gettysburg* in the Panama-Pacific Exposition catalogue, *Official Catalogue of the Department of Fine Arts, Panama-Pacific International Exposition* (San Francisco: Wahlgreen, 1915), #2955.

33. An oil study, privately owned, focuses on this part of the composition.

34. J. Matthew Gallman, *Mastering Wartime: A Social History of Philadelphia During the Civil War* (New York: Cambridge University Press, 1990), 95.

35. Rothermel manuscript, PFR Papers.

36. *Picture of the Battle of Gettysburg*, 32.

37. Ibid., 33.

38. My thanks to Elizabeth Milroy for bringing Hancock's correspondence with Leutze, now in the Manuscript Division of the Library of Congress, to my attention. The letters from Hancock to Rothermel are found in the PFR Papers.

39. Coddington, "Rothermel's Paintings of the Battle of Gettysburg," 20.

40. "Julian Scott's Battle-Picture," *Aldine* 7 (October 1874): 207.

41. John B. Bachelder, *Descriptive Key to the Painting of the Repulse of Longstreet's Assault at the Battle of Gettysburg* (New York: John B. Bachelder, 1870), 31–32.

42. Harold Holzer and Mark E. Neely, Jr., *Mine Eyes Have Seen the Glory: The Civil War in Art* (New York: Orion Books, 1993), 129.

43. W. S. Hancock to Emanuel Leutze, June 22, 1866, Library of Congress, Manuscript Division.

44. Bachelder, *Descriptive Key*, title page.

45. William G. Armstrong Diary, July 24, 1867, Historical Society of Pennsylvania, Philadelphia, Pa. (hereafter HSP). For Rothermel's significance as a history painter, see Thistlethwaite, *Painting in the Grand Manner*.

46. *Picture of the Battle of Gettysburg*, 35.

47. Ibid.

48. Coddington, "Rothermel's Paintings of the Battle of Gettysburg," 5n10.

49. *Picture of the Battle of Gettysburg*, 23.

50. "Permission" came in the form of a note from the Pennsylvania attorney general, who indicated that "there will be no application for an injunction to restrain the Exhibition." Carroll Brewster to James L. Claghorn, December 17, 1870, PFR Papers; "Books and Art in Philadelphia," p. 6.

51. Amy Seville Wolff, "Rothermel and His Gettysburg," *Philadelphia Times*, August 25, 1895, p. 24.

52. Lewis H. Sweeney to Caleb Cope, December 10, 1870, PFR Papers. Similarly, Colonel James Guyer wrote that his wife and daughter "are very much disappointed" that they did not receive tickets (James Guyer to the Committee, December 12, 1870, PFR Papers). The general public was allowed to purchase tickets for the opening.

53. *Picture of the Battle of Gettysburg*, 17.

54. Ibid., 18.

55. Ibid., 22.

56. Ibid.

57. Suddards to the Committee, December 7, 1870, PFR Papers.

58. Quoted from the *Philadelphia Press*, December 21, 1870, in *Picture of the Battle of Gettysburg*, 15.

59. "Fine Arts: Rothermel's 'Battle of Gettysburg,'" 3.

60. *Picture of the Battle of Gettysburg*, 14.

61. "Rothermel's Painting," *Harrisburg Patriot*, December 12, 1870, unpaginated clipping in PFR Papers. A letter of Joseph H. Harrison, Jr., arguing for the artist's right to exhibit the picture appears in *Picture of the Battle of Gettysburg*, 30.

62. Rothermel manuscript, PFR Papers. The site was donated by Colonel Mitchell and his family.

63. Wolff, "Rothermel and His Gettysburg," 24.

64. Rothermel recalled that a young artist took possession of the picture and "claimed a large salvage." The artist's son, a lawyer, was dispatched and the matter was settled amicably ("Venerable Artist," 3). Rothermel may have been approached by the same person who requested recompense from the Chicago Academy of Design for saving pictures during the fire. This unnamed individual was described as an artist "not a member of the academy" ("Acute Artists," *Chicago Times*, November 12, 1872). I am grateful to Patrick Sowle for sharing this article with me. Conservation of the painting undertaken in 1988–90 discovered an upper portion of the canvas having been cut (presumably, at the time of the fire). Coincidentally, Benjamin West's *Death on a Pale Horse*, a work that influenced Rothermel's painting, had to be cut from its stretchers in order to be saved from a fire in the Pennsylvania Academy of the Fine Arts in 1845.

65. P. F. Rothermel to Dr. R. Shelton Mackenzie, January 15, 1872, Gratz Collection, HSP.

66. This gallery owed its existence to the persistence, insistence, and financial backing of Joseph H. Harrison, Jr. Works from Harrison's collection formed the nucleus of this free art gallery (see Carolyn Sue Himelick Nutty, "Joseph Harrison, Jr. [1810–1874]: Philadelphia Art Collector" [Ph.D. diss., University of Delaware, 1993]). Harrison was a commissioner of Fairmount Park, as was General Meade. In 1874 Rothermel was a member of the Park Commission's committee on works of art.

67. Although only the big painting is identified in the resolution, the catalogue for the London exhibition indicates that the four other paintings were also shown; see *Exhibition of Pictures, etc., in the Art Galleries of the American Exhibition, London, 1887* (London: J. J. Garnett and B. W. Dinsmore, 1887), 18.

68. Wolff, "Rothermel and His Gettysburg," 24.

69. George R. Stewart, *Pickett's Charge: A Microhistory of the Final Attack at Gettysburg, July 3, 1863* (Boston: Houghton Mifflin, 1987), 58.

70. Wolff, "Rothermel and His Gettysburg," 24.

71. *Picture of the Battle of Gettysburg*, 18.

72. "Rothermel's Painting of 'The Battle of Gettysburg,'" n.p.

73. J. Thomas Scharf and Thompson Westcott, *History of Philadelphia*, 3 vols. (Philadelphia: L. H. Everts, 1884), 3:1859.

74. *Rand, McNally & Co.'s Handy Guide to Philadelphia and Environs, Including Atlantic City and Cape May*, 6th ed. (Chicago: Rand, McNally, 1901), 81–82.

75. "Rothermel's Painting of 'The Battle of Gettysburg,'" n.p.

76. "Rothermel's Painting," n.p.

77. "Gettysburg," *Philadelphia Press*, December 21, 1870, quoted in *Picture of the Battle of Gettysburg*, 16.

78. "Rothermel's Painting of 'The Battle of Gettysburg,'" n.p.

79. John V. Sears, "Art in Philadelphia," *Aldine* (June 1876): 196.

80. Clarence Cook, "A Centennial Blunder," *New York Tribune*, May 4, 1876, p. 2.

81. S.N.C. [Susan N. Carter], "Art at the Exhibition," *Appleton's Journal*, June 31, 1876, p. 726.

82. Joaquin Miller, "The Great Centennial Fair and Its Future," *Independent*, July 13, 1876, p. 1.

83. "Rothermel's Painting of 'The Battle of Gettysburg,'" n.p.

84. Ibid.

85. *Picture of the Battle of Gettysburg*, 21, 19, 16.

86. Gerdts and Thistlethwaite, *Grand Illusions*, 48.

87. Cook, "Centennial Blunder," p. 2; S.N.C. [Susan N. Carter], "Paintings at the Centennial Exhibition," *Art Journal*, n.s. 2 (September 1876): 284.

88. Sears, "Art in Philadelphia," 196.

89. The illustration makes a fascinating comparison with an image of two one-legged veterans in the April 22, 1865, edition of *Harper's Weekly*. In this cartoon, the former soldiers—one white, one black, and both apparently Union—shake hands in a spirit of reconciliation.

90. *Going to the Centennial: A Guy to the Exhibition* (New York: Collin and Small, 1876), 32–33. Shirley Wadja kindly brought this book to my attention.

91. *1876: American Art at the Centennial* (Washington, D.C.: Smithsonian Institution Press, 1976), 7–8.

92. John Sartain to A. T. Goshorn, July 21, 1876, Sartain Collection, HSP.

93. Cook, "Centennial Blunder," 2.

94. Sears, "Art in Philadelphia," 196.

95. "Fine Arts," *Independent*, May 18, 1876, p. 4.

96. Ibid.

97. "Modern Art and Art Critics," *Potter's American Monthly* 7 (September 1876): 228.

98. Edward Strahan, *Masterpieces of the Centennial International Exhibition* 1 (New York: Garland reprint, 1977), 150.

99. James D. McCabe, *The Illustrated History of the Centennial Exhibition* (Philadelphia: National Publishing, 1876), 586.

100. W[illiam]. D[ean]. Howells, "A Sennlight of the Centennial," *Atlantic Monthly* 38 (July 1876): 94.

101. "Artist Rothermel Died," *Weekly Reading Eagle*, August 24, 1895. I am grateful to Holly K. Green for providing me with a copy of this unpaginated clipping.

102. "Rothermel Passes Away," *Pottstown Daily News*, August 16, 1895, p. 1.

103. For a discussion of this painting, see Thistlethwaite, *Painting in the Grand Manner*, 102–5. I have learned from Sherron R. Biddle that the uniforms of Rothermel's soldiers are those of the 72nd or 95th Pennsylvania (they had the same uniform), not of the 140th New York, as is often supposed. Neither Pennsylvania regiment was at Little Round Top (the 95th was at nearby Devil's Den). Rothermel's desire to highlight Pennsylvania troops, however inaccurate, likely owed to his intention of presenting the work to his Philadelphia friend and supporter, Joseph Harrison, Jr.

104. It is difficult to determine if these are pen and ink drawings or prints. The keys are written in Rothermel's hand.

105. Samuel P. Bates, author of the multivolume *History of the Pennsylvania Volunteers, 1861–65*, wrote Rothermel requesting him to draw the *Fall of Reynolds* as the frontispiece to volume four. Bates wanted "a very spirited picture without attempting to show too much—shells bursting, bullets flying." Samuel P. Bates to P. F. Rothermel, November 7, 1870, PFR Papers. (Rothermel declined the request.)

106. J. William Hofmann to P. F. Rothermel, April 2, 1872, PFR Papers. In the painting, Hofmann's troops are barely visible in the far distance on the right.

107. I am grateful for the assistance provided by David Hedrick, librarian of special collections, Gettysburg College. The study measures approximately 28 x 46 inches and was given to the college in 1932 by the McConaughy family. David McConaughy had been one of the members of the select committee on the commission, and Rothermel found him particularly helpful. It is likely that the artist presented this work to McConaughy as a token of appreciation.

108. S. W. Crawford to P. F. Rothermel, March 8, 1871, PFR Papers.

109. Samuel G. Lane to Reverend Dr. Crawford [the general's father], June 5, 1871, PFR Papers.

110. Robert A. McCoy to P. F. Rothermel, June 20, 1871, PFR Papers.

111. S. W. Crawford to P. F. Rothermel, April 10, 1871, PFR Papers. It is not known whether or not a study was made available to Crawford. In the same letter, the general mentions that Meade informed him that the painting was "progressing finely."

112. James W. Latta to P. F. Rothermel, June 22, 1880, PFR Papers. Rothermel was to be paid $500 for this picture, which was to be hung over the mantel. The painting was exhibited at the annual exhibition of Pennsylvania Academy of the Fine Arts in 1881.

113. Elizabeth D. Kane to P. F. Rothermel, March 28, 1874, PFR Papers. Kane also acknowledged that Rothermel included another anecdote that the general had conveyed to him. It concerned him drawing his pistol, as can be seen in the lower right portion of the composition. I cannot find any other reference to this incident; in fact, Kane was quite ill and hardly participated in this engagement.

114. For more details on this engraving, see Thistlethwaite, *Painting in the Grand Manner*, 108.

115. John Sartain to Emily Sartain, March 19, 1875, Sartain Collection, HSP.

116. John Sartain to unknown, October 1, 1875, Sartain Collection, HSP.

117. Rothermel manuscript, PFR Papers.

118. John M. Jewell to Peter F. Rothermel, [August] 3, August 9, 1880; P. F. Rothermel to John M. Jewell, August 12, 1880. Rothermel file, Kennedy Galleries, New York.

CHAPTER 10. THE BROTHERS' WAR

1. Eric S. Foner, "Ken Burns and the Romance of Reunion," in *Ken Burns's The Civil War: Historians Respond*, ed. Robert Brent Toplin (New York: Oxford University Press, 1996), 112–13.

2. James M. McPherson, *For Cause and Comrades: Why Men Fought in the Civil War* (New York: Oxford University Press, 1997), 117–30.

3. Ibid., 106–10; Elizabeth Fox-Genovese and Eugene D. Genovese, *Fruits of Merchant Capital: Slavery and Bourgeois Property in the Rise and Expansion of Capitalism* (New York: Oxford University Press, 1983), 249–64.

4. Michael Shaara, *The Killer Angels: A Novel* (New York: David McKay Co., 1974), 180.

5. David M. Jordan, *Winfield Scott Hancock: A Soldier's Life* (Bloomington: Indiana University Press, 1988), 34.

6. Robert K. Krick, "Armistead and Garnett: The Parallel Lives of Two Virginia Soldiers," in *The Third Day at Gettysburg and Beyond*, ed. Gary W. Gallagher (Chapel Hill: University of North Carolina Press, 1994), 120–21.

7. E. Porter Alexander, *Fighting for the Confederacy: The Personal Recollections of General Edward Porter Alexander*, ed. Gary W. Gallagher (Chapel Hill: University of North Carolina Press, 1989), 175–76, 445.

8. Phillip Shaw Paludan, *Victims: A True Story of the Civil War* (Knoxville: University of Tennessee Press, 1981). For more on the war's ugly nature, see Michael Fellman's *Inside War: The Guerrilla Conflict in Missouri During the American Civil War* (New York: Oxford University Press, 1989).

9. Lesley J. Gordon, "'In Time of War': Unionists Hanged in Kinston, North Carolina, February 1864," in *Guerrillas, Unionists, and Violence on the Confederate Home Front*, ed. Daniel E. Sutherland (Fayetteville: University of Arkansas Press, 1999), 45–58.

10. Paul Glass and Louis C. Singer, comps., *Singing Soldiers: A History of the Civil War in Song* (1964; rev. ed., New York: DaCapo Press, 1993), 89

11. William Faulkner, *Intruder in the Dust* (New York: Signet New American Library, 1948), 148–49.

12. For an assessment that Gettysburg did not constitute the more important turning point of the war, see Richard M. McMurry, "The Pennsylvania Gambit and the Gettysburg Splash," in *The Gettysburg Nobody Knows*, ed. Gabor S. Borritt (New York: Oxford University Press, 1997), 175–202.

13. Gary W. Gallagher, "'Lee's Army Has Not Lost Any of Its Prestige': The Impact of Gettysburg on the Army of Northern Virginia and the Confederate Home Front," in *The Third Day at Gettysburg and Beyond*, ed. Gary W. Gallagher (Chapel Hill: University of North Carolina Press, 1994), 1–30.

14. Thomas L. Connelly, *The Marble Man: Robert E. Lee and His Image in American Society* (New York: Alfred A. Knopf, 1977), 83–90; Gaines M. Foster, *Ghosts of the Confederacy: Defeat, the Lost Cause, and the Emergence of the New South* (New York: Oxford University Press, 1987), 47–62; Foner, "Romance of Reunion," 104–5.

15. James A. Rawley, *Turning Points of the Civil War* (Lincoln: University of Nebraska Press, 1989); James M. McPherson, *Battle Cry of Freedom: The Civil War Era* (New York: Oxford University Press, 1988), 858.

16. For the assessment on combat footage, see James M. McPherson, "Glory," in *Past Imperfect: History According to the Movies*, ed. Mark C. Carnes (New York: Henry Holt, 1995), 128–31.

CONTRIBUTORS

William Blair is associate professor of U.S. history and director of the Civil War Era Center at The Pennsylvania State University. He also is the editor of *Civil War History*.

Christina Ericson is a librarian in the Special Collections Department of Gettysburg College.

Barbara A. Gannon, a doctoral candidate at The Pennsylvania State University, is writing her dissertation on African-American veterans of the Civil War.

Christian B. Keller, a doctoral candidate at The Pennsylvania State University, is writing a dissertation on Pennsylvania's Germans during the Civil War.

Elizabeth Milroy is associate professor of art at Wesleyan College in Middletown, Connecticut.

Henry O. Pisciotta, formerly of Carnegie Mellon University, is now an arts and architecture librarian at The Pennsylvania State University.

Rachel Filene Seidman is visiting assistant professor of history, Carleton College, Northfield, Minnesota.

Eric Ledell Smith is a historian with the Pennsylvania Historical and Museum Commission in Harrisburg.

Mark Thistlethwaite is professor and holder of the Kay & Velma Kimbell Chair of Art History at Texas Christian University, Fort Worth.

Jim Weeks, a doctoral candidate at The Pennsylvania State University, is writing a dissertation on the marketing of the battle of Gettysburg.

INDEX

Clinton, DeWitt, 107, 108, 124, 290 n. 45
Cochran, Thomas, 75
Coddington, Edwin B., 213, 229, 230, 306 n. 8
Codori's farm, 217, 225
Cole, George, 76
Cole, Thomas, 40–41
colonization, 134–38, 293 nn. 75, 76, 294 n. 78
Colored People's Union League Association, 274 n. 12
Colored Soldiers and Sailors' Monument Association, 180–81
Columbus Landing at America (Leutze), 44
Comly, Willett, 277 n. 64
common soldiers, as source for historical study, xii. *See also* Brock, John C.
Company B, 2nd Virginia Infantry, 14
Company C, 7th Virginia Cavalry, 16
Confederacy
　battle of Gettysburg and, 85–87, 94–95, 281 n. 47
　battle of Gettysburg as turning point for, 254–57
　businessmen in sympathy with, 3, 4–5, 15–16
　charity fairs in, 268 n. 15
　clergy as sympathizers to, 13–14
　estimates of Northern-born soldiers in, 8–10, 262 n. 3, 264 nn. 21, 22
　Fort Pillow massacre and black troops, 183
　language of sympathizers, 10
　marital ties and sympathy with, 16–21, 264 n. 23
　newspapers in sympathy with, 4, 7
　opposition to, after Fort Sumter, 8
　Philadephia sympathy with, 3–6
　reaction to able-bodied unenlisted men in Gettysburg, 194
　reasons for Northerners' sympathy with, xvi, 2–3
　reasons for sympathy with, 10–12, 264 n. 23
　return of Pennsylvania soldiers from, 264 n. 21
　scientists in sympathy with, 15
　slavery issue and, 5, 249–50
　Southern heritage Web sites and, 259
Confederate Ordnance Department, 17
Consumer Rites (Schmidt), 191
Cook, Clarence, 235, 236, 238
Cooke, Jay, 145
Cope, Caleb, 30, 267 n. 13

Cope, Mrs. Caleb, 268 n. 17
Cormany, Rachel, 64, 65, 66, 67
Cormany, Samuel, 64, 65, 66
Cormel, George, 228
The Cotton Trade (McHenry), 12
Couch, Darius N., 144–45
Couture, Thomas, 44
Cowl, John, 111
Craig, Henry Knox, 18
Crawford, Samuel W., 228, 240–41, 310 n. 111
Crawford, Thomas, 105, 134, 135
Cresson, John, 54, 268 n. 18
Crittenden Compromise, 8, 264 n. 18
Crounse, Lorenzo L., 92, 93, 192–93, 205, 281 n. 41
Cruikshank, George, 121, 122, 290 n. 41
Crystal Palace (London), 48, 49, 269 nn. 24, 27
C.S.S. *Louisiana*, 19
Culp, Wesley, xvi, 2, 9, 14–15, 16, 21
Culp's Hill, 87
Cundy, Elijah, 219, 306 n. 15
Cunningham, Sergeant, 220, 225, 306 n. 26
Cuomo, Mario, 103
Curtin, Andrew Gregg, 138, 144, 228
Cushing, Alonzo H., 217
Cushman, Charlotte, 269 n. 36
Cuyler, Theodore, 54

Dana, Edmund L., 219
Daniel Webster (Verhaegen), 109, 110, 284–85 n. 6
Davis, Edward, 296 n. 33
Davis, Jefferson, 20
Davis, Susan G., 182
The Dead Man Restored to Life by Touching the Bones of the Prophet Elisha (Allston), 220
Deane, William M., 16
Death of General Reynolds (Rothermel), 230, 239–40, 309 n. 105
The Death of General Warren at the Battle of Bunker's Hill, June 17, 1775 (Trumbull), 220
Death on a Pale Horse (West), 221, 308 n. 64
death records, military, 170
Delany, Martin
　Anti-Slavery Society and, 286 n. 10
　army recruitment of blacks and, 144
　on colonization, 136–37
　colonization and, 293 nn. 74, 76

Hannibal Guards, 143
Hardin, James, 157
Harper's New Monthly Magazine, 197
Harper's Weekly, 192, 197, 221, 239
Harris, Edward, 185
Harrisburg Patriot, 175
Harrisburg Patriot and Union, 7, 146
Harrison, Joseph H., Jr.
　art gallery of, 269 n. 35, 308 n. 66
　commission for *The Battle of Gettysburg* and,
　　228
　death of, 56
　Fairmont Park commission and, 54, 55
　Great Central Sanitary Fair committees
　　and, 37, 39, 268 n. 18
　as owner of *The Battle of Gettysburg*, 306 n. 25
　Rothermel commission and, 230
　as sponsor of *The Battle of Gettysburg*, 309 n.
　　103
　unveiling of *The Battle of Gettysburg* and,
　　231–32
Harrisonburg Daily Telegraph, 146
Harrisonburg Patriot, 234
Harrisonburg Telegraph, 198
Harte, Bret, 189, 199, 281 n. 41
Haskell, Frank A., 211, 213, 215, 219, 306 n. 20
Hassler's Grand Military Band and Drum
　　Corps, 231
Hastings, Mrs. David, 265 n. 29
Hatcher's Run (Virginia), 159
Hawkins, Thomas R., 146
health care. *See* Great Central Sanitary Fair;
　　United States Sanitary Commission
Hearns, George A., 146
Heart of the Andes (Church), 41, 46, 270 nn.
　　39, 45
Hector, Comrade, 179, 181, 182
Hedrick, David, 309 n. 107
Helper, Hinton Rowan, 137
Henderson, Mr., 178
Hepburn, Moses G., 148
heritage tourism, 207
Hess, Earl, xiv
*High-Mettled Confederates Going to Northern
　　Pastures* (Smith), 46
Hipwell, Henry, 66
Hipwell, Thankful, 66
History and Memory in African American Culture
　　(Fabre, O'Meally, et al.), 168
Hitner, John Kennedy, 12–13, 265 n. 29

Hitner, Mrs. R. K., 265 n. 29
Hoard, Joseph, 74
Hofmann, J. William, 240
Hoge, Sarah, 268 n. 17
Hollinger, Jacob, 90
Hollinger, Liberty, 90, 93, 94
Holmes, Oliver Wendell, 46
Holstein, Anna M., 273 n. 12
Holt, Michael, xi, 125
home front, involvement of. *See* Great Central
　　Sanitary Fair
Homer, Winslow, 46
Hood, John Bell, 254, 258
Hood, Mr., 178–79
Hoogenboom, Ari, 141
Hooker, Joseph T., 86
Hopkins, D. L., 4
"Horticultural" department, 37, 38, 269 n. 33
Howard, H. E., 9
Howe, Samuel Gridley, 267 n. 12
Howe, Thomas M.
　Allegheny Cemetery and, 117, 289 n. 30
　background of, 113, 114
　political activities of, 116, 137, 138, 287 n.
　　17
Howells, William Dean, 238–39
Hughes, Francis W., 4
Hughes, Robert Ball, 105
Hunter, R. M. T., 263 n. 10
Huntington, Daniel, 41

ideology, importance in Civil War, xiv, 6, 10,
　　11–12, 247–48
The Image (Boorstin), 190–91
The Impending Crisis of the South (Helper), 137
Independent, 238
"Indian department," 50–51
Inness, George, 44
Intruder in the Dust (Faulkner), 254
Inventing New England (Brown), 191
Italy (Cole), 41

Jack Paar Show, 206
Jackson, Thomas J. (Stonewall), 1, 2
Jefferson, Thomas, 195
Jewell, John M., 243
Jim Crow laws, 166
Jocylyn, Nathaniel, 291 n. 54
"John Burns of Gettysburg" (Harte), 189,
　　199

Rothermel, Peter Frederick, xviii–xix. *See also*
    The Battle of Gettysburg: Pickett's Charge
    (Rothermel)
    Battle of Gettysburg commission of, 229, 230,
        309 n. 107
    as colorist, 235–36
    commission of, 270 n. 42
    death of, 239
    Great Central Sanitary Fair exhibits of,
        44–45
    influence of other artists on, 220–23, 239–40
    McConaughy and, 309 n. 107
    as member of Fairmont Park Commission's
        committee on works of art, 308 n. 66
    pendant paintings of, 227–28, 230, 239
    permanent displays of art of, 56
    research of, 270 n. 42
    works of, 229–30; Charge of the Pennsyl-
        vania Reserves at Plum Run, 230, 240–41,
        242, 243; Christian Martyrs in the Coli-
        seum, 230; Death of General Reynolds,
        230, 239–40, 309 n. 105; The First Reading
        of the Declaration of Independence, 45;
        Franklin at Versailles, 45; *King Lear,* 230;
        *Patrick Henry in the Virginia House of
        Burgesses, Delivering His Celebrated Speech
        Against the Stamp Act,* 230; *The Pennsyl-
        vania Reserves Charging at Plum Run,*
        227–28; *Repulse of General Johnson's
        Division by General Geary's White Star
        Division,* 230, 241; *Sharpshooters at Round
        Top,* 230; *Sir Walter Raleigh Spreading His
        Cloak for Queen Elizabeth,* 44–45; *State
        House on the Day of the Battle of
        Germantown,* 45
Royal Society of Arts (London), 269 n. 27
Ruggles, Daniel, 19
Ryan, Mary, 74
Rydell, Robert, 266 n. 4

*Sacred Places: American Tourist Attractions in the
    Nineteenth Century* (Sears), 191
Sailor's Requiem, 46
Sanders, Samuel, 143
sanitary fairs. *See also* benevolence societies:
    antebellum; Great Central Sanitary Fair
    definition, 23
    precedents, 266 n. 4, 268 n. 22, 269 n. 27
    soldiers' impressions of, 41
    study of, 25

Sartain, John, 38, 56, 237–38, 241, 242
Saturday Evening Post, 73
Savage, Kirk, 140
Schmidt, Leigh Eric, 191
Schussele, Christian, 38, 270 n. 42
Scientific American, 137
Scott, Anne Firor, 68, 273 n. 11, 278 n. 77
Scott, George Washington, 15
Scott, John, 93, 279 n. 17
Scott, Martha, 279 n. 17
Scudder, John, 284 n. 6
Seafried, Colonel. *See* Sigfried, Joshua K.
Sears, John F., 191, 235, 236
Seated Man (Despair) (Rimmer), 134
secession, 6, 263 n. 12, 264 n. 18
Second Brigade, 152, 233
Second Confiscation Act, 144
2nd Virginia Infantry, 14, 16
Seidman, Rachel, xvii
Sellers, Coleman, 56
Sellers, Escol, 59
Sellers, Jennie, 59–60, 63, 273 n. 8
Sellers, Samuel, 59
Selling God (Moore), 191
separate spheres, 279 nn. 5, 6. *See also* public
    versus private sphere, women and
7th Virginia Cavalry, 16
71st Pennsylvania Regiment, 225
72nd Pennsylvania Regiment, 225, 226
Shaara, Michael, 250
Shafer, Morris, 69
Shafer, Mrs., 69
Shaffer, Donald R., 298 n. 2
Shankman, Arnold, xi, xv, 8–9
Sharpshooters at Round Top (Rothermel), 230
Sharpshooters (Rogers), 46
Shaw, Robert Gould, 172, 174
Sheads, Carrie, 88
Sheridan, Philip, 253
Sherman, William T., 231
Shinn, Asa, 114
Shinn, William M.
    Allegheny Cemetery and, 289 n. 30
    on Avery and private conscious, 140
    Avery will and, 285–86 n. 9
    background of, 114
    colonization and Avery Monument, 138
    as executor of Avery estate, 113
    letter to Whipple on Avery Monument,
        288 n. 26

Webster, Thomas, 145, 146
Weekly Reading Eagle, 239
Weeks, James, xvi, xviii
Weir, Gulian V., 215
Welsh, John, 30, 50, 53, 54, 271 n. 61
West, Benjamin, 221, 230, 308 n. 64
Western Sanitary Commission, 267 n. 13
Western University of Pennsylvania, 292 n. 66
Whig Party, 74, 113, 136
Whipple, George, 114, 115, 288 n. 26
white regiments serving three months, 295 n. 10
Whitnesy, Jane Mariah, 66
Whitney, George, 38, 268 n. 18
Why Pennsylvania Should Become One of the Confederate States (McHenry), 12
The Widow, or Spirit of '64, 46
Wilberforce College, 129, 133, 291 n. 51
Wiley, Bell Irvin, 8
"William Penn Parlor" exhibit, 36–37, 49
William Penn's Treaty with the Indians (West), 221, 230, 306 n. 25
Wills, David, 201, 282 n. 63
Wills Eye Hospital, 32
Wilson, Erasmus, 285 n. 8
Wilson, James R., 219, 306 n. 15
Wilson, Miss, 70
Wilson, Mr., 276 n. 63
Wilson, Mrs., 70
Wilson, Peter, 271 n. 61
Wilstach, William, 38, 270 n. 42
Wilstach family, 56
Windrim, John T., 271 n. 69
WNLL (Women's National Loyal League), 71, 78
Wolf, E. J., 199
Wolf Hill, 90
women. *See also* gender; ladies' aid societies
  during battle of Gettysburg, xvii, 87–88 (*see also* Wade, Jennie (Mary Virginia))
  GAR auxiliaries of black, 174–75, 176, 300 n. 23
  Great Central Sanitary Fair and (*see* Great Central Sanitary Fair)
  Great Central Sanitary Fair Picture Gallery influence on, 45
  interest in war news, 59–61

male attitudes toward sanitary fair efforts of, 29
men during battle of Gettysburg and, 92–95, 281 n. 34
nursing duties during battle of Gettysburg, 96–97
personal ramifications of knowledge of, 67
political ramifications of knowledge of, 66
public's opinion of Gettysburg, 193–94
public versus domestic sphere, 62, 73–75, 78, 83–84, 276 n. 60, 279 n. 5
reaction to deaths in battle, 275 n. 36
recreation to war of Northern versus Southern, 281–82 n. 49
Sanitary Commission and, xiv–xv, 29, 71–73, 98–99
support networks of, 68–69, 274 n. 14, 275 n. 26
themes in writings on Gettysburg, 91–97
wartime bonding of, 64–66, 68–69
writings on Gettysburg, 87–91
Women's Central Relief Association, 266 n. 8
Women's Council, 72
Women's National Loyal League (WNLL), 71, 78
Women's Pennsylvania Branch of the Sanitary Commission, 29–30, 268 n. 17
Women's Relief Corps, 300 n. 23
Women's Relief Corps of Iowa, 198
Woodson, Emma, 293 n. 68
Woodward, George W., 6
Woolsey, Georgeanna, 193–94
Wordabaugh, Mrs., 64
Working for the Fair (Johnson), 46
Worman, Paul W., 306 n. 15
Wounded Scout (Rogers), 46
Wrenshall, John, 286 n. 11
Wright, Albert, 146
Wright, William C., 263 n. 12
Writing the Civil War (McPherson and Cooper), xii

York Pennsylvanian, 73

Zoave Cadets, 143

VOID